# Nihongo ga IPPAI

Elementary Japanese Textbook

# 日本語がいっぱい

[著]
Duck-Young Lee
Naomi Ogi
Masahiro Toma
Yoko Yonezawa

ひつじ書房

Nihongo ga IPPAI



First published 2010
Second printing 2018

Author: Duck-Young Lee, Naomi Ogi, Masahiro Toma and Yoko Yonezawa

Illustrations: Cui Yue Yan



Book Design © Mami Ueda

Hituzi Syobo Publishing
Yamato bldg. 2F, 2-1-2 Sengoku Bunkyo-ku Tokyo, Japan
112-0011

phone +81-3-5319-4916 fax +81-3-5319-4917
e-mail: toiawase@hituzi.co.jp
http://www.hituzi.co.jp/
postal transfer 00120-8-142852

ISBN978-4-89476-4492-1
Printed in Japan

# Acknowledgements

This second edition involves an amendment of typing errors in the first edition. I would like to acknowledge invaluable contributions and comments from my students and anonymous users of the first edition of this textbook.

March 2018, Canberra
Duck-Young Lee

A number of people have made invaluable contributions toward the completion of this textbook in one way or another. Our first and foremost thanks go to our students who have not only been the motivation in developing this textbook, but have also given us direction in our teaching and in producing this book. It has always been a great pleasure to see how their Japanese has improved; without them, it would have been impossible to begin and to complete this textbook.

We would also like to express our sincere gratitude to Kent Anderson, the Director of our faculty; his encouragement has always been a strong support for us to continue our textbook project. Our warm acknowledgement is also paid to William Washington for his patient and tireless contribution as the English editor of this book. Many thanks also to Jim Rowe, for his help with English in early versions of the textbook.

Special thanks go to Tomoko Fujimura, Tokyo University of Foreign Studies, and Chika Maruyama, Yokohama National University, for their invaluable support for the project. We are grateful to Nobu Torao, Han-Byul Moon, Shiori Watanabe, Emi Yoshida, Akane Kawamata and Younghye Seo, for their invaluable help and comments on earlier versions of the textbook. We also wish to acknowledge constructive comments and criticism from anonymous reviewers of an earlier version, which have led to a substantial improvement in this final publication. However, we are solely responsible for all the errors and any misinterpretations.

Finally, we thank Hitsuji Shobo for giving us an opportunity to publish this textbook, which allows us to communicate widely with both teachers and learners in the world-wide community of the Japanese language education.

July 2009, Canberra
Duck-Young Lee
Naomi Ogi
Masahiro Toma
Yoko Yonezawa

# Contents

# Suggestions for use

## Purposes

This textbook is aimed at developing communication skills for beginning learners of the Japanese language. Its primary focus is on developing the learners' abilities in speaking and listening comprehension. However, as it incorporates *hiragana, katakana and kanji* as the basis for instruction, it can also be used as a comprehensive teaching and learning resource for the development of writing and reading skills as well.

## Some special features

Special features of this textbook include:

(1) Systematic learning of the characteristics of spoken Japanese (e.g. frequent use of sentence final particles such as *ne* and *yo*, particle omission, inversion, echo questions, etc.).

(2) Comprehensive Japanese language learning aimed at acquiring a sound balance of knowledge and skills between (i) the systematic understanding of grammar and (ii) a practical-pragmatic use of situational and functional expressions.

(3) Developing a practical conversational ability through a large number of systematically arranged exercises rich in variety.

(4) Aiming at 'easy to learn, easy to teach and easy to use'.

(5) Well-selected situations in the practical use of the Japanese language, with a continuing storyline between a Japanese student and a foreign student.

This textbook has been developed on the belief that the grammatical/structural method of language teaching and the situational/functional method do not conflict with each other; rather, they supplement each other, and both should be employed from the very early stages of language learning, especially when the learners are adults. In this sense, this textbook adopts a holistic approach to Japanese language teaching, which enables learners to master functional/situational expressions as well as grammatical knowledge, systematically. Successful users of this textbook will be able to acquire both grammatical competence and applicable, ready-to-use expressions for various situations, which is of great importance for learners in developing their practical skills and autonomous language-learning abilities.

This textbook organises the exercises in the order of 'sentence level → short dialogue level → discourse level'. This helps the learner to acquire smoothly the expressions and conversation strategies which are necessary for certain situations in a step-by-step manner. Further, the exercises are presented immediately after the explanation of each grammatical or expressional item, so that learners are able to work on what they have just learnt. This encourages the learners' active engagement in the learning process and creates lively interaction between the learners and the instructor.

## Organisation of the book

This textbook consists of three parts, twenty lessons in total. The first part (Lessons 1, 2 and 3) focuses on the basic knowledge of Japanese that learners need to know to begin with (e.g. greetings, basic sentence structures and expressions, etc.). It begins with expressions and situations/functions involving nouns that are conceptually relatively easy to understand. This is followed by the second part (Lessons 4 to 10) and the third part (Lessons 11 to 20), which involve a variety of situational dialogues between Masato, a Japanese student, and Elena, an English speaking student. The overall setting of the second part is Masato meeting Elena while visiting an English-speaking country. Then in the third part Elena is now visiting Japan, and goes to a variety of places with Masato.

Through these practical situations, it is expected that learners will be able to obtain the essential knowledge of the language in a systematic manner so as to gain the skills necessary to speak the language naturally (cf. Contents).

### Estimated learning time

Each lesson is designed to be learnt in approximately 5 to 6 hours and all lessons in approximately 120 hours. With an additional 80 hours for the study of reading and writing, this textbook is organised in such a way that it can be used as core material for an elementary-level Japanese course of 200 hours in total. It may be extended to 7 or 8 hours by taking a detailed approach and/or by adding some extra work if that is felt necessary, or it may be shortened to 3 or 4 hours, by skipping some parts in class, depending on the schedule for the course (Cf. Standard answers are provided in order to assist the learners' self-study.).

### Structure of a lesson

Each lesson basically has the following structure:

(1) Title

(2) Dialogue: Introducing the situation and function dealt with in the lesson. An English translation is provided.

(3) Grammar: Explaining each grammatical item introduced in the lesson concisely yet sufficiently. Drills and exercises are provided.

(4) Natural Conversation Notes: Explaining one or two characteristics or conversation strategies particular to spoken Japanese. Exercises are provided.

(5) Expression Notes: Explaining the expressions introduced in the dialogue of the lesson. Exercises for making sentences are provided.

(6) Communicative Exchanges: Providing work-in-pair or work-in-group type exercises, such as role-play and information gap etc. It is recommended that the tasks listed in *Pre-task* be reviewed prior to the main exercise, using the overhead projector.

(7) Comprehensive Exercises: Providing a dialogue-making exercise where learners can create their own dialogue with their classmates. Students may develop their interactive skills by exploring what they have learnt in the lesson, at the discourse level.

(8) Did you know?: Explaining Japanese culture and the state of affair in Japan related to the theme of the lesson. Not only does this provide some knowledge of these issues, but is also arranged to enable the student to apply them to the process of learning the Japanese language.

(9) Summary of Vocabulary and Expressions: Listing and summarising new vocabulary and expressions introduced in the lesson. Vocabulary and expressions that are essential at the beginner's level are marked with '*'.

### Scripts

A variety of ways of writing the texts is employed on a step-by-step basis, so that learners can develop their reading-writing skills without experiencing much difficulty.

(1) Lessons 1-3: Written in kana with readings in Roman script. Students are expected to become familiar with hiragana before Lesson 3 is finished.

(2) Lessons 4 -10: Written in kana and kanji. Kanji are given their readings in hiragana. Katakana are also given readings in hiragana.

(3) Lessons 11-20: Written in kana and kanji, with hiragana readings for kanji. Katakana is not given readings.

# Kana and pronunciation

## 1. Kana and kanji

Three types of script are commonly used in modern Japanese: they are hiragana (平仮名), katakana (片仮名) and kanji (漢字). Hiragana and katakana are collectively referred to as kana (仮名).

**1.1.** Kanji (漢字)

(i) Kanji were introduced from China nearly 2,000 years ago.
(ii) They are 'ideograms', which represent both sounds and meanings.

(e.g.) 私 reading: *watashi*
meaning: 'I, private'

**1.2.** Kana (仮名)

(i) Hiragana and katakana were developed during the Heian period (A.D. 794–1192).
(ii) They are 'phonograms', which represent sounds only.
(iii) Both kana were derived from kanji

(e.g.)

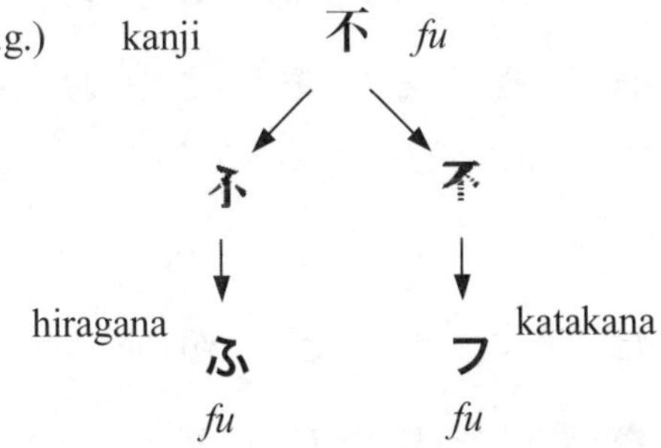


Hiragana: by simplifying kanji
Katakana: by adopting a part of kanji

Note: Only the shape and the sound of kanji influenced the derivation; the meaning of the kanji has nothing to do with the derivation.

## 2. Function of each script

Sentences are normally written in a combination of kana and kanji. Each script type represents:

(i) Kanji: main concept of a word
(ii) Hiragana: grammatical details
(iii) Katakana: loanwords (borrowed words, which are not normally written in kanji)

(e.g.) 私 (watashi) は (wa) 日本人 (Nihonjin) です (desu)。 'I am Japanese.'
'I' [は: topic marker] 'Japanese' [です: Affirmative, non-past, polite]

(e.g.) 私 (watashi) は (wa) オーストラリア人 (Oosutorariajin) です (desu)。 'I am Australian.'
'I' 'Australian'

## 3. Hiragana

### 3.1. Basic hiragana (五十音図 (gojuuonzu) 'fifty-sound chart')

(i) In vowels {*a*, *i*, *u*, *e* and *o*}, *u* does not involve the roundedness of mouth, while the pronunciation of other vowels is similar to that of their English equivalents.

(ii) In the chart, except for the vowels and わ, を and ん, the pronunciation of each kana is a combination between the consonant at the top of that column and the vowel in the rightmost column: e.g. か *ka* = *k* + *a*, す *su* = *s* + *u*.

(iii) There are no *ti* and *tu* sounds in words native to Japanese. They are ち *chi* and つ *tsu*, respectively. Their voiced counterparts are also ぢ *ji* and づ *zu*.

| | | *r* | *y* | *m* | *h* | *n* | *t* | *s* | *k* | | |
|---|---|---|---|---|---|---|---|---|---|---|---|
| | わ<br>wa | ら | や | ま | は | な | た | さ | か | あ | *a* |
| | | り | | み | ひ | に | ち | し | き | い | *i* |
| | | る | ゆ | む | ふ | ぬ | つ | す | く | う | *u* |
| | | れ | | め | へ | ね | て | せ | け | え | *e* |
| ん<br>N | を<br>o | ろ | よ | も | ほ | の | と | そ | こ | お | *o* |

| *p* | *b* | *d* | *z* | *g* | |
|---|---|---|---|---|---|
| ぱ | ば | だ | ざ | が | *a* |
| ぴ | び | ぢ | じ | ぎ | *i* |
| ぷ | ぶ | づ | ず | ぐ | *u* |
| ぺ | べ | で | ぜ | げ | *e* |
| ぽ | ぼ | ど | ぞ | ご | *o* |

> Japanese has a simple five vowel system, {*a*, *i*, *u*, *e* and *o*}.

### 3.2. ん

(i) This is not used in an initial position in any word.

(ii) In isolation or at the end of a word, its pronunciation is like a 'weaker' version of the English –*ng*. To English speakers, it is often not clear whether it is *n*, *m* or *ng*.

(iii) In a medial position, it has several variational pronunciations:

- It is [n] when followed by *t*, *d*, *n*, *s*, *z* or *r*: (e.g.) さんにん *sannin* 'three people'
- It is [m] when followed by *p*, *b* or *m*: (e.g.) さんまん *samman* '30,000'
- It is [ng] when followed by other sounds: (e.g.) げんき ge**ng**ki 'health'

These variations occur naturally when people pronounce the following sound correctly. Therefore, it is not really necessary to try to remember these variations.

**3.3.** お／を, へ and は

(i) Both, お and を represent *o*. を is used only to express a grammatical meaning, i.e. an objective marker, while お is used in all other cases.

kao o araimasu
(e.g.) かお を あらいます。 '(I) wash my face.'
'face' 'wash'
[objective marker]

(ii) When へ and は are used as a particle, 'direction (destination) marker' and 'topic marker' respectively, they are pronounced *e* for the former and *wa* for the latter.

watashi wa Heiwa Kooen e ikimasu
(e.g.) わたし は 平和公園 へ いきます。 'I will go to Peace Park.'
'I' 'Peace Park' 'go'
[topic marker] [direction marker]

**3.4.** Hiragana for *ji* and *zu*: {じ, ず} *vs.* {ぢ, づ}

(i) The sounds *ji* and *zu* are usually written じ and ず.

goji shizukana
(e.g.) ごじ 'five o'clock' しずかな 'quiet'

(ii) ぢ and づ are used (a) after ち and つ respectively; and (b) in a compound word in which ち and つ in the second element are voiced.

chijimu tsuzuku
(e.g.) a. ちぢむ 'shrink' つづく 'continue'

hana chi hanaji
b. はな 'nose' + ち 'blood' → はなぢ 'nosebleed'

ki tsuku kizuku
き 'mind' + つく 'attached' → きづく 'notice, realise'

**3.5.** Others

(i) し: Its sound differs from the English *shi* although we use *shi* for its Roman script. Its sound is close to ひ /hi/ in Tokyo dialect.

(ii) /r/: This differs from the English *r*. Japanese /r/ in {ら り る れ ろ} is a simple tap.

(iii) ふ and /f/: There is no /f/ or /v/ sound in Japanese native words. We represent ふ as *fu* in Roman script just for convenience (cf. *hu* is typically read as [hyu]).

## 4. Special sounds

yooon
**4.1.** Diphthong (twisted sounds): ようおん

(i) These are represented by adding ゃ, ゅ or ょ (smaller size of や, ゆ, よ) to kana which has the *i* sound.

isha kyonen
(e.g.) いしゃ 'medical doctor' きょねん 'last year'

(ii) Compare the two words in each pair below:

(a) きやく *vs.* きゃく (b) じゆう *vs.* じゅう (c) ひよう *vs.* ひょう

**4.2.** Geminate (double consonants): そくおん (sokuon)

(i) These are represented by adding っ (smaller size of つ) to kana which has one of the {*k*, *t*, *p* and *s*} sounds.

(e.g.) もっと (motto) 'more' ゆっくり (yukkuri) 'slowly' すっぱい (suppai) 'sour'

(ii) Compare the two words in each pair below:

(a) して *vs.* しって (b) きて *vs.* きって (c) みつ *vs.* みっつ

**4.3.** Long vowels: ちょうおん (chooon)

(i) Long vowel *a*, *i* and *u*: These are represented by adding あ, い and う, respectively.

(e.g.) おかあさん (okaasan) 'mother' おにいさん (oniisan) 'older brother'
くうき (kuuki) 'air' きゅうじゅう (kyuujuu) 'ninety'

(ii) Long vowel *e*: This is represented by adding basically え in words native to Japanese; and い in words of Chinese origin.

(e.g.) おねえさん (oneesan) 'older sister' えいが (eega) 'movie' とけい (tokee) 'watch, clock'

(iii) Long vowel *o*: This is represented by adding う in most cases.

(e.g.) とうきょう (tookyoo) 'Tokyo' ひこうき (hikooki) 'airplane'

Hiragana お tends to form a long vowel with the preceding kana which ends in the vowel *o*:

(e.g.) おおきい (ookii) 'big' こおり (koori) 'ice'

**Note:** In Japanese, い after the vowel *e* is a long vowel of *e* (examples in (ii) above); and う after *o* is a long vowel of *o* (examples in (iii) above), when there is no morpheme boundary before the い／う.

## 5. Writing a sentence

**5.1.** Question mark '?': In traditional Japanese, the question marker '?' is not used as a question is marked by the question marker か.

(e.g.) 田中さんは (tanakasanwa) 学生ですか。 (gakuseidesuka) 'Is Mr Tanaka a student?'

はい、学生です。 (hai gakuseidesu) 'Yes, (he) is a student.'

In casual writing, the marker may be used as the casual style does not always require か in questions.

| | | |
|---|---|---|
| (e.g.) | tanakasanwa gakusei<br>田中さんは 学生？ | 'Is Mr Tanaka a student?' |
| | u n gakusei<br>うん、学生。 | 'Yeah, (he) is a student.' |

**5.2.** Space between words: In natural Japanese sentences, there is no space between words or phrases. As briefly illustrated below, the use of kanji is crucial for quickly understanding the meaning conveyed by the sentence.

(e.g.) わたしがはじめてきむらさんにあってたなかさんにかんするはなしをきいたのは、わたしがまだ…

→ 私が初めて木村さんに会って田中さんに関する話を聞いたのは、私がまだ

However, words may be written with spaces, while the students do not have much knowledge of kanji and thus sentences are written in kana. When writing sentences with spaces, make sure that no space is given between a dependent word (typically particles; highlighted in grey below) and the preceding independent word (e.g. nouns).

(e.g.) わたしが　はじめて　きむらさんに　あって　たなかさんに　かんする…

## 6. Katakana

(i) The way of representing voiced {g, z, d, b}, aspirated {p} and geminate {ッ} sounds is the same as that in hiragana: (e.g.) ハ (ha) *vs.* バ (ba) *vs.* パ (pa); ヒット (hitto) 'hit'.

(ii) Long vowels are represented by 'ー'. This is applicable for any type of vowel.

(e.g.) コーヒー (koohii) 'coffee'　　コンピューター (konpyuutaa) 'computer'

(iii) There are some sounds which do not exist in words native to Japanese.

(e.g.) パーティー (paatii) 'party'　　ベッド (beddo) 'bed'

| | | *r* | *y* | *m* | *h* | *n* | *t* | *s* | *k* | | |
|---|---|---|---|---|---|---|---|---|---|---|---|
| | ワ<br>wa | ラ | ヤ | マ | ハ | ナ | タ | サ | カ | ア | *a* |
| | | リ | | ミ | ヒ | ニ | チ | シ | キ | イ | *i* |
| | | ル | ユ | ム | フ | ヌ | ツ | ス | ク | ウ | *u* |
| | | レ | | メ | ヘ | ネ | テ | セ | ケ | エ | *e* |
| ン<br>N | ヲ<br>o | ロ | ヨ | モ | ホ | ノ | ト | ソ | コ | オ | *o* |

# Main characters of the textbook

Masato Yamada is a second year student at a Japanese university. His major is International Relations and his hobbies are sports and drawing. He also likes travelling to various places.

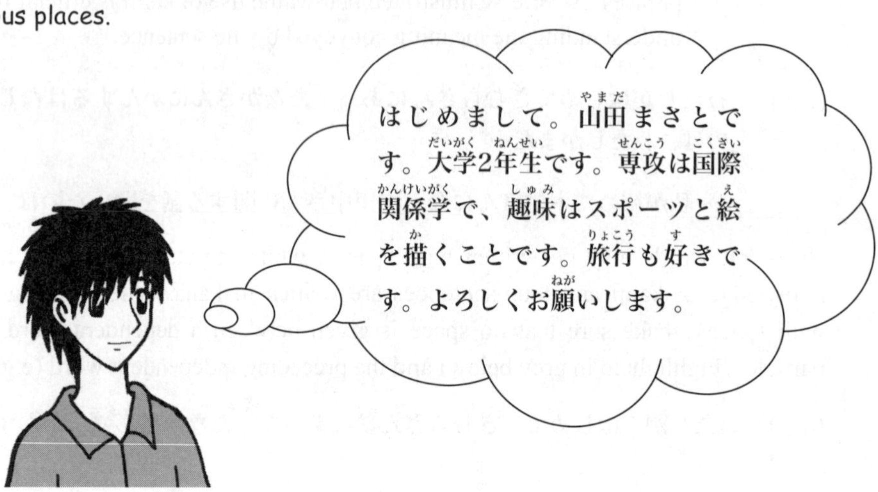
はじめまして。山田まさとです。大学2年生です。専攻は国際関係学で、趣味はスポーツと絵を描くことです。旅行も好きです。よろしくお願いします。

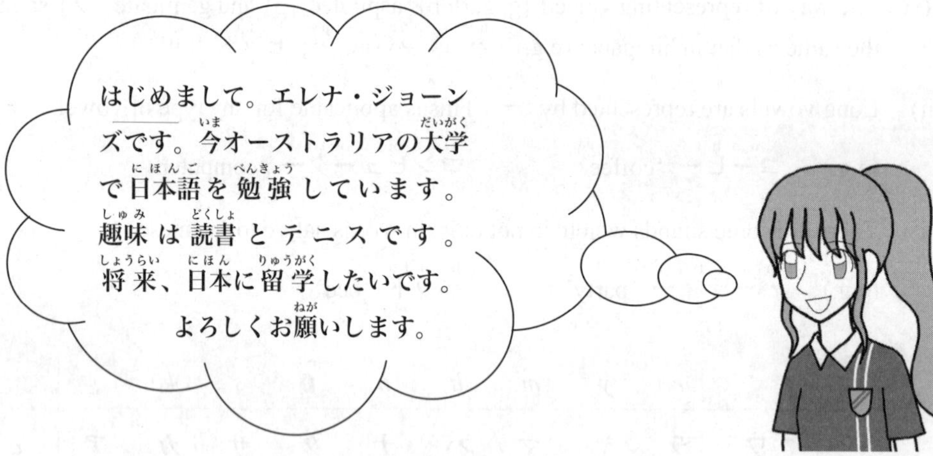
はじめまして。エレナ・ジョーンズです。今オーストラリアの大学で日本語を勉強しています。趣味は読書とテニスです。将来、日本に留学したいです。よろしくお願いします。

Elena Jones is a first year university student in Australia. Her major is Japanese. Her hobbies are reading and playing tennis. She hopes to study in Japan on an exchange program in the near future.

# 第1課（だいいっか）

# はじめまして

## How do you do?

[Elena and Masato meet for the first time]

1 エレナ：　はじめまして。エレナです。よろしく　おねがいします。
Erena　Hajimemashite.　Erena desu.　Yoroshiku onegaishimasu.

2 まさと：　はじめまして。まさとです。よろしく　おねがいします。
Masato　Hajimemashite.　Masato desu.　Yoroshiku onegaishimasu.

3 エレナ：　まさとさんは　がくせいですか。
Erena　Masato san wa　gakusei desu ka.

4 まさと：　はい、そうです。エレナさんは　がくせいですか。
Masato　Hai,　soo desu.　Erena san wa　gakusei desu ka.

5 エレナ：　ええ、わたしも　がくせいです。まさとさんは、りゅうがくせいですか。
Erena　Ee,　watashi mo gakusei desu.　Masato san wa　ryuugakusei desu ka.

6 まさと：　いいえ、りゅうがくせいでは ありません。
Masato　Iie,　ryuugakusei dewa arimasen.

7 にほんの だいがくの　がくせいです。
Nihon no　daigaku no　gakusei desu.

8 エレナ：　あ、そうですか。
Erena　A,　soo desu ka.

### 単語（たんご）と表現（ひょうげん）　Vocabulary and Expressions (Dialogue)

| | | | | | | | |
|---|---|---|---|---|---|---|---|
| 3 | がくせい | gakusei | student | 6 | いいえ | iie | no |
| 4 | はい | hai | yes | 7 | にほん | Nihon | Japan |
| 4 | そう | soo | That's right. | 7 | だいがく | daigaku | university |
| 5 | ええ | ee | yes | 8 | あ | a | oh, ah |
| 5 | りゅうがくせい | ryuugakusei | overseas student | 8 | そうですか | Soo desu ka | I see. |

| | | | |
|---|---|---|---|
| 1 | はじめまして | Hajimemashite | How do you do? (*lit.* I am meeting you for the first time.) |
| 1 | よろしく　おねがいします | Yoroshiku onegaishimasu | Nice to meet you. (*lit.* Please do me a favour, Please be good to me.) |
| 3 | ～さん | san | term of address (Mr., Mrs., Miss.) (cf. Expression Notes 3) |

Dialogue in English

**[Elena and Masato meet for the first time]**

1 E: How do you do? I'm Elena. Nice to meet you.
2 M: How do you do? I'm Masato. Nice to meet you.
3 E: Are you a student, Masato?
4 M: Yes, I am. Are you a student, Elena?
5 E: Yes, I am a student, too. Are you an overseas student, Masato?
6-7 M: No, I'm not an overseas student. I am a student in a university in Japan.
8 E: Oh, I see.

## 文法(ぶんぽう) Grammar

### 1. Xは Yです 'X is Y; As for X, it is Y; Speaking of X, it is Y'
wa desu

*Wa* (topic marker) follows a noun phrase X, and indicates that X is the topic under discussion. The nominal predicate Y *desu* is the description of that topic; *desu* is the copula (polite) which is equivalent to the *be* verb (e.g. am, is, are) in English. (Hiragana は is read as [wa] when used as the topic marker.)

(1) わたしは たなかです。 '(Speaking of myself) I am Tanaka.'
Watashi wa Tanaka desu.

(2) なかおさんは がくせいです。 '(Speaking of Ms Nakao) Ms Nakao is a student.'
Nakao san wa gakusei desu.

(3) ジョンさんは オーストラリアじんです。'(As for Mr John) Mr John is an Australian.'
Jon san wa Oosutoraria jin desu.

In Japanese it is natural to omit the subject of a sentence when it is obvious. For example, when you introduce yourself, *Watashi wa* 'Speaking of myself' may be dropped and only X (the name) *desu* '(I) am X' may be used. So, (1) above could simply be *Tanaka desu* '(I) am Tanaka.' More details on subject omission will be given in later lessons.

### 2. Nouns: Singular-plural distinction

A noun is a word that connotes the name of a person, animal, place or thing. Unlike in English, there is no grammatical item which corresponds to 'a' (e.g. **a** student), or the plural '-s' (e.g. student**s**) in Japanese. Thus, without providing a background to situations, *gakusei* is ambiguous between the singular and the plural interpretations.

(1) がくせい 'student; students' せんせい 'teacher; teachers'
gakusei sensei

The singular-plural interpretation of a given noun often depends on the context, or sometimes remains ambiguous, but without causing problems when the distinction is not the main concern of the sentence. Quantifiers (or counting words) may be used when the number of a noun is specifically to be expressed.

(2) ひとりの がくせい 'one student' ふたりの がくせい 'two students'
hitori no gakusei futari no gakusei

The suffix *–tachi* can be added to the noun in order to indicate its plurality. However, the use of *–tachi* is limited in that it can basically apply only to human beings.

(3) わたしたち 'we'　　　　　がくせいたち 'students'
watashi tachi　　　　　gakusei tachi

**Grammar Exercise 1**

**Rewrite the following sentences in Japanese. Write the answers in Romaji and Hiragana.**

(e.g.) I am Nakamura. Watashi wa Nakamura desu. わたしは　なかむらです。

(1) I am Suzuki.

(2) I am a student.

(3) I am Japanese. (Japanese にほんじん Nihonjin)

(4) Ms Yamada is a teacher.

For practices in Lessons 1-3, refer to a list of occupations, majors and hobbies in Appendix.

**Grammar Exercise 2**

**Look at the pictures and make up sentences with the word listed below. Write the answers in Romaji and Hiragana.**

(e.g.) Takahashi san wa gakusei desu.
たかはしさんは　がくせいです。

(e.g.)

Takahashi

(1) Kimura

(2)

Honda

(3)

Yamada

(4)

Smith

(5)

Shin

| | | |
|---|---|---|
| ~~がくせい 'student'~~<br>gakusei | せんせい 'teacher'<br>sensei | イギリスじん 'English'<br>Igirisu jin |
| いしゃ 'doctor'<br>isha | かんこくじん 'Korean'<br>Kankoku jin | かいしゃいん 'office worker'<br>kaishain |

### 3. か (Interrogative marker)
ka

In Japanese, an interrogative sentence (yes-no question) is formed by simply adding the interrogative marker ***ka*** to the end of a declarative sentence with a rising intonation.

(1) a. なかむらさんは がくせいです。 'Mr Nakamura is a student.'
Nakamura san wa gakusei desu.

b. なかむらさんは がくせいですか。 'Is Mr Nakamura a student?'
Nakamura san wa gakusei desu **ka**.

(2) a. スコットさんは オーストラリアじんです。 'Mr Scott is an Australian.'
Sukotto san wa Oosutoraria jin desu.

b. スコットさんは オーストラリアじんですか。 'Is Mr Scott an Australian?'
Sukotto san wa Oosutoraria jin desu **ka**.

In writing, the question mark '?' is in principle not used with the interrogative marker *ka* in Japanese.

| はい／いいえ |
|---|
| hai　　iie |

In answering a yes-no question, ***hai*** 'yes' and ***iie*** 'no' are used. Also, to negate the sentence X *wa* Y *desu*, *desu* is replaced with ***dewa arimasen***.

(3) なかむらさんは がくせいですか。 'Is Mr Nakamura a student?'
Nakamura san wa gakusei desu ka.

→ はい、(なかむらさんは) がくせいです。 'Yes. He is (a student).'
Hai. Nakamura san wa gakusei desu .

→ いいえ、(なかむらさんは) がくせいでは ありません。 'No. He is not (a student) .'
Iie . Nakamura san wa gakusei dewa arimasen .

(4) スコットさんは オーストラリアじんですか。 'Is Mr Scott an Australian?'
Sukotto san wa Oosutoraria jin desu ka.

→ はい、(スコットさんは) オーストラリアじんです。 'Yes, he is (an Australian).'
Hai. Sukotto san wa Oosutoraria jin desu.

→ いいえ、(スコットさんは) オーストラリアじんでは ありません。
Iie. Sukotto san wa Oosutoraria jin dewa arimasen.
'No, he is not (an Australian).'

**[Note]** ***-dewa (arimasen)*** is often contracted to ***-ja (arimasen)*** in casual conversation.

**Grammar Exercise 3**

**Rewrite the following sentences in Japanese. (Answer in Romaji and Hiragana)**

(e.g.) Is Mr Yamada a student? Yamada san wa gakusei desu ka.

やまださんは がくせいですか。

(1) Is Ms Kim a teacher?

(2) I am not a student.

(3) Is Ms Suzuki a bank employee? (bank employee ぎんこういん ginkooin)

(4) Mr Suzuki is not a bank employee.

(5) Mr Scott is not an American. (American アメリカじん Amerikajin)

**Grammar Exercise 4**

**Provide an affirmative and a negative answer to the following sentences in Japanese. (Write answers in Romaji and Hiragana)**

(e.g.) たなかさんは がくせいですか。
Tanaka san wa gakusei desu ka.

Hai, gakusei desu. はい、がくせいです。

Iie, gakusei dewa arimasen. いいえ、がくせいでは ありません。

(1) おのさんは せんせいですか。
Ono san wa sensei desu ka.

(2) キムさんは かんこくじんですか。
Kimu san wa Kankoku jin desu ka.

(3) すずきさんは だいがくせいですか。
Suzuki san wa daigakusei desu ka.

(4) むらかみさんは かいしゃいんですか。
Murakami san wa kaishain desu ka.

(5) ジョンさんは イギリスじんですか。
Jon san wa Igirisu jin desu ka.

## 4. X の Y 'X's Y; Y associated with X'
no

***No*** is a grammatical item that connects two nouns and basically indicates 'Y associated with X'. The preceding noun 'X' modifies, or adds some information to, the second noun 'Y', describing ownership, location, authorship, genitive proper and so forth.

(1) わたしの　ほん　　　'my book' (*watashi* + *no* = my)
watashi no hon

(2) わたしの　せんせい　　　'my teacher'
watashi no sensei

(3) にほんごの　せんせい　　　'a teacher of Japanese (Japanese teacher)'
Nihongo no sensei

(4) わたしの　にほんごの　せんせい　　　'my Japanese teacher'
watashi no Nihongo no sensei

(5) たなかさんの　おくさん　　　'Mr Tanaka's wife'
Tanaka san no okusan

(6) とうきょうの　だいがく　　　'a university in Tokyo'
Tookyoo no daigaku

### Grammar Exercise 5

**Rewrite the following phrases/sentences in Japanese. Refer to words in the list below. Write the answers in Romaji and Hiragana.**

(e.g.) My teacher ___watashi no sensei___ ___わたしの せんせい___

(1) My book

(2) My university

(3) Mr Tanaka's car

(4) Mary's friend

(5) a teacher of English

(6) Masato's major

(7) Japanese dictionary

(8) My Japanese teacher's book

(9) Yamada-sensei is my Japanese teacher.

(10) Mr Tanaka is not my friend.

| | | | | | |
|---|---|---|---|---|---|
| book | ほん<br>hon | car | くるま<br>kuruma | university | だいがく<br>daigaku |
| friend | ともだち<br>tomodachi | teacher | せんせい<br>sensei | major | せんこう<br>senkoo |
| English (language) | えいご<br>Eigo | Japanese (language) | にほんご<br>Nihongo | dictionary | じしょ<br>jisho |

## 表現（ひょうげん） Expression Notes

### 1 Greetings and some useful expressions

[1] ☛ ・はじめまして 'How do you do? (*lit.* I am meeting you for the first.)'
Hajimemashite

・よろしく おねがいします 'Nice to meet you. (*lit.* Please do me a favour.)'
Yoroshiku onegaishimasu

> They are used when you meet a person for the first time.
>
> (e.g.) *Hajimemashite.* <Name> *desu. Yoroshiku onegaishimasu.*

[2] ☛ ・おはようございます／おはよう (casual) 'Good morning.'
Ohayoo gozaimasu Ohayoo

・こんにちは 'Hello; Good afternoon.'
Konnichiwa

・こんばんは 'Good evening.'
Konbanwa

> (i) *Ohayoo* and *Konnichiwa*
>
> Their use basically depends on whether or not the speaker feels it is still early of the day. So typically at around 10:00 - 11:00 a.m. some might still use *Ohayoo (gozaimasu)*, while some use *Konnichiwa.*
>
> (ii) *Konnichiwa* and *Konbanwa*
>
> - They are not used among family members. (cf. *Ohayoo* is used.)
> - They are not used more than twice to the same person within the day.
>
> (iii) These greetings are often used with bowing.

[3] ☛ ・A: おげんきですか 'How are you?'
Ogenki desu ka

B: ええ、おかげさまで 'Yes, I'm fine. Thank you for asking.'
Ee, okagesama de

> *Ogenki desu ka* is normally used when you have not seen him/her for a long time.

[4] ☛ ・A: いってきます 'So long. (*lit.* I will go and come back.)'
Ittekimasu

B: いっていらっしゃい 'So long. (*lit.* Please go and come back.)'
Itteirasshai

> When leaving home *Ittekimasu* is used, while *Itteirasshai* is used as a response to *Ittekimasu.* (*Itteirasshai* tends to become *Itterasshai.*)

[5] ☛ ・A: ただいま 'I'm home.' (when back home from work, school, etc.)
Tadaima

B: おかえりなさい 'Welcome back home.'
Okaerinasai

[6] ☛ ・では(じゃあ)、また 'Well then…, See you again.'
Dewa (Jaa), mata

・さようなら 'Good-bye.'
Sayoonara

[7] ☛ ・ごめんなさい／ごめん(casual)／すみません 'Excuse me, I'm sorry, Thank you.'
Gomennasai Gomen Sumimasen

> *Sumimasen* mainly has three functions:
> (i) 'I'm sorry' to apologise for the trouble which you have caused.
> (ii) 'Excuse me' to draw the addressee's attention.
> (iii) 'Thank you' to show your appreciation for what the person has done for you.

[8] ☛ ・A: どうも ありがとうございます(formal)／ありがとう 'Thank you.'
Doomo arigatoo gozaimasu Arigatoo

B: いいえ、どういたしまして 'You are welcome.'
Iie, dooitashimashite

> *Dooitashimashite* is often omitted, leaving the simple response *Iie* 'No'.

[9] ☛ ・いただきます 'Thank you for the meal. (*lit*. I will have it.)'
Itadakimasu

・ごちそうさまでした／ごちそうさま (casual) 'Thank you for the meal. (*lit*. It was delicious.)'
Gochisoosamadeshita Gochisoosama

> *Itadakimasu* is used just before eating, while *Gochisoosamadeshita* is used after eating.

[10] ☛ ・おやすみなさい／おやすみ (casual) 'Good night.'
Oyasuminasai Oyasumi

**Expression Exercise 1**

**Introduce yourself to your friends in class as in the example.**

(e.g.) はじめまして。 [Name] です。
Hajimemashite. [Name] desu.

よろしく おねがいします。
Yoroshiku onegaishimasu.

## Expression Exercise 2

**What would you say in each case below?**

(e.g.)

おはようございます
Ohayoo gozaimasu.

(1)

(2)

(3)

(4)

(5)

(6)

(7)

(8)

## 2 Expressions with も (mo) 'also; too; as well'

**[1]☛** The basic meaning of ***mo*** is that the preceding noun shares something in common with others.

(1) わたしは　がくせいです。 'I am a student.'
Watashi **wa** gakusei desu.

たなかさんも　がくせいです。 'Mr Tanaka is a student, too.'
Tanaka san **mo** gakusei desu.

(2) ほんださんは　にほんごの　せんせいです。 'Ms Honda is a Japanese teacher.'
Honda san **wa** Nihongo no sensei desu.

すずきさんも　にほんごの　せんせいです。 'Mr Suzuki is a Japanese teacher, too.'
Suzuki san **mo** Nihongo no sensei desu.

[2]☛ ***Mo*** and ***wa*** are opposite. *Mo* indicates something in common (i.e. 'also'; inclusive), while *wa* indicates something in contrast with others (i.e. 'speaking of this'; exclusive).

(3) わたしは　がくせいです。 たなかさんも　がくせいです。おかださんは
Watashi wa gakusei desu. Tanaka san **mo** gakusei desu. Okada san **wa**

がくせいでは　ありません。
gakusei dewa arimasen.

'I am a student. Mr Tanaka is a student, too. Ms Okada is not a student.'

**Expression Exercise 3**

**Rewrite the following sentences in Japanese. Write the answers in Romaji and Hiragana.**

(e.g.) I am Chinese. Mr Chen is Chinese, too.

→ Watashi wa Chuugoku jin desu. Chen san mo Chuugoku jin desu.

→ わたしは　ちゅうごくじんです。チェンさんも　ちゅうごくじんです。

(1) I am a university student. Miss Yamada is a university student, too.

(2) Mr Tanaka is a teacher. Mr Kimura is a teacher, too.

(3) Mr Suzuki is a company employee. Miss Numata is a company employee, too.

(4) Ms Scott is an American. Mr Smith is an American, too. Miss Johnson is an Australian.

(5) Mr Yamada is my friend. Mr Honda is my friend, too. Mr Nomura is not my friend.

## 3 Address term: ～さん 'Mr., Ms., Mrs., Miss.'
san

☛ ***San*** is used after a name as a generic title. It is never used when one refers to oneself. It is normally used with a family name, but sometimes with a given name when one addresses a close friend. It is also used for both male and female names, and thus it sometimes causes difficulty when people translate Japanese ~ *san* into English, since for example, *Tanaka san* could be Mr Tanaka or Miss Tanaka.

(1) たなかさん 'Miss. Tanaka' まさとさん 'Mr. Masato'
Tanaka san Masato san

スミスさん 'Mrs. Smith' エレナさん 'Miss. Elena'
Sumisu san Erena san

It is sometimes appended to the name of an occupation.

(2) べんごしさん 'lawyer' おいしゃさん 'doctor'
bengoshi san oisha san

Teachers and people in some occupations such as medical doctors and politicians are preferably referred to with the title *sensei* rather than *san*.

(3) やまだせんせい 'Mr. Yamada (Sir)'    すずきせんせい 'Dr. Suzuki'
Yamada sensei    Suuki sensei

Children as well as adults with whom you have a close relationship are sometimes referred to as name-*chan* (also boys as *kun*) rather than *san*.

(4) けいこちゃん 'Keiko'    さっちゃん 'Sachiko'    まなぶくん 'Manabu'
Keiko chan    Sacchan    Manabu kun

## 4 Nationality: ～じん
jin

☛ The combination of the name of a nation and ***jin*** indicates the nationality of a person. See Appendix for an expanded list of the names of countries.

(1) オーストラリアじん 'Australian'    アメリカじん 'American'
Oosutoraria jin    Amerika jin

にほんじん 'Japanese'    かんこくじん 'Korean'
Nihon jin    Kankoku jin

(2) えりこさんは　にほんじんです。 'Miss. Eriko is Japanese.'
Eriko san wa　Nihon jin desu.

チェンさんは　ちゅうごくじんです。 'Mr. Chen is Chinese.'
Chen san wa　Chuugoku jin desu.

### Expression Exercise 4

**Write the nationality of each people, as in the example.**

(e.g) Suzuki san wa Nihon jin desu.    すずきさんは にほんじんです。

(e.g.) [Japan]

すずき
Suzuki

(1) [England]

スコット
Sukotto (Scott)

(2) [Australia]

ジョン
Jon

(3) [Korea]

キム
Kimu

(4) [U.S.A.]

フォード
Foodo (Ford)

(5) [China]

リン
Rin

## <ruby>対話<rt>たいわ</rt></ruby> Communicative Exchanges

**Pre-task:** 〜です／では ありません
Nationalities; Occupations

### Pair practice 1

(i) In the table below, first decide the nationality and occupation of each person—Choose one from the list below. Write your choices on the line in each box.

(ii) In pairs, you then ask your conversation partner (Y.P.) the questions as in the example. This is practice for a closed (*yes-no*) question and you need to guess his/her nationality/occupation by choosing one from the list.

(iii) Write your partner's answers under the line in each box. When you have finished asking/answering the questions, change the roles.

England　Australia　USA　Italy　Japan　Korea　China
doctor　student　office worker　bank employee　housewife

| | | | | |
|---|---|---|---|---|
| | (e.g.)  |  |  |  |
| Name | トニー<br>Tonii | ルーシー<br>Ruushii | エミリー<br>Emirii | アンディ<br>Andii |
| Nationality | English<br>American | | | |
| Occupation | Doctor | | | |

(e.g. 1) You: トニーさんは アメリカじんですか。
Tonii san wa Amerika jin desu ka.

Y.P.: はい、そうです。アメリカじんです。
Hai, soo desu. Amerika jin desu.

You: あ、そうですか。
A, soo desu ka.

(e.g. 2) Y.P.: トニーさんは オーストラリアじんですか。
Tonii san wa Oosutoraria jin desu ka.

You: いいえ、オーストラリアじんでは ありません。イギリスじんです。
Iie, Oosutoraria jin dewa arimasen. Igirisu jin desu.

Y.P.: あ、そうですか。
A, soo desu ka.

**Pair practice 2**

**Pre-task:** First meeting

(i) First decide your nationality and occupation, and write them down in the following table. You may make up your answers for practice.

(ii) In pairs, ask your conversation partner about his/her nationality and occupation as in the example below. In asking the questions, you need to guess your partner's nationality and occupation.

(iii) When you have finished asking/answering the questions, change the roles.

| | (e.g.) You | Y.P. | You | Y.P. 1 | Y.P. 2 |
|---|---|---|---|---|---|
| Name | Daniel Hayes | Chen, Shu Min | | | |
| Nationality | English | Chinese | | | |
| Occupation | Office worker | Doctor | | | |

(Y.P. = Your conversation partner)

(e.g.)

You: はじめまして。ダニエル・ヘイズです。 よろしく おねがいします。
Hajimemashite. Danieru Heizu desu. Yoroshiku onegaishimasu.

Y.P.: はじめまして。チェンシュミンです。 よろしく おねがいします。
Hajimemashite. Chen Shu Min desu. Yoroshiku onegaishimasu.

ヘイズさんは イギリスじんですか。
Heizu san wa Igirisujin desu ka.

You: はい、そうです。 **OR** いいえ、オーストラリアじんです。
Hai, soo desu. Iie, Oosutoraria jin desu.

チェンさんは？
Chen san wa?

Y.P.: わたしは ちゅうごくじんです。ヘイズさんは かいしゃいんですか。
Watashi wa Chuugoku jin desu. Heizu san wa kaishain desu ka.

You: はい、そうです。 **OR** いいえ、ぎんこういんです。
Hai, soo desu. Iie, ginkooin desu.

チェンさんは？
Chen san wa?

Y.P.: わたしは いしゃです。
Watashi wa isha desu.

You: そうですか。
Soo desu ka.

## 知ってた？ Did you know?

### お辞儀 (*ojigi*) 'Bowing'

***Ojigi*** 'bowing' is a very important custom in Japan. Japanese people greet each other by *ojigi* 'bowing' instead of shaking hands. *Ojigi* 'bowing' has many functions such as greeting, expressing a feeling of respect, expressing thanks, apologising, making a request, and asking somebody for a favour.

| 会釈 ***eshaku*** | 敬礼 ***keirei*** | 最敬礼 ***saikeirei*** |
|---|---|---|
| 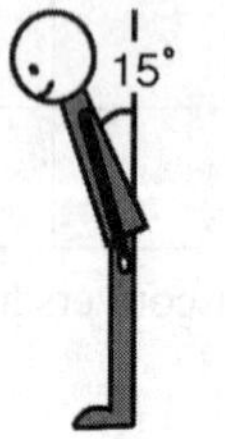 | 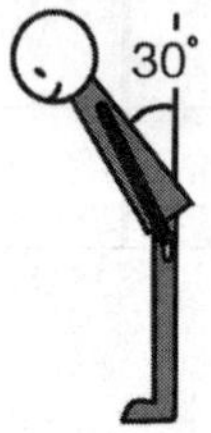 |  |
| Bow of about 15 degrees<br>(e.g.) greeting an acquaintance | Bow of about 30 degrees<br>(e.g.) greeting a guest or one's boss | Bow of about 45 degrees<br>(e.g.) making an important request or thanking and apologising to a person who is of higher status than you are |

Bowing techniques range from a small nod of the head to a 45 degree bow. It depends on the social status or age of the person to whom you bow, as well as the function you are bowing for. If the person is of higher status or older than you , and it is a very important occasion, you should bow deeper and longer.

The proper form for a bow is to bend from the waist with a straight back. Men usually keep their hands at their sides, and women usually put their hands together on their thighs with their fingers touching.

**Exercise**

**Act out an appropriate bowing in the following situations.**

(1) You pass your teacher on the street.

(2) You meet a person who picked up and returned your lost purse.

(3) You enter your teacher's office.

(4) You visit your friend's house and his/her mother pours a cup of tea for you.

(5) You ask your friend to lend you some money.

## Discussions

**Discuss the differences in ways of greeting in different cultures.**

(1) What is a typical or traditional way of greeting in your culture for different times in a day?

- morning - daytime - evening - night - any other time

(2a) When you meet a person for the first time, what is a general or traditional way to greet with him/her in your culture?

- shake hands - bow - hug - any other ways

(2b) Do you have any fixed opening and closing expressions for this occasion?

(Example from Japanese)

Opening: *Hajimemashite* 'I meet you for the first time.'

Closing: *Yoroshiku* (*oneggaishimasu*) 'Please do me a favour.'

## 新(あたら)しい単語(たんご)・表現(ひょうげん) New Vocabulary & Expressions

(Basic words/expressions are marked with '*')

| | |
|---|---|
| あ<br>a | oh, ah |
| アメリカ*<br>America | America, USA |
| いいえ*<br>iie | no |
| いえ*<br>ie | house, home |
| イギリス*<br>Igirisu | English, England |
| いしゃ*<br>isha | doctor |
| えいご*<br>eigo | English |
| ええ*<br>ee | yes |
| オーストラリア*<br>Oosutoraria | Australia |
| おくさん*<br>okusan | wife (someone else's) |
| おじぎ<br>ojigi | bowing |
| かいしゃいん*<br>kaishain | office worker |
| がくせい*<br>gakusei | student |
| かんこく*<br>Kankoku | Korea |
| ぎんこういん<br>ginkooin | bank employer |
| くるま*<br>kuruma | car |
| [country] ご*<br>go | language (of the country) |
| 〜さん*<br>san | Mr., Mrs., Miss. |
| じしょ*<br>jisho | dictionary |
| [country] じん*<br>jin | people (of the country) |

| | |
|---|---|
| せんこう*<br>senkoo | major |
| せんせい*<br>sensei | teacher |
| そう<br>soo | That's right. |
| そうですか*<br>soo desu ka | Is that so?, I see. |
| だいがく*<br>daigaku | university |
| だいがくせい*<br>daigakusei | university student |
| ちゅうごく*<br>Chuugoku | China |
| とうきょう*<br>Tookyoo | Tokyo |
| ともだち*<br>tomodachi | friend |
| にほん*<br>Nihon | Japan |
| はい*<br>hai | yes |
| はじめまして*<br>hajimemashite | How do you do? |
| フランス<br>Furansu | France |
| べんごし<br>bengoshi | lawyer |
| ほん*<br>hon | book |
| よろしく*<br>yoroshiku | Please be good to me. |
| りゅうがくせい<br>ryuugakusei | overseas student |
| わたし*<br>watashi | I |

# 第2課（だいにか）

# しゅみは　なんですか
## What is your hobby?

[Elena and Masato are talking]

1 まさと：　エレナさんの　しゅみは　なんですか。
Masato　Erena san no　shumi wa　nan desu ka.

2 エレナ：　わたしの　しゅみは　どくしょです。
Erena　Watashi no　shumi wa　dokusho desu.

3 まさと：　そうですか。それは　にほんごの　ほんですか。
Masato　Soo desu ka.　Sore wa　Nihongo no　hon desu ka.

4 エレナ：　はい、そうです。まさとさんの　しゅみは　なんですか。
Erena　Hai,　soo desu.　Masato san no　shumi wa　nan desu ka.

5 まさと：　やきゅうです。
Masato　Yakyuu desu.

6 エレナ：　やきゅう？　やきゅうって
Erena　Yakyuu?　Yakyuu tte

7 　えいごで　なんですか。
Eigo de　nan desu ka.

8 まさと：　Baseball です。
Masato　'Baseball' desu.

9 エレナ：　あ、そうですか。
Erena　A,　soo desu ka.

## 単語と表現（たんご　ひょうげん） Vocabulary and Expressions (Dialogue)

| | | | | | | | |
|---|---|---|---|---|---|---|---|
| 1 | しゅみ | shumi | hobby | 2 | どくしょ | dokusho | reading books |
| 1 | なん | nan | what | 3 | それ | sore | that |
| 6-7 | Xって　えいごで　なんですか (tte　Eigo de　nan desu ka) | | What is X in English ? | | | | |

**Dialogue in English**

**[Elena and Masato are talking]**

1 M: What is your hobby, Elena?
2 E: My hobby is reading books.
3 M: I see. Is that a Japanese book?
4 E: Yes, it is. What is your hobby, Masato?
5 M: (My hobby) is 'yakyuu'.
6-7 E: 'Yakyuu'? What is 'yakyuu' in English?
8 M: It is baseball.
9 E: Oh, I see.

## 文法 Grammar

(ぶんぽう)

### 1. X は なんですか／X は どこですか 'What/Where is X?"

wa nan desu ka wa doko desu ka

#### 1.1. *Wh* questions

In Japanese, a *wh*-question (or open question) is made up by adding an interrogative word and the interrogative marker *ka*. An interrogative word appears in the position at which information sought by the interrogative word appears. As in the *yes-no* question, *ka* appears at the end of a sentence with a rising intonation.

(1) しゅみは ＿＿ です。 '(My) hobby is ...........'
Shumi wa desu.

→ *Wh* question: しゅみは なんですか。 'What is (your) hobby?'
Shumi wa nan desu ka.

→ Descriptive: しゅみは どくしょです。 '(My) hobby is reading books.'
Shumi wa dokusho desu.

(NB. Both a question and the answer have the same sentence structure.)

You may answer *wh* questions simply by providing the required information (and with ～です *desu* in polite speech).

(2) しゅみは なんですか。 'What is (your) hobby?'
Shumi wa nan desu ka.

→ どくしょです。 '(My hobby) is reading books.'
Dokusho desu.

Study the following examples, in which words in ( ) are not normally repeated in answers; [ご] and [お] are honorific prefix (See below, for details):

(3) [ご] しゅみは なんですか。 'What is (your) hobby?'
[Go] shumi wa nan desu ka.

→ (しゅみは) つりです。 '(My hobby) is fishing.'
(Shumi wa ) tsuri desu.

(4) [ご] しゅっしんは どこ（どちら）ですか。 'Where is (your) place of birth? (Where are you from?)'
[Go] shusshin wa doko (dochira) desu ka.

→ (しゅっしんは) オーストラリアです。 '(My place of birth) is Australia. (I'm from Australia.)'
(Shusshin wa) Oosutoraria desu.

(5) [お] すまいは どこ（どちら）ですか。 'Where is (your) living place?'
[O] sumai wa doko (dochira) desu ka.

→ (すまいは) とうきょうです。 '(My living place) is in Tokyo.'
(Sumai wa) Tookyoo desu.

### 1.2. なん／なに 'what'
nan nani

The interrogative word for 'what' has two pronunciations, *nan* and *nani*. *Nan* is used immediately before *desu ka,* or to form a compound such as *nan ji* 'what time', *nan nin* 'how many people', *nan kai* 'how many times', etc., whereas *nani* is used before a particle or with the suffix *-jin* '*nani jin*' (which nationality).

(6) なん： なんですか 'what is it' なんじ 'what time' なんにん 'how many people'
nan nan desu ka nanji nannin

なに： なにを 'what-(objective marker)' なにが 'what-(subjective marker)'
nani nani o nani ga

### 1.3. どこ／どちら 'where'
doko dochira

*Dochira* is more formal than *doko* and preferably used in formal situations.

(7) しゅっしんは どこですか。
Shusshin wa doko desu ka.

ごしゅっしんは どちらですか。
Goshussin wa dochira desu ka.

'Where is (your) place of birth? (Where are you from?)'

### 1.4. お／ご '(Honorific prefix)'
o go

In Lesson 2, we just focus on the use of o/go in several expressions as in (8).

The prefix *o* or *go* is added to nouns which refer to respected person talked about or people/things that are associated with that person: *O* is basically used with Yamato-Japanese (or words native to Japanese) and *go* with Sino-Japanese (or words of Chinese origin).

(8) おすまい 'living place' おしごと 'occupation; work' おなまえ 'name'
**o**sumai **o**shigoto **o**namae

ごせんこう 'major' ごしゅっしん 'place of birth' ごしゅみ 'hobby'
**go**senkoo **go**shusshin **go**shumi

They may not be used to refer to the speaker him/herself:

(9) *わたしの おなまえは きむらです。 [ungrammatical] 'My name is Kimura.'
Watashi no onamae wa Kimura desu.

*わたしの ごしゅみは どくしょです。[ungrammatical] 'My hobby is reading books.'
Watashi no goshumi wa dokusho desu.

### 1.5. The use of あなた 'you'
anata

The use of the second-person pronoun *anata* 'you' is restricted to a very limited context; for example, when people fight, when a wife calls her husband, or towards indefinite audience/readers as in an advertisement. Thus, *anata* is, in general, not used in 'normal' conversation. Instead, name-*san*, kin terms, or occupational terms may be used to address the second person. Note also that second-person references are often not overtly specified (Sentences without a second-person reference, or a first person reference (e.g. *watashi*), are still fully understandable by the discourse or the situational context).

(10) Second person reference is omitted (thus, *anata* may not be overtly used):

おなまえは なんですか。 'What is (your) name?'
Onamae wa nan desu ka.

→ [Less common] <u>あなたの</u> おなまえは なんですか。 'What is your name?'
<u>Anata no</u> onamae wa nan desu ka.

(11) Make use of the listener's name (thus, the second-person pronoun *anata* may not be used):

スミスさんの ごしゅっしんは どちらですか。
Sumisu san no goshusshin wa dochira desu ka.
'Ms. Smith, where is (your) place of birth?'

→ [Less common] <u>あなたの</u> ごしゅっしんは どちらですか。
<u>Anata no</u> goshusshin wa dochira desu ka.
'Where is your place of birth?'

**Grammar Exercise 1**

**Rewrite the following sentences in Japanese. Write the answers in Romaji and Hiragana.**

(e.g.) A: What's your name? <u>Onamae wa nan desu ka.</u> <u>おなまえは なんですか。</u>

B: (My name is) Tanaka. <u>(Watashi no namae wa) Tanaka desu.</u>
<u>（わたしの なまえは）たなかです。</u>

(1) A: What is your name?

B: (My name is) Sakamoto.

(2) A: Where is your place of birth? (Where are you from?)

B: It is China. (I'm from China.) (China ちゅうごく *Chuugoku*)

(3) A: What is your occupation?

B: It is a bank employee.

(4) A: What is your major?

B: It is Japanese.

(5) A: What is your hobby?

B: It is reading books. (reading books どくしょ *dokusho*)

(6) A: Where is your living place? (Where do you live?)

B: It is in Sydney. (Sydney シドニー *Shidonii*)

## 2. Demonstratives: [これ --- それ --- あれ] *vs.* [この --- その --- あの]

kore sore are kono sono ano

**'this, that, that (over there)'**

### 2.1. General features of *ko-so-a*

When the speaker refers to a thing/person/place, the demonstrative words *ko-*, *so-* and *a-* are distinctively used, based on proximity to the speaker or the listener:

(a) ***Ko***- refers to a thing/person/place that is close to the speaker.

(b) ***So***- refers to a thing/person/place that is close to the listener.

(c) ***A***- refers to a thing/person/place that is far from both the speaker and the listener.

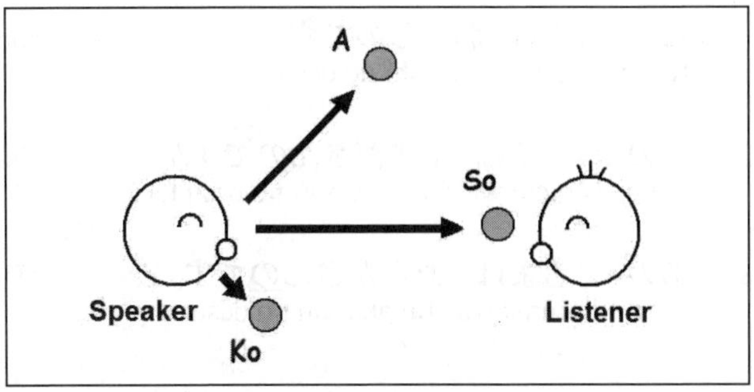


### 2.2. Differences between *kore – sore – are* and *kono – sono – ano*

***Kore***, ***sore***, and ***are*** stand alone to mean 'this thing', 'that thing (near you)' and 'that thing over there', while ***kono***, ***sono***, and ***ano*** are grammatically dependent, and always precede nouns to modify them. Compare:

(1) これは わたしの ほんです。 'This is my book.'
Kore wa watashi no hon desu.

この ほんは わたしの ほんです。 'This book is my book.'
Kono hon wa watashi no hon desu.

(2) それは わたしの ほんです。 'That (near you) is my book.'
Sore wa watashi no hon desu.

その ほんは わたしの ほんです。 'That book (near you) is my book.'
Sono hon wa watashi no hon desu.

(3) あれは わたしの ほんです。 'That one over there is my book.'
Are wa watashi no hon desu.

あの ほんは わたしの ほんです。 'That book over there is my book.'
Ano hon wa watashi no hon desu.

Some further examples for the use of *kono*, *sono* and *ano*:

(4) この ひとは たなかさんです。 'This person is Mr Tanaka.'
Kono hito wa Tanaka san desu.

(5) その ほんは やまださんの ほんですか。 'Is that book Miss Yamada's book?'
Sono hon wa Yamada san no hon desu ka.

(6) あの くるまは たなかさんの くるまです。 'That car over there is Mr Tanaka's car.'
Ano kuruma wa Tanaka san no kuruma desu.

## 2.3. Indefinite pronoun の
no

A noun 'Y' may be omitted in the possessive phrase 'X の Y'. The phrase 'X の' then indicates something that belongs to X, in which の refers to an indefinite entity. Compare two sentences in (1) below.

(1) この　ほんは　わたしの　ほんです。　'This book is my book.'
Kono　hon wa　watashi no　hon desu.

この　ほんは　わたしのです。　'This book is mine.'
Kono　hon wa　watashi no desu.

(2) その　カメラは　やまださんのですか。　'Is that camera Miss Yamada's?'
Sono　kamera wa　Yamada san no desu ka.

(3) あの　くるまは　たなかさんのです。　'That car over there is Mr Tanaka's.'
Ano　kuruma wa　Tanaka san no desu.

**Grammar Exercise 2**

**Rewrite the following sentences in Japanese. Write the answers in Romaji and Hiragana.**

(e.g.) This is a book.　Kore wa hon desu.　これは　ほんです。

(1) This is my car.

(2) That is Ms Suzuki's hat.　(hat ぼうし *booshi*)

(3) That one over there is Mr Smith's watch.　(watch とけい *tokei*)

(4) This dictionary is a Japanese dictionary.

(5) That pen is Miss Nakamura's pen.　(pen ペン *pen*)

(6) That house over there is my teacher's house.

(7) This bag is not my bag. That bag is not my bag either.　(bag かばん *kaban*)

(8) That person over there is not an Australian. (He) is an American.　(person ひと *hito*)

(9) A: Is that a newspaper over there?　(newspaper しんぶん *shinbun*)
B: No, that over there is not a newspaper. (That) is a magazine.　(magazine ざっし *zasshi*)

(10) A: Is this umbrella Mr Yamada's umbrella?　(umbrella かさ *kasa*)
B: Yes, it is.

(11) A: What is that?
B: This is my Japanese book.

(12) A: What is that over there?
B: That over there is the library.　(library としょかん *toshokan*)

## 3. Reading numerals

### 3.1. Numbers 0~100

| | | | | | |
|---|---|---|---|---|---|
| 0 | ゼロ/れい<br>zero / rei | | | | |
| 1 | いち<br>ichi | 11 | じゅういち<br>juuichi | 30 | さんじゅう<br>sanjuu |
| 2 | に<br>ni | 12 | じゅうに<br>juuni | 40 | よんじゅう<br>yonjuu |
| 3 | さん<br>san | 13 | じゅうさん<br>juusan | 50 | ごじゅう<br>gojuu |
| 4 | し/よん (i)<br>shi / yon | 14 | じゅうし/じゅうよん<br>juushi / juuyon | 60 | ろくじゅう<br>rokujuu |
| 5 | ご<br>go | 15 | じゅうご<br>juugo | 70 | ななじゅう<br>nanajuu |
| 6 | ろく<br>roku | 16 | じゅうろく<br>juuroku | 80 | はちじゅう<br>hachijuu |
| 7 | しち/なな (ii)<br>shichi / nana | 17 | じゅうしち/じゅうなな<br>juushichi / juunana | 90 | きゅうじゅう<br>kyuujuu |
| 8 | はち<br>hachi | 18 | じゅうはち<br>juuhachi | 100 | ひゃく<br>hyaku |
| 9 | きゅう (iii)<br>kyuu | 19 | じゅうきゅう/じゅうく<br>juukyuu / juuku | 1,000 | せん<br>sen |
| 10 | じゅう<br>juu | 20 | にじゅう<br>nijuu | 10,000 | まん<br>man |

[Note] Readings for 4, 7 and 9 vary, basically depending on the counting words (or quantifiers) which these numbers are used with. Below are some examples.

In isolation: 4 = よん or し (yon, shi)　7 = しち or なな (shichi, nana)　9 = きゅう (kyuu) (not read as く (ku) in isolation)

(i) 4(よん)さい '4 year old' — yon sai
4(よん)しゅうかん 'for 4 weeks' — yon shuukan
4(よ)じ '4 o'clock' — yo ji
4(よ)にん '4 persons' — yo nin

> In general, *shi* (for 4) is not used with counting words.

(ii) 7(なな)さつ '7 books' — nana satsu
7(しち)じ '7 o'clock' — shichi ji
7 (なな/しち) にん '7 persons' — nana / shichi nin

(iii) 9(きゅう) かい '9th floor' — kyuu kai
9(く)じ '9 o'clock' — ku ji
9 (きゅう/く) にん '9 persons' — kyuu / ku nin

## 3.2. Counting numbers

In English a new unit (thousand, million or billion) is used for every three digits and readings up to 999 are reduplicated within the unit.

```
555,555,555   →   5    5    5    5    5    5    5    5    5
                  |    |    |    |    |    |    |    |    |
               hundred |    | hundred |    | hundred |    |
                      ten   |        ten   |        ten   |
                         million       thousand        (none)
```

five hundred and fifty-five **million**, five hundred and fifty-five **thousand**, five hundred and fifty-five **(none)**

(e.g.) 34 thirty four
34,000 thirty-four **thousand**
34,000,000 thirty-four **million**

This basic principle is also applicable to the Japanese reading, but where it differs from the English reading is that a new unit (*man*, *oku* or *choo*) is used for every four digits.

```
555,555,555   →   5    5    5    5    5    5    5    5    5
                  |    |    |    |    |    |    |    |    |
                  |   sen   |    |    |   sen   |    |    |
                  |      hyaku   |    |      hyaku   |    |
                  |            juu    |            juu    |
                 oku                 man                (none)
```

go **oku**, go-sen go-hyaku go-juu go **man**, go-sen go-hyaku go-juu go **(none)**

(e.g.) 26 ni-juu roku
260,000 ni-juu roku **man**
2600,000,000 ni-juu roku **oku**

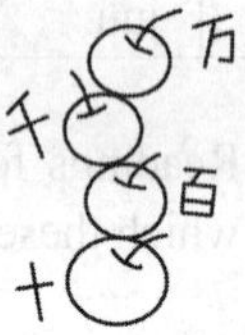


[Note] Typical mistake made by English-speaking learners:
(e.g.) 65,000 → **roku-juu go sen* (should be '*roku man go sen*')

**Grammar Exercise 3**

**Write the readings of the following numbers in Romaji and Hiragana.**

(e.g.) 27 Nijuu nana にじゅうなな

| | | | |
|---|---|---|---|
| (1) 32 | (2) 670 | (3) 448 | (4) 901 |
| (5) 5,524 | (6) 3,303 | (7) 76,100 | (8) 32,000 |
| (9) 320,000 | (10) 183,000 | (11) 92,176 | (12) 275,505 |

## ひょうげん
## 表　現　Expression Notes

### 1 Asking and telling time: なんじですか／３じです 'What time is it?/It's three o'clock.'
Nan ji desu ka　San ji desu

**[1]** ☛ なんじですか　'What time is it?' (cf. *nan -ji* 'what-o'clock').
Nanji desu ka

(1) A: いま　なんじですか。　'What time is it now?'
Ima　nan ji desu ka.

B: １０じです。　'It's ten o'clock.'
Juu ji desu.

(2) A: パーティーは　なんじですか。　'What time is the party? (What time does the party start?)'
Paatii wa　nan ji desu ka.

B: ７じです。　'It's seven o'clock.'
Shichi ji desu.

**[2]** ☛ **Summary of time**

Hours

| | |
|---|---|
| 1 o'clock | いちじ<br>ich iji |
| 2 o'clock | にじ<br>ni ji |
| 3 o'clock | さんじ<br>san ji |
| 4 o'clock | よじ<br>yo ji |
| 5 o'clock | ごじ<br>go ji |
| 6 o'clock | ろくじ<br>roku ji |
| 7 o'clock | しちじ<br>shich iji |
| 8 o'clock | はちじ<br>hach iji |
| 9 o'clock | くじ<br>ku ji |
| 10 o'clock | じゅうじ<br>juu ji |
| 11 o'clock | じゅういちじ<br>juuichi ji |
| 12 o'clock | じゅうにじ<br>juuni ji |

Minutes (Minutes are *fun* or *pun*, depending on the preceding number)

| | | | |
|---|---|---|---|
| 1 | いっぷん<br>ip pun | 11 | じゅういっぷん<br>juuip pun |
| 2 | にふん<br>ni fun | 12 | じゅうにふん<br>juuni fun |
| 3 | さんぷん<br>san pun | 13 | じゅうさんぷん<br>juusan pun |
| 4 | よんぷん<br>yon pun | 14 | じゅうよんぷん<br>juuyon pun |
| 5 | ごふん<br>go fun | 15 | じゅうごふん<br>juugo fun |
| 6 | ろっぷん<br>rop pun | 16 | じゅうろっぷん<br>juurop pun |
| 7 | ななふん<br>nana fun | 17 | じゅうななふん<br>juunana fun |
| 8 | はっぷん<br>hap pun | 18 | じゅうはっぷん<br>juuhap pun |
| 9 | きゅうふん<br>kyuu fun | 19 | じゅうきゅうふん<br>juukyuu fun |
| 10 | じゅっぷん<br>jup pun | 20 | にじゅっぷん<br>nijup pun |
| | | 30 | さんじゅっぷん<br>sanjup pun |
| | | 40 | よんじゅっぷん<br>yonjup pun |
| | | 50 | ごじゅっぷん<br>gojup pun |

[Notes] (1) As in English, 30 minutes are also read as *han* 'half'.

(e.g.) 3じ はん 'half past three' 8じ はん 'half past eight'
san ji han hachi ji han

(2) The use of *mae* 'before, front'.

(e.g.) 5 (minutes) to 3 (o'clock) [= 2:55] → 3じ 5ふん まえ
san ji go fun **mae**

(3) ごぜん *gozen* 'a.m.' and ごご *gogo* 'p.m.

(*gozen* and *gogo* are placed before the time)

(e.g.) 9:00 a.m. → ごぜん 9じ 9:00 p.m.→ ごご 9じ
gozen ku ji gogo ku ji

(4) No specific word is available for 'quarter'. It is simply 15 minutes.

(e.g.) 2:15 [= a quarter past two] → 2じ 15ふん
ni ji juugo fun

In the exercises below we focus on 5 minutes, 10 minutes, 15 minutes, 20 minutes, 25 minutes, etc.

**Expression Exercise 1**

**Look at the following pictures and write the time in Romaji and Hiragana.**

(e.g.) Rokuji gojuu go fun desu. ろくじ ごじゅうごふんです。

(e.g.)

(1)

(2)

(3)

(4)

(5)

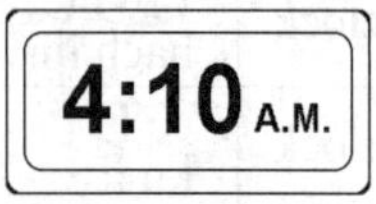


(6)

(7)

(8)

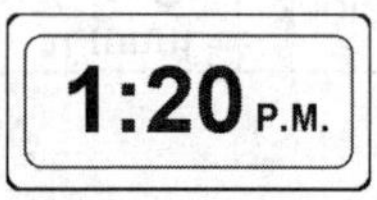

**Expression Exercise 2**

**Rewrite the following sentences in Japanese. Write the answers in Romaji and Hiragana.**

(e.g.) A: What time is it now? Ima nanji desu ka. いま なんじですか。

B: It's 4:00 (now). (Ima) yoji desu. （いま） 4じです。

(1) A: What time is it now?

B: It's 11:25.

(2) A: What time is the movie? (What time does the movie start?) (movie えいが *eiga*)

B: It's 9:30.

(3) A: What time is the party? (What time does the party start?)

B: Its' 7:00 p.m.

(4) A: What time is the exam? (What time does the exam start?) (exam しけん *shiken*)

B: It's 10:50 p.m.

## 2 Useful expressions

**[1] ☛ Xって えいごで なんですか 'What is *X* in English?'**

tte Eigo de nan desu ka

This expression is useful when you do not know the meaning of Japanese words or expressions, you can ask someone what it is in English. Similarly, **X *tte Nihongo de nan desu ka*** 'What is X in Japanese?' may be used to ask the Japanese equivalent for English words.

(1) A: せんこうは げんごがくです。 'My major is *Gengogaku*.'
Senkoo wa Gengogaku desu.

B: げんごがくって えいごで なんですか。 'What is *Gengogaku* in English?'
Gengogaku tte Eigo de nan desu ka.

A: Linguistics です。 'It's Linguistics.'
Linguistics desu.

B: そうですか。 'I see.'
Soo desu ka.

(2) A: しゅみは なんですか。 'What is your hobby?'
Shumi wa nan desu ka.

B: Swimming って にほんごで なんですか。 'What is 'swimming' in Japanese?'
Swimming tte Nihongo de nan desu ka.

A: すいえいです。 'It's *suiei*.'
Suiei desu.

B: そうですか。わたしの しゅみは すいえいです。 'I see. My hobby is swimming.'
Soo desu ka. Watashi no shumi wa suiei desu.

**[2] ☛ Other useful expressions**

(1) もういちど いって もらえませんか。 'Could you say it again?'
Moo ichido itte moraemasen ka.

もういちど いって いただけませんか。 [formal]
Moo ichido itte itadakemasen ka.

(2) ゆっくり いって もらえませんか。 'Could you please speak slowly?'
Yukkuri itte moraemasen ka.

ゆっくり いって いただけませんか。 [formal]
Yukkuri itte itadakemasen ka.

## 対話（たいわ） Communicative Exchanges

### Pair practice 1

**Pre-task:** Expressions on なまえ, しゅっしん, すまい, せんこう, しゅみ

**Ask five classmates about their places of birth, living places, fields of study, and hobbies, and write their answers in the table below. In answering the questions, you may make up your answers for the purpose of practice.**

| なまえ<br>namae | しゅっしん<br>shusshin | すまい<br>sumai | せんこう<br>senkoo | しゅみ<br>shumi |
|---|---|---|---|---|
| (e.g.) Lisa | Sydney | Reid | History, Japanese | Reading books |
| | | | | |
| | | | | |
| | | | | |
| | | | | |
| | | | | |

(e.g.) You: リサさんの ごしゅっしんは どちらですか。
Lisa san no goshussin wa dochira desu ka.

Lisa: (わたしの しゅっしんは) シドニーです。
Watashi no shussin wa Shidonii desu.

You: そうですか。おすまいは どちらですか。
Soo desu ka. Osumai wa dochira desu ka.

Lisa: すまいは リードです。
Sumai wa Riido desu.

: :

You: そうですか。ありがとうございます。
Soo desu ka. Arigatoo gozaimasu.

## Pair practice 2

**Pre-task:** telling time

(i) First decide for yourself what time each activity/event in each question begins (Write the time in the row, 'You').

(ii) In pairs, ask the other person what time each activity/event begins and then write his/her answers in the row, 'Y.P.' (Y.P. = 'Your (Conversation) Partner').

(iii) When you have finished asking/answering the questions, change the roles.

(e.g.) You: えいがは　なんじですか。
Eiga wa　nan ji desu ka.

Y.P.: えいがは　８じはん（or ８じさんじゅっぷん）です。
Eiga wa　hachi ji han (hachi ji sanjup pun) desu.

You: そうですか。ありがとうございます。
Soo desu ka.　Arigatoo gozaimasu.

| | (e.g.) えいが eiga 'movie' | じゅぎょう jugyoo 'class' | でんしゃ densha 'train' | パーティー paatii 'party' | デート deeto 'a date' | コンサート konsaato 'concert' |
|---|---|---|---|---|---|---|
| You | 9:00 | | | | | |
| Y.P. | 8:30 | | | | | |

## Pair practice 3

**Pre-task:** ～って　にほんごで／えいごで　なんですか

**In pairs, ask what given items are called in Japanese (or English).**

(i) In pairs, one checks the Japanese or English words equivalent to those in [A] and the other, those in [B] below. You may wish to check in your dictionaries, internet dictionaries, or to ask your instructor.

(ii) Then ask your partner for at least 5 English words and 3 Japanese words in the list that you have not checked. (i.e. If you have verified Japanese/English words for those in [A], ask about the words in [B]; your partner should be able to give you the correct answers.)

(iii) When you have finished asking/answering the questions, change the roles.

[A] check words below; then ask the words in [B]

| | | |
|---|---|---|
| dictionary | umbrella | hat |
| Law | Psychology | Mathematics |
| Politics | Sociology | music |
| うみ | あたま | じてんしゃ |
| あし | おなか | め |

[B] check words below; then ask the words in [A]

| | | |
|---|---|---|
| newspaper | bird | breakfast |
| Science | Accounting | Physics |
| Literature | History | songs |
| やま | かお | ひこうき |
| うで | て | みみ |

(e.g.) A: Newspaper って にほんごで なんですか。
Newspaper tte Nihongo de nan desu ka.

B: しんぶんです。
Shinbun desu.

A: そうですか。 ありがとうございます。
Soo desu ka. Arigatoo gozaimasu.

## 知(し)ってた？ Did you know?

## 日本人(にほんじん)の名前(なまえ) 'Japanese names'

**Nihonjin no namae**

A Japanese name consists of a family name (苗字 *myooji*, or 姓 *sei*) and a given name (名前 *namae*). In Japanese the family name is usually written before the given name: for example, in 渡辺花子 *Watanabe Hanako*, 渡辺 *Watanabe* is the family name and 花子 *Hanako* is the given name. Japanese people do not have middle names.

### 苗字 *myooji* 'family names'

Until the 19th century when the new Meiji government decided that all people must have family names, only the aristocracy and *bushi* (samurai) had family names. The others, including farmers, merchants and craftsman or 80 per cent of Japanese people, had only given names.

There are thousands of family names in Japan. A family name commonly consists of two kanji such as 鈴木 *Suzuki*, 田中 *Tanaka*, 青木 *Aoki*, and 高橋 *Takahashi* or three kanji such as 佐々木 *Sasaki* and 五十嵐 *Igarashi*. Many Japanese family names derive from features of the rural landscape (e.g. 田中 *Tanaka* 'the middle of the ricefield', 山本 *Yamamoto* 'the base of the mountain' and 北村 *Kitamura* 'the north village').

### 名前 *namae* 'given names'

Most Japanese given names are normally written in one or more kanji, although some names use hiragana or katakana only, or a mixture of kanji and hiragana. The reading of a particular kanji for a given name may vary because each kanji has several possible pronunciations. Boys are sometimes given names indicating the order in which they were born (e.g. 一郎 *Ichiroo* (一 'first, one') first son' and 次郎 *Jiroo* (次 'next') 'second son'). In girl's names, a common final kanji has been 子 *ko* meaning 'child' (e.g. 明子 *Akiko*) or 美 *mi* meaning 'beauty' (e.g. 良美 *Yoshimi*).

**Some popular given names (male):**

| | | Meaning of the 1st kanji | Meaning of the 2nd kanji |
|---|---|---|---|
| 学 | *Manabu* | study, learning | (not applicable) |
| 蓮 | *Ren* | lotus | (not applicable) |
| 大輝 | *Dai・ki* | large, big | radiance, to shine |
| 大樹 | *Hiro・ki* | large, big | tree |
| 翔太 | *Shoo・ta* | to soar, to fly | thick, stout |

**Some popular given names (female):**

| | | Meaning of the 1st kanji | Meaning of the 2nd kanji | Meaning of the 3rd kanji |
|---|---|---|---|---|
| 愛 | *Ai* | love, affection | (not applicable) | (not applicable) |
| 舞 | *Mai* | dance, to dance | (not applicable) | (not applicable) |
| 愛美 | *Mana・mi* | love, affection | beauty, beautiful | (not applicable) |
| 直美 | *Nao・mi* | straight, erect, honesty | beauty, beautiful | (not applicable) |
| 陽子 | *Yoo・ko* | sun, sunshine | child | (not applicable) |
| 由美子 | *Yu・mi・ko* | cause, reason | beauty, beautiful | child |

## Foreign names

Foreign names, except those which may be written in kanji (e.g. most of Korean and Chinese names), are written in katakana (e.g. スミス 'Smith'). When the foreign names are written in Japanese (katakana), the given names are written first, and followed by the family names as in English. A '・' or '=' is often used between the family name and the given name:

| | | | | |
|---|---|---|---|---|
| (e.g.) | トム・クルーズ<br>Tomu Kuruuzu | or | トム=クルーズ<br>Tomu Kuruuzu | Tom Cruise |
| | ジュリア・ロバーツ<br>Juria Robaatsu | or | ジュリア=ロバーツ<br>Juria Robaatsu | Julia Roberts |

### Discussions

**Discuss with your classmates the differences and similarities between names in different cultures. You may wish to refer to, but are not limited to, the following items.**

(1) What is the order of names in your culture? [family name]-[given name]? or [given name]-[family name], or any other ways?

(2) Do you have middle names or some other type of names (rather than family and given names) in your culture?

(3) Are there any other special features in names or naming in your culture?— e.g. meaning of name, length, etc.

## <ruby>新<rt>あたら</rt></ruby>しい<ruby>単語<rt>たんご</rt></ruby>・<ruby>表現<rt>ひょうげん</rt></ruby> New Vocabulary & Expressions

(Basic words/expressions are marked with '*')

| | |
|---|---|
| あなた<br>anata | you |
| あの*<br>ano | that (over there) |
| あれ*<br>are | that one (over there) |
| いま*<br>ima | now |
| えいが*<br>eiga | movie |
| かさ*<br>kasa | umbrella |
| かばん*<br>kaban | bag |
| カメラ*<br>kamera | camera |
| くつ*<br>kutsu | shoes |
| げんごがく<br>Gengogaku | Linguistics |
| ごご*<br>gogo | p.m. |
| ごぜん*<br>gozen | a.m. |
| この*<br>kono | this |
| これ*<br>kore | this one |
| コンサート*<br>konsaato | concert |
| ざっし*<br>zasshi | magazine |
| しごと*<br>shigoto | occupation, job |
| シドニー<br>Shidonii | Sydney |
| じゃあ<br>jaa | then |
| じゅぎょう*<br>jugyoo | class |
| しゅっしん*<br>shusshin | place of birth |
| しゅみ*<br>shumi | hobby |
| しんぶん*<br>shinbun | newspaper |
| すいえい<br>suiei | swimming |
| すまい*<br>sumai | living place |
| その*<br>sono | that (near you) |
| それ*<br>sore | that one (near you) |
| つり<br>tsuri | fishing |
| デート<br>deeto | date |
| てがみ *<br>tegami | letter |
| でんしゃ*<br>densha | train |
| どくしょ*<br>dokusho | reading books |
| とけい*<br>tokei | watch, clock |
| どこ *／どちら*<br>doko dochira | where |

| | |
|---|---|
| としょかん* toshokan | library |
| なまえ* namae | name |
| なん (なに)* nan (nani) | what |
| パーティー* paatii | party |
| ひと* hito | person, people |
| ペン* pen | pen |
| ぼうし* booshi | hat |
| みょうじ myooji | family name |
| もう いちど* moo ichido | one more time |
| やきゅう yakyuu | baseball |
| ゆっくり* yukkuri | slowly |

# 第3課（だいさんか）

# としょかんは あそこに あります
## The library is over there

[Elena and Masato are talking]

1 まさと： あの〜、エレナさん。
Masato Anoo, Erena san.

2 としょかんは どこに ありますか。
Toshokan wa doko ni arimasu ka.

3 エレナ： えっと、としょかんは あそこに あります。
Erena Etto, toshokan wa asoko ni arimasu.

4 まさと： あ、あの たてものですか。ほんやは どこに ありますか。
Masato A, ano tatemono desu ka. Honya wa doko ni arimasu ka.

5 エレナ： ほんやは としょかんの となりに あります。
Erena Honya wa toshokan no tonari ni arimasu.

6 まさと： あ、ゆうびんきょくは どこに ありますか。
Masato A, yuubinkyoku wa doko ni arimasu ka.

7 エレナ： ゆうびんきょくは だいがくに ありません。
Erena Yuubinkyoku wa daigaku ni arimasen.

8 まさと： あ、そうですか。
Masato A, soo desu ka.

## 単語と表現（たんご と ひょうげん） Vocabulary and Expressions (Dialogue)

| | | | | | | | |
|---|---|---|---|---|---|---|---|
| 2 | あります | arimasu | exist, be | 4 | ほんや | honya | book shop |
| 3 | あそこ | asoko | over there | 5 | となり | tonari | next to |
| 4 | たてもの | tatemono | building | 6 | ゆうびんきょく | yuubinkyoku | post office |
| 1 | あの〜 | anoo | Well (*Anoo* and *Etto* are used before starting speech and indicate that you have some reservations about saying what you are going to say next.) | | | | |
| 3 | えっと | etto | | | | | |

### Dialogue in English

**[Elena and Masato are talking]**

1-2 M: Well, Elena. Where is the library?
3 E: Well, the library is over there.
4 M: Oh, (it is) that building over there.
Where is the bookshop?
5 E: The bookshop is next to the library.
6 M: Oh, where is the post office?
7 E: There is no post office in the university.
8 M: Oh, I see.

## 文法 Grammar

(ぶんぽう)

### 1. X は Y に あります／います 'Speaking of X, X is in (on) Y' (locations)'

wa ni arimasu imasu

The initial noun X marked by *wa* is the topic, and the second noun Y is a place where X exists. As a whole, the sentence indicates the location of X, where the location, Y, is marked by *ni*. The final word ***arimasu/imasu*** are 'existence' verbs meaning broadly 'to exist' or 'to be'. The use of the existence verb, *arimasu* or *imasu* depends on whether X is inanimate or animate. *Arimasu* is used when X is an inanimate thing, whereas *imasu* is used when it is a living thing.

**Inanimate subjects**

(1) オペラハウスは シドニーに あります。
Opera hausu wa Shidonii ni arimasu.
'The Opera House is in Sydney.'

(2) ピラミッドは エジプトに あります。
Piramiddo wa Ejiputo ni arimasu.
'The pyramids are in Egypt.'

(3) わたしの だいがくは きょうとに あります。
Watashi no daigaku wa Kyooto ni arimasu.
'My university is in Kyoto.'

(4) わたしの いえは とうきょうに あります。
Watashi no ie wa Tookyoo ni arimasu.
'My home is in Tokyo.'

**Animate subjects**

(5) たなかさんは としょかんに います。
Tanaka san wa toshokan ni imasu.
'Mr Tanaka is in the library.'

(6) なかむらさんは いま ちゅうごくに います。
Nakamura san wa ima Chuugoku ni imasu.
'Ms Nakamura is in China now.'

(7) やまださんは いま タイに います。
Yamada san wa ima Tai ni imasu.
'Ms Yamada is in Thailand now.'

(8) わたしの いぬは いま たなかさんの いえに います。
Watashi no inu wa ima Tanaka san no ie ni imasu.
'My dog is now in Mr Tanaka's home.'

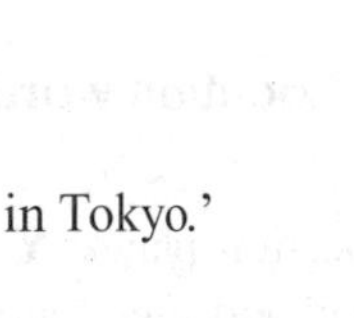

**Grammar Exercise 1**

**Rewrite the following sentences in Japanese. Write the answers in Romaji and Hiragana.**

(e.g.) My school is in Brisbane. Watashi no gakkoo wa Burisuben ni arimasu.

わたしの がっこうは ブリスベンに あります。

(1) My university is in Melbourne.

(2) Parliament House is in Tokyo. (Parliament House こっかいぎじどう *kokkaigijidoo*)

(3) Mr Okada is in Singapore now.

(4) Mr Kimura's wife is in America.

(5) My bag is in my office. (office オフィス *ofisu*)

(6) My cat is in Ms Yamada's home. (cat ねこ *neko*)

## 2. Location words: うえ (ue) 'on, above', した (shita) 'under, beneath', etc

A location phrase **Y** in [X *wa* Y *ni arimasu/imasu*] may include a location word such as *ue* 'on, above' and *shita* 'under, beneath', for a further specific location of a thing/person.

(1) りんごは テーブルの うえ に あります。
Ringo wa teeburu no ue ni arimasu.
'The apple is on the table.'

(2) ほんは テーブルの した に あります。
Hon wa teeburu no shita ni arimasu.
'The book is under the table.'

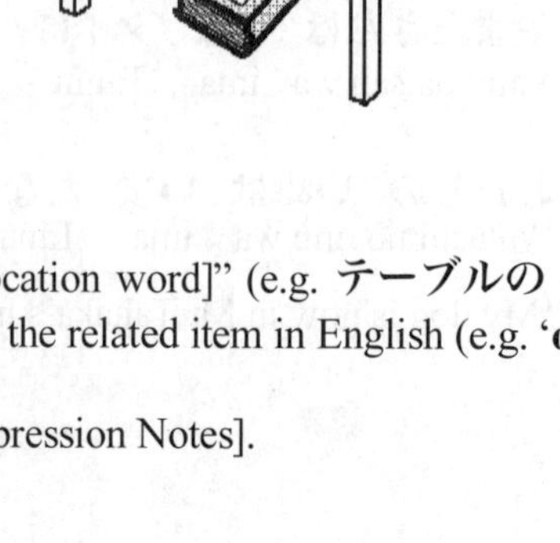

**[Note]**

(i) Be aware that the word order is "[related item] no [location word]" (e.g. テーブルの うえ *teeburu no* ***ue***), whereas a location word appears before the related item in English (e.g. '**on** the table').

(ii) An expanded list of location words will be given in [Expression Notes].

Grammar Exercise 2

**Make up sentences which indicate the location of items in the picture below. Write the answers in Romaji and Hiragana.**

| | |
|---|---|
| ue 'on' | shita 'under' |
| soba 'by' | naka 'inside' |

(e.g.)

Hon wa teeburu no ue ni arimasu.

ほんは テーブルの うえに あります。

(1)

(2)

(3)

(4)

(5)

(6)

## 3. ありません／いません '(negative expressions)'
arimasen imasen

(1) ペンは テーブルの うえに ありません。 'The pen is not on the table.'
Pen wa teeburu no ue ni arimasen.

(2) わたしの ほんは ソファの うえに ありません。 'My book is not on the sofa.'
Watashi no hon wa sofa no ue ni arimasen.

(3) オペラハウスは キャンベラに ありません。 シドニーに あります。
Opera Hausu wa Kyanbera ni arimasen. Shidonii ni arimasu.
'The Opera House is not in Canberra. It is in Sydney.'

(4) たなかさんは いま うちに いません。 'Tanaka-san is not at home now.'
Tanaka san wa ima uchi ni imasen.

(5) やまださんは としょかんに いません。 'Yamada-san is not in the library.'
Yamada san wa toshokan ni imasen.

**Grammar Exercise 3**

**Rewrite the following sentences in Japanese. Write the answers in Romaji and Hiragana.**

(e.g.) My school is not in Sydney. Watashi no gakkoo wa Shidonii ni arimasen.
わたしの がっこうは シドニーに ありません。

(1) My office is not in Kyoto.

(2) Parliament House is not in Osaka.

(3) Ms Ogi is not in China now.

(4) My bag is not in my car.

(5) Mr Kimura is not in America now. (He) is in Australia.

## 4. X は どこに ありますか／いますか 'Where is X?'
wa doko ni arimasu ka imasu ka

This is the interrogative sentence to ask the location of something/someone, X: the interrogative word ***doko*** 'where' is used with the particle ***ni***; and ***ka*** is added to the end of the sentence with a rising intonation.

(1) A: オペラハウスは どこに ありますか。 'Where is the Opera House?'
Opera Hausu wa doko ni arimasu ka.

B: (オペラハウスは) シドニーに あります。 '(It) is in Sydney.'
(Opera Hausu wa) Shidonii ni arimasu.

(2) A: たなかさんは いま どこに いますか。 'Where is Mr Tanaka now?'
Tanaka san wa ima doko ni imasu ka.

B: (たなかさんは いま) だいがくに います。 '(He) is in the university (now).'
(Tanaka san wa ima) daigaku ni imasu.

**Grammar Exercise 4**

**Ask the location of items in Japanese, and then answer, using the given location in [ ]. Write the answers in Romaji and Hiragana.**

(e.g.) Toda-san's book / [ on the table ]

Q: Toda-san no hon wa doko ni arimasuka. とださんの ほんは どこに ありますか。

A: Teeburu no ue ni arimasu. テーブルの うえに あります。

(1) pen / [ under the table ]

(2) apple / [on the TV]

(3) Japanese dictionary / [ inside my bag ]

(4) Saito-san / [ in Sapporo ]

(5) Suzuki-san / [ in the office (company) ]

### [Note] Yに Xが あります／います 'There is X in Y (Neutral description)'

ni ga arimasu imasu

This sentence pattern may also be used to indicate a location of something/someone. However, grammatically and cognitively it differs from *X wa Y ni arimasu/imasu*. In *X wa Y ni arimasu/imasu* ('Speaking of X, it is located in Y'), the focus is placed on X, and that is why X is topicalised and marked by *wa*. In *Y ni X ga arimasu/imasu*, the speaker describes the 'scenery' that involves a location of something/someone as a whole, without focusing on any part of the situation, and that is why *wa* is not used.

Broadly speaking, *X wa Y ni arimasu/imasu* is close to the phrase 'X is (located) in Y', while *Y ni X ga arimasu/imasu* is close to 'There is X in Y'.

| (a) | | (b) |
|---|---|---|
| ほんは テーブルの うえに あります。<br>Hon wa teeburu no ue ni arimasu.<br>'The book is on the table.' | *vs.* | テーブルの うえに ほんが あります。<br>Teeburu no ue ni hon ga arimasu.<br>'There is a book on the table.' |

While we focus on *X wa Y ni arimasu/imasu* in this lesson, some examples of *Y ni X ga arimasu/imasu* are:

(1) はこの なかに カメラが あります。 'There is a camera in the box.'
Hako no naka ni kamera ga arimasu

(2) くるまの そばに たなかさんが います。 'There is Mr Tanaka near the car.'
Kuruma no soba ni Tanaka san ga imasu

# ひょうげん
# 表現 Expression Notes

## 1 Words describing locations

[1] ☛ **ここ－そこ－あそこ (cf. どこ 'where')**
koko soko asoko doko

**'this place, here; that place, there; that place, over there'**

These are a group of demonstrative expressions the initial syllables of which are *ko-*, *so-*, and *a-*. Grammatically, they stand alone as nouns, and mean 'here', 'there (near the listener)' and 'over there', respectively.

(1) たなかさんの ほんは ここに あります。 'Mr Tanaka's book is here.'
Tanaka san no hon wa koko ni arimasu.

(2) としょかんは あそこに あります。 'The library is over there.'
Toshokan wa asoko ni arimasu.

(3) たなかさんは そこに いますか。 'Is Mr Tanaka there?'
Tanaka san wa soko ni imasu ka.

(4) たなかさんは ここに いません。 'Ms Tanaka is not here.'
Tanaka san wa koko ni imasen.

(5) ここは わたしの へやです。 'Here (This) is my room.'
Koko wa watashi no heya desu.

**Expression Exercise 1**

**Rewrite the following sentences in Japanese. Use ここ, そこ or あそこ.**

(e.g.) My book is here. Watashi no hon wa koko ni arimasu.
わたしの ほんは ここに あります。

(1) My car is over there.

(2) My pen is there (near you).

(3) The telephone is over there.

(4) Ms Ogi is over there.

(5) Mr Kimura's wife is here.

(6) My book is not here.

(7) Ms Yoshida is not here now.

[2] ☛ **Location words:**

| |
|---|
| うえ 'on; above', した 'under' , なか 'inside', となり 'next to',<br>ue shita naka tonari<br>そば ' by, near', まえ 'front, in front of', うしろ 'behind'<br>soba mae ushiro |

(1) ほんは　つくえの　うえに　あります。　'The book is on the desk.'
Hon wa tsukue no ue ni arimasu.

(2) ねこは　テーブルの　したに　います。　'The cat is under the table.'
Neko wa teeburu no shita ni imasu.

(3) ペンは　かばんの　なかに　あります。　'The pen is inside of the bag.'
Pen wa kaban no naka ni arimasu.

(4) ゆうびんきょくは　きっさてんの　となりに　あります。
Yuubinkyoku wa kissaten no tonari ni arimasu.
'The post office is next to the coffee shop.'

(5) ほんやは　としょかんの　そばに　あります。
Honya wa toshokan no soba ni arimasu.
'The book shop is near the library.'

(6) ゆうびんきょくは　としょかんの　まえに　あります。
Yuubinkyoku wa toshokan no mae ni arimasu.
'The post office is in front of the library.'

(7) レストランは　きっさてんの　うしろに　あります。
Resutoran wa kissaten no ushiro ni arimasu.
'The restaurant is behind the coffee shop.'

**Expression Exercise 2**

**Make up sentences which indicate the location of items/animals/people in the picture below. Some questions have more than two possible answers.**

(e.g.) Tanaka san wa denwa no soba ni imasu.

たなかさんは でんわの そばに います。

(e.g.)

Mr Tanaka

(1)

Miss Kimura

(2)

(3)

(4)

(5)

(6)

(7)

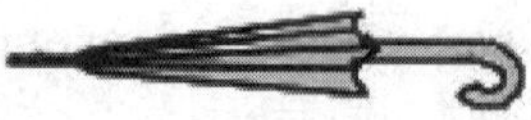

**Expression Exercise 3**

**Rewrite the following sentences in Japanese. Write the answers in Romaji and Hiragana.**

(e.g.) My watch is on the table.

Watashi no tokee wa teeburu no ue ni arimasu.

わたしの とけいは テーブルの うえに あります。

(1) My bag is inside my car.

(2) Mr Nakamura's wife's car is next to my car.

(3) The university is near the park. (park こうえん *kooen*)

(4) The book shop is behind the shoe shop. (shoe shop くつや *kutsuya*)

(5) The bus stop is in front of the post office. (bus stop バスてい *basutei*)

## 2 (X は) Y が あります 'X possess Y; an event , Y will take place'
wa ga arimasu

[1] ☛ The existence verbs ***arimasu/imasu*** can be used to indicate possession, *X wa Y ga arimasu/imasu* 'X possesses Y'. The verb is normally translated as 'have'. As shown in (3) below, X may be omitted; as in (4), *arimasu* may be used when Y is a family member even though he/she is animate.

(1) わたしは くるまが あります。 'I have a car.'
Watashi wa kuruma ga arimasu.

(2) おかねが ありません。 'I don't have money.'
Okane ga arimasen.

(3) じかんが ありますか。 'Do you have (free) time?'
Jikan ga arimasu ka.

(4) すずきさんは いもうとさんが あります／います。
Suzuki san wa imooto san ga arimasu/imasu.
'Ms Suzuki has a younger sister.'

[2] ☛ ***Arimasu*** is also used to indicate that an event marked by *ga* will take place.

(1) きょう テストが あります。 'There will be an exam today; I have a test today.'
Kyoo tesuto ga arimasu.

(2) あした アルバイトが あります。 'There will be a part-time job tomorrow.'
Ashita arubaito ga arimasu.

(3) こんばん パーティーが あります。 'There will be a party tonight.'
Konban paatii ga arimasu.

### Expression Exercise 4

**Rewrite the following sentences in Japanese. Write the answers in Romaji and Hiragana.**

(e.g.) I have a car. Watashi wa kuruma ga arimasu. わたしは くるまが あります。

(1) I have a bicycle. (bicycle じてんしゃ *jitensha*)

(2) I have siblings. (siblings きょうだい *kyoodai*)

(3) Mr Tanaka has a dog.

(4) Ms Sato has an older brother. (older brother おにいさん *oniisan*)

(5) Do you have any money?

(6) There will be a concert next weekend. (next weekend こんどの しゅうまつ *kondo no shuumatsu*)

(7) There will be a Japanese exam tomorrow. (= I have a Japanese exam tomorrow.)

## 対話（たいわ） Communicative Exchanges

### Pair practice 1

**Pre-task: ～に ありります／ありません**

(i) Randomly choose 5 items in (a)-(g) below. Locate them in the picture. You can locate them by your own decision.

(ii) In pairs, ask your conversation partner the location of each item in his/her picture. Then mark the locations in your picture. When your partner asks about items you did not choose in (i), answer, using ～は ありません.

(iii) When you have finished asking/answering the questions, change the roles.

(e.g.)

(a)

(b)
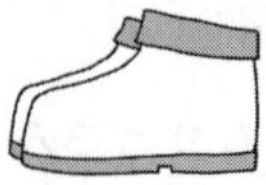

(c)

(d)

(e)

(f)
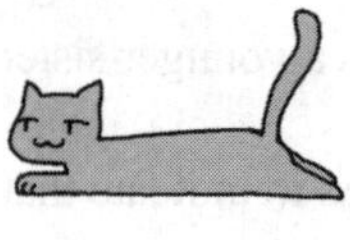

(g)

(e.g.)

A: ほんは どこに ありますか。
Hon wa doko ni arimasu ka.

B: ほんは ベッドの うえに あります。
Hon wa beddo no ue ni arimasu.

A: そうですか。ありがとうございます。
Soo desuka. Arigatoo gozaimasu.

A: くつは どこに ありますか。
Kutsu wa doko ni arimasu ka.

B: くつは ここに ありません。
Kutsu wa koko ni arimasen.

A: そうですか。ありがとうございます。
Soo desuka. Arigatoo gozaimasu.

**Pair practice 2**

Pre-task: ～が あります／ありません

**In pairs, ask your friend if he/she has the following things/people/animals. Write "Yes" in [ ] if he/she does, and "No" if he/she does not. When you have finished asking/answering the questions, change the roles.**

(e.g.) A: [name of B] さんは じてんしゃが ありますか。
san wa jitensha ga arimasu ka.

B: はい、あります。 OR いいえ、ありません。
Hai, arimasu. Iie, arimasen.

A: あ、そうですか。
A, soo desu ka.

| | | |
|---|---|---|
| (e.g.) じてんしゃ [ Yes ] jitensha | (1) いぬ [ ] inu | (2) きょうだい [ ] kyoodai |
| (3) コンピューター [ ] konpyuutaa | (4) くるま [ ] kuruma | (5) おねえさん [ ] oneesan |
| (6) にほんごの じしょ [ ] Nihongo no jisho | (7) けいたいでんわ [ ] keitai denwa | (8) ねこ [ ] neko |

## 知(し)ってた？ Did you know?

### 日本(にほん) (*Nihon*) 'Japan'

Japan is an island nation in East Asia. It consists of four main islands, structured into 8 regions, or 47 prefectures (see below).

Japan has four distinct seasons (四季 *shiki*), however, due to the large North-South extension of the country, regional variations of the climate range from cool in 北海道 *Hokkaidoo* to subtropical in 九州 *Kyuushuu* and further in 沖縄 *Okinawa*. For example, 北海道 *Hokkaidoo* is cold and has heavy snow in winter, whereas 沖縄 *Okinawa* still has 16 degrees Celsius in January. The central area of Japan has hot and humid summers and short winters, while south-western Japan has long, hot, humid summers and mild winters. Japan is also characterised as a country which experiences frequent earthquakes and occasional volcanic activity because it is located in a region where several continental plates meet.

Hokkaidoo Honshuu Shikoku Kyuushuu Okinawa
**4 main islands:** 北海道, 本州, 四国, 九州 (including 沖縄)

Hokkaidoo Toohoku Kantoo Chuubu Kinki Chuugoku Shikoku Kyuushuu
**8 regions:** 北海道, 東北, 関東, 中部, 近畿, 中国, 四国, 九州

Hokkaidoo Tookyooto Kyootofu Oosakafu
**47 prefectures:** 北海道, 東京都, 京都府, 大阪府;

ken Aomoriken
All other prefectures are referred to as ～県 (e.g. 青森県)

| | ken 県 'prefecture' | kenchooshozaichi 県庁所在地 'the seat of prefectural government' |
|---|---|---|
| 1 | Hokkaidoo 北海道 | Sapporoshi 札幌市 |
| 2 | Aomoriken 青森県 | Aomorishi 青森市 |
| 3 | Iwateken 岩手県 | Moriokashi 盛岡市 |
| 4 | Akitaken 秋田県 | Akitashi 秋田市 |
| 5 | Miyagiken 宮城県 | Sendaishi 仙台市 |
| 6 | Yamagataken 山形県 | Yamagatashi 山形市 |
| 7 | Fukushimaken 福島県 | Fukushimashi 福島市 |
| 8 | Ibarakiken 茨城県 | Mitoshi 水戸市 |
| 9 | Tochigiken 栃木県 | Utsunomiyashi 宇都宮市 |
| 10 | Gunmaken 群馬県 | Maebashishi 前橋市 |
| 11 | Chibaken 千葉県 | Chibashi 千葉市 |
| 12 | Saitamaken 埼玉県 | Saitamashi さいたま市 |
| 13 | Tookyooto 東京都 | Tookyoo 東京 Shinjukuku (新宿区) |
| 14 | Kanagawaken 神奈川県 | Yokohamashi 横浜市 |
| 15 | Niigataken 新潟県 | Niigatashi 新潟市 |
| 16 | Toyamaken 富山県 | Toyamashi 富山市 |
| 17 | Ishikawaken 石川県 | Kanazawashi 金沢市 |
| 18 | Naganoken 長野県 | Naganoshi 長野市 |
| 19 | Gifuken 岐阜県 | Gifushi 岐阜市 |
| 20 | Fukuiken 福井県 | Fukuishi 福井市 |
| 21 | Yamanashiken 山梨県 | Koofushi 甲府市 |
| 22 | Shizuokaken 静岡県 | Shizuokashi 静岡市 |
| 23 | Aichiken 愛知県 | Nagoyashi 名古屋市 |

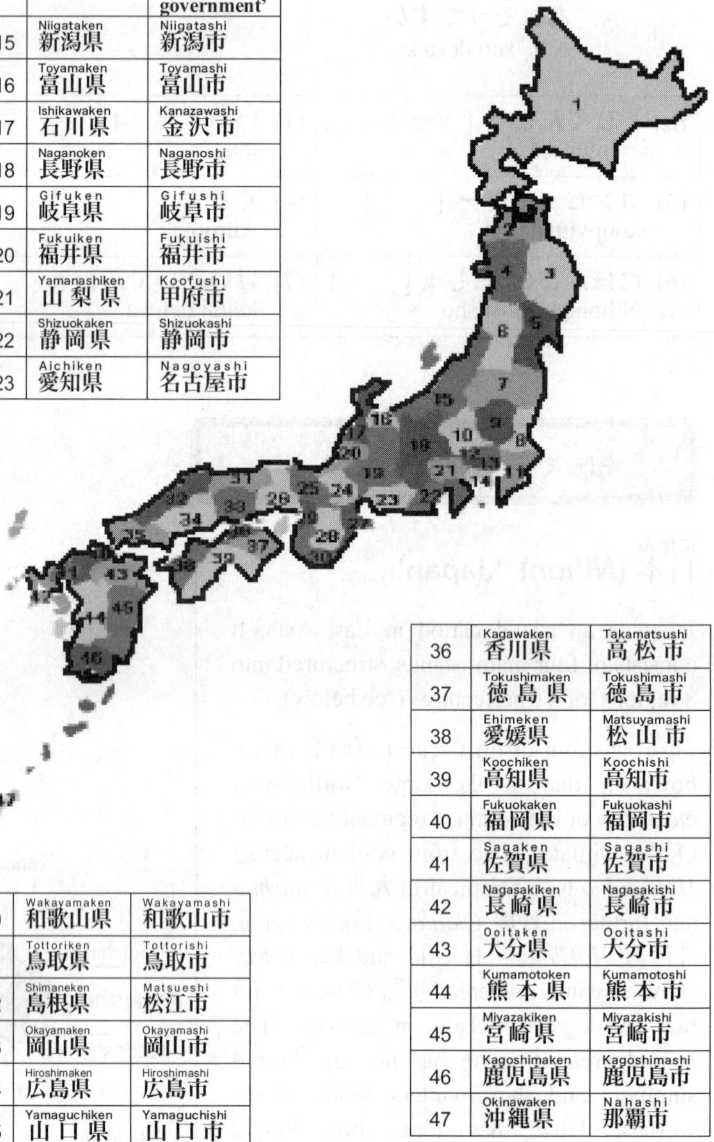

| | | |
|---|---|---|
| 24 | Shigaken 滋賀県 | Ootsushi 大津市 |
| 25 | Kyootofu 京都府 | Kyootoshi 京都市 |
| 26 | Hyoogoken 兵庫県 | Koobeshi 神戸市 |
| 27 | Mieken 三重県 | Tsushi 津市 |
| 28 | Naraken 奈良県 | Narashi 奈良市 |
| 29 | Oosakafu 大阪府 | Oosakashi 大阪市 |
| 30 | Wakayamaken 和歌山県 | Wakayamashi 和歌山市 |
| 31 | Tottoriken 鳥取県 | Tottorishi 鳥取市 |
| 32 | Shimaneken 島根県 | Matsueshi 松江市 |
| 33 | Okayamaken 岡山県 | Okayamashi 岡山市 |
| 34 | Hiroshimaken 広島県 | Hiroshimashi 広島市 |
| 35 | Yamaguchiken 山口県 | Yamaguchishi 山口市 |
| 36 | Kagawaken 香川県 | Takamatsushi 高松市 |
| 37 | Tokushimaken 徳島県 | Tokushimashi 徳島市 |
| 38 | Ehimeken 愛媛県 | Matsuyamashi 松山市 |
| 39 | Koochiken 高知県 | Koochishi 高知市 |
| 40 | Fukuokaken 福岡県 | Fukuokashi 福岡市 |
| 41 | Sagaken 佐賀県 | Sagashi 佐賀市 |
| 42 | Nagasakiken 長崎県 | Nagasakishi 長崎市 |
| 43 | Ooitaken 大分県 | Ooitashi 大分市 |
| 44 | Kumamotoken 熊本県 | Kumamotoshi 熊本市 |
| 45 | Miyazakiken 宮崎県 | Miyazakishi 宮崎市 |
| 46 | Kagoshimaken 鹿児島県 | Kagoshimashi 鹿児島市 |
| 47 | Okinawaken 沖縄県 | Nahashi 那覇市 |

**Note:**

Tookyooto ku shi machi/choo mura
東京都 consists of 23 city wards (区), 26 cities (市), 5 towns ( 町 ) and 8 villages ( 村 ).

**Research**

**Provide the name of the prefecture for the places in the following questions. If you do not know the place, search for it via the internet.**

(e.g.) 富士山（ふじさん）は どこに ありますか。 → Fujisan wa Shizuoka ken ni arimasu.
Fujisan wa doko ni arimasu ka.
ふじさんは しずおかけんに あります。

(1) 琵琶湖（びわこ）は どこに ありますか。
Biwako wa doko ni arimasu ka.

(2) 成田国際空港（なりたこくさいくうこう）は どこに ありますか。
Narita Kokusai Kuukoo wa doko ni arimasu ka.

(3) 草津温泉（くさつおんせん）は どこに ありますか。
Kusatsu onsen wa doko ni arimasu ka.

(4) 原爆ドーム（げんばくどーむ）は どこに ありますか。
Genbaku doomu wa doko ni arimasu ka.

(5) 松島（まつしま）は どこに ありますか。
Matsushima wa doko ni arimasu ka.

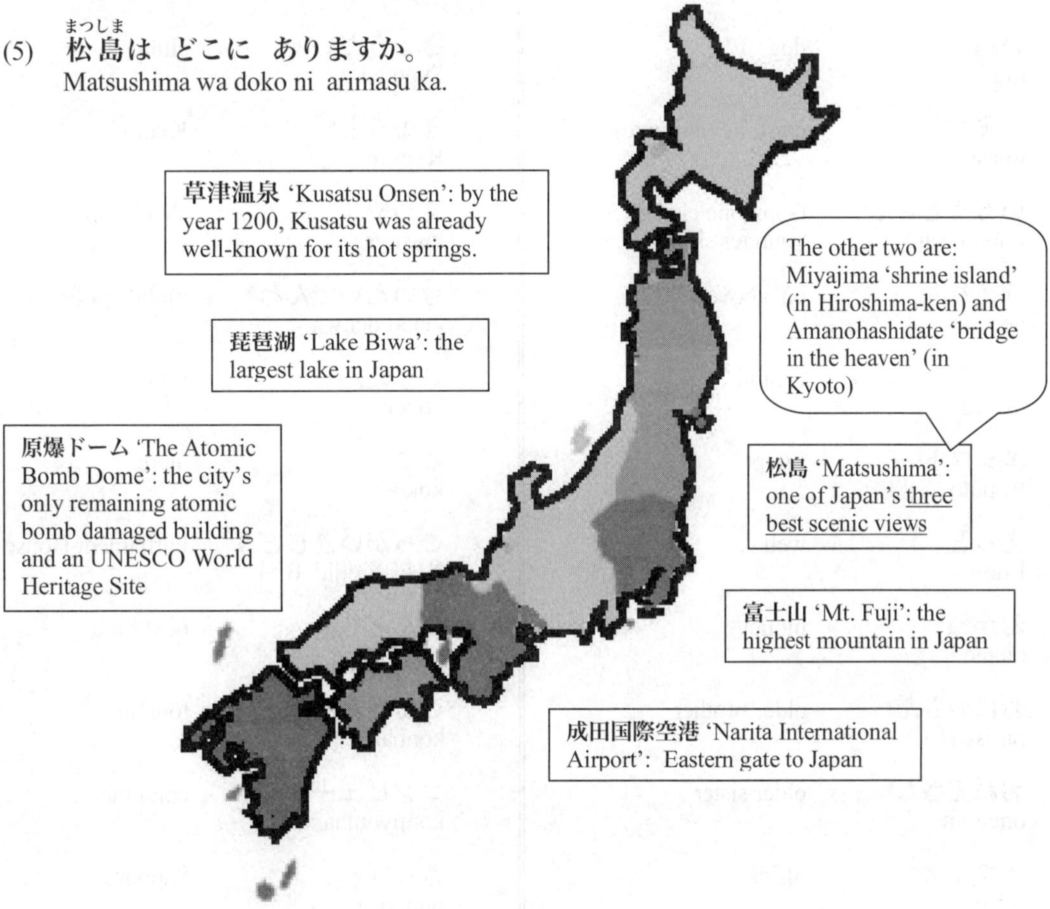
草津温泉 'Kusatsu Onsen': by the year 1200, Kusatsu was already well-known for its hot springs.
琵琶湖 'Lake Biwa': the largest lake in Japan
原爆ドーム 'The Atomic Bomb Dome': the city's only remaining atomic bomb damaged building and an UNESCO World Heritage Site
The other two are: Miyajima 'shrine island' (in Hiroshima-ken) and Amanohashidate 'bridge in the heaven' (in Kyoto)
松島 'Matsushima': one of Japan's three best scenic views
富士山 'Mt. Fuji': the highest mountain in Japan
成田国際空港 'Narita International Airport': Eastern gate to Japan

## <ruby>新<rt>あたら</rt></ruby>しい<ruby>単語<rt>たんご</rt></ruby>・<ruby>表現<rt>ひょうげん</rt></ruby> New Vocabulary & Expressions

(Basic words/expressions are marked with '*')

| | |
|---|---|
| あした* ashita | tomorrow |
| あそこ* asoko | over there |
| あの〜 anoo | well … |
| あります* arimasu | exist, be (inanimate) |
| アルバイト* arubaito | part-time job |
| いす* isu | chair |
| いぬ* inu | dog |
| います* imasu | exist, be (animate) |
| いもうとさん* imooto san | (someone else's) younger sister |
| うえ* ue | on, above |
| うしろ* ushiro | behind |
| エジプト Ejiputo | Egypt |
| えっと Etto | well … |
| おかね* okane | money |
| おにいさん* oniisan | older brother |
| おねえさん* oneesan | older sister |
| オフィス ofisu | office |
| オペラハウス Opera hausu | Opera House |
| がっこう* gakkoo | school |
| カップ kappu | cup |
| きっさてん* kissaten | coffee shop |
| キャンベラ kyanbera | Canberra |
| きょう* kyoo | today |
| きょうだい kyoodai | siblings |
| きょうと* Kyooto | Kyoto |
| くつや kutsuya | shoe shop |
| けいたいでんわ* keitai denwa | mobile phone |
| こうえん* kooen | park |
| ここ* koko | here |
| こっかいぎじどう Kokkai gijidoo | Parliament House |
| こんど* kondo | next time |
| こんばん* konban | tonight |
| コンピューター* konpyuutaa | computer |
| さっぽろ Sapporo | Sapporo |

| | |
|---|---|
| じかん<br>jikan | time |
| した*<br>shita | under, beneath |
| じてんしゃ<br>jitensha | bicycle |
| しゅうまつ*<br>shuumatsu | weekend |
| シンガポール*<br>Shingapooru | Singapore |
| そこ*<br>soko | there |
| そば*<br>soba | near |
| ソファ<br>sofa | sofa |
| タイ*<br>Tai | Thai |
| たてもの*<br>tatemono | building |
| つくえ*<br>tsukue | desk |
| テーブル*<br>teeburu | table |
| テスト*<br>tesuto | test, exam |
| デパート*<br>depaato | department store |
| テレビ*<br>terebi | TV |
| でんわ*<br>denwa | telephone |
| となり*<br>tonari | next, next to |
| なか*<br>naka | inside |
| ねこ*<br>neko | cat |
| はこ<br>hako | box |
| バスてい<br>basutei | bus stop |
| ピラミッド<br>Piramiddo | Pyramid |
| ブリスベン<br>Burisuben | Brisbane |
| へや*<br>heya | room |
| ほんや *<br>honya | book shop |
| まえ*<br>mae | front, in front of |
| まんが*<br>manga | manga, comics |
| めがね*<br>megane | glasses |
| メルボルン<br>Meruborun | Melbourne |
| ゆうびんきょく*<br>office<br>yuubinkyoku | post |
| ラジオ<br>rajio | radio |
| りんご*<br>ringo | apple |
| レストラン*<br>resutoran | restaurant |

# 第4課（だいよんか）

## 7じに あさごはんを たべます
## I have breakfast at 7

[Elena and Masato are talking]

まさと： エレナさん、あさ たいてい なんじに おきますか。

エレナ： そうですね、たいてい 6じはんごろ おきます。それから 7じに あさごはんを たべます。

まさと： はやいですね。

エレナ： ええ。

まさと： なんじごろ だいがくに いきますか。

エレナ： 7じはんごろです。

まさと： だいがくの あと、 いつも なにを しますか。

エレナ： ええと、げつようびと すいようびは いつも アルバイト（あるばいと）を します。もくようびは たいてい テニス（てにす）を します。たまに すいえいも します。

まさと： そうですか。たのしそうですね。

エレナ： ええ。

### 単語（たんご）と表現（ひょうげん） Vocabulary and Expressions (Dialogue)

| | | | | | |
|---|---|---|---|---|---|
| 1 | あさ | morning | 6 | だいがく | university |
| 1 | たいてい | usually | 6 | いきます | go |
| 1 | なんじ | what time | 8 | あと | after |
| 1 | おきます | get up, wake up | 8 | いつも | always |
| 2 | そうですね | let me think..., well... | 9 | げつようび | Monday |
| 2 | ～ごろ | around, about (for time) | 9 | すいようび | Wednesday |
| 2 | それから | (and) then | 10 | もくようび | Thursday |
| 3 | あさごはん | breakfast | 10 | たまに | occasionally |
| 3 | たべます | eat | 10 | すいえい | swimming |
| 4 | はやい | early, quick, fast | 11 | たのしそう(な) | sounds/looks/seems fun |

**Dialogue in English**

**[Elena and Masato are talking]**

1 M: Elena, what time do (you) usually get up in the morning?
2-3 E: Well, (I) usually get up around 6:30. Then (I) have breakfast at 7.
4 M: (It's) early, isn't it?
5 E: Yes.
6 M: About what time do (you) go to university?
7 E: Around 7:30.
8 M: What do (you) always do after uni?
9-10 E: Mmm, (I) work part-time on Mondays and Wednesdays. (I) usually play tennis on Thursdays. I occasionally swim (go swimming).
11 M: I see. (It) sounds/seems fun.
12 E: Yes.

## 文法 (ぶんぽう) Grammar

### Verb phrase and the *masu* form

A verb is a word which basically expresses an action, event or movement. Within a sentence, it forms a verb phrase with other grammatical elements to indicate a variety of grammatical meanings such as tense, negation, politeness, and so forth. Below we focus on the *masu* form of the verb phrase.

Details apart, *masu* indicates several grammatical meanings: polite style (*vs.* casual style), affirmative (*vs.* negative), non-past (present or future) tense (*vs.* past tense), and so forth. In this regard, it has the same function as *desu*, but *masu* is exclusively used with a verb while *desu* is used with nouns and adjectives.

#### 1. [Object]を V-ます； [Destination]に(へ) V-ます

The particle を indicates that the preceding noun is an object of the action that is expressed by the verb phrase, V-ます. For example, in (a) below, コーヒー [coffee] is an object of an action "drink" and is thus marked by を. Similarly, に marks a destination, and for example in (b), だいがく [university] is a destination someone "goes" to, and is marked by に. Note that while に is used as the destination marker, it may be replaced by へ (read as 'e' not 'he' in this case).

The object (marked by を) or the destination (marked by に) has a 'core' relationship (or 'strong connection') with the verb — Consider a naturally perceivable connection with the action, as in "drink-[what]" or "go to-[where]".

(a) **を-type:** "drink"

[ coffee ]
コーヒー(こーひー)[を] のみます

(b) **に-type:** "go"

[ university ]
だいがく[に] いきます

(c) **Zero-type:** "get up"

[ (none) ]
おきます

Some verbs, however, do not have such a noun that is in a 'core' relationship. For example, the action "get up" as in (c) above does not have an object or destination. Other types of information, such as time, may be included in a sentence with such a verb (e.g. 7じに おきます '(I) get up at 7 o'clock'). See below for more examples of basic verbs.

Some verbs may have an object-like noun marked by が (e.g. にほんごが わかります '(I) understand Japanese').

**を-type verbs**

| (1) "write" | (2) "read" | (3) "eat" | (4) "buy" |
|---|---|---|---|
|  |   |  |  |
| [letter] てがみを かきます | [book] ほんを よみます | [cake] ケーキを たべます | [bag] かばんを かいます |

| (5) "see, look, watch" | (6) "listen to, hear" | (7) "play, do" | (8) "study" |
|---|---|---|---|
|  |  |  |   |
| [movie] えいがを みます | [music] おんがくを ききます | [tennis] テニスを します | [Japanese] にほんごを べんきょうします |

**に-type verbs**

| (9) "come" | (10) "return, go back" | (11) "get on, ride" | (12) "meet, see" |
|---|---|---|---|
|   |  |   |  |
| [(my) home] うちに きます | [home] うちに かえります | [bus] バスに のります | [friend] ともだちに あいます |

(The use of に in (11) and (12) needs special attention.)

**Zero-type verbs**

| (13) "get up, wakeup" | (14) "sleep, go to bed" | (15) "swim" | (16) "laugh" |
|---|---|---|---|
|  |  |  |  |
| [(none)] おきます | [(none)] ねます | [(none)] およぎます | [(none)] わらいます |

**文法練習（ぶんぽうれんしゅう） 1**

**Make up your own expression of either an [object]を～ます or [destination]に～ます, using words given below. Also provide their English meaning.**

(e.g.1) だいがく → だいがくに いきます '(I) go to university.'

(e.g.2) ほん → ほんを かいます '(I) buy books.'

(1) りんご

(2) アフリカ（あふりか）

(3) にほんちゃ 'Japanese tea'

(4) テレビ（てれび）

(5) ちゅうかりょうり 'Chinese food'

(6) まんが 'Manga, comic books'

(7) かんこくご

(8) たなかせんせい

(9) うち

(10) でんしゃ 'train'

## 2. ～ますか；～ません (Interrogative ; negative)

As in the case of ～です and ～ですか, an interrogative sentence (*yes-no* question) with a verbal (polite) predicate is made by adding か to the end of an affirmative sentence (i.e. ～ますか) with a rising intonation. Its negative sentence ending is ～ません. In answers, the object phrase (ほんを) is often omitted.

(1) ほんを よみますか。 'Do you read books?'

→ はい、（ほんを） よみます。 'Yes, I read (books).'

→ いいえ、（ほんを） よみません。 'No, I don't read (books).'

**文法練習（ぶんぽうれんしゅう） 2**

**For practising the structural formation of ～ますか, ～ません as well as ～ます, make up your own questions and answers (both cases of 'Yes' and 'No'), using given words as in the example.**

(e.g.) だいがく： だいがくに いきますか。 → はい、だいがくに いきます。

→ いいえ、だいがくに いきません。

(1) ほん

(2) しんぶん

(3) パーティー（ぱーてぃー）

(4) しゅくだい ('homework')

(5) タクシー（たくしー）

(6) きっぷ ('tickets')

(7) ジュース（じゅーす）

(8) はがき ('post cards')

### 3. なにを 'what -を', どこに 'where -に'

なにを 'what-を' and どこに 'where-に' are interrogative words for open questions to ask what someone does or where someone goes. With ますか they normally indicate future or habitual events.

| | | | |
|---|---|---|---|
| (1) | A： | あした なにを しますか。 | 'What do/will (you) do tomorrow?' |
| | B： | ラグビーをします。 | 'I will play rugby.' |
| (2) | A： | なにを のみますか。 | 'What do/will (you) drink?' |
| | B： | コーヒーを のみます。 | 'I (will) drink coffee.' |
| (3) | A： | こんばん どこに いきますか。 | 'Where do/will you go tonight?' |
| | B： | しんじゅくに いきます。 | 'I (will) go to Shinjuku.' |

**文法練習 3**

**Refer to the pictures and make up a question sentence and an answer for the question. Feel free to use future time words below. Some questions have more than one possible answer.**

| | | |
|---|---|---|
| あした 'tomorrow' | こんばん 'tonight' | げつようび 'Monday' |
| かようび 'Tuesday' | すいようび 'Wednesday' | もくようび 'Thursday' |
| きんようび 'Friday' | どようび 'Saturday' | にちようび 'Sunday' |

(See also "Did you know?" for Japanese days of the week.)

(e.g.) A: こんばん なにを しますか。

B: テニスを します。

(e.g.)

(1) study Japanese

(2)

(3) meet a friend

(4) go to Kimura's house

(5)

## 自然(しぜん)な日本語(にほんご) Natural Conversation Notes

### Filled pauses or fillers: そうですね；ええと

The filled pauses or fillers are a special feature of natural speech. Their basic function is to fill gaps or to indicate the speaker's hesitancy. Japanese 'そうですね', 'ええと', and '(う)んんん' are of this kind. English counterparts to these are '*let me see/think…*', '*well*', '*um*' and '*er*', etc. They often reflect a speaker's alertness or emotional state and/or for the planning of words yet to come, and may serve as an indication that the speaker is now thinking of what to say and/or how to respond appropriately. Appropriate use of these devices helps one to sound more natural and smooth.

#### 1. そうですね 'let me see/think', 'well'

そうですね is used when one is asked a question or invited to do something, and cannot come up with an immediate answer or response. It is also used when one is hesitant to respond to someone's question/invitation, or when one is deciding what/how to respond.

(1) A: たいてい なんじに おきますか。 'What time do (you) usually get up?'

B: そうですね, たいてい 6じに おきます。

'Let me think/Well, (I) usually get up at 6.'

(2) A: レストラン(れすとらん)に いきませんか。 'Why don't (we) go to a restaurant?'

B: そうですね…。 'Let me see / Well...,'

Note: そうですね has another usage: It is used to indicate the speaker's agreement to someone's utterance which one normally expects the other to agree to. When そうですね is used in this way, the final ね tends to be pronounced in rather short length with a more definite tone, while it (i.e. ね) tends to be lengthened in a lingering manner when used as a filler. The usage of the agreement そうですね will be discussed in Lesson 6.

#### 2. ええと '*Well...*'

ええと is quite similar to そうですね in that it is used when the speaker cannot give an immediate response and wants to gain some time to come up with some appropriate words/expressions. In this regard, these two expressions are interchangeable in many cases. However, ええと is normally used when the speaker responds to certain types of inquiry which require one to refer to one's knowledge or memory in order to answer, while そうですね is typically used when the speaker tries to fill a time gap for making a decision.

(3) A: にちようびは たいてい なにを しますか。'What do (you) usually do on Sundays?'

B: ええと、ともだちと サッカーをします。 'Well, (I) play soccer with (my) friends.'

(4) A: すみません。ゆうびんきょくは どこですか。'Excuse me, where is the post office?'

B: ええと、デパートの となりです。 'Well, (it) is next to the department store.'

ええと and そうですね often occur together when one needs more time to respond.

(5) A: どようびに パーティーに いきませんか。 'Why don't (we) go to a party?'

B: そうですね、ええと、はい、いいですよ。いきます。

'Let me see... well... yes, ok. I will go (with you).'

**自然な日本語：練習**

**Complete the responses of B by filling the blanks with appropriate fillers. Refer to the clues in [  ] when you choose them. You may use the same filler more than once.**

(e.g.) A: たいてい なんじに ねますか。 'What time do (you) usually sleep?'

B: <u>そうですね</u>、たいてい １２じに ねます。

'Let me think/Well, (I) usually sleep at 12.'

(1) A: きょう ひるごはんは なにを たべますか。 'What do you eat for lunch today?'

B: ________、ちゅうかりょうりを たべます。[thinking]

(2) A: にほんごの ほんは どこに ありますか。 'Where is the Japanese book?'

B: ________、わたしの つくえの うえに あります。[remembering]

(3) A: きんようびの よる なにを しますか。 'What do you do on Friday night?'

B: ________、にほんごを べんきょうします。[remembering Friday's schedule]

(4) A: なんじに うちに かえりますか。'What time do you return home today?'

B: ________、６じはんに かえります。[checking his/her schedule]

## 表現（ひょうげん） Expression Notes

### 1 Particle : (time/day) に

[1] ☛ The particle に may be used to mark the time and/or day in which a certain action/event takes place. Note that a particle may have more than two usages: e.g. に for 'destination' and 'time/day', (and some more).

| | | |
|---|---|---|
| (1) | あさ 6じ<u>に</u> おきます。 | '(I) get up at 6 in the morning.' |
| (2) | かようび<u>に</u> やきゅうを します。 | '(I) play baseball on Tuesday.' |
| (3) | 8じ<u>に</u> がっこうに いきます。 | '(I) go to school at 8 am.' |

#### 表現練習（ひょうげんれんしゅう）1

**Describe what each person does in each picture, as in the example.**

(e.g.) たなかさんは たいてい 6じはんに おきます。

(e.g.) たなか；6:30

(1) きむら；8:00

(2) やまだ；9:30

(3) おかだ；4:30 pm

(4) なかむら；10:30

(5) ジョン（じょん）；Friday

(6) やまだ；Saturday

(7) ほんだ；Sunday

(8) すずき；Thursday

**[2]** ☛ To make an open question to ask a time when a particular action/event occurs, なんじ 'what time' or いつ 'when' is normally used with the interrogative marker か with a rising intonation.

(1) A： なんじに おきますか。 'What time do (you) get up?'

B： ６じに／６じごろに おきます。 '(I) get up at 6 o'clock/ around 6 o'clock.'

(2) A： いつ ロンドン(ろんどん)に いきますか。 'When are you going to London?'

B： すいようびに いきます。 '(I) will go (there) on Wednesday.'

Note: あさ, ひる, ゆうがた, よる are not normally accompanied by the time/day marker に (see Lesson 7 for details).

## 表現(ひょうげん)練習(れんしゅう) 2

**Refer to the pictures, and make up Shigeru's questions and Hanako's responses. Use either なんじ or いつ in your question.**

(e.g.) しげる： はなこさんは なんじに おきますか。

はなこ： あさ６じに おきます。

For (7) and (8):
[noun] and [noun] ～と～
(e.g.) ほん<u>と</u>ペン
'books and pens'

(e.g.) 6:00 am

(1) 12:30 pm (lunch)

(2) Tuesday (magazines ざっし)

(3) 10:30 am (tea)

(4) Thursday

(5) Saturday (shopping)

(6) 11:00 pm

(7) Wednesday and Friday

(8) Monday and Sunday

## 2 たいてい 'usually'； いつも 'always'； よく 'often'； ときどき 'sometimes'； たまに 'occasionally'

☛ These adverbials express the frequency of a certain action/event to take place.

(1) わたしは たいてい 7じに ばんごはんを たべます。

(2) わたしは いつも 6じに おきます。

(3) たなかさんは よく ロンドン(ろんどん)に いきます。

(4) たなかさんは ときどき テニス(てにす)を します。

(5) たなかさんは たまに にほんの えいがを みます。

In an independent sentence, they normally occur after the topic as in (6) below, although they may also occur rather freely in other locations as in (7) and (8).

(6) わたしは たいてい 7じに ばんごはんを たべます。

(7) たいてい わたしは 7じに ばんごはんを たべます。

(8) わたしは 7じに たいてい ばんごはんを たべます。

The general meaning of the sentences is 'I usually have dinner at 7 o'clock': (6) and (7) are virtually the same; in (8), prominence is given to the phrase ばんごはんを たべます and it is interpreted as 'What I usually do at 7 o'clock is eating dinner'.

### 表現(ひょうげん) 練習(れんしゅう) 3

**Rewrite the following sentences in Japanese.**

(e.g.) I usually get up at 5 in the morning. わたしは たいてい あさ5じに おきます。

(1) Tanaka-san always buys a newspaper on Monday.

(2) I occasionally eat cakes at around 3:00 pm. (at around ごろ)

(3) Katoo-san sometimes plays golf on Sunday.

(4) I usually study Japanese on Friday.

(5) Suzuki-san often drinks tea.

(6) I occasionally watch movies.

(7) Yamada-san sometimes reads Japanese magazines.

(8) Nomura-san always play tennis on Saturday and Sunday.

## 対話（たいわ） Communicative Exchanges

### 対話練習（たいわれんしゅう）1

**Pre-task:** なんじですか
Words of frequency

(i) Write the time when you do the things indicated in the pictures (write your own time at 'You: ______').

(ii) In pairs, ask your partner what time he/she usually does the things illustrated in the pictures. Then write the time at 'Y.P.: ______'.

(iii) After answering, your conversation partner asks you (e.g. たなかさんは？ 'What about you, Tanaka-san?') as shown in the example.

(e.g.)

You: 7:30

Y.P.: 7:00

A: [B] さんは たいてい なんじに あさごはんを たべますか。

B: わたしは たいてい 7じに（あさごはんを）たべます。
[A] さんは？

A: わたしは 7じはんごろに（あさごはんを）たべます。

B: そうですか。

(1)

You: ______

Y.P.: ______

(2)

You: ______

Y.P.: ______

(3)

You: ______

Y.P.: ______

(4)

You: ______

Y.P.: ______

(5)

You: ______

Y.P.: ______

(6)

You: ______

Y.P.: ______

(7)

You: ______

Y.P.: ______

(8)

You: ______

Y.P.: ______

((7) take a shower シャワー（しゃわー）を あびます)

## 対話練習2

**Pre-task:** Words of frequency

(i) Ask 3 to 5 of your classmates if they do the activities listed in the table below.
(ii) If their answer is 'yes', fill in the table with the expression of frequency. Write いいえ when their answer is 'no'.
(ii) In answering the questions, if your answer is はい 'yes', include an appropriate frequency word in your answers.

> いつも 'always'　よく 'often'　たまに 'occasionally'　ときどき 'sometimes',
> まいにち 'everyday'　まいしゅう 'every week'　まいつき 'every month'

(e.g.1)
A: えいがを　みますか。
B: はい、ときどき みます。
A: あ、そうですか。

(e.g.2)
A: テニスを　しますか。
B: いいえ、しません。
A: あ、そうですか。

| activities \ names | e.g. John | 1 | 2 | 3 | 4 | 5 |
|---|---|---|---|---|---|---|
| えいが | ときどき | | | | | |
| しんぶん | | | | | | |
| テニス | いいえ | | | | | |
| アルバイト | | | | | | |
| にほんごの べんきょう | | | | | | |
| ワイン | | | | | | |

## 対話練習3

**Pre-task:** なに

**In pairs, ask your partner questions using either なにを しますか 'what do you do?' or なにを たべますか 'what do you eat?': Choose an appropriate one in accordance with the given key word. When you have finished asking/answering the questions, change the roles.**

(e.g.) breakfast

You: toast
Y.P.: bread and an egg

A: あさごはんは たいてい なにを たべますか。
B: たいてい パンと たまごを たべます。
A: あ、そうですか。

(1) breakfast

You: ____________

Y.P.: ____________

(2) lunch

You: ____________

Y.P.: ____________

(3) dinner

You: ____________

Y.P.: ____________

(4) after class

You: ____________

Y.P.: ____________

(5) after dinner

You: ____________

Y.P.: ____________

(6) Sunday

You: ____________

Y.P.: ____________

(after class じゅぎょうの あと, after dinner ばんごはんの あと)

## 対話作り（たいわづくり） Comprehensive Exercises

✍ **In pairs, create a dialogue for the given situation. Please feel free to ask the instructor if you have any questions about Japanese expressions for your dialogue.**

**Situation:**

You and your friend are talking about what you do and he/she does each day or week. Tell him/her some of your daily or weekly routines, and ask his/hers.

You may choose either (i) daily routine or (ii) weekly activities.

You may also want to focus on one or two of the following:

(a) what time you (and your conversation partner) usually have breakfast, lunch or dinner, and what you have for these meals.

(b) what time you usually come to university and return home.

(c) what you often do after class.

(d) what you usually do on week days (i.e. Mon, Tues, Wed, Thurs, Fri, Sat, and Sun).

Please try to incorporate the following expressions into your dialogue:

- [object] を／ [direction] に(へ)
- [verb] ます／ますか／ません
- [time word] に
- たいてい／いつも／よく／ときどき／たまに／まいにち／まいしゅう
- そうですね／ええと

**[Sample Dialogue 1]** Michael and Sayuri are talking about what they will eat for dinner.

マイケル(まいける)： さゆりさん、こんばんは なにを たべますか。

さゆり： そうですね, わたしは パスタ(ぱすた)と サラダ(さらだ)を たべます。マイケル(まいける)さんは？

マイケル： こんばんは ええと カレー(かれー)を つくります。

さゆり： そうですか。よく カレー(かれー)を たべますか。

マイケル： はい、よく たべます。

**[Sample Dialogue 2]** Michael and Sayuri are talking about what sports they normally play.

マイケル： さゆりさん、どようびに たいてい なにを しますか。

さゆり： わたしは たいてい アルバイト(あるばいと)を します。マイケル(まいける)さんは？

マイケル： わたしは スポーツ(すぽーつ)を よく します。

さゆり： そうですか。

マイケル： たいてい ラグビー(らぐびー)を します。でも、ときどき サッカー(さっかー)も します。さゆりさんは？

さゆり： わたしは たまに テニス(てにす)と すいえいを します。

マイケル： あ、そうですか。

[Dialogue 1]

M: Sayuri, what do you eat tonight?

S: Well/Let me think. I will have pasta and salad. What about you, Michael?

M: Tonight, well, (I) will cook curry.

S: I see. Do (you) often have curry?

M: Yes, (I) often have (curry).

[Dialogue 2]

M: Sayuri, what do you usually do on Saturday?

S: I usually do my part-time work. What about you, Michele?

M: I often play sports.

S: Is that so?

M: I usually play rugby. But I sometimes play soccer too. What about you, Sayuri?

S: I occasionally play tennis and go swimming.

M: Oh, I see.

## 知(し)ってた？ Did you know?

## 曜日(ようび) 'Japanese days of the week'

| Hiragana | げつようび | かようび | すいようび | もくようび | きんようび | どようび | にちようび |
|---|---|---|---|---|---|---|---|
| Kanji | 月曜日 | 火曜日 | 水曜日 | 木曜日 | 金曜日 | 土曜日 | 日曜日 |
| Literal | 'Moon' day | 'Fire' day | 'Water' day | 'Wood' day | 'Gold' day | 'Earth' day | 'Sun' day |
| English | Monday | Tuesday | Wednesday | Thursday | Friday | Saturday | Sunday |
| Stars named after | Moon 月(つき) | Mars 火星(かせい) | Mercury 水星(すいせい) | Jupiter 木星(もくせい) | Venus 金星(きんせい) | Saturn 土星(どせい) | Sun 太陽(たいよう)(日(にち/ひ)) |

It is thought that the Japanese names for the days of the week originate from the ancient Chinese astrological method of recording days according to the Sun, Moon, and five planets: Mars, Mercury, Jupiter, Venus and Saturn. By observing these, it was found that seven days made one week, which was repeated in a cycle. This concept was brought to Japan with Buddhism in around 6th century.

The first kanji in the name of each day is related to an elemental force of nature such as fire, water, wood, gold, earth and sun. The middle character 曜(よう) means 'sunlight' or 'luminary; shining body'. The final character 日(ひ) is pronounced as び and means 'sun' or 'day'. 曜日(ようび) is used as a single expression meaning 'day of the week' to all intents and purposes. The seven astral bodies were called 'seven luminaries' by the ancient Chinese, although it is not used in modern Chinese.

**Useful Expressions**

(1) A: きょうは なんようびですか。　(なんようび what day (of the week))
'What day (of the week) is today?'

B: (きょうは) すいようびです。
'(Today) is Wednesday.'

(2) わたしは きんようびに にほんに いきます。
'I will go to Japan on Friday.'

(3) げつようびと すいようびに アルバイト(あるばいと)を します。
'(I) work part-time on Mondays and Wednesdays.'

## 練習（れんしゅう）しましょう Exercise

(i) First write down the given activities for each day in the table below.
(ii) In pairs, ask your partner what day of the week he/she does the given activities. When you receive his/her response, write it down, as shown in the example.
(iii) When you have finished asking/answering the questions, change the roles.

(e.g.1) A: なんようびに バーベキュー（ばーべきゅー）を しますか。
B: げつようびです。
A: そうですか。

A: On what day (of the week) will you have a BBQ?
B: On Monday.
A: I see.

(e.g.2) B: なんようびに レストラン（れすとらん）に いきますか。
A: げつようびです。
B: そうですか。

B: On what day (of the week) will you go to a restaurant?
A: On Monday.
B: I see.

**Activities**
Have a BBQ　Work part-time　Go to a restaurant　Go to Japan　Play tennis
Have a Japanese class　Watch a movie　Go shopping　Meet a friend

| ようび | スケジュール（すけじゅーる） (schedule) | |
|---|---|---|
| | You | Your conversation partner |
| げつようび | (e.g.1) Have a BBQ | (e.g.2) Go to a restaurant |
| げつようび | | |
| かようび | | |
| すいようび | | |
| もくようび | | |
| きんようび | | |
| どようび | | |
| にちようび | | |

## 新(あたら)しい単語(たんご)・表現(ひょうげん) New Vocabulary & Expressions

(Basic words/expressions are marked with '*')

| | |
|---|---|
| あいます* | meet |
| あさ* | morning |
| あさごはん* | breakfast |
| あと* | after |
| あに | older brother |
| あびます | take (a shower) |
| アフリカ(あふりか) | Africa |
| いきます* | go |
| いつ* | when |
| いつも* | always |
| うた | song |
| うち* | house, home |
| ええと | well |
| おきます* | wake up, get up |
| およぎます* | swim |
| おんがく | music |
| かいます* | buy |
| かいもの* | shopping |
| かえります* | return |
| かきます* | write |
| かようび* | Tuesday |
| カレー(かれー) | curry |
| かんこくご* | Korean (language) |
| かんこく りょうり | Korean food |
| ききます* | listen to, hear |
| きっぷ | ticket |
| きます* | come |
| きょうしつ | classroom |
| きんようび* | Friday |
| ケーキ(けーき) | cake |
| げつようび* | Monday |
| コーヒー(こーひー)* | coffee |
| ～ごろ* | around, about (time) |
| サッカー(さっかー) | soccer |
| サラダ(さらだ) | salad |
| ～します* | do |
| シャワー(しゃわー) | shower |
| ジュース(じゅーす) | juice |
| しゅくだい* | homework |
| すいようび* | Wednesday |
| スポーツ(すぽーつ)* | sports |
| それから | then |
| たいてい* | usually |
| タクシー(たくしー)* | taxi |
| たのしそう(な) | look fun |
| たべます* | eat |
| たまご | egg |
| たまに* | occasionally |
| ちゅうかりょうり* | Chinese food |
| ドイツ(どいつ)／ドイツご(どいつ) | Germany/German language |
| どうやって | how, in what way |
| ときどき* | sometimes |
| どようび* | Saturday |
| なに* | what |
| にちようび* | Sunday |

| | |
|---|---|
| にほんちゃ | Japanese tea |
| ねます* | sleep, go to bed |
| のみます* | drink |
| のります* | get on, board, ride |
| バーベキュー（ばーべきゅー） | barbecue, BBQ |
| はがき | postcard |
| バス*（ばす） | bus |
| パスタ（ぱすた） | pasta |
| はやい* | early, fast, quick |
| パン*（ぱん） | bread |
| ばんごはん* | dinner |
| ひるごはん* | lunch |
| べんきょうします* | study |
| まいしゅう* | every week |
| まいつき* | every month |
| まいにち* | everyday |
| みます* | watch, see, look |
| もくようび* | Thursday |
| よく* | often, frequently |
| よみます* | read |
| よる* | night |
| ラグビー（らぐびー） | rugby |
| ロンドン*（ろんどん） | London |
| ワイン（わいん） | wine |
| わかります* | understand, know |
| わらいます* | laugh, smile |

# 第5課（だいごか）

## いっしょに テニスを しませんか
## Why don't we play tennis together?

[Elena and Masato are talking]

1 エレナ：　いいてんきですね。
2 まさと：　そうですね。ほんとうに いいてんきですね。
3 エレナ：　ところで まさとさん、よく スポーツ（すぽーつ）を しますか。
4 まさと：　そうですね、よく にちようびに こうえんで
5 　　　　　やきゅうを します。エレナさんは？
6 エレナ：　わたしは ときどき ともだちと テニス（てにす）を します。
7 まさと：　そうですか。いいですね。
8 エレナ：　よかったら こんしゅうの どようびに いっしょに テニス（てにす）を しませんか。
9 まさと：　あ、いいですね。そうしましょう。
10 エレナ：　ええ。テニス（てにす）のあと ばんごはんでも たべましょうか。
11 まさと：　いいですよ。

### 単語と表現（たんごとひょうげん） Vocabulary and Expressions (Dialogue)

| | | | | | |
|---|---|---|---|---|---|
| 1 | いい | good, nice | 4 | こうえん | park |
| 1 | てんき | weather | 8 | よかったら | if you like, if it's alright |
| 2 | ほんとうに | really | 8 | こんしゅう | this week |
| 3 | ところで | by the way | 8 | いっしょに | together (with) |
| 3 | スポーツ（すぽーつ） | sport(s) | 10 | Xでも | *X* or something |

### Dialogue in English

**[Elena and Masato are talking]**

1 E: It's fine weather, isn't it?
2 M: Yes, indeed. It's really fine weather.
3 E: By the way, do you often play sport?.
4 M: Well, (I) often play baseball in the park.
5 How about you, Elena?
6 E: I sometimes play tennis with (my) friend.
7 M: I see. That's good.
8 E: If you like, why don't we play tennis together on Saturday this week?
9 M: Oh, that sounds good. Let's play.
10 E: Yes. Shall we have dinner or something after tennis?
11 M: That's good.

## 文法 Grammar

(ぶんぽう)

### 1. Sentence structure: Predicate and case particles

Making up a sentence requires two types of basic knowledge (before you consider the various detailed rules of the language). One is knowing how the things and concepts in question are 'named' or 'termed' in that language and the other is knowing the way those names and terms are linearly 'ordered'. Suppose you are trying to describe the following situation 'Mr Tanaka watches TV at 7 o'clock at home' in Japanese:

First we need to know the Japanese words for 'Mr Tanaka', '7 o'clock', 'TV', 'home' and 'watch': They are the nouns, たなかさん, 7じ, テレビ and うち and a verb, みます, respectively. We then need to know how these words are arranged to form a sentence: i.e., how we put them one by one in order. What is at issue here is the fact that a verb (or 'predicate' in a more broad sense) is the 'core' of the sentence in the sense that all the other words within the sentence are related to the verb directly or indirectly. For example, 'Mr Tanaka' is the doer of the action 'watch', '7 o'clock' is the time, 'home' is the location, and 'TV' is the object, for the action. Put differently, each word has a certain relationship with the verb: i.e. doer, time, location, object, etc of the action that is expressed by the verb.

In some language such a relationship is usually indicated by the word order. For example, in English *Mary hits John* (doer=Mary; John=object) and *John hits Mary* (doer=John; Mary=object) reverses the meaning, i.e. the opposite meaning being expressed by the different word order. In Japanese such a relationship is in principle expressed by case particles. In the example above, the relationship (or role) of たなかさん as the doer is marked by が (or topic marker は if topicalised), and similarly the time 7じ by に, the object テレビ by を, and the location うち by で. In this regard, case particles in Japanese are like 'in', 'from' and 'to' in English (e.g. *I walked 'from the bus stop to my office' vs. I walked 'to my office from the bus stop'*: The two sentences have the same meaning despite the difference in word order).

It is a basic rule in Japanese that a verb appears at the end of a sentence. Apart from this basic rule, any word order as shown below is grammatically possible so long as the case particles are properly used, since in any order the role (or relationship with the verb) of each noun is the same so long as it is marked by the same particle. This is why it is sometimes said that the word order is very flexible in Japanese. Note, however, that the sentence (a) with the order 'topic-time-location-object-verb' is a 'neutral' sentence and the most preferred when used in isolation. Other sentences with a different word order may be used to indicate a certain effect (such as prominence or emphasis on a particular word of the sentence).

(a) たなかさんは　７じに　うちで　テレビ(てれび)を　みます。
(b) ７じに　たなかさんは　うちで　テレビ(てれび)を　みます。
(c) うちで　たなかさんは　７じに　テレビ(てれび)を　みます。
(d) テレビ(てれび)を　たなかさんは　７じに　うちで　みます。
(e) たなかさんは　７じに　テレビ(てれび)を　うちで　みます。

For this reason the accurate use of case particles is important for properly expressing the intended meaning in Japanese. Conversely, this also means that you do not have to worry too much about the word order if you use the case particles properly.

## 2. Basic Japanese word order and particles

topic-は　time-(に)　subject-が　place-で　destination-に／へ　object-を　[verb]

| | *topic* | *time* | *subject* | *place* | *object / destination* | *verb* |
|---|---|---|---|---|---|---|
| 1 | わたしは | あした* | | うちで | テレビを | みます |

'I will watch TV at home tomorrow.'

| | | | | | | |
|---|---|---|---|---|---|---|
| 2 | たなかさんと わたしは | かようびに | | しんじゅくで | ちゅうかりょうりを | たべます |

'Tanaka-san and I will eat Chinese food in Shinjuku on Tuesday.'

| | | | | | | |
|---|---|---|---|---|---|---|
| 3 | たなかさんは | ８じに | | | かいしゃに | いきます |

'Tanaka-san goes to his/her office (company) at 8 o'clock.'

| | | | | | | |
|---|---|---|---|---|---|---|
| 4 | | あした | ともだちが | | うちに | きます |

'My friend will come to my home tomorrow.'

| | | | | | | |
|---|---|---|---|---|---|---|
| 5 | わたしは | あした | | しぶやで | デパートと えいがかんに | いきます |

'I will go to a department store and a cinema in Shibuya tomorrow.'

| | | | | | | |
|---|---|---|---|---|---|---|
| 6 | ちちは | たいてい ６じに | | | | おきます |

'My father usually gets up at 6 o'clock.'

(*Some time words including あした are normally used without the particle に.)

## 文法練習 1
(ぶんぽうれんしゅう)

**Put an appropriate particle in __ and then make up Japanese sentences. You need to consider the relationship between the nouns in [box] and the verb in [ ].**

(e.g.) 7:00 に breakfast を [ eat ]

→ 7じに　あさごはんを　たべます。

(1) 6:00 ____ [ get up ]

(2) Friday ____ pool ____ [ swim ]

(3) department store ____ bag ____ [ buy]

(4) department store ____ [ go]

(5) Wednesday ____ Japan ____ [ return ]

(6) 5:00 ____ coffee shop ____ Katoo-san ____ [ meet]

(7) Saturday ____ park ____ soccer ____ [play/do]

(8) 4:30 ____ library ____ Japanese language ____ [study]

(9) Kimura-san ____ Friday ____ Ikebukuro ____ movie ____ [see/watch]

## 文法練習 2
(ぶんぽうれんしゅう)

**Make up Japanese sentences which describe what each person does in each picture.**

(e.g.) たなかさんは　7じに　うちで　ばんごはんを　たべます。

(e.g.) たなか

(1) きむら

(2) よしだ

(3) さとう

(4) はやし

(5) すずき

(6) まつだ

(7) たかだ

(8) くどう

## 文法練習３ (ぶんぽうれんしゅう)

**Make up a Japanese sentence which describes the situation in each picture.**

〜と ‘with, and’
〜で ‘(instrument; means) by, with’

(e.g.) たなかさんは ８じはんに はやしさんと だいがくに いきます。

(e.g.) Tanaka / with Hayashi

8:30 am / university

(1) Okada / by bus

8:00 am / office (company)

(2) Tanaka / with Kimura

Friday / movie

(3) I / with (my) friend

library / study Japanese

(4) Suzuki

Saturday / Sydney

(5) Yoshida

Sunday / Japan

### 3. Past tense of verbs (polite form): ～ました

The past expression of ～ます (affirmative polite verbal predicate) is ～ました. The past interrogative expression is ～ましたか and the negative is ～ませんでした [～ません negative + ～でした past].

(1) きのう わたしは おおさかに いきました。 'I went to Osaka yesterday.'

(2) たなかさんは きょう 6じに おきました。 'Tanaka-san got up at 6 today.'

(3) やまださんは きのう がっこうに きませんでした。 'Yamada-san did not come to school yesterday.'

(4) あさごはんを たべましたか。 'Did you eat breakfast?'

→ はい、(あさごはんを) たべました。 'Yes, I ate (breakfast).'

→ いいえ、(あさごはんを) たべませんでした。 'No, I didn't eat (breakfast).'

**文法練習(ぶんぽうれんしゅう) 4**

**For practising the structural formation of ～ましたか；～ませんでした as well as ～ました, make up your own questions and their answers, using given words, as in the example.**

(e.g.) きのう、 だいがく

Q: きのう だいがくに いきましたか。

[Yes] はい、だいがくに いきました。

[No] いいえ、だいがくに いきませんでした。

(1) ゆうべ、 テレビ(てれび)

(2) おととい、 まち、 コーヒー(こーひー)

(3) ゆうべ、 にほんご

(4) きのう、 おかださん

(5) せんしゅうの どようび、 かいもの

きのう 'yesterday' おととい 'the day before yesterday' ゆうべ 'last night'
まち 'town' せんしゅう 'last week' (せんしゅうの どようび 'last Saturday')

## 自然(しぜん)な日本語(にほんご) Natural Conversation Notes

# そうですね *vs.* そうですか

Involving the combination of そうです 'That's right' and the interactive particle (or sentence-final particle) ね and よ, respectively, these may be used in response to someone's comments (ね and よ will be discussed in a later lesson). However, they denote quite different meanings.

### 1. そうですね 'Yes, it is / Indeed'

The fundamental function of ね is to indicate agreement (or alignment) with the other speaker (See later lesson for more details). In the examples below, A states his/her evaluative feeling about the weather, the speed of a car and the price of petrol, respectively, and seeks agreement or alignment from B, which is expressed by ね.

(1) A： きょうは あついですね。 'It is hot today, isn't it?' (あつい 'hot')

B： そうですね。 'Yes, it is. / Indeed.'

(2) A： この くるまは はやいですね。 'This car is fast, isn't it?' (はやい 'fast, early')

B： ほんとうに そうですね。 'Yes, it really is.'

(3) A： ガソリン(がそりん)が たかいですね。 'Petrol is expensive, isn't it?' (たかい 'expensive')

B： そうですね。たかいですね。 'Indeed. It's expensive.'

The other speaker B uses そうですね, to show his/her full agreement/alignment with what A has said. Without ね, B's responses would sound unnatural and even blunt, since they lose the nuance that shows the listener's full agreement. (Note that そうですね in this usage is different from the one used as a filled pause or filler and means 'Let me think/see', 'Well…", which we studied in Lesson 4.)

### 2. そうですか 'I see / is that so?'

そうですか is used to express acknowledgement that he/she did not know and has now understood what was just said.

(4) A： わたしは だいがくせいです。 'I am a university student.'

B： そうですか。 'I see. / Is that so?'

(5) A： たなかさんは くつを かいました。 'Tanaka-san bought shoes.'

B： そうですか。 'I see. / Is that so?'

(6) A： らいしゅう にほんに いきます。 'I will go to Japan next week.'

B： そうですか。いいですね。 'Is that so? That's good.'

か at the end of a sentence usually indicates a question and is normally pronounced with a rising intonation. However, it usually has a falling intonation when used to show acknowledgement, as in the case of そうですか. If か were said with a rising intonation in the context of acknowledgement, it would sound as if he/she has some doubt about what the speaker has said.

## 自然(しぜん)な日本語(にほんご)：練習(れんしゅう)

**Choose either そうですね or そうですか to respond to the speaker's comments or statements and cross out any inappropriate ones as in the example. Both may be acceptable in some cases, but each conveys a different nuance.**

(e.g.) A：たなかさんは こうこうの せんせいです。 'Tanaka-san is a high school teacher.'
B：~~そうですね。~~ ／ そうですか。

(1) A: きょうは さむいですね。 'It's cold today, isn't it?'
B: そうですね。／ そうですか。

(2) A: きょう いい てんきですね。 'It's fine weather today, isn't it?'
B: そうですね。／ そうですか。

(3) A: あのひとは べんごしです。 'That person is a lawyer.'
B: そうですね。／ そうですか。

(4) A: このケーキ(けーき)は おいしいですね。 'This cake is delicious, isn't it?'
B: そうですね。／ そうですか。

(5) A: わたしの しゅっしんは ほっかいどうです。 'I am from Hokkaido.'
B: そうですね。／ そうですか。

(6) A: この もんだいは むずかしいですね。 'This question is difficult/hard, isn't it?'
B: そうですね。／ そうですか。

(7) A: ゆうべ まちで コーヒー(こーひー)を のみました。 'I drank coffee in town last night.'
B: そうですね。／ そうですか。

(8) A: きんようびに しけんが ありますね。 'We have an exam on Friday, don't we?'
B: そうですね。／ そうですか。

(9) A: わたしの りょうしんは オーストラリア(おーすとらりあ)に います。'My parents are in Australia.'
B: そうですね。／ そうですか。

(10) A: きのう たなかさんと テニス(てにす)を しました。
'I played tennis with Tanaka-san yesterday.'
B: そうですね。／ そうですか。

## 表現 Expression Notes

### 1 ～ませんか, ～ましょう and ～ましょうか

**'Inviting someone to do something together or suggesting / proposing doing something with someone'**

These expressions are interchangeable in many cases when the speaker expresses an invitation or makes a suggestion which seeks the listener's response on his/her participation in an activity. However, each expression differs from the others. The specific features of these expressions are as follows.

**[1]** ☛ [～ませんか] (by asking the listener's intention) may be used to express a polite invitation or suggestion: 'Why don't we ~?'.

(1) いっしょに テニスを しませんか。 'Why don't we play tennis together?'

[～ましょう] is a polite, volitional form and is primarily used to propose an action, or to suggest doing something together with another or others: 'Let's…'

(2) いっしょに テニスを しましょう。 'Let's play tennis together.'

[～ましょうか] (～ましょう followed by the question particle か) indicates that the speaker seeks agreement with a suggestion / proposal: 'Shall we ~?'.

(3) いっしょに テニスを しましょうか。 'Shall we play tennis together?'

**[2]** ☛ Generally, the listener has two ways to respond to such an invitation or suggestion, namely, accepting it or refusing it. Acceptance may be expressed in a straightforward way, while refusal may include extra elements such as an apology and reason/excuse to mitigate the impact of refusing, or the manipulation of an incomplete sentence to imply refusal (please refer to Lesson 8 for details aboutrefusals in Japanese).

(4) あした いっしょに テニスを しませんか。
'Why don't we play tennis together tomorrow?'

[Accepting] ええ、いいですね。しましょう。
'Yes, that sounds good. Let's play (tennis).'

[Refusing] (a) すみません。じゅぎょうが あります。 'Sorry, but I have class.'
(b) ええと テニスは ちょっと… 'Well, tennis is a little bit... I'm afraid...'
(c) あの～ あしたは ちょっと…
'Well, tomorrow is a little bit... I'm afraid...'

## 表現練習 1

**For sentence-pattern practice, change the given sentences into expressions of ～ませんか, ～ましょう and ～ましょうか. Feel free to use いっしょに 'together'.**

(e.g.) きょう まちで ばんごはんを たべます。

きょう まちで いっしょに ばんごはんを たべませんか。

きょう まちで いっしょに ばんごはんを たべましょう。

きょう まちで いっしょに ばんごはんを たべましょうか。

(1) もくようびに えいがを みます。

(2) としょかんで にほんごを べんきょうします.

(3) きっさてんで コーヒーを のみます。

(4) たいいくかんで バドミントンを します。 (たいいくかん 'gym')

(5) ３じごろに かとうさんに あいます。

## 表現練習 2

**Look at the pictures and make up short conversations between [A] and [B], which describe the situations. In each situation, [A] makes an invitation, or makes a suggestion or proposal and [B] responds to it as in the examples.**

(e.g.1) A: いっしょに おちゃを のみましょうか。 'Shall we have tea?'

B: いいですね。のみましょう。 'That sounds good. Let's have (some).'

(e.g.2) A: いっしょに サッカーを しませんか。 'Why don't we play soccer?'

B: すみません。しゅくだいが あります。 'Sorry, but I have homework (to do).'

or あ、サッカーは ちょっと…。 'Oh, soccer is a bit....'

(e.g.1) suggestion/proposal

Drink tea

(e.g.2) invitation

Play soccer / Homework to do

(1) invitation

Go to the party

(2) suggestion / proposal

Study Japanese

(3) invitation

See a movie

(4) suggestion/proposal

Play tennis / Cold

(5) invitation

Go shopping / No money
(shopping かいもの)

(6) suggestion/proposal

Go to the park

(7) suggestion/proposal

Swim / Busy
(busy いそがしい)

## 対話(たいわ) Communicative Exchanges

### 対話練習(たいわれんしゅう) 1

**Pre-task:** ようび; なにを しますか;
[place]-で, [time]-に, [people]-と

(i) First decide your own schedule (you can make it up) for each day and write it in the column 'You' in the table below. If necessary, you may include the time, location and person with whom you will do the things.

(ii) In pairs, ask each other about his/her schedule for each day as in the example.

(iii) When you have finished asking/answering the questions, change the roles.

(e.g. 1) A: [B] さん、げつようびに なにを しますか。

B: 1じに まちで ともだちと コーヒーを のみます。

A: そうですか。

(e.g. 2) B: [A] さん、げつようびに なにを しますか。

A: だいがくの としょかんで にほんごを べんきょうします。

B: そうですか。

| ようび | スケジュール (schedule) | |
|---|---|---|
| | You [A] | Your conversation partner [B] |
| (e.g.) げつようび | (1) Studying at the library | (2) Drinking coffee with friends: in town at 1 pm |
| げつようび | | |
| かようび | | |
| すいようび | | |
| もくようび | | |
| きんようび | | |
| どようび | | |
| にちようび | | |

## 対話練習2

Pre-task: ～ました; なにを しましたか

**Ask 5 of your classmates what they did (i) last night (ゆうべ) and (ii) last Saturday (せんしゅうの どようび).**

(e.g.) A: [B] さんは ゆうべ なにを しましたか。

B: うちで テレビを みました。

A: そうですか。せんしゅうの どようびには なにを しましたか。

B: え～と、ともだちと かいものを しました。

| Classmates | Last night (ゆうべ) | Last Saturday (せんしゅうの どようび) |
|---|---|---|
| (e.g.) [B] さん | Watched TV at home | Went shopping with a friend |
| | | |
| | | |
| | | |
| | | |
| | | |

## 対話練習3 (たいわ れんしゅう)

**Pre-task: 〜ませんか／ましょう／ましょうか**

(i) Choose 5 activities/events, which you would like to do with your conversation partner.
(ii) In pairs, then invite your partner to do the activities/events together. In addition to the activity/event, try to include the time/day and place, if possible. (Refer to the lists below.)
(iii) When you have finished asking/answering the questions, change the roles.
(iv) In responding to the suggestion/invitation, you can decide your own answers. You can also make up an excuse when you reject the suggestion/invitation.

(e.g.1) A: げつようびに まちで いっしょに えいがを みませんか。
B: あ、いいですね。みましょう。

(e.g.2) B: きょうの ごご プール(ぷーる)で いっしょに およぎましょうか。
A: あ、きょうの ごごは ちょっと…／ すみません。じゅぎょうが あります。
B: そうですか。じゃあ、こんどに しましょう。　（こんど 'next time'）

**Activities/events**

See a film　Study Japanese　Have a BBQ
Swim　Clean the house　Go to Tokyo
Drink coffee　Go to Japan　Do shopping
or Your own choice

**Time/day**

Tonight　This afternoon　Tomorrow
Monday　Wednesday　Friday
Saturday　Sunday　Summer holiday
Next Tuesday　or Your own choice

**Places**

Town
University
Library
Home
Swimming pool
Park
Coffee shop in town
Movie/cinema in town
Sydney
or Your own choice

**[Take notes below]**

| | My activities/events | Conversation partner's activities/events |
|---|---|---|
| e.g. | See a film; Monday; in town (Partner's response: OK) | Swim in the pool; this afternoon (My response: No, don't want to / uni classes) |
| 1 | | |
| 2 | | |
| 3 | | |
| 4 | | |
| 5 | | |

## 対話作り Comprehensive Exercises

(たいわ づく)

✍ **In pairs, create a dialogue for the given situation. Please feel free to ask the instructor if you have any questions about Japanese expressions for your dialogue.**

**Situation:**

You are inviting your friend to do certain activities. You may want to refer to one of the following things to do:

(a) having lunch/dinner　　(b) seeing a movie

(c) playing some sport　　(d) buying clothes/shoes/CDs etc.

or something that is your own

Please incorporate the following expressions into your dialogue:

- いっしょに
- ～ませんか／～ましょうか／～ましょう
- ～は ちょっと
- そうですね／そうですか

**[Sample Dialogue]** Satoko and Kenji are talking about an exam.

さとこ： らいしゅう しけんが ありますね。

けんじ： そうですね。

さとこ： わたしは どようびに えいごを べんきょうします。

けんじ： そうですか。

さとこ： よかったら いっしょに べんきょうしませんか。

けんじ： いいですね。しましょう。

さとこ： じゃ、どようびの １０じに としょかんで あいましょうか。

けんじ： はい。

S: There is an exam next week, isn't there?
K: Yes, there is.
S: I will study English on Saturday.
K: I see.
S: If it is all right, why don't we study together?
K: Sounds good. Let's (do so).
S: Then, shall we meet in the library at 10 o'clock on Saturday?
K: Yes.

## 知ってた？ Did you know?

### 日本のスポーツ 'Popular sports in Japan'

Japanese of all ages enjoy sporting activities, both as participants and as spectators. In Japan, sport is regarded as a healthy pastime that develops good discipline, builds character, encourages fair play, and instills sportsmanship.

Win, lose, or draw, Japanese will enthusiastically cheer the athlete who makes a determined and sincere effort. At sporting events, competitors are invariably urged by shouts of がんばって！'Do your best!' or 'Hang in there!'

Whether you actually play some sports yourself or simply like to see them as a spectator, sport is part of our daily life these days and it is often an interesting topic we talk about, for example, professional baseball games, World Cup soccer, the Olympic games, etc. Thus, understanding sports in Japan and the Japanese words for sports terminology will be very useful when you are talking with Japanese people.

**Sports in Japanese:**

Aikido 合気道

Badminton バドミントン

Basketball バスケットボール(バスケット)

Cycling サイクリング

Gymnastics 体操

Hockey ホッケー

Ice hockey アイスホッケー

Jogging ジョギング

Karate 空手

Marathon マラソン

Scuba diving スキューバダイビング

Snowboarding スノーボード

Softball ソフトボール

Swimming 水泳

Ten pin bowling ボーリング

Volleyball バレーボール (バレー)

Athletic sports 陸上

Baseball 野球

Boxing ボクシング

Golf ゴルフ

Handball ハンドボール

Horse (back) riding 乗馬

Ice skating アイススケート

Judo 柔道

Kendo 剣道

Rugby ラグビー

Skiing スキー

Soccer サッカー

Sumo 相撲

Table tennis 卓球

Tennis テニス

**Useful Words/Expressions**

| | |
|---|---|
| Amateur　アマチュア（あまちゅあ） | draw　引（ひ）き分（わ）けます |
| games, matches　試合（しあい） | lose　（試合（しあい）に）負（ま）けます |
| Olympic Games　オリンピック（おりんぴっく）（オリンピック（おりんぴっく）・ゲーム（げーむ）、五輪（ごりん）） | |
| player　選手（せんしゅ） | professional baseball　プロ野球（ぷろやきゅう） |
| professional team　プロチーム（ぷろちーむ） | sports　スポーツ（すぽーつ）、運動（うんどう） |
| stadium　スタジアム（すたじあむ） | team　チーム（ちーむ） |
| win（試合（しあい）に）勝（か）ちます | The score is 2-3　スコア（すこあ）は　2対（たい）3です |

## 話（はな）し合（あ）いましょう Discussions

1. **What sports do you often play?**
2. **What sports are popular in Japan and your country?**
3. **Who are the famous sports players in Japan and your country? And what sports do they play?**

## 練習（れんしゅう）しましょう Exercise

**As mentioned earlier, sport is one of the interesting topics Japanese people talk about. Refer to the example below and ask 5 of your classmates what sports they like.**

(e.g.) A: なんの　スポーツ（すぽーつ）が　すきですか。
'What sports do you like?'

B: わたしは　やきゅうが　すきです。
'I like baseball. How about you?'
[A]さんは？
'What about you, A-san?'

A: わたしは　サッカー（さっかー）が　すきです。
'I like soccer.'

| Classmates | Favorite sports |
|---|---|
| (e.g.)　[B] さん | やきゅう |
| | |
| | |
| | |
| | |
| | |

**～が　すきです** 'I like ....'　(a) わたしは　さしみが　すきです。　'I like sashimi.'
(b) わたしは　たなかさんが　すきです。　'I like Tanaka-san.'

## 新しい単語・表現 New Vocabulary & Expressions

(Basic words/expressions are marked with '*')

| | |
|---|---|
| あつい* | hot |
| いい* | good, nice |
| いそがしい* | busy |
| いっしょに* | together |
| えいがかん* | movie theatre |
| おいしい* | delicious |
| おおさか | Osaka |
| おちゃ* | tea |
| おととい* | day before yesterday |
| かいしゃ* | company |
| ガソリン（がそりん） | gasoline, petrol |
| きのう* | yesterday |
| こうこう* | high school |
| こんしゅう* | this week |
| さしみ* | sashimi |
| さむい* | cold |
| すきです* | I like |
| せんしゅう* | last week |
| そうじします* | clean (rooms, house) |
| たいいくかん | gym |
| たかい* | expensive, high |
| ちち* | father |
| ちょっと* | a bit, little, few |
| ～でも | or something |
| てんき* | weather |
| ところで* | by the way |
| なつやすみ* | summer holiday |
| バドミントン（ばどみんとん） | badminton |
| はやい* | fast, early |
| ひこうき* | airplane |
| プール（ぷーる） | pool |
| ほっかいどう* | Hokkaido |
| ほんとうに* | really |
| まち* | town |
| むずかしい* | difficult, hard |
| もんだい | question |
| ゆうべ* | yesterday evening, last night |
| よかったら | if you like, if it's all right |
| らいしゅう* | next week |
| りょうしん* | parents |

# 第6課(だいろっか)

## やすいですね
### It's cheap, isn't it?

[Masato and Elena are looking at a leaflet of a department store]

まさと：　あ、デパート(でぱーと)の ちらしですか。

エレナ：　ええ。いろいろな 服(ふく)が ありますね。ほら、このシャツ(しゃつ)は １０ドル(どる)ですよ。

まさと：　へえ、安(やす)いですね。

エレナ：　はい。わたしは このデパート(でぱーと)で シャツ(しゃつ)と スカート(すかーと)を 買(か)います。いっしょに 行(い)きませんか。

まさと：　ええ、行(い)きましょう！

[After shopping]

まさと：　とても にぎやかな ところでしたね。それに いろいろな ものが 安(やす)かったです。

エレナ：　ええ。でも わたしの スカート(すかーと)は 安(やす)く ありませんでした。

まさと：　いくらでしたか。

エレナ：　２５０ドル(どる)でした。

まさと：　うわ、それは 高(たか)かったですね。

エレナ：　ええ。ところで そのジャケット(じゃけっと)は 小(ちい)さく ありませんか。

まさと：　いいえ、小(ちい)さく ありません。ちょうど いいです。

エレナ：　そうですか。それは よかったですね。

## 単語（たんご）と表現（ひょうげん） Vocabulary and Expressions (Dialogue)

| | | | | | |
|---|---|---|---|---|---|
| 1 | (こうこく)ちらし | leaflet, flyer | 8 | もの | thing, item |
| 2 | いろいろ(な) | various | 11 | いくら | how much |
| 2 | シャツ（しゃつ） | shirt | 13 | 高（たか）い | expensive |
| 4 | 安（やす）い | cheap | 14 | ジャケット（じゃけっと） | jacket |
| 5 | スカート（すかーと） | skirt | 14 | 小（ちい）さい | small |
| 8 | とても | very, so | 15 | ちょうど | just |
| 8 | にぎやか(な) | lively, busy | 15 | いい | (is) good, right |
| 8 | ところ | place | 16 | よかった | (was) good, right |

### Dialogue in English

**[Masato and Elena are looking at a leaflet of a department store]**

1 M: Oh, is it a leaflet of a department store?
2-3 E: Yes. There are / They have various (types of) clothes. Look, this shirt is 10 dollars.
4 M: Hm, it's cheap, isn't it?
5-6 E: Yes. I'll buy a shirt and a skirt at this department store. Why don't we go together?
7 M: Yes, let's go.

**[After shopping]**

8-9 M: It was a very lively place, wasn't it? And, various things/items were cheap.
10 E: Yea, but my skirt wasn't cheap.
11 M: How much was it?
12 E: (It was) 250 dollars.
13 M: Wow, that was expensive.
14 E: Yes. By the way, isn't the jacket small (for you)?
15 M: No, it isn't. (It's) just right/good.
16 E: Is that so? That's good.

## 文法（ぶんぽう） Grammar

## Adjectives (い-adjectives and な-adjectives)

### 1. Functions of adjectives:

An adjective is a word that describes a state or situation. Generally, adjectives can be used in both attributive and predicative ways to describe nouns. That is, they can come before nouns and modify them directly, or they can appear at the end of a sentence to form a predicate or part of it, which gives information about the grammatical subject of the situation.

| Attributive | Predicative |
| --- | --- |
| やすい くるま 'cheap car'<br>adjective noun | このくるまは やすいです。'This car is cheap.'<br>noun adjective |
| しんせつな ひと 'kind person'<br>adjective noun | あのひとは しんせつです。'That person is kind.'<br>noun adjective |

Adjectives can be modified by some adverbs such as とても 'very' and ほんとに 'really':

(e.g.) とても やすい 'very cheap' ほんとに やすい 'really cheap'

## 2. Two types of adjectives in Japanese

Japanese adjectives are basically categorised into two types, namely, い-adjectives and な-adjectives.

### 2.1. い-adjectives

い-adjectives are so called because their non-past affirmative forms (as well as dictionary form) ends in ～い. い-adjectives always end in *-ai* (e.g. ちいさい *chiisai* 'small'), *-ii* (e.g. おいしい *oishii* 'delicious'), *-ui* (e.g. ひくい *hikui* 'low') or *-oi* (e.g. ひろい *hiroi* 'wide, spacious'), and never end in *-ei* (cf. きれい(な) *kirei(na)* is a な-adjective).

(1) たかい ほん 'expensive book' (2) ふるい うち 'old house'

In the polite style, い-adjectives are followed by です when they are used at the end of a sentence.

(3) このほんは たかいです。 'This book is expensive.'

(4) わたしのうちは ふるいです。 'My house is old.'

### 2.2. な-adjectives

な-adjectives are so called because their non-past affirmative form is ～な.

(5) しずかな まち 'quiet town' (6) げんきな おとこのこ 'healthy / cheerful boy'

When な-adjectives are used as a predicate at the end of a sentence, they do not need な, but だ (plain)／です(polite). In this sense, な-adjectives are very similar to nouns in their behaviour when they are used to form a predicate.

(7) わたしの まちは しずかです。 'My town is quiet.'
(*しずかなです is ungrammatical.)

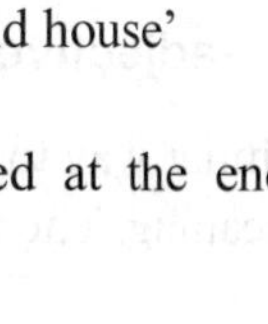

(8) この こうえんは きれいです。 'This park is clean/beautiful.'
(*きれいなです is ungrammatical.)

## 文法練習 1
(ぶんぽうれんしゅう)

**Rewrite the following English phrases and sentences in Japanese. Refer to the words listed below.**

(れい) a. small town ちいさい まち

b. This town is small. このまちは ちいさいです。

(1) new book (2) That book is new.

(3) big / large building (4) That building over there is big.

(5) spacious house (6) Tanaka-san's house is spacious.

(7) famous singer (8) That singer is very famous.

(9) kind person (10) Nara-san is very kind.

| | | | | | |
|---|---|---|---|---|---|
| new | 新しい (あたら) | big, large | 大きい (おお) | spacious, wide | 広い (ひろ) |
| famous | 有名な (ゆうめい) | singer | 歌手 (かしゅ) | kind | 親切な (しんせつ) |
| person | 人 (ひと) | | | | |

### 3. Negative forms

#### 3.1. い-adjectives in negative forms

In a similar way to verbs, い-adjectives conjugate their endings in order to convey a negative and past meaning. The negative meaning for い-adjectives is conveyed as follows:

(1) おもいです → おもく ありません
'is/are heavy' 'is/are not heavy'

(2) やすいです → やすく ありません
'is/are cheap' 'is/are not cheap'

**いい** The familiar adjective いい 'good' is actually a spoken version of よい, so, various grammatical forms of いい are derived from its original version よい.

(3) いいです → よく ありません
'is/are good' 'is/are not good'

Note: *いくありません is ungrammatical.

#### 3.2. な-adjectives in negative forms

Like nouns, な-adjectives indicate different grammatical meanings by changing だ／です. [〜じゃ･･･ is a spoken version of 〜では･･･]

(4) きれいです → きれいでは(じゃ) ありません
'is/are clean' 'is/are not clean'

(5) げんきです → げんきでは(じゃ) ありません
'is/are cheerful' 'is/are not cheerful'

There is another version of negative expressions, which makes use of the negative suffix ～ない:

(6) やすく ないです 'is/are not cheap'

(7) しずかでは ないです 'is/are not quiet'

These expressions indicate the negative feeling more strongly, compared to ～く ありません and ～では ありません. We focus on the ～ありません expressions here.

**文法練習(ぶんぽうれんしゅう) 2**

**Change the following affirmative sentences into negative ones.**

(れい) きょうは あついです。→ きょうは あつく ありません。

(1) たなかさんの いえは ちいさいです。

(2) この じてんしゃは あたらしいです。

(3) きょう わたしは げんきです。

(4) いま としょかんは しずかです。

(5) この もんだいは むずかしいです。

(6) あのひとは しんせつです。

(7) わたしの いえは だいがくから ちかいです。

## 4. Past forms

### 4.1. い-adjectives in the past form

The past tense of い-adjectives is formed by dropping the final い and adding かった.

(1) おいしいです → おいしかったです
'is/are delicious' 'was/were delicious'

(2) やすいです → やすかったです
'is/are cheap' 'was/were cheap'

(3) いいです → よかったです (いかったです is wrong)
'is/are good' 'was/were good'

Typical mistakes: *おいしいでした, *やすいでした, *いいでした

### 4.2 な-adjectives in the past form

The past tense is simply expressed by でした (だった for casual expressions) in the case of な-adjectives, i.e. the same as in the case of a noun.

(4) きれいです → きれいでした
'is/are pretty' 'was/were pretty'

(5) しずかです → しずかでした
'is/are quiet' 'was/were quiet'

**文法練習 3** (ぶんぽうれんしゅう)

**Rewrite the following sentences in Japanese. Refer to the words listed below.**

(れい) My car was small. わたしの くるまは ちいさかったです。

(1) Tokyo was very big.

(2) My jacket was very expensive.

(3) Katoo-san's car was fast.

(4) The party was very (really) fun.

(5) The movie was scary.

(6) Suzuki-san's house was big.

(7) Okada-san was very kind.

(8) Sydney was very lively.

(9) Yesterday's exam was easy.

(10) I was busy last week.

| | | |
|---|---|---|
| big 大(おお)きい | fast 速(はや)い | fun 楽(たの)しい |
| scary 怖(こわ)い | easy, simple 簡単(かんたん)な | |

### 4.3. Negative past forms of い-adjectives and な-adjectives

The negative past forms of い-adjectives and な-adjectives are formed by combining their negative forms with past forms, i.e. by just adding 〜でした to 〜く ありません (for い-adjectives) or 〜では(じゃ) ありません (for な-adjectives).

(1) おいしく ありません ＋ でした → おいしく ありませんでした (い-adjective)
'is/are not delicious' past 'was/were not delicious'

(2) きれいでは(じゃ) ありません ＋ でした
'is/are not clean' past
→ きれいでは(じゃ) ありませんでした (な-adjective)
'was/were not clean'

ぶんぽうれんしゅう
**文法練習 4**

**Rewrite the following sentences in Japanese.**

(れい) My car wasn't big. わたしの くるまは おおきくありませんでした。

(1) The movie wasn't interesting. (interesting おもしろい)

(2) The cake wasn't delicious.

(3) I wasn't busy yesterday.

(4) Satoo-san wasn't cheerful yesterday. [use げんき(な)]

(5) The teacher wasn't kind.

(6) The beach wasn't clean. (beach ビーチ(びーち))

(7) My university was not so far from my home.

**Summary:**

| | Non-past | | Past | |
|---|---|---|---|---|
| | Affirmative | Negative | Affirmative | Negative |
| **い-adj** | あついです<br>'is hot' | あつくありません<br>'is not hot' | あつかったです<br>'was hot' | あつくありませんでした<br>'was not hot' |
| **な-adj** | しずかです<br>'is quiet' | しずかではありません<br>'is not quiet' | しずかでした<br>'was quiet' | しずかではありませんでした<br>'was not quiet' |
| **Noun** | ほんです<br>'is a book' | ほんではありません<br>'is not a book' | ほんでした<br>'was a book' | ほんではありませんでした<br>'was not a book' |

## 自然(しぜん)な日本語(にほんご) Natural Conversation Notes

### あいづち 'Back channelling/Response tokens'

Japanese continuously use verbal as well as non-verbal signals to indicate that the listener is paying attention and understanding the speaker. This behaviour is called 'Aizuchi', which is the Japanese term for frequent interjections, back-channelling or response tokens during a conversation. A recent study of aizuchi found that it occurs every few seconds in an average Japanese conversation.

This form of aizuchi is to indicate the speaker's concern to assure the conversation partner that 'I'm paying attention', 'I'm surprised', and/or 'I'm listening, so please go ahead/keep going'. As such, their use is normally meant to encourage the speaker to go on and to make the conversation flow smoothly. They are often followed by additional comments such as しらなかった 'I didn't know', そうだったんですか 'Was that so?', and そういうこともあるんですか 'Can that be true?/Could that kind of thing happen?'. Some examples of aizuchi are shown below.

- ・そうですね 'Yes, it is. / Yes, indeed.'  ・そうですか 'I see. / Is that so?'
- ・はい／ええ 'Yes (formal)' - often repeated like はい、はい／ええ、ええ 'Yes, yes'
- ・うん 'Yeah (casual)' - often repeated like うん、うん 'Yeah, yeah'
- ・ほんとう？／ほんとに？ 'Really? / Truly?'
- ・すごい！ 'Excellent!, Wonderful!, Fantastic!'
- ・へえ 'Huh'  ・うわ（あ） 'Wow' 'Oh'
- ・Nodding (sometimes with うん、うん) 'I am listening / I agree with you.'

## 自然(しぜん)な日本語(にほんご)：練習(れんしゅう)

**In pairs, practise the following conversation. Provide an appropriate aizuchi in B's responses. Try to use a variety of aizuchi. You may also add further comments following the aizuchi.**

**[練習(れんしゅう) 1: A has come back from a park and is now talking to B. ]**

| [Speaker A] | [Speaker B] |
|---|---|
| 1 きのう こうえんに いきました。さくらを みました。 | ………………………… |
| 2 とても きれいでした。でも かぜが つよかったです。 | ………………………… |
| 3 さくらまつりも みました。(まつり 'festival') | ………………………… |
| 4 はい。とても たのしかったです。 | ………………………… |

**[練習(れんしゅう) 2: A is talking to B about what happened to her yesterday. ]**

| [Speaker A] | [Speaker B] |
|---|---|
| 1 きのう ゆうめいな かしゅを みました。 | ………………………… |
| 2 デパート(でぱーと)で みました。 | ………………………… |
| 3 とても きれいでした。 | ………………………… |
| 4 せも たかかったです。 | ………………………… |
| 5 いっしょに しゃしんを とりました。 | ………………………… |

# 表現（ひょうげん） Expression Notes

## 1 Describing objects, things and people using adjectives

### 表現練習（ひょうげんれんしゅう）1

**Look at the pictures which illustrate your feelings. Describe them using adjectives given in the words listed below. Some questions may have more than one answer.**

(れい)

うれしいです

(1)

(2)

(3)

(4)

(5)

(6)

(7)

(8)

| | | | | | |
|---|---|---|---|---|---|
| 寒（さむ）い | 痛（いた）い | 元気（げんき）（な） | 暑（あつ）い | 嬉（うれ）しい | たいくつ (な) |
| 楽（たの）しい | 悲（かな）しい | 強（つよ）い | 暖（あたた）かい | 気持（きも）ちが いい | |

## 表現練習 2

(ひょうげん れんしゅう)

**Each picture indicates what you experienced in the past. State your experience using adjectives.**

(れい)　ふじさんは とても きれいでした。(or おおきかったです。)

(れい)　ふじさん

(1)　べんきょう

(2)　にほん

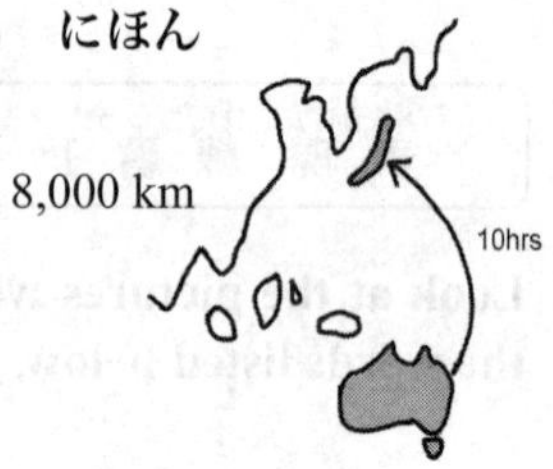


(3)

(4)　テスト (てすと)

(5)

(6)

(7)　1,000,000 えん

(8)

### 2 Negative expressions: あまり ...(negative)... 'not so...'

あまり is often added to negative expressions in order to soften the negative tone involved. When あまり is used for this function, it is always followed by a negative expression.

(e.g.)　このくるまは <u>あまり</u> たかく <u>ありません</u>。

やまださんは <u>あまり</u> しんせつでは <u>ありません</u>。

とても 'very' is not normally used for such function in negative expressions while it is all right in the affirmative.

(e.g.)　このくるまは <u>とても</u> たかいです。

このくるまは <u>あまり</u> たかく <u>ありません</u>。

(*このくるまは とても たかく ありません is not normally used.)

## 表現練習 3

**State your feeling when you found something was different from what you had imagined or expected. Feel free to use あまり.**

(れい) Expectation: Mt Fuji would be beautiful/pretty.

→ ふじさんは あまり きれいじゃ ありませんでした。

(1) Expectation: The movie would be interesting.

(2) Expectation: The mobile phone would be cheap.

(3) Expectation: The restaurant (food) would be delicious.

(4) Expectation: Satoo-san would be kind/gentle.

(5) Expectation: Okinawa would be warm.

(6) Expectation: The exam would be difficult.

(7) Expectation: The teacher would be strict.

(8) Expectation: The singer would be good (at singing). (good いい, じょうず(な))

(9) Expectation: Tanaka-san's car would be fast.

(10) Expectation: The chair would be comfortable. (comfortable らく(な))

# 対話 Communicative Exchanges

## 対話練習 1

Pre-task: ～い です
～く ありません

**Ask 5 of your classmates the following questions in Japanese.**

(1) Whether or not his/her home (or residence) is far (とおい) from here (where you are now).

(2) Whether or not his/her room is spacious (ひろい).

(3) Whether or not he/she feels Japanese is difficult (むずかしい) to learn.

| なまえ: | (れい) みか | | | | | |
|---|---|---|---|---|---|---|
| Home; とおい？ | はい | | | | | |
| Room; ひろい？ | いいえ | | | | | |
| Japanese; むずかしい？ | いいえ | | | | | |

(れい)　You:　みかさん、うちは ここから とおいですか。

みか:　はい、とおいです。

You:　そうですか。みかさんの へやは ひろいですか。

みか:　いいえ、あまり ひろくありません。

You:　そうですか。にほんごは むずかしいですか。

みか:　いいえ、あまり むずかしくありません。

## 対話練習 2 (たいわれんしゅう)

**Pre-task:** い-adj, な-adj

**Describe special features of people, using adjectives.**

(i) In pairs, ask your partner about the special features of each person, using ～さんの とくちょうは なんですか？ 'What is a special feature of ~san?'. (とくちょう 'special features, characteristics')

(ii) Answer the question by describing the feature, using the expression, ～さんは X (point to be described) が Y (adjective) です 'As for ~san, his/her X is Y'. You may also make up your own answers.

(iii) When you have finished asking/answering the questions, change the roles.

(れい)　かとう

A:　かとうさんの とくちょうは なんですか。

B:　かとうさんは せが たかいです。　or

かとうさんは めが ちいさいです。

はな nose　　みみ ear
あし leg　　かみの け hair
ながい long　　くろい black

## 対話練習 3

**Pre-task:** い-adj, な-adj (past)

**In pairs, create a short dialogue about something that one of you has experienced.**

(i) Refer to the prompts below and ask the other a question **～は どうでしたか** 'How was ~?'.

(ii) The other replies stating his/her own impression about what is indicated in the prompts.

(iii) When you have finished asking/answering the questions, change the roles.

(れい) えいが

A: えいがは　どうでしたか。
B: とても　おもしろかったです。 or
あまり　おもしろくありませんでした。
A: あ、そうですか。

(1) じゅぎょう

(2) アルバイト

(3) しょくじ

(4) りょこう

(5) テスト

(6) コンサート

## 対話作り Comprehensive Exercises

✍ **In pairs, create a dialogue for the given situation. Please feel free to ask the instructor if you have any questions about the Japanese expressions for your dialogue.**

**Situation:**

You have just come back from your trip to one of the following places. Your friend asks you about it.

[Japan, Tasmania, London, Hong Kong, or you can choose one from your own experience]

Please incorporate the following expressions into your dialogue:

- Adjectives (non-past, past, negative, negative past)
- Aizuchi including へえ, おお, ええ etc (exclamation)
- ～は どうでしたか
- とても

**[Sample Dialogue]**

(けん has just come back from Korea)

みか：　かんこくりょこうは どうでしたか。

けん：　とても たのしかったです。かんこくの ひとは とても しんせつでした。

みか：　そうですか。よかったですね。

けん：　はい。やきにくも おいしかったです。

みか：　たかかったですか。

けん：　いいえ。５００えんぐらいでした。

みか：　へえ！それは やすいですね。

けん：　はい。らいねん また いきます。

M: How was your trip to Korea?
K: It was very (really) fun. Korean people were very kind.
M: Was it so? That was good.
K: Yes. (Korean)BBQ was also delicious.
M: Was it expensive?
K: No, (it) was about 500yen.
M: Huh, that's cheap, isn't it?
K: Yes. I will go (there) again next year.

## 知(し)ってた？ Did you know?

## お客(きゃく)様(さま)は神様(かみさま)です 'A customer is a god'

A famous Japanese expression/saying, 'お客様は神様です' literally meaning 'a customer is a god', reflects the concept that shop assistants should treat their customers respectfully and make them feel important. Indeed, Japanese customer service is usually very friendly, attentive and at the same time very polite. This is frequently commented on by foreign visitors to the country as well as by Japanese people themselves.

This idea of how to treat customers is also reflected in the use of the shop assistants' language; that is, they use honorific forms of language and speak in a humble and deferential manner. This degree of service can be observed in various situations ranging from local rental video shops to department stores.

**[Some polite expressions typically used by shop assistants at a department store]**

| | |
|---|---|
| ・いらっしゃいませ。 | 'Welcome.' |
| ・承知(しょうち)いたしました。or かしこまりました。 | 'I understood.' |
| ・なにか おさがしでしょうか。 | 'Are you looking for something?' |
| ・こちらは1万(まん)4千円(せんえん)でございます。 | 'This (item) is 14,000 yen.' |
| ・2万円(まんえん) お預(あず)かりいたします。 | 'I temporarily keep 20,000 yen (that you've just paid).' |

## 話(はな)し合(あ)いましょう Discussions

**1. Discuss the differences in the types of services or goods at a department store between your country and Japan.**

(1) What time does a department store generally open and close?

(2) What is the structure of a department store?

(3) What/Who do you see in the elevator?

(4) You bought a dish as your friend's birthday present at a department store. Can you ask a shop assistant to wrap the item with wrapping paper and ribbon for free?

(5) You bought a bag at a department store yesterday, but found that it was an inferior product. When you return it to the department store, what do you expect from the shop assistant?

**Useful Words/Expressions**

| | | | |
|---|---|---|---|
| 営業時間(えいぎょうじかん) | 食料品売り場(しょくりょうひんうりば) | 屋上(おくじょう) | エレベーター・ガール(えれべーたー・がーる) |
| 無料包装(むりょうほうそう) | レストラン街(れすとらんがい) | お客様のクレームへの対処(きゃくさま くれーむ たいしょ) | |

**2. Discuss the services at various types of public establishments (e.g. restaurant, hair salon, petrol station) in your country and in Japan.**

# Supplementary: At a department store

This is to supplement and reinforce what we have studied in previous lessons, by looking at expressions commonly used at a department store in Japan. We particularly focus on verbal exchanges to make enquiries at an information desk, and to buy goods at a variety of sales sections.

## 1. Where is the toilet?: At the information desk

I.L. = Information lady

| | | |
|---|---|---|
| 1 | 田中（たなか）： | あの、すみません。 |
| 2 | 案内嬢（あんないじょう）： | いらっしゃいませ。 |
| 3 | 田中（たなか）： | あの、紳士服（しんしふく）売り場（ば）は 何階（なんかい）ですか。 |
| 4 | 案内嬢（あんないじょう）： | 紳士服（しんしふく）売り場（ば）は 5階（かい）でございます。 |
| 5 | 田中（たなか）： | 5階（かい）ですね。 |
| 6 | 案内嬢（あんないじょう）： | はい。 |
| 7 | 田中（たなか）： | あの～、お手洗い（てあら）は どこですか。 |
| 8 | 案内嬢（あんないじょう）： | 3階（かい）の 時計（とけい）売り場（ば）の となりで ございます。 |
| 9 | 田中（たなか）： | どうも ありがとうございました。 |
| 10 | 案内嬢（あんないじょう）： | いいえ。 |

1 T: Excuse me.
2 I.L.: Yes, madam. May I help you?
3 T: Which floor can I find the men's clothing on?
4 I.L.: The men's clothing section is on the 5th floor, madam.
5 T: The 5th floor, is it?
6 I.L.: Yes.
7 T: Sorry, but where is the bathroom?
8 I.L.: (It's) next to the watch/clock section on the 3rd floor.
9 T: Thank you very much.
10 I.L.: It was my pleasure.

### Related words

**Sales sections（～売り場（うりば））**

| | | | |
|---|---|---|---|
| ・家具（かぐ） 売り場（うりば） | 'furniture section' | ・かばん 売り場（うりば） | 'bag section' |
| ・くつ 売り場（うりば） | 'shoe section' | ・化粧品（けしょうひん） 売り場（うりば） | 'cosmetics section' |
| ・食料品（しょくりょうひん） 売り場（うりば） | 'food section' | ・紳士服（しんしふく） 売り場（うりば） | 'men's clothing section' |
| ・電気製品（でんきせいひん） 売り場（うりば） | 'electronic goods section' | ・時計（とけい） 売り場（うりば） | 'watch/clock section' |
| ・婦人服（ふじんふく） 売り場（うりば） | 'women's clothing section' | ・文房具（ぶんぼうぐ） 売り場（うりば） | 'stationery section' |

**Facilities**

| | | | |
|---|---|---|---|
| ・レストラン（れすとらん） | 'restaurant' | ・お手洗い（てあら） (トイレ（といれ）) | 'bathroom', 'toilet' |
| ・きっさてん | 'café', 'coffee shop' | ・階段（かいだん） | 'stairs' |
| ・エスカレーター（えすかれーたー） | 'escalator' | ・エレベーター（えれべーたー） | 'elevator' |
| ・駐車場（ちゅうしゃじょう） | 'parking space' | | |

**Levels**

・いっかい '1st floor'　・にかい '2nd floor'　・さんかい／さんがい '3rd floor'

・よんかい '4th floor'　・ごかい '5th floor'　・ろっかい '6th floor'

・ななかい '7th floor'　・はっかい／はちかい '8th floor'　・きゅうかい '9th floor'

・じっかい／じゅっかい '10th floor'　・ちか 'basement'; ちか いっかい '1st basement'

**Locations**

・まえ 'front'　・となり 'next to'　・よこ 'side'

・なか 'in, inside'　・みぎ 'right'　・ひだり 'left'

## 練習 1

**Make a sentence to ask on what floor the given section is and/or where the given facility is, as in the examples.**

(れい 1) Women's clothing section → すみません。ふじんふく売り場は 何階ですか。

(れい 2) Escalator → すみません。エスカレーターは どこですか。

(1) Furniture section　(2) Watch/clock section　(3) Bag section　(4) Shoe section

(5) Stairs　(6) Elevator　(7) Café　(8) Escalator

## 練習 2

**Provide the location of each sales section/facility, referring to the information on the right.**

(れい 1) 食料品うりばは ちかいっかいに あります。

(れい 2) おてあらいは にかいの 時計うりばの となりに あります。

(e.g.1) Food section　(e.g.2) Bathroom/toilets

(1) Shoe section　(2) Stairs

(3) Furniture section　(4) Men's clothing section

(5) Café　(6) Restaurant

| | |
|---|---|
| 5F | [Restaurant] [Café] |
| 4F | [Furniture section] [Stationery section] |
| 3F | [Men's clothing section] [Shoe section] |
| 2F | [Women's clothing section] [Watch section]-[Toilets] |
| 1F | [Cosmetics section]-[Stairs] |
| B1 | [Food section] |
| B2 | Car park |

## 練習(れんしゅう) 3

(i) Sketch your own plan of a department store, by locating sales sections and facilities on various floors. Locate all sections and facilities given in the list below.

(ii) Then in pairs, ask your conversation partner the location of the sales sections and facilities of his/her department store, as in the example. Write his/her answers (the locations) in [ ] in the list below.

(れい 1)

A： すみません。時計(とけい)うりばは なんかいですか。

B： 時計(とけい)うりばは いっかいです。

A： いっかいですね。ありがとうございます。

A: Excuse me. On what floor can I find the watch section?

B: The watch section is located on the first floor.

A: On the first floor, is it? Thank you very much.

(れい 2)

A： あの、おてあらいは どこですか。

B： おてあらいは いっかいの 時計(とけい)うりばの となりです。

A： 時計(とけい)うりばの となりですね。ありがとう ございます。

A: Sorry but where is the bathroom?

B: The bathroom is next to the watch section on the first floor.

A: Next to the watch section, is it? Thank you very much.

[List]

food section [ ]
bag section [ ]
electronic goods section [ ]
shoe section [ ]
watch section [ ]
furniture section [ ]
stationery section [ ]
women's clothing section [ ]
men's clothing section [ ]
restaurant [ ]; car park [ ]
toilets [ ]
stairs [ ]
escalator[ ]
elevator [ ]

(For the location of these facilities, use location words such as まえ, となり, みぎ, ひだり, etc.)

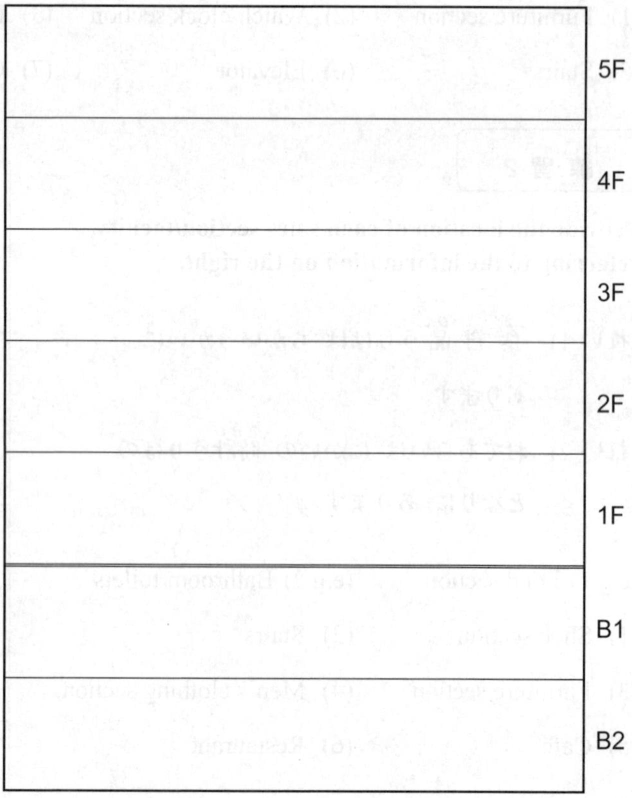

## 2. How much is the red one?: At the men's clothing section

1 田中(たなか)：　あの、すみません。

2 店員(てんいん)：　はい、いらっしゃいませ。

3 田中(たなか)：　これは、オーストラリア(おーすとらりあ)の セーター(せーたー)ですか。

4 店員(てんいん)：　いいえ、日本(にほん)のでございます。

5 田中(たなか)：　そうですか。オーストラリア(おーすとらりあ)のは ありますか。

6 店員(てんいん)：　はい、ございます。これです。

7 田中(たなか)：　いくらですか。

8 店員(てんいん)：　５０００円(えん)でございます。

9 田中(たなか)：　そうですか。もっと 安(やす)いのは ありませんか。

10 店員(てんいん)：　そうですね、４０００円(えん)のが ございます。

11 田中(たなか)：　じゃあ、４０００円(えん)のを おねがいします。 Or じゃあ、けっこうです。

12 店員(てんいん)：　はい、かしこまりました。 Or もうしわけありません。

ありがとうございました。

1 T: Excuse me.
2 SA: Yes, sir.
3 T: Is this an Australian sweater?
4 SA: No, it is a Japanese one, sir.
5 T: I see. Do you have an Australian one?
6 SA: Yes, we do, sir. This is (the one).
7 T: How much is it?
8 SA: It is 5000 yen, sir.
9 T: I see. Do you have a cheaper one?
10 SA: Well, we have a 4000 yen one, sir.
11 T: Then I will take the 4000 yen one. (or, Then, no thank you.)
12 SA: Certainly. (or, I am very sorry, sir. Thank you for coming.)

SA = shop assistant

の is an indefinite pronoun, which is used in place of a noun when the noun follows an adjective or another noun, and when what it refers to is clear from the context or the situation. (See Lesson 2 for more details.)

(1) おおきいのを かいます。 'I will buy a big one.'

(2) にほんのは たかいです。 'The Japanese one is expensive.'

Note: の may also be used as a grammatical item that connects two nouns and basically indicates 'Y associated with X'. (e.g. わたしの ほん 'my book'; Cf. Lesson 1)

## Related words

### Countries

アメリカ（あめりか） 'America'　　イギリス（いぎりす） 'England'　　オーストラリア（おーすとらりあ） 'Australia'
韓国（かんこく） 'Korea'　　シンガポール（しんがぽーる） 'Singapore'　　タイ（たい） 'Thailand'
中国（ちゅうごく） 'China'　　ドイツ（どいつ） 'Germany'　　日本（にほん） 'Japan'
フランス（ふらんす） 'France'

### Colours

赤い（あか） 'red'　　青い（あお） 'blue'　　黄色い（きいろ） 'yellow'　　黒い（くろ） 'black'　　白い（しろ） 'white'

### Sizes

小さい（ちい） 'small'　　大きい（おお） 'big, large'

### Prices

安い（やす） 'cheap'　　高い（たか） 'expensive'

### 練習（れんしゅう）4

**Rewrite the following sentences in Japanese. Refer to the words in the list above.**

（れい１）　Do you have a French wine?　　フランス（ふらんす）の ワイン（わいん）、ありますか。

（れい２）　How much is the red one?　　あかいのは　いくらですか。

(1) Do you have an Australian sweater?　　(2) Is this a German one?

(3) Do you have a white one?　　(4) How much is this Chinese one?

(5) Do you have a cheap camera?　　(6) Is this a Thai one?

(7) Do you have a big sweater?　　(8) This hat is two thousand five hundred yen.

(9) I have a black one.　　(10) Is that a Japanese watch?

(11) Do you have a small one?　　(12) Do you have a Singapore beer?

(13) Do you have a blue bag?　　(14) I have a Korean one.

## 練習(れんしゅう) 5

**This is a role-play practice of a conversation between a customer and shop staff.**

(i) Provide your own information about each item given in the table: i.e. item's product country, colour, etc. Table [A] is for your role as a customer and [B] is for your partner's role as shop staff. Some types of information are not important these are marked '------'. In these cases, just ignore this element.

(ii) Then, in pairs, try to buy/sell the items. Use words given earlier in 'Related words'.

(iii) When you have finished asking/answering questions, change the roles.

A (customer): I am looking for,

| Item | Country | Colour | Size | Price |
|---|---|---|---|---|
| (e.g.) sweater | English | blue or black | small | 6000 yen |
| (1) bag | ------- | | | |
| (2) hat | ------- | | | |
| (3) wine | | ------- | ------- | |
| (4) shoes | | ------- | | |
| (5) camera | | | ------- | |

B (shop staff): My shop has,

| Country | Colour | Size | Price |
|---|---|---|---|
| English, Canada | black, red, white | small, large | 5500 yen |
| ------- | | | |
| ------- | | | |
| | ------- | ------- | |
| | | ------- | |
| | | ------- | |

(れい)

A: すみません。イギリス(いぎりす)のセーター(せーたー)、ありますか。

B: はい、ございます。

A: あおいの ありますか。

B: もうしわけ ありません。ございません。

A: じゃあ、くろいの ありますか。

B: はい、ございます。

A: いくらですか。

B: ５５００円(えん)で ございます。

A: じゃあ、それ おねがいします。

B: かしこまりました。

A: Excuse me. Do you have an English sweater?

B: Yes, we do, sir/madam.

A: Do you have a blue one?

B: I am so sorry, sir/madam. We don't (have one).

A: Do you have a black one, then?

B: Yes, we do, sir/madam.

A: How much is it?

B: It is 5500 yen, sir/madam.

A: Then I will take it.

B: Certainly.

## 新しい単語・表現（あたらしいたんご・ひょうげん） New Vocabulary & Expressions

(Basic words/expressions are marked with '*')

| | |
|---|---|
| あおい* | blue |
| あかい* | red |
| あし* | leg (脚（あし）), foot (足（あし）) |
| 暖かい（あたたかい）* | warm |
| 案内嬢（あんないじょう） | information lady |
| 新しい（あたらしい）* | new |
| あまり* | not very ... |
| いくら* | how much |
| 痛い（いたい）* | sore, hurt |
| いろいろ(な)* | various |
| 嬉しい（うれしい）* | glad |
| 売り場（うりば）* | sales section |
| エスカレーター（えすかれーたー） | escalator |
| エレベーター（えれべーたー） | elevator |
| 大きい（おおきい）* | big, large |
| お客さん（おきゃくさん）* | customer, guest, visitor, client |
| お手洗い（おてあらい）* | bathroom, toilet |
| 重い（おもい）* | heavy |
| 面白い（おもしろい）* | interesting |
| ～階（かい）* | -th floor |
| 階段（かいだん） | stairs |
| 家具（かぐ） | furniture |
| 歌手（かしゅ） | singer |
| 風（かぜ）* | wind |
| 悲しい（かなしい）* | sad |
| 髪の毛（かみのけ）* | hair |
| かわいい* | cute |
| かわいそう(な)* | pitiful |
| 簡単（かんたん）(な)* | easy, simple |
| 黄色い（きいろい）* | yellow |
| 厳しい（きびしい）* | strict |
| 気持ちが いい（きもちが いい）* | feel good |
| きれい(な)* | pretty, clean |
| 黒い（くろい）* | black |
| 化粧品（けしょうひん） | cosmetics |
| 元気（げんき）(な)* | healthy, fine |
| ございます | (formal of あります) |
| 怖い（こわい）* | scary, scared, afraid |
| さくら | cherry blossom |
| 静か（しずか）(な)* | quiet |
| ジャケット（じゃけっと） | jacket |
| 写真（しゃしん）* | photo |
| シャツ（しゃつ） | shirt |
| 上手（じょうず）(な)* | be good at, skilled |
| 食事（しょくじ）* | meal |
| 食料品（しょくりょうひん） | grocery, food |
| 親切（しんせつ）(な)* | kind, gentle |
| 白い（しろい）* | white |
| 紳士服（しんしふく） | men's clothes |
| スカート（すかーと）* | skirt |
| セーター（せーたー）* | sweater |
| 背が 高い（せが たかい）* | tall |
| 退屈（たいくつ）(な)* | bored, boring |
| 大丈夫（だいじょうぶ）(な)* | It's OK; Not to worry. |
| 楽しい（たのしい）* | fun, enjoyable |
| 小さい（ちいさい）* | small, little |
| 地下（ちか） | underground, basement |

| | |
|---|---|
| ちか<br>近い* | close, near |
| ちゅうしゃじょう<br>駐車場 | car park |
| ちょうど* | just |
| ちらし | leaflet, flyer |
| つよ<br>強い* | strong |
| でんきせいひん<br>電気製品 | electronic goods |
| といれ<br>トイレ* | toilets |
| どう* | how |
| とお<br>遠い* | far |
| とくちょう<br>特徴 | special features, characteristics |
| ところ* | place |
| とても* | very |
| とります* | take |
| なが<br>長い* | long |
| にぎ<br>賑やか(な)* | vivid, lively |
| はな<br>鼻* | nose |
| はや<br>速い* | fast (cf. 早い(はや) early) |
| びーち<br>ビーチ | beach |
| びーる<br>ビール* | beer |
| ひだり<br>左* | left |
| ひろ<br>広い* | spacious, wide |
| ふじさん<br>富士山 | Mt. Fuji |
| ふじんふく<br>婦人服 | women's clothes |
| ふる<br>古い* | old |
| ぶんぼうぐ<br>文房具 | stationery |
| また* | again |
| まつ<br>祭り | festival |
| みぎ<br>右* | right |
| みみ<br>耳* | ear |
| むずか<br>難しい* | difficult, hard |
| め<br>目* | eye |
| もの* | thing, item |
| もっと* | more |
| や　にく<br>焼き肉 | yakiniku, Korean style BBQ |
| やす<br>安い* | cheap |
| ゆうめい<br>有名(な)* | famous, well known |
| よこ<br>横 | side |
| らいねん<br>来年* | next year |
| らく<br>楽(な)* | comfortable |
| りょこう<br>旅行 | travel, trip |

# 第７課

## バーベキューを する つもりです
## We are planning to have a barbecue

[Elena and Masato are talking]

1 まさと： 週末は、何を しますか。
2 エレナ： ええと、週末は、買い物に 行きます。
3 ケイトさんの 誕生日プレゼントを 買うつもりです。
4 まさと： そうですか。ケイトさんの誕生日は、いつですか。
5 エレナ： １５日です。
6 まさと： じゃあ、あさってですね。
7 エレナ： ええ、まさとさんも パーティーに 来ませんか。
8 まさと： えっ、いいんですか。
9 エレナ： もちろん。
10 まさと： あ、ぜひ 行きたいです。
11 場所は どこですか。
12 エレナ： 湖の近くの 公園です。
13 その公園で、バーベキューを するつもりです。
14 まさと： そうですか。じゃあ、飲み物を 持っていきますね。

### ♣ 単語と表現 Vocabulary and Expressions (Dialogue)

| | | | | | |
|---|---|---|---|---|---|
| 3 | 誕生日 | birthday | 11 | 場所 | place |
| 3 | プレゼント | present | 12 | 湖 | lake |
| 3 | ～つもりです | intend to.., be planning to... | 12 | 近く | close |
| 6 | あさって | the day after tomorrow | 13 | バーベキュー | barbecue, BBQ |
| 9 | もちろん | of course | 14 | 飲み物 | drinks |
| 10 | ぜひ | definitely | 14 | 持っていく | bring (thing) |

**Dialogue in English**

**[Elena and Masato are talking]**

1 M: What will you do on the weekend?
2 E: I will go shopping.
3 I intend to buy a birthday present for Kate.
4 M: I see. When is Kate's birthday?
5 E: The fifteenth.
6 M: Then, the day after tomorrow, right?
7 E: Yes, will you come to the party with me?
8 M: May I? (Is it OK?)
9 E: Of course.
10 M: Well then, I definitely want to go.
11 Where is the place?
12 E: It's the park near the lake. We are
13 planning to have a barbecue in the park.
14 M: That's good. Then, I will bring some drinks.

## 文法(ぶんぽう) Grammar

## Verb Conjugation

'Conjugation' (also known as 'inflection') is linguistic behaviour by which various grammatical functions of words (more precisely, 'predicates': verbs, I-adjectives and copula) are indicated. It is like the paradigm observed in *close*, *closes*, *closed*, *is closing* and *not close*, etc. in English. On the one hand, these are the same in that all commonly share the meaning (lexical meaning) of the action 'closing'. On the other hand, they differ from each other in that each indicates different functions (grammatical meanings): For example, *close* indicates 'non-past, affirmative, the subject being first or second person'; *closes* indicates 'the subject being third person'; *closed* indicates 'past', and so forth.

In Japanese a verb consists of a stem and suffix(es). The stem carries the lexical meaning of the verb, and suffixes indicate grammatical functions. For example, the verb form *tabemasu* is composed of the stem *tabe* 'the action of eating' and the suffix *masu* 'non-past, affirmative, polite'. Japanese verbs are divided into three groups according to their conjugation patterns.

### 1. 1-base verbs: Those with a fixed stem shape.

| | 食(た)べる 'eat' | | | 見(み)る 'see, watch, look' | | |
|---|---|---|---|---|---|---|
| Negative | tabe | -nai | たべない<br>'do not eat' (plain) | mi | -nai | みない<br>'do not see' (plain) |
| Affirmative, Polite | | -masu | たべます<br>'(I) eat' (polite) | | -masu | みます<br>'(I) see' (polite) |
| Base, casual, Noun-modifying | | -ru | たべる<br>'(I) eat' (plain) | | -ru | みる<br>'(I) see' (plain) |
| Imperative (Command) | | -ro | たべろ<br>'Eat it' (plain) | | -ro | みろ<br>'See it' (plain) |
| Conditional ('if') | | -re-ba | たべれば<br>'If (you) eat it' | | -re-ba | みれば<br>'If (you) see it' |
| Volitional ('Let's (casual)') | | -yo-o | たべよう<br>'Let's eat it' (plain) | | -yo-o | みよう<br>'Let's see it' (plain) |

Some further 1-base verbs are (base forms are given):

起きる ok**i**-ru 'get up'　落ちる och**i**-ru 'drop'　信じる shinj**i**-ru 'believe'
開ける ak**e**-ru 'open'　閉める shim**e**-ru 'close'　考える kanga**e**-ru 'think'

As shown above, 1-base verbs end with る preceded by either *i* or *e* in their base forms: [i/e]る
Also notice that a verb in this group retains its stem-final vowel, *i* or *e*, throughout all different conjugational variations. That is, its conjugational paradigm is based on one vowel and that is the reason for its name, '1-base verb'.

## 2. 5-base verbs: Those in which the stem takes various shapes for different suffixes.

| | 書く 'write' | | | 飲む 'drink' | | |
|---|---|---|---|---|---|---|
| Negative | kak**a** | -nai | かかない<br>'do not write' (plain) | nom**a** | -nai | のまない<br>'do not drink' (plain) |
| Affirmative, Polite | kak**i** | -masu | かきます<br>'(I) write' (polite) | nom**i** | -masu | のみます<br>'(I) drink' (polite) |
| Base, casual, Noun-modifying | kak**u** | — | かく<br>'(I) write' (plain) | nom**u** | — | のむ<br>'(I) drink' (plain) |
| Imperative (Command) | kak**e** | — | かけ<br>'Write it' (plain) | nom**e** | — | のめ<br>'Drink it' (plain) |
| Conditional ('if') | kak**e** | -ba | かけば<br>'If (you) write it' | nom**e** | -ba | のめば<br>'If (you) drink it' |
| Volitional ('Let's (casual)') | kak**o** | -o | かこう<br>'Let's write it' (plain) | nom**o** | -o | のもう<br>'Let's drink it' (plain) |

Note: For those verbs ending with う in their base form (e.g. 買う 'buy', 会う 'meet'), their Nai-form is *wa*-ない:

買う 'buy' + ない → 買<u>わ</u>ない 'do not buy'
会う 'meet' + ない → 会<u>わ</u>ない 'do not meet'

Some further 5-base verbs are (base forms are given):

買う 'buy'　話す 'speak'　待つ 'wait'　泳ぐ 'swim'
取る 'take'　読む 'read'　遊ぶ 'play'　死ぬ 'die'

As shown above, a 5-base verb changes its final vowel through *a*, *i*, *u*, *e* and *o* for different suffixes. This is the reason for its name, '5-base verb'.

**3. Irregular verbs:** There are two verbs which do not follow the conjugational pattern of 1-base or 5-base verbs. Because each of these verbs does not share its pattern with others, we need to become familiar with their patterns separately.

| | 来(く)る 'come' | | する 'do' | |
|---|---|---|---|---|
| Negative | ko -nai | こない<br>'do not come' (plain) | shi -nai | しない<br>'do not do' (plain) |
| Affirmative, Polite | ki -masu | きます<br>'(I) come' (polite) | shi -masu | します<br>'(I) do' (polite) |
| Base, casual, Noun-modifying | kuru — | くる<br>'(I) come' (plain) | suru — | する<br>'(I) do' (plain) |
| Imperative (Command) | koi — | こい<br>'Come here' (plain) | shiro — | しろ<br>'Do it' (plain) |
| Conditional ('if') | kure -ba | くれば<br>'If (you) come' | sure -ba | すれば<br>'If (you) do it' |
| Volitional ('Let's (casual)') | ko -yo-o | こよう<br>'Let's come' (plain) | shi -yo-o | しよう<br>'Let's do it' (plain) |

**行(い)く**

行(い)く 'go' is also sometimes treated as an irregular verb because the pattern for its Te-form differs from other 5-base verbs. However its pattern is otherwise exactly the same as that of other 5-base verbs. We will regard it as regular 5-base throughout the textbook with an acknowledgement of its exceptional behaviour in the Te-form. (See later lesson for Te-form.)

## 4. Some notes on verb conjugation

**4.1.** Base forms: Japanese verbs, without exception, end with *–u* in their base form. That is, a verb ends with one of the hiragana in the *u*-vowel row, i.e. う, く, す, つ, ぬ...., in the chart below.

| | | | | | | | | | | | | | | |
|---|---|---|---|---|---|---|---|---|---|---|---|---|---|---|
| ぱ | ば | だ | ざ | わ | ら | や | ま | は | な | た | さ | か | あ | a |
| ぴ | び | ぢ | じ | | り | | み | ひ | に | ち | し | き | い | i |
| ぷ | ぶ | づ | ず | | る | ゆ | む | ふ | ぬ | つ | す | く | う | u |
| ぺ | べ | で | ぜ | | れ | | め | へ | ね | て | せ | け | え | e |
| ぽ | ぼ | ど | ぞ | を | ろ | よ | も | ほ | の | と | そ | こ | お | o |

(i) There is no verb that ends with ず, づ, ゆ or ぶ in Modern Japanese.

(ii) 死(し)ぬ 'die' is the only verb that ends with ぬ.

(iii) Base forms are also referred to as 'dictionary form' since they are used in dictionaries to indicate the lexical meaning of the verb.

**4.2.** If a given verb is a 1-base verb, its stem-final hiragana is one of either *i*-vowel line, i.e. い, き, し..., or *e*-vowel line, i.e. え, け, せ..., in the above chart (cf. it ends in –{i/e}る). If a given verb is a 5-base verb, it makes use of five hiragana in the same column as the final hiragana in its base form: e.g. for の<u>む</u> 'drink', -ま, -み, -む, -め and -も for its conjugational variables. (cf. Table in Section 2 above)

**4.3.** Some 5-base verbs end in –{i/e}る in their base form and are not distinguishable from 1-base verbs in terms of the base form.

帰(かえ)る 'return'　滑(すべ)る 'slip'　切(き)る 'cut'　走(はし)る 'run'

These verbs can be identified by observing the pattern of their Masu-form. If a given verb is 1-base, the final る will simply be replaced by ます; if it is 5-base, the final る will be changed to り before ます.

[1-base] 変(か)え<u>る</u> → 変(か)えます
[5-base] 帰(かえ)<u>る</u> → 帰(かえ)<u>り</u>ます

**4.4.** A particular stem may be used for more than two different suffixes:

書(か)き -ます '(polite)' → 書(か)きます 'I will write it (speaking politely).'
-たい 'want to...' → 書(か)きたい 'I want to write it.'
-ながら 'while ...' → 書(か)きながら 'While I write it, ...'

It is predetermined that a particular suffix is required to connect to a particular stem.

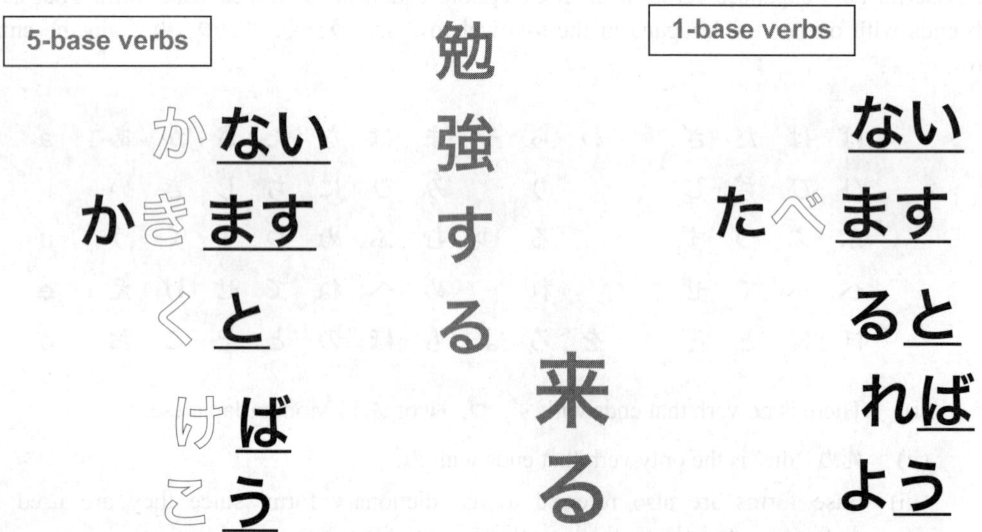

## 文法練習 1

**Complete the following table, by filling in the blanks with an appropriate form. For those verbs we have not yet learnt, please try to identify the group of the given verb, by comparing its base and ます forms. That will give you a clue for its ない form.**

| | *Base form* | *gloss* | ない *form* | ます *form* |
|---|---|---|---|---|
| (e.g.) | 書く | write (a letter) | かかない | かきます |
| (1) | 食べる | eat | ______ | ______ |
| (2) | 行く | go | ______ | ______ |
| (3) | 勉強する | study | ______ | ______ |
| (4) | 聞く | listen | ______ | ______ |
| (5) | とる | take | ______ | とります |
| (6) | 買う | buy | ______ | ______ |
| (7) | 出す | take out | ______ | だします |
| (8) | 着る | wear | ______ | きます |
| (9) | 起きる | get up | ______ | ______ |
| (10) | 来る | come | ______ | ______ |
| (11) | 読む | read | ______ | ______ |
| (12) | 見る | see, watch | ______ | ______ |
| (13) | 帰る | return, go home | ______ | ______ |
| (14) | 休む | rest | ______ | ______ |
| (15) | 出かける | go out | ______ | ______ |
| (16) | 借りる | borrow | ______ | かります |
| (17) | いる | be, stay | ______ | ______ |
| (18) | 待つ | wait | ______ | ______ |
| (19) | 寝る | sleep | ______ | ______ |
| (20) | 走る | run | ______ | はしります |

## 自然な日本語 Natural Conversation Notes

### Subject Omission

In Japanese, the subject (or 'Doer' or 'Agent') is frequently omitted. Especially in spoken conversation, the omission of the following types of subjects is a pervasive phenomenon.

(i) First and second person subjects
(ii) Subject which has already been referred to in previous discourse
(iii) Subject which can be readily identified in the situational context
(iv) Generic subjects

First, in a two-way conversation, the first and second person pronouns are defined by the conversational role: the speaker is the first person and the listener is the second. Subjects in declarative and interrogative sentences are often omitted even from the beginning of a conversation as they are commonly identifiable as the speaker (first person) in declaratives and the listener (second person) in interrogative.

(1) A: あした、Ø　学校に　行きますか？　'Will (you) go to school tomorrow?
B: ええ、Ø　行きますよ。　'Yes, (I) will go.'

Secondly, when the subject is identifiable from the context because it has already been mentioned previously, it is generally omitted.

(2) 田中さんは、たいてい　7時に　おきます。 Ø　8時に　朝ごはんを　食べます。
'Mr Tanaka usually gets up at seven. (He) has breakfast at eight.'

In the second sentence in example (2), the subject 'Mr Tanaka' is not expressed. In English, a pronoun 'he' is used in this case while in Japanese omission is generally adopted.

Thirdly, unexpressed subjects are normally understandable from the situation.

(3) Ø おいしい！　'(This food is) delicious!'
(4) Ø なんの音ですか。'What is (that) sound (we heard just now)?'

Fourthly, generic subjects are often omitted such as 'we', 'people', 'one' in English. Also, there are some cases where an unexpressed subject has no particular relevance.

(5) Ø　公園で　バーベキューが　できます。 'We/one/people can do barbecue in the park.'
(6) Ø　いい　天気ですね。 '(It's) lovely weather, isn't it?'
(7) Ø　8時ですよ。　'(It's) eight o'clock.'

You will see many sentences with subject omission throughout the textbook. In this lesson, try to omit subjects wherever possible in the exercises. It will soon become natural for you.

## 自然(しぜん)な日本語(にほんご)：練習(れんしゅう)１

**Underline the subjects which may be omitted.**

(れい)　わたしは 学校(がっこう)へ 行(い)きます。

(1)　わたしは、来年(らいねん)、中国(ちゅうごく)に 行(い)きます。そして わたしは、中国(ちゅうごく)で 勉強(べんきょう)します。

(2)　あなたは あした 出(で)かけますか。

(3)　A:　きのうのニュース、田中(たなか)さんは 見(み)ましたか。　(ニュース 'news')

B:　いいえ、わたしは 見(み)ませんでした。
そのニュースは どんな ニュースでしたか。

A:　それは さつじんの ニュースでした。　(さつじん 'murder')
さつじんは このあたりで ありました。　(このあたり 'around here')

B:　ええ？ それは ほんとうですか。それは こわいですね。　(ほんとう 'real')

## 自然(しぜん)な日本語(にほんご)：練習(れんしゅう)２

**Rewrite the following sentences in Japanese. Omit the subject wherever possible.**

(れい)　I will go to school tomorrow.　→　あした 学校(がっこう)へ 行(い)きます。

(1)　I am Tanaka.

(2)　It's hot, isn't it?

(3)　Wow, this is big!

(4)　I will go to Japan next year.

(5)　I had dinner with my teacher last night.

(6)　Will you come to the party next Sunday?

(7)　What time do you usually get up in the morning?

(8)　A:　Will you drink coffee?

B:　Yes, I will.

## 表現　Expression Notes

### 1　〜つもりです　Expressing one's plan: 'I am planning to..., I intend to...'

☛ [Verb base form (or 'dictionary' form)] + つもりです expresses what a person is planning to do in the future. What one is planning not to do or what one intends not to do is expressed by the Nai form, plus つもりです.

(1) あした 買い物に 行くつもりです。 'I am planning to go shopping tomorrow.'

(2) 新しい 車を 買うつもりです。 'I intend to buy a new car.'

(3) この本は 読まないつもりです。 'I am planning not to read this book.'

(4) 今年は、くにに 帰らないつもりです。 'I am planning not to go back to my hometown this year.'

#### 表現練習 1

**Make up sentences that describe the pictures below, using 〜つもりです.**

(れい) こんばん 高田さんに 会うつもりです。

(e.g.) Tonight

(1) Today

(2) Friday night

(3) Next year

(4) Tomorrow

(5) Tonight

## 2 ～たいです　Expressing one's desire: '(I) want to…'

☛ [Masu-stem ] + たい indicates that one desires to do something (e.g. I want to eat sushi ; I want to go to Japan, etc.). The ～たい form itself behaves as an *I-adjective.* Note that in the ～たい construction, the original object is marked by either が or を in affirmative sentences and by を in negative sentences. (The object may be marked by other particles such as は '(topic)' or も 'also'.)

{Objectが／を}　Masu-stem + たいです　'I want to …'

{Objectを}　Masu-stem + たくありません　'I do not want to …'

(1) すしが（すしを）食(た)べたいです。　'I want to eat sushi.'

(2) 映画(えいが)が（映画(えいが)を）見(み)たいです。　'I want to see a movie.'

(3) パーティー(ぱーてぃー)に 行(い)きたいです。　'I want to go to the party.'

(4) きょうは、映画(えいが)を 見(み)たくありません。'I don't want to watch a movie today.'

These patterns in principle indicate the desire of the first person (i.e. the speaker) in an affirmative statement, and of the second person (i.e. the other speaker) in questions.

(5) すしを 食(た)べたいですか。　'Do you want to eat sushi?'

(6) パーティー(ぱーてぃー)に 行(い)きたいですか。　'Do you want to go to the party?'

Note, however, that in the question form ～たいですか sounds too direct and is not normally used, especially when asking about the desire of one's superiors or in a formal situation. Some other expressions such as いかがですか 'What about ...?' and ～ませんか 'Would you like to ...?' are used in this case.

(7) すしは いかがですか。　'What about sushi (Would you like to have some)?'

(8) パーティー(ぱーてぃー)に 行(い)きませんか。'Would you like to come to a party?'

～たい is not normally used to indicate a third person's desire. Different expressions are used in this case (e.g. ～ようです 'It seems ...'; ～たがっています 'He/she wants to ...').

(9) 田中(たなか)さんは、車(くるま)を 買(か)いたいようです。
'It seems that Mr. Tanaka wants to buy a car.'

(10) ねこが さかなを 食(た)べたがっています。'A cat wants to eat a fish.'

### 表現(ひょうげん)練習(れんしゅう) 2

**Rewrite the following sentences in Japanese with ～たいです.**

（れい）　I want to meet Kimura-san.　→　<u>きむらさんに 会(あ)いたいです。</u>

(1)　I want to wear a kimono.

(2)　I want to eat Thai food.

(3)　I want to listen to J-pop.

(4)　I don't want to meet Yamada-san tonight.

(5)　I don't want to eat sashimi.

### 表現(ひょうげん)練習(れんしゅう) 3

**Answer the following questions using ～たいです**

(1)　いま、何(なに)が したいですか。

(2)　（あなたは）来週(らいしゅう) 日本(にほん)に 行(い)きます。日本(にほん)で 何(なに)が したいですか。

(3)　休(やす)みに、何(なに)が したいですか。

(4)　卒業(そつぎょう)のあと、何(なに)が したいですか。　（卒業(そつぎょう) 'graduation'）

(5)　１００００ドルが あります。何(なに)が したいですか。

## 3 Days and months

**[1] ☛ Months**

| | | | | | |
|---|---|---|---|---|---|
| いちがつ | （一月） | January | しちがつ | （七月） | July |
| にがつ | （二月） | February | はちがつ | （八月） | August |
| さんがつ | （三月） | March | くがつ | （九月） | September |
| しがつ | （四月） | April | じゅうがつ | （十月） | October |
| ごがつ | （五月） | May | じゅういちがつ | （十一月） | November |
| ろくがつ | （六月） | June | じゅうにがつ | （十二月） | December |

**[2] ☛ Days [Please first focus on the 1st – 10th of the month]**

| Sunday<br>日曜日<br>にちようび | Monday<br>月曜日<br>げつようび | Tuesday<br>火曜日<br>かようび | Wednesday<br>水曜日<br>すいようび | Thursday<br>木曜日<br>もくようび | Friday<br>金曜日<br>きんようび | Saturday<br>土曜日<br>どようび |
|---|---|---|---|---|---|---|
| | | | **1**<br>一日<br>ついたち | **2**<br>二日<br>ふつか | **3**<br>三日<br>みっか | **4**<br>四日<br>よっか |
| **5**<br>五日<br>いつか | **6**<br>六日<br>むいか | **7**<br>七日<br>なのか | **8**<br>八日<br>ようか | **9**<br>九日<br>ここのか | **10**<br>十日<br>とおか | **11**<br>十一日<br>じゅういち<br>にち |
| **12**<br>十二日<br>じゅうににち | **13**<br>十三日<br>じゅうさん<br>にち | **14**<br>十四日<br>じゅうよっか | **15**<br>十五日<br>じゅうごにち | **16**<br>十六日<br>じゅうろく<br>にち | **17**<br>十七日<br>じゅうしち<br>にち | **18**<br>十八日<br>じゅうはち<br>にち |
| **19**<br>十九日<br>じゅうくにち | **20**<br>二十日<br>はつか | **21**<br>二十一日<br>にじゅういち<br>にち | **22**<br>二十二日<br>にじゅうに<br>にち | **23**<br>二十三日<br>にじゅうさん<br>にち | **24**<br>二十四日<br>にじゅう<br>よっか | **25**<br>二十五日<br>にじゅうご<br>にち |
| **26**<br>二十六日<br>にじゅうろく<br>にち | **27**<br>二十七日<br>にじゅうしち<br>にち | **28**<br>二十八日<br>にじゅうはち<br>にち | **29**<br>二十九日<br>にじゅうく<br>にち | **30**<br>三十日<br>さんじゅう<br>にち | **31**<br>三十一日<br>さんじゅういち<br>にち | |

(i) 1st – 10th of the month have readings peculiar to the day of the month.

(ii) After 11th, the normal numeral reading with ～にち is used, except for 14th (じゅうよっか), 20th (はつか) and 24th (にじゅうよっか).

(iii) A question word to ask the day of the month is 何日 (なんにち).

(1) きょうは 何日(なんにち)ですか。　きょうは ４月(がつ)１７日(にち)、金曜日(きんようび)です。
What day is today?　It's the 17th of April, Friday, today.

(2) ４月(がつ)２６日(にち)は 日曜日(にちようび)です。　The 26th of April is Sunday.

(3) コンサート(こんさーと)は ６月１０日(がつとおか)です。　The concert is on the 10th of June.

(4) お姉(ねえ)さんの結婚式(けっこんしき)は ８月６日(がつむいか)です。　My older sister's wedding day is the 6th of Aug.

(5) 田中(たなか)さんの 誕生日(たんじょうび)は １１月(がつ) ２０日(はつか)です。　Tanaka-san's birthday is the 20th of Nov.

**Year**: The year is read in just the same way as a normal numeral, followed by 年(ねん):

(e.g.) １９００年　せんきゅうひゃく ねん

２０３５年　にせんさんじゅうご ねん

The date is read (and written as well) in the order of year, month and then day:

(e.g.) １９１１年(ねん)１２月(がつ)２５日(にち)　25th of December, 1911

**昭和(しょうわ)／平成(へいせい)**: The year may also be indicated by the name of the era, such as 昭和(しょうわ) and 平成(へいせい). For the year of 昭和(しょうわ) and 平成(へいせい), plus 1925 and 1988, respectively, in order to indicate the equivalent Solar calendar year.

(e.g.) 昭和(しょうわ)３４年(ねん)１月(がつ)２７日(にち)　27th of January, 1959 (← 34 + 1925)

平成(へいせい)３年(ねん)３月(がつ)１１日(にち)　11th of March, 1991 (← 3 + 1988)

## 表現(ひょうげん) 練習(れんしゅう) 4

**Read the following time expressions in Japanese.**

(れい) 13th of January → いちがつ じゅうさんにち（1月(がつ) １3日(にち)）

(1) 1st of January　　(2) 20th of March

(3) 5th of November　　(4) 9th of September

(5) 14th of August　　(6) 24th of December

(7) 31st of December, 1995　　(8) 9th of September, 2000

### [3] ☛ Other time words

| | 3 before | 2 before | 1 before | now | 1 after | 2 after | 3 after |
|---|---|---|---|---|---|---|---|
| Day | みっかまえ<br>3日前 | おととい<br>一昨日 | きのう<br>昨日 | きょう<br>今日 | あした<br>明日 | あさって<br>明後日 | しあさって<br>明々後日 |
| Week | さんしゅうかんまえ<br>3週間前 | せんせんしゅう<br>先々週 | せんしゅう<br>先週 | こんしゅう<br>今週 | らいしゅう<br>来週 | さらいしゅう<br>再来週 | さんしゅうかんご<br>3週間後 |
| Month | さんかげつまえ<br>3ヶ月前 | せんせんげつ<br>先々月 | せんげつ<br>先月 | こんげつ<br>今月 | らいげつ<br>来月 | さらいげつ<br>再来月 | さんかげつご<br>3ヶ月後 |
| Year | さんねんまえ<br>3年前 | おととし<br>一昨年 | きょねん<br>去年 | ことし<br>今年 | らいねん<br>来年 | さらいねん<br>再来年 | さんねんご<br>3年後 |

(i) 3ヶ月 is read さんかげつ and indicates a duration, 'for three months'; 'ヶ' is from 箇; It is also written as 3ヵ月 or 3か月.

(ii) '々' indicates the repeat of the preceding kanji: e.g. 先々月(せんせんげつ) 'the month before last, 色々(いろいろ) 'various'.

(iii) Last year is 去年(きょねん), and not 先年.

**[4] ☛ Time words and に**

Particle に may be used with 'countable' time words (year, month, day of the month/week, time), and normally not with 'un-countable' time words (all words except those words in the column '3 before' and '3 after' — they may be used with に).

(1) わたしは ２００５年に 日本に 行きました。／ ５月５日に テストが あります。
I went to Japan in 2005. There will be an exam on the 5th of May.

(2) 来週の 火曜日に 映画を 見ます。／ きょう__ ９時に 起きました。
I will see a film next Tuesday. I got up at 9 o'clock today.

(3) きのう__ 町で 山田さんに 会いました。／ 来月__ 日本に 行きます。
I met Yamada-san in town yesterday. I will go to Japan next month.

### 表現練習５

**Answer the following questions using expressions for days and months.**

(れい) いつ 日本に 帰りますか。 → １２月１２日に 帰ります。

(1) きょうは 何日ですか。

(2) 誕生日は、いつですか。

(3) 今学期は、いつ 終わりますか。（今学期 'this semester'）

(4) あしたは、何月何日ですか。

(5) 来週の金曜日は、何月何日ですか。

### 表現練習６

**Rewrite the following sentences in Japanese. Pay special attention to the time word.**

(れい) I will go to Japan next year. → わたしは 来年 日本に 行きます。

(1) I will meet my friend in Tokyo next week.

(2) My dog died last year.

(3) The day after tomorrow is Monday the 20th of May.

(4) I studied Japanese in Japan last year.

(5) Tanaka-san came to Australia 3 years ago.

## 対話(たいわ) Communicative Exchanges

### 対話練習(たいわれんしゅう) 1

**Pre-task: 〜つもりです**

**Ask 4 of your classmates what they will do on the weekend and where they will do these activities.**

(れい) A: 週末(しゅうまつ)、何(なに)を しますか。

B: 本(ほん)を 読(よ)むつもりです。(or 勉強(べんきょう)するつもりです, DVD を 見(み)るつもりです, etc.)

A: そうですか。どこで 読(よ)みますか。

B: 図書館(としょかん)で 読(よ)むつもりです。

| Friend's name | Activity | Place of activity |
|---|---|---|
| (e.g.) Bさん | Reading books | library |
| さん | | |
| さん | | |
| さん | | |
| さん | | |

### 対話練習(たいわれんしゅう) 2

**Pre-task:** Day of month

(i) Decide your own date, month and day of the week for each event in the table below.

(ii) Ask 2 of your classmates when each event is scheduled in their list.

(れい) A: テスト(てすと)は 何日(なんにち)ですか。

B: 5月(がつ)13日(にち)です。

A: そうですか。5月(がつ)13日(にち)は 何曜日(なんようび)ですか。

B: 木曜日(もくようび)です。

| Events | You | Classmate (1) | Classmate (2) |
|---|---|---|---|
| (e.g.) Test | 2nd of Sep; Mon | 13th of May; Thurs | 25th of Jan; Tue |
| Birthday | | | |
| Japanese exam | | | |
| BBQ | | | |
| Party | | | |

## 対話練習 3

**Pre-task: 〜たいです**

(i) Decide what you want to do in the following situations.
(ii) Ask 2 classmates what they want to do in the same situations.
(iii) Answer your partner's questions.

(れい) A: 夏休みに、何を しますか。
B: そうですね、まだ わかりませんが (I am not sure, but)、日本に 行きたいです。
A: いいですね。日本で 何を しますか。
B: たくさん 買い物を したいです。

| Events | You | Classmate (1) | Classmate (2) |
|---|---|---|---|
| (e.g.) Summer holiday | See friends | Go to Japan | |
| Your birthday | | | |
| Christmas holiday | | | |
| After graduation | | | |

## 対話作り Comprehensive Exercises

✍ **In pairs, create a dialogue for the given situation. Please feel free to ask the instructor if you have any questions about Japanese expressions for your dialogue.**

**Situation:**
You would like to go out together with your friend on the weekend. First, ask each other what you are planning to do on the weekend. Then, decide what to do and arrange the time and place to meet, and so forth.

Please incorporate the following expressions into your dialogue:

- いっしょに 〜ませんか／〜ましょうか／〜ましょう
- 〜つもりです
- 〜たいです
- Time words
- Subject omission wherever applicable

**[Sample Dialogue]**

エレナ：　今週の週末は、何を しますか。

まさと：　土曜日は、買い物を するつもりです。

日曜日は まだ わかりません。エレナさんは？　（まだ 'yet'）

エレナ：　そうですね。わたしも まだ わかりません。

まさと：　じゃあ、日曜日に いっしょに 出かけませんか。

エレナ：　いいですね。どこが いいですか。

まさと：　そうですね。映画を 見ましょうか。

エレナ：　いいですね。

まさと：　あ、日曜日は １７日ですね。「リング」が 始まりますよ。　（始まる 'begin, start'）

エレナ：　あの…、すみません。わたし、こわい映画は ちょっと…。

まさと：　あ、そうですか。じゃあ、「シャルウィーダンス？」は どうですか。

エレナ：　いいですね。

まさと：　じゃあ それを 見ましょうか。

エレナ：　はい。映画は、何時に 始まりますか。

まさと：　２時です。

エレナ：　じゃあ、１時半ごろ 会いましょうか。

まさと：　そうですね。どこで 待ち合わせますか。　（待ち合わせる 'arrange to meet'）

エレナ：　町の噴水の前は どうですか。　（噴水 'fountain'）

まさと：　あ、いいですね。じゃあ、日曜日の１時半に、噴水の前で。

エレナ：　ええ。じゃあ また。

E: What will you do on the weekend?
M: I am planning to go shopping on Saturday, but for Sunday, I don't know yet. How about you Elena?
E: Well... I also don't know yet.
M: Then, why don't we go out together?
E: Sounds good. Where do you want to go?
M: Let me see. Shall we watch a movie?
E: Sounds good.
M: Oh, Sunday is the 17th, isn't it? "The Ring" is starting on that day.
E: Well... I'm sorry, but, I don't like a scary movie.
M: Oh, I see. Then, what about "Shall we dance"?
E: Sounds good.
M: OK then, shall we watch that movie?
E: Yes. What time is the movie starting?
M: Two o'clock.
E: So, shall we meet at around 1.30?
M: Sounds good. Where shall we meet?
E: How about in front of the fountain in Civic?
M: Oh, that's good. Then, see you at 1.30 on Sunday, in front of the fountain.
E: Yeah. See you.

## 知（し）ってた？ Did you know?

## 日本（にほん）の四季（しき） 'Four seasons in Japan'

Although four seasons exist in many regions of the world, Japanese people particularly appreciate the four seasons as if the distinction of four seasons is something unique to their country.

### 調（しら）べましょう Research

**1. Fill in the table below with the name of the four seasons in Japanese and the months for each season.**

| English | Japanese | Months of each season in Japan |
|---|---|---|
| Spring | | |
| Summer | | |
| Autumn | | |
| Winter | | |

**2. The words in the table below are conceptually associated with a certain season. What is the meaning of each word? Which season are they associated with?**

| Word | Meaning | Season |
|---|---|---|
| 梅雨（つゆ） | | |
| さくら | | |
| 台風（たいふう） | | |
| 雪（ゆき）だるま | | |
| 花火（はなび） | | |
| 入学式（にゅうがくしき） | | |
| 卒業式（そつぎょうしき） | | |
| 紅葉（こうよう） | | |
| 花見（はなみ） | | |
| 新年（しんねん） | | |
| 運動会（うんどうかい） | | |

## National holidays

Below is a list of National Holidays in Japan. We will learn more about the ways of celebrating seasons and festivals in [Did you know?] in Lesson 9.

January 1 - **New Year's Day** (元日)

The second Monday in January - **Adult's Day** (成人の日)

February 11 - **National Founding Day** (建国記念日)

March 20 or 21 - **Vernal Equinox** (春分の日)

April 29 – **Day of Showa** (昭和の日); used to be Green Day (緑の日) until 2007

May 3 - **Constitution Memorial Day** (憲法記念日)

May 4 - **Greenery Day** (緑の日; used to be National People's Day (国民の休日) until 2007

May 5 - **Children's Day** (子供の日)

The third Monday in July - **Marine Day** (海の日)

The third Monday in September - **Respect-for-the-Aged Day** (敬老の日)

September 23 or 24 - **Autumnal Equinox** (秋分の日)

The second Monday in October - **Health/Sports Day** (体育の日)

November 3 - **Culture Day** (文化の日)

November 23 - **Labor Thanksgiving Day** (勤労感謝の日)

December 23 - **Emperor's Birthday** (天皇誕生日)

## 新(あたら)しい単語(たんご)・表現(ひょうげん) New Vocabulary & Expressions

(Basic words/expressions are marked with '*')

| | |
|---|---|
| 会(あ)う* | meet, see |
| 開(あ)ける* | open |
| あさって* | the day after tomorrow |
| 遊(あそ)ぶ* | play, hang around |
| 姉(あね)* | older sister |
| いつ* | when |
| 落(お)ちる* | drop, fell down |
| 音(おと) | sound, noise |
| 変(か)える | change |
| 借(か)りる* | borrow |
| 考(かんが)える* | think |
| 着物(きもの)* | kimono |
| 着(き)る* | wear, put on |
| 切(き)る* | cut |
| 結婚式(けっこんしき) | wedding ceremony |
| このあたり | around here |
| 今学期(こんがっき) | this semester |
| 殺人(さつじん) | murder |
| 四季(しき) | four seasons |
| 死(し)ぬ* | die |
| 閉(し)める* | close |
| 信(しん)じる* | believe |
| 滑(すべ)る | slip |
| ぜひ* | definitely |
| 卒業(そつぎょう) | graduation |
| タイ(たい)料理(りょうり) | Thai food |
| 誕生日(たんじょうび)* | birthday |
| 出(で)かける* | go out |
| 取(と)る* | take |
| 飲(の)み物(もの)* | drinks |
| ニュース(にゅーす)* | news |
| 始(はじ)まる* | begin, start |
| 場所(ばしょ)* | place, location, venue |
| 走(はし)る* | run |
| プレゼント(ぷれぜんと) | present |
| 噴水(ふんすい) | fountain |
| 本当(ほんとう)* | real, really |
| まだ* | yet |
| 待(ま)ち合(あ)わせる | arrange to meet |
| 待(ま)つ* | wait for |
| 湖(みずうみ) | lake |
| もちろん* | of course |
| 持(も)っていく | take (thing) |
| 休(やす)む* | have a break, rest |
| 分(わ)かる* | understand |

# 第8課（だいはちか）

# 笑（わら）ってください
## Smile!

[Masato and Elena are talking about where to go]

エレナ：　まさとさん、きょう タワー（たわー）に 行（い）きませんか。
まさと：　タワー（たわー）？
エレナ：　あそこを 見（み）てください。あの山（やま）の 頂上（ちょうじょう）の タワー（たわー）です。景色（けしき）が きれいですよ。
まさと：　そうですか。でも ぼくは 高（たか）いところは ちょっと…。
エレナ：　あ、そうですか。
まさと：　ええ、すみません。
エレナ：　じゃあ、国立美術館（こくりつびじゅつかん）へ 絵（え）を 見（み）に 行（い）きませんか。
まさと：　それは いいですね。ぼくは アボリジナルアート（あぼりじなるあーと）が 見（み）たいです。

[In the National Gallery]

エレナ：　ほら、見（み）てください。あれが アボリジナルアート（あぼりじなるあーと）ですよ。
まさと：　うわあ、いいですね。あのう、ここで 写真（しゃしん）を とってもいいですか。
エレナ：　ええ、いいですよ。私（わたし）が とりましょうか。
まさと：　じゃあ、お願（ねが）いします。
エレナ：　まさとさん、笑（わら）ってください。はい、チーズ（ちーず）！
まさと：　どうも ありがとう。

## 単語と表現 Vocabulary and Expressions (Dialogue)

| | | | | | |
|---|---|---|---|---|---|
| 1 | タワー | tower | 8 | 絵 | paintings, drawings |
| 3 | 頂上 | top, summit | 9 | アボリジナルアート | Aboriginal art |
| 4 | 景色 | landscape, scenery | 10 | ほら | look! (drawing attention) |
| 5 | でも | However, but | 12 | 写真 | photo |
| 5 | ぼく | I (casual; male) | 12 | とる | take (photo) |
| 5 | ところ | place | 15 | 笑う | smile, laugh |
| 8 | 国立美術館 | National Gallery | 15 | チーズ | cheese |

### Dialogue in English

**[Elena and Masato are talking about where to go]**

1 E: Masato, why don't we go to the Tower today? .
2 M: Tower?
3 E: Look over there. It's the tower on the top of that
4 mountain. We can see a beautiful landscape from there.
5 M: I see. However, I am not good at heights.
6 E: Oh, aren't you?
7 M: No, I'm sorry.
8 E: Then, why don't we go to the National Gallery to see the paintings?
9 M: Sounds good. I want to see some Aboriginal art.

**[In the National Gallery]**

10 E: See, look. That's Aboriginal art.
11 M: Wow, great, isn't it.
12 Um, may I take a photo here?
13 E: Yes, you may. Shall I take it?
14 M: Please.
15 E: Masato. Smile! Cheese!
16 M: Thank you.

## 文法 Grammar

## Verb て form

### 1. Usages

The て form is a conjugational variation of predicates (verbs, *I*-adjectives and copula (for *Na*-adjectives and nouns)). It plays an important grammatical role in Japanese. The form itself may be used as an imperative expression in casual conversation (e.g. 見て！ 'look!'). However, its fundamental function is to connect two actions, events or states within a sentence. In this lesson, we focus on the case of verb (cf. Lesson 9 for the cases of *I*-adjective and copula).

Verb て form can form a sentence which describes two or more activities/events.

(1) これから 買い物をして、映画を見て、家に帰ります。

'Now, I will do some shopping, see a movie and then go back home.'

(2)　きのう 買い物をして、映画を見て、家に帰りました。

‘Yesterday, I did some shopping, saw a movie and then went back home.’

(3)　私は 買い物をして、田中さんは 映画を見ました。

‘Yesterday, I did some shopping and Mr. Tanaka saw a movie.’

The て form itself does not indicate the tense (i.e. past, present or future); its tense is determined by the tense of the final verb in the sentence: i.e. It is basically the same as that of the final verb. In (1) above, the final verb 帰ります indicates future and thus the underlined て forms will also be interpreted as future. By the same token, in (2) and (3), the underlined て forms are interpreted as past given that the final verb in their sentences is also past ～ました.

The て form is also used in a number of phrases/constructions.

- ～て ください　‘Please ...’
- ～ても いいですか　‘May I ...?’
- ～ている　‘I'm doing ...’
- ～てみる　‘try to ...’
- 持っていく　‘take (something) somewhere’
- 連れていく　‘take (someone) somewhere’

## 2. Formation

The formation rule for the て form varies depending on the type of verb.

**2.1. 5-base verbs:** These vary, depending on the final syllable of the base form

| | Base form | | | て form |
|---|---|---|---|---|
| ～う、つ、る → ～って | 買う | buy | → | 買って |
| | 待つ | wait for | → | 待って |
| | 売る | sell | → | 売って |
| ～く → ～いて* | 書く | write | → | 書いて |
| ～ぐ → ～いで | 泳ぐ | swim | → | 泳いで |
| ～す → ～して | 話す | speak | → | 話して |
| ～ぬ、む、ぶ → ～んで | 死ぬ | die | → | 死んで |
| | 飲む | drink | → | 飲んで |
| | 遊ぶ | play | → | 遊んで |

**行く**

行く ‘go’ is an exception to this rule. If the verb followed this rule, its て form would be 行いて: Its て form is in fact 行って. This is the only exceptional form for 行く and all its other conjugational patterns are the same as those of other 5-base verbs.

**2.2. 1-base verbs**: take the final る off and add て

| | Base form | | | て form |
|---|---|---|---|---|
| 〜{i/e}る → 〜{i/e}て | 見(み)る | see | → | 見(み)て |
| | 食(た)べる | eat | → | 食(た)べて |

**2.3. Irregular verbs:**

| | Base form | | | て form |
|---|---|---|---|---|
| ________ | 来(く)る | come | → | 来(き)て |
| | する | do | → | して |

**文法練習(ぶんぽうれんしゅう) 1**

**Complete the following chart, by filling in the blanks with an appropriate form. For those verbs we have not yet learnt, please try to identify the group of the given verb, by comparing its base and ます forms. That will give you a clue to its て form.**

| | *Base form* | | *ます form* | *て form* | *glossary* |
|---|---|---|---|---|---|
| (e.g.1) | 書(か)く | [5-base verb] | 書(か)きます | 書(か)いて | write (a letter) |
| (e.g.2) | 食(た)べる | [1-base verb] | 食(た)べます | 食(た)べて | eat |
| (1) | (友達(ともだち)を) 待(ま)つ | | 待(ま)ちます | ________ | wait (for a friend) |
| (2) | (子供(こども)を) 呼(よ)ぶ | | 呼(よ)びます | ________ | call (a child) |
| (3) | (本(ほん)を) 読(よ)む | | ________ | ________ | read (a book) |
| (4) | (友達(ともだち)に) 会(あ)う | | ________ | ________ | meet (a friend) |
| (5) | 歩(ある)く | | ________ | ________ | walk |
| (6) | (写真(しゃしん)を) とる | | とります | ________ | take (a photo) |
| (7) | 起(お)きる | | ________ | ________ | wake up |
| (8) | 寝(ね)る | | ________ | ________ | sleep |
| (9) | 死(し)ぬ | | ________ | ________ | die |

| | | | | |
|---|---|---|---|---|
| (10) | (音楽を) 聞く | | | listen to (music) |
| (11) | (学校に) 行く | | | go (to school) |
| (12) | (鳥が) 飛ぶ | 飛びます | | (a bird) flies |
| (13) | 急ぐ | 急ぎます | | hurry |
| (14) | (韓国語を) 話す | | | speak (Korean) |
| (15) | (日本語を) 勉強する | | | study (Japanese) |
| (16) | (学校に) 来る | | | come (to school) |

## 文法練習 2

**Look at the pictures and make up sentences using the て form. Decide the tense of the sentence by referring to the clue given in parentheses.**

(れい) わたしは 毎朝 起きて コーヒーを 飲みます。

(e.g.) [every morning]

(1) [usually]

(2) [usually]

(3) [yesterday]

(4) [every night]

(5) [last Sunday]

## 自然な日本語 Natural Conversation Notes

### Various usages of ちょっと

The word ちょっと literally means 'a small amount', 'a little' or 'a bit'.

(1) しおを ちょっと 入れてください。 'Put a bit of salt in, please.'

(2) 野菜を ちょっとだけ 買いました。 'I bought a small amount of vegetables.'

Further, ちょっと may be used to mitigate the force of an utterance and thus is often used as a softener (or hedger) of speech by making the speaker's purpose seem lighter.

(3) A: 今晩、出かけますか。 'Are you going out tonight?'

B: ええ、ちょっと 買い物に。 'Yes, (I'm) just going for shopping.'

(4) ちょっと 用事が ありますので、きょうは ここで 失礼します。 (用事 'errand')

'I have an errand to run, so, today please excuse me here.'

(5) ちょっと 質問しても いいですか。 'May I ask a question?' (質問 'question')

As shown in (3), (4) and (5), ちょっと is often used in cases where a speaker talks about his/her own activities, or where a speaker asks, requests, or makes an excuse for, something.

Finally, ちょっと is also frequently used in expressions that may otherwise give the listener a negative impression: e.g. refusal, disagreement, complaint.

(6) A: 映画を 見ませんか。 'Would you like to see a movie?'

B: 映画は ちょっと.... 'A movie is a little bit....'

(7) A: 日曜日は、どうですか。 'How about Sunday?'

B: あ、日曜日は ちょっと.... 'Oh, Sunday is a little bit....'

(8) これは ちょっと よく ありませんね。 'This is not good.'

In such a case, the rest of the sentence is often omitted; for example, in (6) 好きではありません 'don't like it' and in (7) 行けません 'cannot go', 忙しいです 'I'm busy', etc. By doing so, the speaker can avoid a direct expression of refusal or disagreement and at the same time, with ちょっと he/she can express his/her 'feeling' of inconvenience or excuse, which is as a whole interpreted as more polite. In this way, the use of ちょっと is seen as an important strategy to convey politeness in this kind of expression.

## 自然(しぜん)な日本語(にほんご)：練習(れんしゅう) 1

**Rewrite the sentences in Japanese, using ちょっと.**

（れい） I want to eat sashimi. → <u>わたしは ちょっと さしみが 食(た)べたいです。</u>

(1) I want to see this movie.

(2) I want to drink coffee.

(3) Japanese is a bit difficult.

(4) This car is a bit expensive.

(5) I will study Japanese a little bit tonight.

## 自然(しぜん)な日本語(にほんご)：練習(れんしゅう) 2

**Refuse or disagree with A's suggestions/comments, using ちょっと….**

（れい） A: 日曜日(にちようび)に いっしょに バーベキュー(ばーべきゅー)を しましょうか。

B: <u>わたし、日曜日(にちようび) (or バーベキュー(ばーべきゅー)) は ちょっと…。</u>

(1) A: いっしょに サッカー(さっかー)を しませんか。

B: ______________________________

(2) A: 土曜日(どようび)は どうですか。

B: ______________________________

(3) A: あした いっしょに パーティー(ぱーてぃー)に 行(い)きませんか。

B: ______________________________

(4) A: 来週(らいしゅう)の 月曜日(げつようび)に 映画(えいが)を 見(み)ましょうか。

B: ______________________________

(5) A: リング(りんぐ)、おもしろいですね。 （リング(りんぐ) '*Ring*, the movie'）

B: そうですか？ わたしは ______________________________

(6) A: この宿題(しゅくだい)、あした 出(だ)して くださいね。 （出(だ)して ください 'please submit'）

B: ええっ？ ______________________________

## 表現(ひょうげん) Expression Notes

### 1 〜てください Making a request 'Please do ...'

[1] ☛ 〜てください is a 'typical' expression for making a request.

(1) 教科書(きょうかしょ)を 見(み)てください。 'Please look at your textbook.'

(2) 窓(まど)を 開(あ)けてください。 'Please open the windows.'

(3) 9時(じ)に 学校(がっこう)へ 来(き)てください。 'Please come to school at 9 o'clock.'

Note that 〜てください is more suitable in situations where the request is reasonable or could be expected. For example, in (1) above, the teacher requests students to look at their textbooks, which is perfectly normal in the class situation.

[2] ☛ In a formal situation, 〜てください is somewhat too direct and does not sound very polite. In such a case, more polite expressions such as 〜ていただけませんか and 〜ていただけないでしょうか are preferable.

(4) a. 先生(せんせい)、すみません。 推薦状(すいせんじょう)を 書(か)いてください。(?)
b. 先生(せんせい)、すみません。 推薦状(すいせんじょう)を 書(か)いていただけないでしょうか。
'Could you please write a recommendation letter for me?'

[3] ☛ Note also that if 〜てください is used to make a request which is to the listener's benefit, it functions as a suggestion and invitation as in the following examples. どうぞ 'please' is often used together with 〜てください in such a usage.

(5) どうぞ、ここに 座(すわ)ってください。 'Please have a seat here.'

(6) どうぞ、お茶(ちゃ)を 飲(の)んでください。 'Please have some tea.'

### 表現練習(ひょうげんれんしゅう) 1

**Rewrite the following sentences in Japanese, using 〜てください.**

(1) Please get up at 6 o'clock.
(2) Please read this book.
(3) Please open the window.
(4) Please write a letter.
(5) Please stand up. (stand up 立(た)つ)
(6) Please wait. (wait 待(ま)つ)
(7) Please hurry. (hurry いそぐ)
(8) Please speak slowly. (slowly ゆっくり)

**表現(ひょうげん) 練習(れんしゅう) 2**

**Look at the pictures and make up sentences, using ～てください and the given key words.**

(れい)　窓(まど)を 閉(し)めてください。

(e.g.) 閉(し)める close

(1) 貸(か)す lend

(2) 救急車(きゅうきゅうしゃ)を 呼(よ)ぶ call ambulance

(3) 食(た)べる

(4) 開(あ)ける

(5) 待(ま)つ

## 2 ～てもいい／～てはいけない Permission and prohibition

**[1]** ☛ ～ても いいです expresses the giving of permission 'you may do…'. An interrogative sentence ～ても いいですか "May I do...?' seeks a person's permission.

(1) この水(みず)、飲(の)んでも いいですよ。　'You may drink this water.'

(2) ここで 寝(ね)ても いいですよ。　'You may sleep here.'

(3) A: このペン(べん)を 使(つか)っても いいですか。　'May I use this pen?'

B: ええ、使(つか)っても いいですよ。　'Yes, you may.'

**[2]** ☛ ～ては いけません indicates that the speaker is forbidding someone from doing something, and may be used as a negative answer to a question that seeks permission.

(4) ここで 寝(ね)ては いけません。　'You may not sleep here.'

(5) A: このペン(べん)を 使(つか)っても いいですか。　'May I use this pen?'

B: いいえ、使(つか)っては いけません。　'No, you may not.'

However, 〜ては いけません has an 'official tone' and is often too direct in many cases. In this case, ちょっと, with the omission of the rest of the sentence, is more frequently used in conversation.

(6) A: このペンを 使っても いいですか。 'May I use this pen?'

B: すみません、そのペンは ちょっと…。 'Sorry, that pen is a bit….'

(7) A: ここで 寝ても いいですか。 'May I sleep here?'

B: ここでは ちょっと…。 'Here is a bit….'

(8) A: この部屋に 入っても いいですか。 'May I enter this room?'

B: あの、この部屋は ちょっと…。 'Well, this room is a bit….'

### 表現練習3

**Look at the pictures and make up sentences, using 〜てもいいですか and 〜てもいいです／〜てはいけません, as in the example.**

(れい) A: ここで たばこを 吸っても いいですか。

B: いいえ、吸っては いけません。

(e.g.) [No]

Here

(1) [Yes]

Park

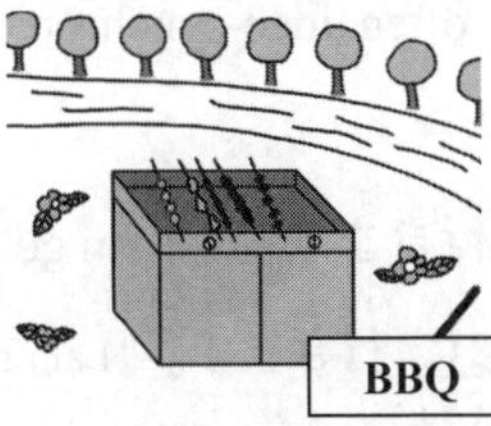


(2) [No]

Concert

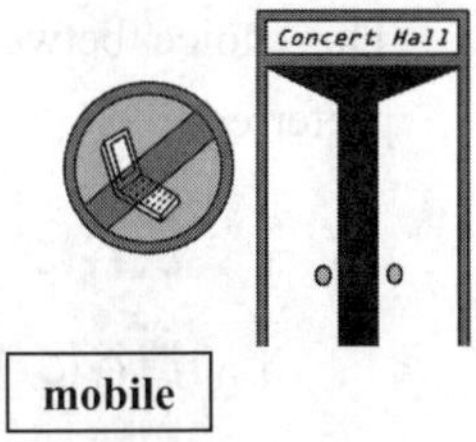


(3) [No]

This room

(4) [Yes]

Here

(5) [No]

High school student

## 3 [Masu-stem/Dynamic noun]に 行く／来る

**'go/come (to a place) to do something'**

**[1]** ☛ [Masu-stem]に 行く／来る indicates the purpose of going/coming somewhere.

(1) きょう 図書館に 勉強しに 行きます。 'I am going to the library to study today.'

(2) 町へ すしを 食べに 行きました。 'I went to town to eat sushi.'

(3) みかが 家に CD を 借りに 来ました。 'Mika came to my home to borrow CDs.'

(4) A: 日本へ 何を しに 行きましたか。 'What did you go to Japan for?'

B: 友達に 会いに 行きました。 'I went to see my friend.'

(5) A: ここへ 何を しに 来ましたか。 'What did you come here for?'

B: コーヒーを 飲みに 来ました。 'I came here to drink coffee.'

**[2]** ☛ [Dynamic noun]に 行く／来る: A (dynamic) noun may be used in this construction. Dynamic nouns include shopping, work, study, concerts, movies and all sorts of sports.

(1) きょう 渋谷に 買い物に 行きます。 'I am going to Shibuya for shopping today.'

(2) あした 大学へ テニスに 行きます。 'I am going to uni to play tennis tomorrow.'

(3) A: 日本へ 何を しに 行きましたか。 'What did you go to Japan for?'

B: 日本語の勉強に 行きました。 'I went there to study Japanese.'

**[3]** ☛ In some cases both constructions with [Masu-stem] and [Dynamic noun] are available. The choice between them is often ideo-synchronic, although the [Dynamic noun] is preferred.

(1) a. 渋谷に 買い物に 行きます。 'I am going to Shibuya for shopping.'

b. 渋谷に 買い物を しに 行きます。 'I am going to Shibuya to do some shopping.'

(2) a. 日本へ 日本語の勉強に 行きました。

'I went to Japan for studying Japanese.'

b. 日本へ 日本語を 勉強しに 行きました。

'I went to Japan to study Japanese.'

---

Typical mistake: Learners tend to use で for the destination in this construction.

(e.g.) 渋谷で 買い物に 行きました

This sentence is in itself grammatical but it means 'I went shopping in Shibuya', which differs from the intended meaning, 'I went to Shibuya (destination) to do some shopping'.

---

## 表現練習４

**Rewrite the following sentences in Japanese, using the [Masu-stem/Dynamic noun]に 行く／来る construction.**

(れい)　I'm going to my friend's house to study today.

きょう 友達のうちに 勉強しに 行きます。

(1) I'm going to the post office to buy stamps. (post stamps きって)

(2) Susan is going to Sydney to meet her parents next holiday.

(3) I'm going to the coffee shop to drink a cup of coffee with Tanaka-san.

(4) Okada-san went to town to see a movie last week.

(5) Kimura-san is coming to Australia to study English next year.

(6) Sasaki-san is coming here to teach Japanese. (teach おしえる)

(7) I didn't go to Sydney to buy clothes with my friend last weekend.

(8) Yamada-san did not come to my house to have dinner last Saturday.

(9) I want to go to China to see the Great Wall. (The Great Wall 万里の長城)

(10) I want to go to Hong Kong to buy a watch and a CD player.

## 表現練習５

**Complete the following sentences by providing a purpose for going/coming to the places given. Make up your own purposes.**

(れい)　町に コーヒーを 飲みに 行きます。

(1) わたしは 来週 日本に ____________________ に 行きます。

(2) デパートに ____________________ に 行きます。

(3) 町に ____________________ に 行きました。

(4) 日本の友達が オーストラリアへ ____________________ に 来ます。

(5) 木村さんが あした うちに ____________________ に 来ます。

(6) 来年 エジプトへ ____________________ に 行きたいです。

## 対話（たいわ） Communicative Exchanges

### 対話練習（たいわれんしゅう）1

**Pre-task:** ～ても いいです／
～ては いけません

(i) In pairs, one of you is a student who is doing home stay and the other is the host parent.

Student: Ask your host parent for permission to do the following things.

Host parent: Give, or refuse to give, permission to the student (Make up your own answers).

(ii) When you have finished asking/answering the questions, change roles.

(れい) A: テレビを 見（み）てもいいですか。

B: ええ、見（み）てもいいですよ。 or あ、テレビは ちょっと…

A: ありがとうございます。 or そうですか。わかりました。

(e.g.) [ Yes No ] (Yes circled)

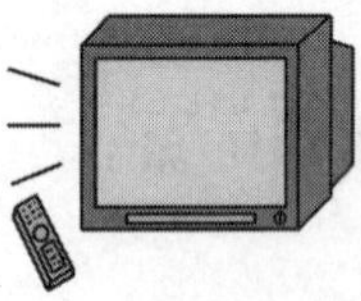

(1) [ Yes No ]

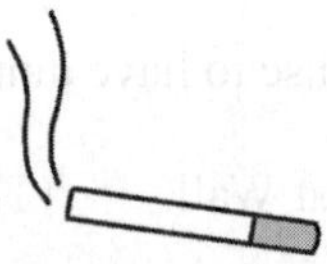

(2) [ Yes No ]

party

(3) [ Yes No ]

cooking

(4) [ Yes No ]

shower

(5) [ Yes No ]

**Further, make up three of your own questions and ask the host whether or not you are allowed to do them. When you play the role of the host parent, provide your own answers.**

(6) [ Yes No ]

Your own question;
Your own answer

(7) [ Yes No ]

Your own question;
Your own answer

(8) [ Yes No ]

Your own question;
Your own answer

## 対話(たいわ)練習(れんしゅう)2

**Pre-task: ～て ください**

**Work in pairs, A and B: A is a secretary and B is his/her boss. Ask when, or what time, B (boss) wants A (secretary) to do the following things. In answering the questions, make up your own answers. When you have finished asking/answering the questions, change roles.**

(れい)　A: あした 何時(なんじ)に オフィス(おふぃす)に 来(き)ましょうか。
　　　　B: 朝(あさ)8時(じ)に 来(き)てください。
　　　　A: わかりました。

| **Activities** | (e.g.) come to office   | (1) send a fax  | (2) call a taxi   |
|---|---|---|---|
| **Time** Yours: Partner's: | 9.00 am / 8.00 am | ______ / ______ | ______ / ______ |
| **Activities** | (3) go to Hong Kong  | (4) start a meeting  | (5) lunch with Noda-san   |
| **Time** Yours: Partner's: | ______ / ______ | ______ / ______ | ______ / ______ |
| **Activities** | (6) meet Kimura-san   | (7) phone to Tanaka-san  | (8) start a party  |
| **Time** Yours: Partner's: | ______ / ______ | ______ / ______ | ______ / ______ |

send 送(おく)る　　fax ファックス(ふぁっくす)　　start 始(はじ)める　　meeting 会議(かいぎ)
phone (to someone) 電話(でんわ)をかける

## 対話練習3

Pre-task: [Masu-stem/Noun]に 行く／来る

**Work in pairs, A and B: Invite your friend to do something together using** [Masu-stem/Noun]に 行く／来る. **Make up your invitation sentences on the basis of you own choice of the day/time, place to go and activity to do. Also respond to your friend's invitation appropriately.**

(れい)　A:　あした、町へ 映画を 見に 行きませんか。

　　　　B:　いいですね、行きましょう。(or すみません、あしたは ちょっと…。)

| Day/time | Place to go/come | Activity to do | Partner's answer |
|---|---|---|---|
| (e.g.) tomorrow | town | see a movie | Yes (No) |
| (1) | | | |
| (2) | | | |
| (3) | | | |
| (4) | | | |
| (5) | | | |

## 対話(たいわ)作(づく)り Comprehensive Exercises

✍ **In pairs, create a dialogue for the given situation. Please feel free to ask the instructor if you have any questions about Japanese expressions for your dialogue.**

> **Situation:**
>
> One of you is a student (渡辺(わたなべ)さん) and has just rented a room in an apartment owned by the landlord 田中(たなか)さん. While talking about your daily routine, ask the owner whether or not you are allowed to do certain things. The owner gives permission or forbids you from doing something.

Please incorporate the following expressions into your dialogue:

- ・～て、～ます
- ・～てもいいです／～てはいけません
- ・～に 行(い)く／来(く)る
- ・～てください
- ・～は ちょっと…

**[Sample Dialogue]** 田中(たなか) --- landlord 渡辺(わたなべ) --- student

田中(たなか)：渡辺(わたなべ)さんは たいてい 何時(なんじ)に 起(お)きますか。
渡辺(わたなべ)：そうですね、たいてい 6時(じ)ごろです。
田中：早(はや)いですね。わたしは たいてい 8時(じ)ごろです。
渡辺：そうですか。朝(あさ)7時(じ)ごろ シャワー(しゃわー)を
あびてもいいですか。うるさいですか。
田中：だいじょうぶですよ。あびてもいいですよ。
渡辺：すみません。
田中：夜(よる)は たいてい 何(なに)をしますか。
渡辺：たいてい、すこし 勉強(べんきょう)して、音楽(おんがく)を
聞(き)いて、寝(ね)ます。
田中：そうですか。
渡辺：あのう、ねこを 飼(か)ってもいいですか。
田中：ああ、ペット(ぺっと)は ちょっと…
渡辺：そうですか。わかりました。
田中：ええと、それから… これが 洗濯機(せんたくき)です。
どうぞ 使(つか)ってください。
渡辺：ありがとうございます。

> ペット(ぺっと) 'pet';
> 洗濯機(せんたくき) 'washing machine'

T: What time do you usually get up?
W: Well, around 6 o'clock.
T: It's early. I usually wake up at 8 o'clock.
W: I see. May I have a shower around 7 o'clock? Is it noisy?
T: No problem. You may have a shower.
W: Thank you.
T: At night, what do you usually do?
W: Usually, I study a little bit and listen to music and then go to bed.
T: I see.
W: Uhm, may I keep a cat?
T: Ah, a pet is a little bit…
W: I see. I understand.
T: Well, and next… this is the washing machine. Please use it anytime.
W: Thank you.

## 知ってた？ Did you know?

### 日本の名所 'Sightseeing places in Japan'

**調べましょう Research**

**Search the popular sightseeing places in 札幌，東京，大阪，京都 and 広島 via the internet and share what you have found in class.**

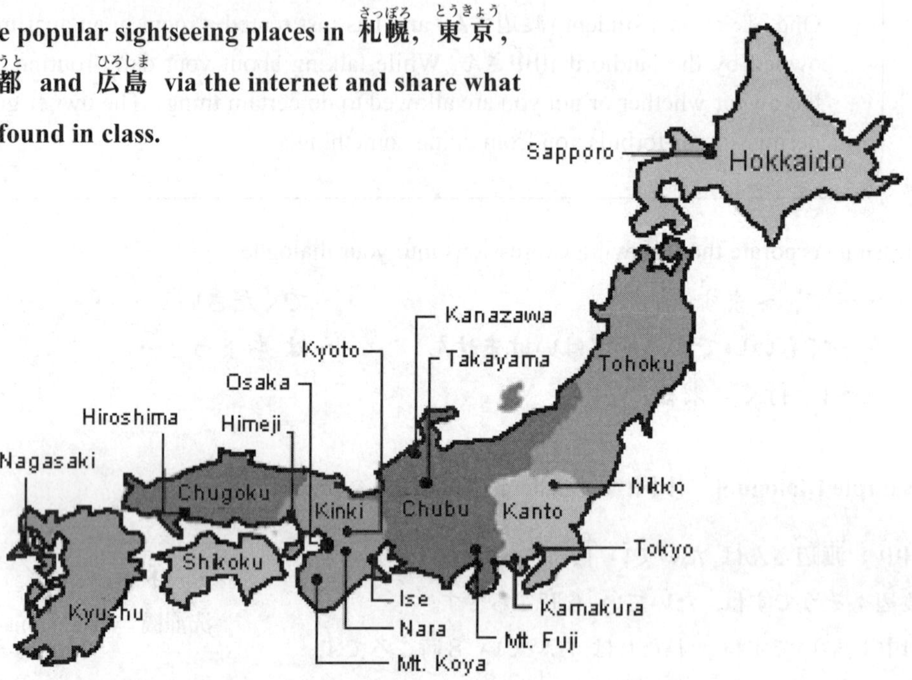


**練習しましょう Exercise**

**Based on what you have found above, make a sentence using [place]で ～たいです as in the example.**

(れい)　札幌で <u>ゆきまつりが</u> みたいです。　(雪まつり 'snow festival')

(1)　東京で ________________________ たいです。

(2)　大阪で ________________________ たいです。

(3)　京都で ________________________ たいです。

(4)　広島で ________________________ たいです。

## 新しい単語・表現 (あたらしいたんご・ひょうげん) New Vocabulary & Expressions

(Basic words/expressions are marked with '*')

| | | |
|---|---|---|
| 歩く* | ある | walk |
| 急ぐ* | いそ | hurry |
| 入れる* | い | put in |
| 売る* | う | sell |
| うるさい* | | noisy |
| 送る* | おく | send |
| お酒 | さけ | Osake, alcohol drinks |
| 教える* | おし | teach |
| 会議* | かいぎ | meeting |
| 飼う | か | keep pets |
| 貸す* | か | lend |
| 切手* | きって | post stamp |
| 救急車 | きゅうきゅうしゃ | ambulance |
| 教科書 | きょうかしょ | textbook |
| 景色* | けしき | landscape |
| 国立 | こくりつ | national |
| しお* | | salt |
| 質問* | しつもん | question |
| 失礼する* | しつれい | excuse (me) |
| 推薦状 | すいせんじょう | recommendation letter |
| 座る* | すわ | sit |
| 洗濯機 | せんたくき | washing machine |
| 出す* | だ | submit, take (thing) out |
| 立つ* | た | stand up |
| タワー | たわー | tower |
| チーズ | ちーず | cheese |
| 頂上 | ちょうじょう | top |
| 使う* | つか | use |
| つれていく | | take (someone) somewhere |
| 電話を かける* | でんわ | make a phone call |
| ところ* | | place |
| 飛ぶ* | と | fly |
| 寝る* | ね | sleep, go to bed |
| 始める* | はじ | start (something) |
| 万里の 長城 | ばんり ちょうじょう | The Great Wall |
| 美術館* | びじゅつかん | fine art museum |
| ファックス | ふぁっくす | fax |
| ペット | ぺっと | pet |
| ほら | | look! (drawing attention) |
| 香港 | ほんこん | Hong Kong |
| 毎朝* | まいあさ | every morning |
| 毎晩* | まいばん | every night |
| 窓* | まど | window |
| 名所 | めいしょ | sightseeing places |
| 野菜* | やさい | vegetable |
| 雪祭り | ゆきまつ | snow festival |
| 用事* | ようじ | errand |
| 呼ぶ* | よ | call |
| 料理* | りょうり | food, cooking |
| 笑う* | わら | laugh, smile |

# 第9課(だいきゅうか)

## 友達(ともだち)に 会(あ)ったり、そうじを したりします

I do things like meeting friends and cleaning my room

[Masato and Elena are talking]

まさと： エレナさん、こんにちは。

エレナ： こんにちは。

まさと： きょうも いい天気(てんき)ですね。

エレナ： ほんとうに いい天気(てんき)ですね。さあ、ここに 座(すわ)ってください。

まさと： あ、すみません。この町(まち)は いつも 空(そら)が 青(あお)くて、気持(きも)ちいいですね。

エレナ： ええ、でも 冬(ふゆ)は 寒(さむ)いですよ。

まさと： ああ、そうですか。ところで、エレナさん、学校(がっこう)の 休(やす)みには たいてい 何(なに)を しますか。

エレナ： そうですねえ。ええと、買(か)い物(もの)に 行(い)ったり、友達(ともだち)に 会(あ)ったり、そうじを したりします。たまに 映画(えいが)にも 行(い)きます。

まさと： そうですか。今度(こんど)の 週末(しゅうまつ)は 連休(れんきゅう)ですね。

エレナ： そうですね。

まさと： エレナさんは 何(なに)を しますか。

エレナ： 実家(じっか)に 帰(かえ)るつもりです。

まさと： へえ～、いいですね。

エレナ： ええ。日本(にほん)の大(おお)きい休(やす)みは いつですか。

まさと： お盆(ぼん)と お正月(しょうがつ)です。5月(がつ)には ゴールデンウィーク(ごーるでんうぃーく)も ありますよ。

エレナ： そうですか。

### 単語(たんご)と表現(ひょうげん) Vocabulary and Expressions (Dialogue)

| | | | | | |
|---|---|---|---|---|---|
| 5 | 空(そら) | sky | 14 | 実家(じっか) | one's own home |
| 5 | 気持(きも)ち いい | feel good | 17 | お盆(ぼん) | The Bon Festival |
| 6 | 冬(ふゆ) | winter | 17 | お正月(しょうがつ) | New Year's day |
| 11 | 連休(れんきゅう) | long weekend | 17 | ゴールデンウィーク(ごーるでんうぃーく) | Golden Week |

**Dialogue in English**

**[Elena and Masato are talking]**

1 M: Hi, Elena. Good afternoon.
2 E: Good afternoon.
3 M: It's nice weather again today.
4 E: It's really nice weather. Please sit here.
5 M: Oh, thank you. In this town, the sky is always blue and it makes us feel good, doesn't it?
6 E: Yes, but winter is cold.
7-8 M: Ah, I see. By the way, Elena, what do you usually do during university holidays?
9-10 E: Well... I do things like going shopping, meeting friends, and cleaning my room. Occasionally I go to watch a movie.
11 M: I see. Next weekend is a long weekend.
12 E: Yes, that's right.
13 M: Elena, what will you do?
14 E: I will go home.
15 M: Wow. That's good.
16 E: Yes. When are the long holidays in Japan?
17 M: Obon and New Year's Day. In May, we have 'Golden Week' as well.
18 E: I see.

## 文法(ぶんぽう) Grammar

### 1. The て form: い-adjective and Copula

The て form of an い-adjective is formed by replacing the final い by く, and then adding て. That of the copula is formed by simply adding で to the stem/base of the な-adjective or the noun.

**い-adjectives:** ～い → ～く＋て
たかい → たかくて
おおきい → おおきくて
(*Be careful) いい → よくて

**Copula:** Add ～で
**な-adjectives:**
しずか（な） → しずかで
しんせつ（な） → しんせつで
**Nouns:**
がくせい → がくせいで
にほんじん → にほんじんで

As in the case of verbs, the て form of い-adjectives and copula functions to connect two attributes.

(1) 田中(たなか)さんの 家(いえ)は 広(ひろ)くて きれいです。 'Mr. Tanaka's house is spacious and clean.'
(2) わたしは オーストラリア人(おーすとらりあじん)で、学生(がくせい)です。 'I am an Australian and a student.'
(3) この町(まち)は 静(しず)かで きれいです。 'This town is quiet and beautiful.'

The first て form of two events or situations often expresses the cause for the second statement.

(4) 映画(えいが)が おもしろくて、2度(ど) 見(み)ました。 'The movie was interesting and I saw it twice.'
(5) 車(くるま)は 高(たか)くて 買(か)いませんでした。 'The car was expensive, so I didn't buy it.'
(6) わたしは 学生(がくせい)で お金(かね)が ありません。 'I am a student, so don't have money.'

## 文法練習 1
(ぶんぽうれんしゅう)

**Provide the て form for the given words.**

| い-*adjective* | て *form* | *Copula (な-adj / Noun)* | て *form* |
|---|---|---|---|
| (れい) たかい expensive | たかくて | げんき(な) fine | げんきで |
| (1) やすい cheap | ________ | (2) にぎやか(な) lively | ________ |
| (3) おおきい big | ________ | (4) しずか(な) quiet | ________ |
| (5) ふるい old | ________ | (6) きれい(な) pretty, clean | ________ |
| (7) つまらない boring | ________ | (8) しんせつ(な) kind | ________ |
| (9) むずかしい difficult | ________ | (10) りっぱ(な) respectful | ________ |
| (11) あつい hot (weather) | ________ | (12) じみ(な) plain | ________ |
| (13) いい good, nice | ________ | (14) にほんじん Japanese | ________ |
| (15) あおい blue | ________ | (16) せんせい teacher | ________ |

## 文法練習 2
(ぶんぽうれんしゅう)

**Rewrite the following sentences in Japanese.**

(れい) My house is old and small. → わたしの家(いえ)は、古(ふる)くて小(ちい)さいです。

(1) My car is small and old.

(2) Tokyo is big and lively.

(3) That restaurant is delicious and not expensive.

(4) Yamamoto-san's house is very spacious and clean.

(5) My cat is small and cute. (cute かわいい)

(6) Sato-san is pretty and gentle.

(7) Suzuki-san is smart and handsome. (smart 頭(あたま)がいい)

(8) James is English, Jane is American and Lucy is Australian.

(9) I am sick today, so I don't go to school. (sick, sickness 病気(びょうき))

(10) The wine was very expensive, so I did not buy it.

## 2. 'and' in Japanese

The word 'and' is used in various contexts in English. In Japanese, it may be manifested as different expressions in different contexts. Typical examples are:

(i) [noun] and [noun] → [noun]と [noun]

(1) 本とペンを 買いました。 'I bought a book and a pen.'

(ii) .... [predicate]...., and ... [predicate] → ～て、...

(2) 山田さんは テニスをして、川口さんは サッカーをしました。

'Yamada-san played tennis and Kawaguchi-san played soccer.'

(iii) .... [predicate]. And, .... → ～[predicate]。そして ...

(3) 田中さんは 8時に 家に 帰りました。そして、木村さんに 電話しました。

'Tanaka-san went back home at 8 o'clock. And then he called Kimura-san.'

### 文法練習 3

**Rewrite the following sentences in Japanese.**

(れい) I met Noda-san and Kimura-san.

→ わたしは のださんと きむらさんに あいました。

(1) I bought a pen and a book yesterday.

(2) I ate a hamburger and a meat pie.

(3) I went to Kyoto and Nara last year.

(4) This is a library and that is the students' accommodation. (students' accommodation 寮)

(5) Yesterday, I met my friend and we had coffee together.

(6) The park is beautiful and quiet.

(7) My car is small and old.

(8) Yoshiko-san is cute and kind.

(9) Yesterday, I came back home at 6 o'clock. And I had a shower, and had dinner.

(10) I went to Sydney yesterday. And, I met Nomura-san and Okada-san there.

### 3. Listing nouns: と 'exhaustive'; や 'representative'; か 'alternative'

To list more than two things or events that are represented by nouns と, や or か may be used. と indicates items that are an exhaustive list (i.e. all items are listed), や indicates items that are representative (i.e. listed items are some examples) and か indicates items that are alternative to another. など 'etc.' may also be added at the end of the list.

(i) [noun] と [noun]

(1) 本(ほん)とペン(ぺん)を 買(か)いました。 'I bought a book and a pen.'

(2) 田中(たなか)さんと木村(きむら)さんに 会(あ)います。 'I will meet Tanaka-san and Kimura-san.'

(ii) [noun] や [noun]

(3) 本(ほん)やペン(ぺん)を 買(か)いました。 'I bought some things like a book and a pen.'

cf. 本(ほん)やペン(ぺん) などを 買(か)いました。 'I bought a book and a pen, etc.'

(4) 東京(とうきょう)や大阪(おおさか)に 行(い)きます。 'I am going to places like Tokyo and Osaka.'

(iii) [noun] か [noun]

(5) 本(ほん)かペン(ぺん)を 買(か)います。 'I will buy a book or a pen.'

(6) ビデオ(びでお)か DVD を 見(み)てください。 'Please watch video or DVD.'

**文法練習(ぶんぽうれんしゅう) 4**

**Rewrite the following sentences in Japanese. Use と, や or か.**

(れい) I had toast and apples this morning.

→ わたしは 今朝(けさ) トースト(とーすと)と りんごを 食(た)べました。

(1) I will meet Tanaka-san, Kimura-san and Yamada-san tomorrow.

(2) I studied Japanese and Economics yesterday.

(3) I bought a TV, a DVD player, a mobile phone, etc.

(4) Okada-san plays sports like soccer, hockey and swimming, etc.

(5) Either Nomura-san or I will go to Japan next week.

(6) I will go to Osaka or Kyoto.

## 自然な日本語 Natural Conversation Notes

### Various usages of すみません

(i) <u>'I'm sorry'</u> — When the speaker apologizes for something caused by him/herself.

(1) あっ、すみません！　'Oh, I'm sorry!' [When you step on someone's foot in a train.]

(2) 先生、教科書を 忘れました。すみません。　'Teacher, I forgot my textbook. I'm sorry.'

(ii) <u>'Excuse me'</u> — When you want to draw the attention of someone.

(3) すみません。注文、お願いします／ 勘定、お願いします。[At a restaurant]
'Excuse me. Could you please take my order/ Could I have the bill?'

(注文 'order', 勘定 'bill')

(iii) <u>'Thank you'</u> — すみません is often used in the same context where 'thank you' is normally used in English. The use of すみません in such a context underlines the meaning 'Thank you for what you've done and I am sorry for bothering you'.

(4) A: お茶です。どうぞ。　'Tea is ready. Please have some.'
B: あ, すみません。　'Oh, thank you.'

#### 自然な日本語：練習

**Look at the pictures and write the phrase that you should say in each situation. Try to add some further expressions such as 大丈夫ですか 'Are you all right?' as in the example.**

(れい) <u>すみません！ 大丈夫ですか。</u>

(e.g.)

(1) call a waiter

(2) receive a present

(3) someone drops some thing

(4)

(5)

## 表現(ひょうげん) Expression Notes

### 1 ～たり、～たりする 'do things like .... and ....'

**[1]** ☛ The construction ～たり ～たりする is useful for representatively listing some activities.

(1) 今週末(こんしゅうまつ)は 家(いえ)で 音楽(おんがく)を 聞(き)いたり 本(ほん)を 読(よ)んだりします。

'This weekend, I will do things like listening to music and reading a book at home.'

The て form of verbs indicates an exhaustive list of activities.

(2) 今週末(こんしゅうまつ)は 家(いえ)で 音楽(おんがく)を 聞(き)いて 本(ほん)を 読(よ)みます。

'This weekend, I will listen to music and read a book at home.'

**[2]** ☛ To make the たり form, just replace the て in the て form with たり. Note that the final verb needs to be たりする and it expresses the tense of the sentence.

(3) 休(やす)みのあいだ、買(か)い物(もの)を したり、レストラン(れすとらん)に 行(い)ったりしました。

'I did things like shopping and going to restaurants during the holiday.'

### 表現練習(ひょうげんれんしゅう) 1

**Complete the following table, by filling in the blanks with the appropriate form.**

| | *Base form* | *て form* | *たり form* | *gloss* |
|---|---|---|---|---|
| (e.g.1) | 書(か)く [5-base verb] | かいて | かいたり | write |
| (e.g.2) | 食(た)べる [1-base verb] | たべて | たべたり | eat |
| (1) | (コーヒー(こーひー)を) 飲(の)む | ______ | ______ | drink (coffee) |
| (2) | (映画(えいが)を) 見(み)る | ______ | ______ | watch (a movie) |
| (3) | (友達(ともだち)に) 会(あ)う | ______ | ______ | meet (a friend) |
| (4) | (友達(ともだち)を) 待(ま)つ | ______ | ______ | wait for (a friend) |
| (5) | (写真(しゃしん)を) とる | ______ | ______ | take (a photo) |
| (6) | (6時(じ)に) 起(お)きる | ______ | ______ | get up (at 6) |
| (7) | (ジョン(じょん)に) 話(はな)す | ______ | ______ | speak (to John) |
| (8) | (音楽(おんがく)を) 聞(き)く | ______ | ______ | listen to (music) |
| (9) | (学校(がっこう)に) 行(い)く | ______ | ______ | go (to the library) |
| (10) | (日本語(にほんご)を) 勉強(べんきょう)する | ______ | ______ | study (Japanese) |

## 表現練習2（ひょうげんれんしゅう）

**Make up sentences, using the given cues. Use the ～たり～たりする construction.**

(れい) Last weekend: reading a book, watching TV, etc.

→ <u>先週末（せんしゅうまつ）は、本（ほん）を 読（よ）んだり、テレビ（てれび）を 見（み）たりしました。</u>

(1) This weekend: driving, going to a restaurant, etc.

(2) Last year: meeting friends, shopping, etc. in Japan.

(3) Tomorrow: cleaning my room, doing the washing, etc. (do the washing 洗濯（せんたく）する)

(4) Tonight: making a phone call to my family, writing an email to a friend, etc.

(5) Usually on a weekend: going to the coast, watching movies, drinking coffee in town, etc.

## 2 Adjective +そうです 'It looks ...; It sounds ...'

**[1]** ☛ An [adjective + そうです] indicates that the impression expressed by the adjective is based on visual (or sometimes 'auditory') information.

(1) あのケーキ（けーき）は とても おいしそうですね。 'That cake looks very delicious.'

(2) このＣＤプレイヤー（ぷれいやー）は 高（たか）そうですね。 'This CD player looks expensive.'

(3) 田中（たなか）さんは 元気（げんき）そうでしたよ。 'It looked like Mr. Tanaka was fine.'

**[2]** ☛ To make the そうです expression, take off the final い in the い-adjective and add そうです. For a な-adjective, replace な with そうです.

**い-adjectives:** ～<u>い</u> → ～∅そうです　おもしろ<u>い</u> → おもしろ<u>そうです</u>

おいし<u>い</u> → おいし<u>そうです</u>

(*Be careful) い<u>い</u> → よ<u>さそうです</u>

**な-adjectives:** ～<u>な</u> → ～<u>∅</u>そう　しずか<u>な</u> → しずか<u>そうです</u>

げんき<u>な</u> → げんき<u>そうです</u>

**[3]** ☛ (i) ～そうです is not used with nouns. Other similar expressions such as ようです 'it seems…' are used in this case.

(ii) ～そうです may also be used with verbs (the Masu-stem). This case will be discussed in a later lesson.

(iii) ～そうです itself basically behaves as a な-adjective:

(e.g.) おいしそう<u>な</u> ケーキ（けーき） 'cake that looks delicious'

## 表現練習3

（ひょうげん れんしゅう）

**Provide the ～そうです expression for the given adjectives.**

| い-adjective | ～そうです | な-adjectives | ～そうです |
|---|---|---|---|
| (e.g.) たかい expensive | たかそうです | げんき(な) fine | げんきそうです |
| (1) やすい cheap | ________ | (2) にぎやか(な) lively | ________ |
| (3) あまい sweet | ________ | (4) しずか(な) quiet | ________ |
| (5) にがい bitter | ________ | (6) きれい(な) pretty, clean | ________ |
| (7) まずい not tasty | ________ | (8) しんせつ(な) kind | ________ |
| (9) あたたかい warm | ________ | (10) りっぱ(な) respectful | ________ |
| (11) さむい cold (weather) | ________ | (12) ひま(な) free | ________ |
| (13) いい good, nice | ________ | (14) 上手(じょうず)(な) skillful, good at | ________ |

## 表現練習4

（ひょうげん れんしゅう）

**Look at the pictures and make up sentences using ～そうですね.**

(れい) この料理(りょうり)は、おいしそうですね。

(e.g.) looks delicious

(1) looks warm

(2) [outside] looks cold

(3) looks expensive

(4) looks sweet

(5) [movie] looks interesting

(6) looks fast

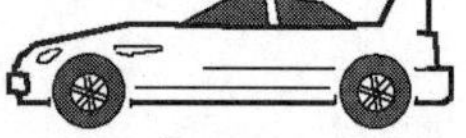

(7) [movie] looks scary

(8) looks comfortable

## 対話(たいわ) Communicative Exchanges

### 対話練習(たいわれんしゅう) 1

**Pre-task**: [adjective]て； ～けど

(i) First describe the given places/things, using appropriate words in the list below, or your own words. You may make up expressions for the purpose of practice.

(ii) Use more than two words: In connecting them use either the て form 'and' or けど 'but', depending on the relationship between the first and second words.

(iii) In pairs, then ask your friend about his/her places/things, as in the example.

| | | | |
|---|---|---|---|
| ふるい old | あたらしい new | あかるい bright | くらい dark |
| おおきい large, big | ちいさい small | おおい many | すくない few |
| しずかな quiet | うるさい noisy | はでな colorful | じみな plain |
| おもい heavy | かるい light | ひろい spacious, wide | せまい narrow |
| きれいな clean, pretty | きたない dirty | はやい fast, early | おそい slow |

(れい) まさと： エレナ(えれな)さんの家(いえ)は どうですか。
エレナ(えれな)： わたしの家(いえ)は ひろくて きれいです。
まさと： そうですか。
エレナ(えれな)： まさとさんの家(いえ)は どうですか。
まさと： わたしの家(いえ)は ひろいけど、ちょっと ふるくて きたないです。
エレナ(えれな)： そうですか。

| | My own | Friend's |
|---|---|---|
| (e.g.) House [ いえ ] | - ひろくて きれい | - ひろいけど、ふるくて きたない |
| Room [ へや ] | | |
| University [ 大学(だいがく) ] | | |
| Car [ 車(くるま) ] | | |
| Mobile phone [ けいたい電話(でんわ) ] | | |
| Computer [ コンピューター(こんぴゅーたー) ] | | |
| High school [ 高校(こうこう) ] | | |

## 対話練習２

**Pre-task:** ～たり ～たりします； adj.+そうですね

**Ask your classmates what they normally do on the weekend and for their health. In answering the questions, you may refer to the activities in the list below or you can make up your own activities. When you hear the answers, please also try to make a comment.**

| | | |
|---|---|---|
| 買い物を する | CD／音楽を きく | DVD／テレビ／映画を 見る |
| 寝る | 料理を する | 読書を する |
| そうじを する | 洗たくを する | 友達と 会う |
| スポーツを する | 野菜を たくさん 食べる | ジョギングする (jog) |
| キャンプを する | 水泳を する | エアロビクスを する (aerobics) |
| サーフィンを する | 釣りを する | 山登りを する (mountain climb) |
| ダンスを する | サイクリングを する | 何も しない (do nothing) |

(れい)　週末 (On weekends)

田中：　ジョンさん、週末は いつも 何を しますか。
ジョン：　家で テレビを 見たり、音楽を 聞いたりします。
田中：　そうですか。楽しそうですね。

(れい)　健康のために (For one's health)

田中：　ジョンさん、健康のために たいてい 何を しますか。
ジョン：　そうですね…。スポーツを したり、野菜を たくさん 食べたりします。
田中：　そうですか。それは いいですね。

| ともだちの名前 | On weekends | For health |
|---|---|---|
| (e.g.) John | ・テレビを 見る<br>・音楽を きく, etc. | ・スポーツを する<br>・野菜を たくさん 食べる, etc. |
| | | |
| | | |
| | | |
| | | |

## 対話作り Comprehensive Exercises

✍ **In pairs, create a dialogue for the given situation. Please feel free to ask the instructor if you have any questions about Japanese expressions for your dialogue.**

> **Situation:**
> You meet your friend and talk about final exams, your next holiday and other related things.

Please incorporate the following expressions into your dialogue:

- Greetings with expressions about the weather
- The て form of adjectives or copula ; ～けど
- ～たり～たりする
- Adjective +そうです
- すみません

Also refer to [Useful Words/Expressions] on the next page.

**[Sample Dialogue]**

エレナ： まさとさん、こんにちは。

まさと： こんにちは、エレナさん。きょうも 暑いですね。

エレナ： ええ、そうですね。ゆうべは 暑くて ぜんぜん 勉強しませんでした。

まさと： そうですか。日本語のテストは いつですか。

エレナ： 来週の 火曜日です。

まさと： もうすぐですね。僕が 日本語の勉強を 手伝いますよ。

エレナ： すみません。ほんとうに 助かります。

まさと： いいえ。ところで、試験のあとは 夏休みですね。何をしますか。

エレナ： そうですねえ。実家に 帰ります。家族と いっしょに おいしい料理を 食べたり、買い物に 行ったりします。

まさと： それは 楽しそうですね。

エレナ： ええ。

E: Hi, Masato.
M: Hi, Elena. It's hot again today.
E: Yes, indeed. Last night, it was so hot that I didn't study.
M: I see. When is the Japanese test?
E: Next Tuesday.
M: That's soon. I'll help you with your Japanese study.
E: Thank you. That's really helpful.
M: You're welcome. By the way, aft the test, it's the summer holiday. What will you do?
E: Well, I'll go back home. I'll do things like eating delicious foo and shopping with my family.
M: It sounds fun.
E: Yes.

[ぜんぜん '(not) at all'; もうすぐ 'soon'; 手伝う 'help'; ほんとうに 'really 助かる 'helpful, saved']

**Useful Words/Expressions**

暖(あたた)かい 'warm'　暑(あつ)い 'hot'　涼(すず)しい 'cool'　寒(さむ)い 'cold'

いい天気(てんき) 'nice weather, sunny'　いやな天気(てんき) 'awful weather, cloudy'

よく 降(ふ)りますね 'It's raining a lot, isn't it?'　暑(あつ)いですね (cf. we don't say 暑(あつ)い天気(てんき)ですね)

期末(きまつ)テスト 'final exam'　たいへんです 'It's tough'　難(むずか)しいです 'difficult, hard'

がんばってください 'good luck'　旅行(りょこう)する 'travel'

家(うち)に いる 'stay home'　アルバイト(あるばいと) 'part-time work'

## 知(し)ってた？ Did you know?

## 年中行事(ねんちゅうぎょうじ) 'Seasonal celebrations and national holidays in Japan'

### 調(しら)べましょう Research

**The following are some of the seasonal celebration days of Japan. Choose a picture that best illustrates the given day below. Further, research through the internet and other means what and how Japanese people celebrate on each day.**

(1) May 5 - 子供(こども)の日(ひ) 'Children's Day'

(2) February 3 - 節分(せつぶん) 'The beginning of spring'

(3) March 3 - ひな祭(まつ)り 'Doll Festival/Girls' Day'

(4) July 7 - 七夕(たなばた) 'Star Festival'

(5) November 15 - 七五三(しちごさん) 'Seven-Five-Three Festival'

(6) The second Monday of January - 成人(せいじん)の日(ひ) 'Coming-of-Age Day'

(a)

(b)

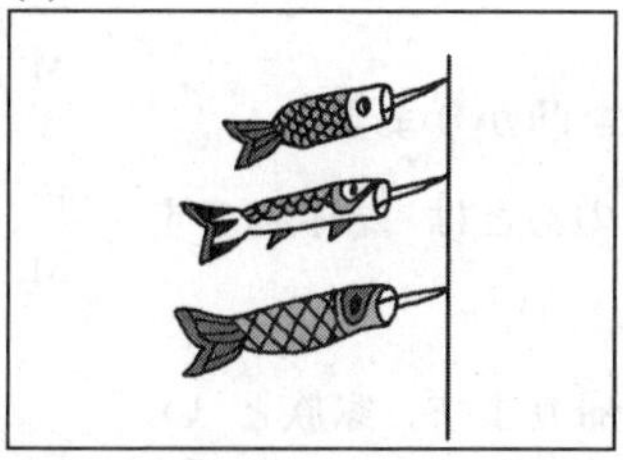

(c)

(d)

(e)

(f)

## 話(はな)し合(あ)いましょう Discussions

**Below is the list of national holidays of Japan. Refer to the list and discuss the similarities and differences between holidays in Japan and your country.**

### [National holidays of Japan]

January 1 — **New Year's Day** (元旦(がんたん))

The second Monday of January — **Coming-of-Age Day** (成人(せいじん)の日(ひ))

February 11 — **National Founding Day** (建国記念日(けんこくきねんび))

March 20 or 21 — **Vernal Equinox Day** (春分(しゅんぶん)の日(ひ))

April 29 — **Shoowa Day** (昭和(しょうわ)の日(ひ))

May 3 — **Constitution Memorial Day** (憲法記念日(けんぽうきねんび))

May 4 — **Greenery Day** (緑(みどり)の日(ひ))

May 5 — **Children's Day** (子供(こども)の日(ひ))

July 20 — **Marine Day** (海(うみ)の日(ひ))

The third Monday of September — **Respect-for-the-Aged Day** (敬老(けいろう)の日(ひ))

September 23 or 24 — **Autumnal Equinox Day** (秋分(しゅうぶん)の日(ひ))

The second Monday of October — **Health/Sports Day** (体育(たいいく)の日(ひ))

November 3 — **Culture Day** (文化(ぶんか)の日(ひ))

November 23 — **Labour Thanksgiving Day** (勤労感謝(きんろうかんしゃ)の日(ひ))

December 23 — **Emperor's Birthday** (天皇誕生日(てんのうたんじょうび))

## 新(あたら)しい単語(たんご)・表現(ひょうげん) New Vocabulary & Expressions

(Basic words/expressions are marked with '*')

| | |
|---|---|
| 間(あいだ)* | during, between |
| 青(あお)い* | blue |
| 明(あか)るい* | bright |
| 頭(あたま)がいい* | smart |
| イーメール(いーめーる) | email |
| エアロビクス(えあろびくす) | aerobics |
| 多(おお)い* | many, lots |
| お正月(しょうがつ)* | New Year's day |
| お盆(ぼん)* | the Bon Festival |
| 家族(かぞく)* | family |
| 軽(かる)い* | light (weight) |
| 勘定(かんじょう) | bill |

| | |
|---|---|
| 汚い*（きたな） | dirty |
| キャンプ（きゃんぷ） | camp, camping |
| 暗い*（くら） | dark |
| 経済学*（けいざいがく） | Economics |
| 健康（けんこう） | health |
| コースト（こーすと） | coast |
| ゴールデンウィーク（ごーるでんうぃーく） | Golden Week |
| サーフィン（さーふぃん） | surfing |
| サイクリング（さいくりんぐ） | cycling |
| 実家（じっか） | one's parents' home |
| 地味(な)*（じみ） | plain |
| ジョギング（じょぎんぐ） | jog |
| すぐに* | soon |
| 涼しい*（すず） | cool |
| 狭い*（せま） | narrow |
| 全然*（ぜんぜん） | (not) at all |
| 洗濯する（せんたく） | do the washing |
| 空*（そら） | sky |
| たくさん* | many, much, lots |
| 助かる*（たす） | be saved |
| ダンス（だんす） | dance |
| 注文（ちゅうもん） | order |
| つまらない* | boring |
| 手伝う*（てつだ） | help |
| トースト*（とーすと） | toast |
| 苦い（にが） | bitter |
| 2度（ど） | twice |
| 年中行事（ねんちゅうぎょうじ） | seasonal cerebrations |
| 派手(な)*（はで） | loud, colourful |
| ハンバーガー（はんばーがー） | hamburger |
| 暇(な)*（ひま） | free, have free time |
| 病気*（びょうき） | sickness, sick |
| 冬*（ふゆ） | winter |
| まずい* | not tasty |
| ミートパイ（みーとぱい） | meat pie |
| もうすぐ* | soon |
| 山登り*（やまのぼ） | mountain climb |
| 立派(な)*（りっぱ） | wonderful |
| 寮*（りょう） | students' accommodation |
| 連休（れんきゅう） | long weekend |
| 忘れる*（わす） | forget |

# 第10課

## ３００キロぐらいだと 思います

## I think it's about 300 km

[Elena and Masato are talking]

まさと： エレナさん、シドニーは ここから 遠いですか？

エレナ： そんなに 遠く ありませんよ。３００キロぐらいだと 思います。

まさと： あ、そうですか。

エレナ： よかったら あした 行きましょうか。

まさと： えっ ほんとうですか。ぜひ お願いします。

[In Sydney]

まさと： とても にぎやかな ところですね。

エレナ： はい。シドニーは オーストラリアで 一番 大きいんですよ。

まさと： そうですか。人口は どのくらいですか。

エレナ： ４００万人ぐらいだと 思います。

まさと： いろいろな 国の人が いますね。

エレナ： ええ。この国には 移住者が たくさん いて、いろいろな 国の店や レストランが たくさん ありますよ。

まさと： へえ、いいですね。

エレナ： ところで、オペラハウスに 行った ことが ありますか。

まさと： いいえ、ありませんけど、オペラハウスは 日本でも 有名です。

エレナ： そうですか。じゃあ、行ってみましょうか。

まさと： あ、いいですね。

## 単語と表現　Vocabulary and Expressions (Dialogue)

| | | | | | |
|---|---|---|---|---|---|
| 2 | そんなに | that much, that many | 8 | 人口 | population |
| 2 | ぐらい | about, approximately | 10 | 国 | country |
| 2 | ～と 思う | I think that … | 11 | 移住者 | immigrant(s) |
| 7 | 一番 | most, first, best | 11 | 店 | shop |
| 16 | 行ってみる | go and find out what happens/what it looks like | | | |

### Dialogue in English

**[Elena and Masato are talking]**

1 M: Elena, is Sydney far from here?
2 E: (It's) not that far. I think it's about 300km.
3 M: I see.
4 E: Shall we go (there) tomorrow?
5 M: Really? Please (take me there).

**[In Sydney]**

6 M: (It's) a very lively place, isn't it?
7 E: Yes. You know, Sydney is the biggest (city) in Australia.
8 M: I see. What is the population (of Sydney)?
9 E: I think it's about four million.
10 M: There are people of various nationalities, aren't there?
11-12 E: Yes. In this country, there are a lot of immigrants and we have a number of shops and restaurants representing different nationalities.
13 M: Huh, that's good.
14 E: By the way, have you been to the Opera House?
15 M: No, I haven't, but the Opera House is famous even in Japan.
16 E: Is that so? Then, shall we go there?
17 M: Oh, that's good (I'd love to).

## 文法 Grammar

## Plain forms

Plain forms are grammatical variations of predicates, which are in opposition to the polite forms represented by the *desu-masu* styles. Plain forms are typical endings of predicates in casual conversation. They may also be used in various constructions or embedded clauses.

In each predicate (verb, い-adjective or copula (for a な-adjective or noun)), a plain 'non-past form' and plain 'past form' exist as shown below — they are equivalent to the polite forms, ます／です and ました／でした, respectively.

**1. Verbs: ～る *vs.* ～た**

(i) The る form represents different non-past (or dictionary) forms of various verbs: Their actual endings vary as in 買う 'buy', 書く 'write', 話す 'speak', 待つ 'wait for', … or 売る 'sell'.

(ii) The た form indicates past. Below is a summary of the た form of the three verb groups:

| | Summary | Non-past (る form) | | Past (た form) | |
|---|---|---|---|---|---|
| 5-base verbs: | ～う、つ、る → ～った | 買う | buy | 買った | bought |
| | | 待つ | wait for | 待った | waited for |
| | | 売る | sell | 売った | sold |
| | ～く → ～いた | 書く | write | 書いた | wrote |
| | ～ぐ → ～いだ | 泳ぐ | swim | 泳いだ | swam |
| | ～す → ～した | 話す | speak | 話した | spoke |
| | ～ぬ、む、ぶ → ～んだ | 死ぬ | die | 死んだ | died |
| | | 飲む | drink | 飲んだ | drank |
| | | 呼ぶ | call | 呼んだ | called |
| 1-base verbs: | ～{i / e}る → ～{i / e}た | 見る | see | 見た | saw |
| | | 食べる | eat | 食べた | ate |
| Irregular verbs | ―― | 来る | come | 来た | came |
| | | する | do | した | did |

た forms

The た form of a particular verb is also obtainable from its て form, by simply replacing て with た without exception.

(e.g.) 買う → 買って／買った； 書く → 書いて／書いた

## 文法練習(ぶんぽうれんしゅう) 1

**Fill in the blanks with an appropriate form. For those verbs we have not yet learnt, please try to identify the group of the given verb, by comparing its base and ます forms.**

| | *Base form* | *ます form* | *た form* | *gloss* |
|---|---|---|---|---|
| (e.g.1) | 書(か)く [5-base verb] | かきます | かいた | write (a letter) |
| (e.g.2) | 食(た)べる [1-base verb] | たべます | たべた | eat |
| (1) | (棒(ぼう)を 手(て)で) 持(も)つ | | | hold (a stick with hand) |
| (2) | (大(おお)きい 声(こえ)で) 叫(さけ)ぶ | | | shout (in a loud voice) |
| (3) | (本(ほん)を) 読(よ)む | | | read (books) |
| (4) | (友達(ともだち)に) 会(あ)う | | | meet (a friend) |
| (5) | (歯(は)を) みがく | | | clean (one's teeth) |
| (6) | (本(ほん)を) 借(か)りる | かります | | borrow (books) |
| (7) | (本(ほん)を) 返(かえ)す | | | return (books) |
| (8) | (家(うち)に) 帰(かえ)る | かえります | | return (home) |
| (9) | (窓(まど)を) 開(あ)ける | あけます | | open (the window) |
| (10) | (自転車(じてんしゃ)に) 乗(の)る | | | ride (a bicycle) |
| (11) | (日本語(にほんご)を) 勉強(べんきょう)する | | | study (Japanese) |
| (12) | (友達(ともだち)が 家(うち)に) 来(く)る | | | come (to my home) |

**2. い-adjectives: ～い *vs.* ～かった**

| | Polite forms | | Plain forms | | English |
|---|---|---|---|---|---|
| Non-past | ～いです | 高(たか)いです | ～い | 高(たか)い | is high/expensive |
| | | 大(おお)きいです | | 大(おお)きい | is big |
| Past | ～かったです | 高(たか)かったです | ～かった | 高(たか)かった | was high/expensive |
| | | 大(おお)きかったです | | 大(おお)きかった | was big |

**3. Copula (な-adjectives and nouns): ～だ *vs.* ～だった**

| | Polite forms | | Plain forms | | English |
|---|---|---|---|---|---|
| Non-past | ～です | 静(しず)かです | ～だ | 静(しず)かだ | is quiet |
| | | 学生(がくせい)です | | 学生(がくせい)だ | is a student |
| Past | ～でした | 静(しず)かでした | ～だった | 静(しず)かだった | was quiet |
| | | 学生(がくせい)でした | | 学生(がくせい)だった | was a student |

## 文法練習(ぶんぽうれんしゅう) 2

**Convert the following polite expressions to their plain form counterparts:**

(れい) 私(わたし)は 学生(がくせい)です。 → わたしは 学生(がくせい)だ。

(1) この本(ほん)は とても おもしろいです。

(2) 私(わたし)の 車(くるま)は 古(ふる)いです。

(3) テスト(てすと)は 難(むずか)しかったです。

(4) きのう とても 忙(いそが)しかったです。

(5) ここは いつも 静(しず)かですね。

(6) 私(わたし)は すしが 好(す)きです。

(7) さとしは とても まじめです。

(8) あの人(ひと)は 私(わたし)の 妹(いもうと) ですよ。

(9) 田中(たなか)さんは 去年(きょねん)まで 学生(がくせい)でした。

(10) 東京(とうきょう)は とても にぎやかでした。

### 4. Negative plain forms

The negative meaning is expressed by ない in plain form for all types of predicates. We first summarise the basic facts about ない below.

**ない** It may be used as an independent predicate, or as a suffix attached to other (main) predicates.

| | As an independent predicate | As a suffix |
|---|---|---|
| Meaning | 'absent, do not exist, do not have'<br>(e.g) ここに ない (It) is not here.<br>お金(かね)が ない (I) don't have money. | Negative (of the main predicate)<br>(e.g) 見(み)ない don't see.<br>高(たか)くない not high. |
| Opposite word | ある *vs.* ない (We do not have *あらない in Standard Japanese)<br>(e.g) あした テスト(てすと)は ない<br>I don't have a test tomorrow. | Affirmative expression of predicates<br>(e.g) 見(み)る *vs.* 見(み)ない<br>高(たか)い *vs.* 高(たか)くない |
| Polite expression | ないです／ありません<br>(e.g) あした テスト(てすと)は ありません<br>I don't have a test tomorrow. | Polite negative expressions<br>(e.g) 見(み)ません<br>高(たか)くありません |
| Past form | なかった<br>(e.g) きのう テスト(てすと)は なかった<br>I didn't have a test yesterday. | ～なかった<br>(e.g) 見(み)なかった didn't see<br>高(たか)くなかった wasn't high |

ない behaves as an い-adjective in both uses:

(1) なかった didn't have; なくて don't have and …; なければ if (I) don't have; etc.

(2) 見(み)なかった didn't see; 見(み)なくて don't see and …; 見(み)なければ if (I) don't see; etc.

**4.1.** Verbs (negative): V-ない *vs.* V-なかった

| | Polite forms | Plain forms | English |
|---|---|---|---|
| Non-past | ～ません 書(か)きません<br>見(み)ません | ～ない 書(か)かない<br>見(み)ない | do not write<br>do not watch |
| Past | ～ませんでした<br>書(か)きませんでした<br>見(み)ませんでした | ～なかった<br>書(か)かなかった<br>見(み)なかった | did not write<br>did not watch |

ない forms:

- 5-base verbs: ～u → ～a ない
  - (1) 書(か)く(kak**u**) → 書(か)か(kak**a**) ＋ない
  - (2) 飲(の)む(yom**u**) → 飲(の)ま(yom**a**) ＋ない
  - (3) 買(か)う(ka**u**) → 買(か)わ(ka**wa**) ＋ない
- 1-base verbs: ～{i / e}る → ～{i / e}ない
  - (4) 食(た)べる → 食(た)べ＋ない
  - (5) 見(み)る → 見(み)＋ない
- Irregular verbs: [no common rules]
  - (6) 勉強(べんきょう)する → 勉強(べんきょう)し＋ない
  - (7) 来(く)る → 来(こ)＋ない

**文法練習(ぶんぽうれんしゅう)３**

**Convert the following polite expressions to their plain form counterparts:**

(れい) かばんを 買(か)いません。→ <u>かばんを 買(か)わない。</u>

(1) まりは いつも 朝(あさ)ご飯(はん)を 食(た)べません。

(2) 私(わたし)は パーティー(ぱーてぃー)に 行(い)きません。

(3) 私(わたし)は テレビ(てれび)を 見(み)ません。

(4) そのかばんを 買(か)いませんでした。

(5) 田中(たなか)さんに 会(あ)いませんでした。

(6) さとしは きょう 学校(がっこう)に 来(き)ませんでした。

(7) あした テスト(てすと)は ありません。

(8) きのう テスト(てすと)は ありませんでした。

**4.2.** い-adjectives (negative): ～く ない *vs.* ～く なかった

| | Polite forms | Plain forms | English |
|---|---|---|---|
| Non-past | ～く ありません<br>高(たか)くありません | ～く ない<br>高(たか)くない | <br>is not high |
| Past | ～く ありませんでした<br>高(たか)くありませんでした | ～く なかった<br>高(たか)くなかった | <br>was not high |

N.B. ない form of いい is よくない (*いくない is ungrammatical).

**4.3.** Copula (negative): ～では ない *vs.* ～では なかった

| | Polite forms | Plain forms | English |
|---|---|---|---|
| Non-past | ～では ありません<br>静(しず)かではありません<br>学生(がくせい)ではありません | ～では ない<br>静(しず)かではない<br>学生(がくせい)ではない | <br>is not quiet<br>is not a student |
| Past | ～では ありませんでした<br>静(しず)かではありませんでした<br>学生(がくせい)ではありませんでした | ～では なかった<br>静(しず)かではなかった<br>学生(がくせい)ではなかった | <br>was not quiet<br>was not a student |

N.B. ～では tends to become ～じゃ in spoken conversation, particularly in casual conversation, or in casual writing.

### 文法練習(ぶんぽうれんしゅう) 4

**Rewrite the following polite expressions in their plain form counterparts:**

(れい) この山(やま)は 高(たか)く ありません。→ <u>この山(やま)は 高(たか)くない。</u>

(1) きょうは 寒(さむ)く ありません。

(2) 私(わたし)の 車(くるま)は 新(あたら)しく ありません。

(3) このいすは 楽(らく)じゃ ありません。

(4) さしみは 好(す)きじゃ ありません。

(5) 私(わたし)の 部屋(へや)は 大(おお)きく ありません。

(6) しげるは 学生(がくせい)では ありませんでしたよ。

(7) なおこは あまり まじめじゃ ありませんでした。 (あまり ～ない 'not so ...')

(8) この映画(えいが)は あまり おもしろく ありませんでしたね。

## 自然な日本語 Natural Conversation Notes

## Particle omission

Particle omission is a key phenomenon that characterises the naturalness or the 'spokeness' of Japanese conversation. It is typically observed in face-to-face conversation (but also in emails and postcards), and occurs more frequently in casual conversation than in formal conversation.

**1. Which particles can be omitted?**

が (or は when topicalised) for the subject with any kind of predicate; を (or は when topicalised) for the object with a transitive; に／へ for the destination with a 'transport-movement' verb (e.g. 行く 'go', 来る 'come', 入る 'enter'); に for location with いる／ある 'exist'.

(1) 私 [は] カレーライス[を] 食べます。 'I will eat curry rice.'

(2) 私 [は] あした 学校[に] 行きません。 'I won't go to school tomorrow.'

Other types of particles are not normally omitted: e.g. で for the place of a dynamic event,; に for the indirect object; から for a starting point; etc.

(3) 私 [は] 田中さんに 手紙[を] 書きました。 'I wrote a letter to Tanaka-san.'

(4) 7時から 私の家で 勉 強[を] しませんか。 'Shall we study together from 7 o'clock at my home?'

**2. When can particles be omitted?**

Strong feeling/emotion: Particle omission may occur more readily when the speaker is strongly expressing his/her feelings/emotions towards the hearer:

(5) ご飯_ 食べない！ 'I won't eat dinner!'

(6) 私_ すし_ 大好き！ 'I like sushi!'

This is the reason for its more frequent occurrence in casual conversation. Speakers are normally in a close relationship in casual conversation, and are allowed to expose their feelings/emotions more strongly and in a straightforward manner to the hearer, while this is not the case in a formal situation.

(7) 私は すしが 好きです。 ↑ more formal ; less strong emotion

(8) 私_ すし_ 好きですよ。

(9) 私_ すし_ 大好き！ ↓ more casual ; stronger emotion

(All have the meaning 'I like sushi'.)

Difficult for nouns in contrastive relation: Particle omission does not normally occur when the particle marks a noun phrase that is in a contrastive relationship with other noun phrases:

(10) まさとは 行(い)くけど、 私(わたし)は 行(い)かない。 'Masato will go (there), but I won't go.'

However, if the sentence involves a strong expression of the speaker's feeling/emotions, the particle may be omitted even in this case:

(11) まさと_ 行(い)くけど、 私(わたし)_ 行(い)かないよ！ 'Masato will go (there), but I won't!'

We will practise particle omission further throughout this textbook, especially when we learn casual expressions in later lessons. But, in the current lesson, we focus on identifying particles that may be omitted.

### 自然(しぜん)な日本語(にほんご)：練習(れんしゅう) 1

**Underline the particles which may be omitted.**

(れい) 私(わたし)は いま 大学(だいがく)で 日本語(にほんご)を 勉強(べんきょう)しています。

(1) まさと君(くん)は エレナ(えれな)と 町(まち)で コーヒー(こーひー)を 飲(の)んでいますよ。

(2) シドニー(しどにー)で 新(あたら)しい かばんを 買(か)いましたよ。

(3) 私(わたし)は 9時(じ)から 10時半(じはん)まで クラス(くらす)が あります。

(4) あした 鈴木先生(すずきせんせい)に 電話(でんわ)を して ください。

(5) まさと君(くん)は 日本(にほん)に 行(い)かないと 思(おも)う。

### 自然(しぜん)な日本語(にほんご)：練習(れんしゅう) 2

**Rewrite the following sentences in Japanese with particles omitted whenever applicable. Use polite (i.e. *Desu-Masu*) endings, but feel free to strongly express the emotion that is involved in the sentence.**

(1) I won't go to school!

(2) I won't see Okada-san any more!

(3) I won't watch this movie.

(4) Tanaka-san has come!

(5) I like fish a lot.

(6) I wrote a letter to Tanaka-san yesterday.

(7) This movie was really interesting, wasn't it?

(8) Mika-san did not come to school yesterday.

## 表現(ひょうげん) Expression Notes

### 1 Expressing one's experience: ～た ことが あります／ありません

☛ '[Verb]た ことが ある' is used to express one's experience; 'I have done such and such a thing', 'I have the experience of doing such and such'.

(1) 私(わたし)は 日本(にほん)に 行(い)った ことが あります（ありません）。
'I have (have not) been to Japan.'

(2) A: 日本(にほん)に 行(い)った ことが ありますか。 'Have you ever been to Japan?'
B: はい、あります。 ／ いいえ、ありません。
'Yes, I have.' 'No, I haven't.'

### 表現(ひょうげん) 練習(れんしゅう) 1

**Make up sentences that are related to the pictures, using ～た ことが あります. There is more than one possibility in most cases.**

(れい) 京都(きょうと)に 行(い)った ことが あります。

(e.g.) 京都(きょうと)

(1) すし sushi

(2) 時代劇(じだいげき) *samurai* drama

(3) お酒(さけ) Sake

(4) 日本(にほん)の小説(しょうせつ) Japanese novel

(5) サーフィン(さーふぃん) surfing

## 2 一番(いちばん)～ 'the most ….'

[1] ☛ 一番(いちばん) literally means 'number one'. It may be used in a superlative expression which means 'the most ~' or 'the best'. It is normally followed by an adjective; or by some adverbs (e.g. たくさん 'a lot', よく 'frequently, often') further followed by a verb (e.g. 私(わたし)が 一番(いちばん) たくさん 食(た)べました 'I ate it the most').

[2] ☛ The range of items (things or people) in a comparison is marked by で.

(1) 日本(にほん)で 富士山(ふじさん)が 一番(いちばん) 高(たか)いです。 'Mt. Fuji is the highest in Japan.'

(2) たかしが クラス(くらす)で 一番(いちばん) 背(せ)が 高(たか)いです。 'Takashi is the tallest in the class.'

(3) シドニー(しどにー)が オーストラリア(おーすとらりあ)で 一番(いちばん) 大(おお)きいです。 'Sydney is the biggest (city) in Australia.'

**表現(ひょうげん) 練習(れんしゅう) 2**

**Make up a sentence for each picture as in the example, using 一番(いちばん).**

(れい) 富士山(ふじさん)が 日本(にほん)で 一番(いちばん) 高(たか)いです。

(e.g.) Mt. Fuji / in Japan

(1) this car

(2) air plane

(3) Australia

(4) this watch / in this shop

(5) Mayumi / in my class

## 3 〜と 思います 'I think that .....'

**[1]** ☛ This is a useful expression when a speaker expresses his/her thoughts about something that he/she is not certain of; it is often used even when the speaker is certain, in order to soften his/her assertiveness (e.g. これから 日本の社会について 話したいと 思います 'Now I will talk about Japanese society (*literally*: Now I think I will talk about Japanese society)').

**[2]** ☛ [.......... **plain form**] と 思う

contents Q.M. think (Q.M.= quotation marker)

Within the content clause (what the speaker is thinking of), predicates are always in the plain form; the different level of politeness is expressed in the main verb (e.g. 思う *vs.* 思います).

(1) 田中さんは あした 学校に 来る（来ない）と 思います。

'I think that Tanaka-san will come (not come) to school tomorrow.'

(2) 田中さんは きのう 日本に 行った（行かなかった）と 思います。

'I think that Tanaka-san went (did not go) to Japan yesterday.'

(3) この映画は おもしろい（おもしろくない）と 思います。

'I think that this movie is (is not) interesting.'

(4) この 車 は 高かった（高くなかった）と 思います。

'I think that this car was (was not) expensive.'

(5) このいすは 楽だ（楽ではない）と 思います。

'I think that this chair is (is not) comfortable.'

(6) スミスさんは アメリカ人だ（ではない）と 思います。

'I think that Mr Smith is (is not) an American.'

(7) 田中さんは きょねん 学生だった（ではなかった）と 思います。

'I think that Tanaka-san was (was not) a student last year.'

**[3]** ☛ This expression is basically restricted to the speaker's own thoughts (or the hearer's when used in a question); a third person's thought is expressed as 〜と 思っている.

(8) まさとは あした 雨が 降ると 思っています。

'Masato thinks that it will rain tomorrow.'

(9) 木村さんは 田中さんが 学生だと 思っています。

'Kimura-san thinks that Tanaka-san is a student.'

## 表現練習 3

**Rewrite the following sentences in Japanese. Use 〜と 思います.**

(れい) I think Tanaka-san is a student. → 田中さんは 学生だと 思います。

(1) I think that Tanaka-san is going to buy a new car.

(2) I think that Tanaka-san didn't go to Sydney yesterday.

(3) I think that Kimura-san was a student last year.

(4) I think that this car is not so expensive.

(5) I think that the test was easy. (use 簡単だ 'easy, simple')

(6) I think that Tanaka-san is the tallest in the class.

# 対話 Communicative Exchanges

## 対話練習 1

**Pre-task: た forms; 〜た ことが あります**

(i) In pairs, ask your partner whether or not he/she has ever experienced the things or situations that are indicated by the words in [ ].
(ii) If he/she has, further ask his/her opinion or impression of the experience, as in the example.
(iii) When you have finished asking/answering the questions, change the roles.

(e.g.)
A: すしを 食べた ことが ありますか。
B: はい、(食べた ことが) あります。or いいえ、(食べた ことが) ありません。
A: そうですか。どうでしたか。 or そうですか。 (Move to next question)
B: おいしかったです。／おいしく ありませんでした。

(e.g.) [すし]

(1) [日本のまんが]

(2) [日本語でE メール]

(3) [BBQ]

(4) [カラオケ]

(5) [サーフィン]

(6) [ディズニーランド]

(7)

| |
|---|
| Make up your own question |

(8)

| |
|---|
| Make up your own question |

## 対話練習 2

**Pre-task: ～と思います**

(i) In pairs, ask your partner about his/her opinion or impression of the things, situations or people that are illustrated in the picture, using ~と思いますか 'Do you think~?'.

(ii) For the answers, you can choose a word from [ ], or make up your own expression.

(iii) When you have finished asking/answering the questions, change the roles.

Questions have the structure, [.... plain form (without か)] と 思いますか, in which か appears at the end of sentence, and not in the embedded clause.

(e.g.) 田中さんは 行きますか。 → 田中さんは 行くと思いますか。
'Would Tanaka-san go (there)?' 'Do you think Tanaka-san would go (there)?'

The embedded clause may include a question word (Q.W.):
→ [...Q.W... plain form (without か)] と 思いますか。

(e.g.) いま 何時ですか。 → いま 何時だと 思いますか。
'What time is it now?' 'What time do you think it is now?'

| | |
|---|---|
| (e.g.)<br> | A: あした 晴(は)れると 思(おも)いますか。<br>Do you think that it will be fine tomorrow?<br>B: いいえ、雨(あめ)が 降(ふ)ると 思(おも)います。<br>[ 晴(は)れる clear, 雨(あめ)が 降(ふ)る rain, 曇(くも)る get cloudy ] |
| (1)<br><br> | A: __________<br>Do you think Tanaka-san will come to the party tomorrow?<br>B: __________<br>[ はい, いいえ, わからない don't know ] |
| (2)<br><br> | A: __________<br>What do you think Nakamura-san's occupation is?<br>B: __________<br>[ 医者(いしゃ) doctor, 科学者(かがくしゃ) scientist, 床屋(とこや) barber ] |
| (3)<br><br> | A: __________<br>Where do you think Suzuki-san has been?<br>B: __________<br>[ 香港(ほんこん), ハワイ(はわい) Hawaii, イギリス(いぎりす), カナダ(かなだ) ] |
| (4)<br> | A: __________<br>How do you think the food was?<br>B: __________<br>[ おいしい, まずい, 高(たか)い, 安(やす)い] |
| (5)<br> | A: __________<br>What do you think is the most interesting place in Japan?<br>B: __________<br>[ 東京(とうきょう), 京都(きょうと), 大阪(おおさか), 横浜(よこはま), 札幌(さっぽろ) ] |

## 対話作り Comprehensive Exercises

✍ **In pairs, create a dialogue for the given situation. Please feel free to ask the instructor if you have any questions about Japanese expressions for your dialogue.**

> **Situation:**
>
> You are thinking of doing the following activities. Obtain some information on these activities from your friend. You may choose one from the following:
>
> (i) Going on a trip during summer holidays
> (ii) Starting a new sport

Please incorporate the following expressions in your dialogue:

- ～た ことが あります／ありません
- ～と 思います
- 一番 [adjectives]

Also please omit particles whenever applicable. In the following sample dialogue, the particles which can be omitted are specified by □.

**[Sample Dialogue]** You are thinking of cooking dinner for the party next weekends.

エレナ： まさとさん、日本料理[を] 作った こと[が] ありますか。
まさと： もちろん ありますよ。 (もちろん of course)
エレナ： 今度の 週末、日本人の友達と 家で パーティーを します。どんな 日本料理が いいと 思いますか。
まさと： 肉じゃがは どうですか。一番 簡単だと 思いますよ。 (肉じゃが Nikujaga)
エレナ： そうですか。じゃあ、 作り方[を] 教えてください。
まさと： いいですよ。

| | |
|---|---|
| Elena: | Masato, have you ever cooked Japanese food? |
| Masato: | Of course I have. |
| Elena: | Next weekend I will have a party at my place with my friends. What kind of Japanese food do you think is good? |
| Masato: | How about 'Nikujaga'? I think it's the easiest one to cook. |
| Elena: | I see. Well, please tell me how to cook it. |
| Masato: | Sure. |

## 知ってた？ Did you know?

## 日本について　'Some facts about Japan'

### 調べましょう Research

**Complete the table below. You may search the necessary information in the internet.**

| | 日本 Japan | [ ] (Your country) |
|---|---|---|
| 面積 size of land | | |
| 人口 population | | |
| 国花 national flower | | |
| 首都 capital city | | |
| 一番 大きい 都市 biggest city | | |
| 一番 高い 山 highest mountain | | |
| 一番 長い 川 longest river | | |
| 公式言語 official language | | |
| その他の言語 other languages used | | |

### 発表しましょう Present

**Present in Japanese to your group what you have found above.**

(e.g.1)　日本の面積は 377,835 $km^2$ で、人口は約1億2600万人です。

(e.g.2)　日本で 一番 高い山は 富士山です。

## 新(あたら)しい単語(たんご)・表現(ひょうげん) New Vocabulary & Expressions

(Basic words/expressions are marked with '*')

| | |
|---|---|
| 雨(あめ)* | rain |
| 移住者(いじゅうしゃ) | immigrants |
| 一番(いちばん)* | first, best, most |
| 妹(いもうと) * | younger sister |
| 思(おも)う* | think |
| 返(かえ)す* | return (something) |
| 帰(かえ)る* | go back, return |
| 科学者(かがくしゃ) | scientist |
| [noun]から* | from |
| カラオケ(からおけ) | karaoke |
| カレーライス(かれーらいす) | curry rice |
| 川(かわ)* | river |
| キロ(きろ) | kilometre, kilogram |
| 国(くに)* | nation, country |
| 曇(くも)る | to get cloudy |
| くらい／ぐらい* | about / approximately |
| クラス(くらす)* | class |
| 公式言語(こうしきげんご) | official language |
| 声(こえ)* | voice |
| 国花(こっか) | national flower |
| ご飯(はん)* | meal |
| 魚(さかな) | fish |
| 叫(さけ)ぶ* | shout |
| 時代劇(じだいげき) | samurai drama |
| 社会(しゃかい)* | society |
| 首都(しゅと) | capital city |
| 小説(しょうせつ) * | novel |
| 人口(じんこう) | population |
| 背(せ)が 低(ひく)い／高(たか)い* | short/tall (people) |
| その他(た) | others |
| そんなに | that much, that many |
| 大好(だいす)き(な)* | like a lot |
| 作(つく)り方(かた) | how to make/cook |
| 手(て)* | hand |
| 床屋(とこや) | barber |
| 都市(とし) | city |
| 肉(にく)じゃが | Nikujaga (Japanese food made with beef, potato and ginger) |
| 乗(の)る* | get on, board, ride |
| 歯(は)* | teeth, tooth |
| 晴(は)れる | to become clear |
| ハワイ(はわい) | Hawaii |
| 降(ふ)る* | fall (rain/snow) |
| 棒(ぼう) | stick, rod |
| 真面目(まじめ)(な) * | diligent, hard-working |
| 磨(みが)く* | clean, polish |
| 店(みせ)* | shop |
| 面積(めんせき) | size of land |
| 持(も)つ* | to hold |
| 横浜(よこはま) | Yokohama |

# 第11課(だいじゅういっか)

## つまらないものですが…
## It's a little something...

[Elena has come to visit her friend Masato in Japan. She arrived at Tokyo International Airport, Masato came to pick her up, and they are both now at his home.]

[At Masato's house]

まさと：　ただいま。お母(かあ)さん、エレナさんだよ。

まさとの母(はは)：　おかえり。

まさと：　僕(ぼく)の母(はは)です。

エレナ：　はじめまして。エレナと申(もう)します。よろしくお願(ねが)いします。

まさとの母(はは)：　はじめまして。まさとの母(はは)です。こちらこそ、よろしく。さあさあ、どうぞ、あがってください。

エレナ：　おじゃまします。

[In a Japanese-style room]

まさとの母(はは)：　長旅(ながたび)で、疲(つか)れたでしょう。

エレナ：　いえ、大丈夫(だいじょうぶ)です。あの、これ、つまらないものですが…。

まさとの母(はは)：　あら、まあ、そんな…。

エレナ：　お口(くち)に合(あ)うかどうかわかりませんが…。

まさとの母(はは)：　すみません、気(き)をつかっていただいて。

エレナ：　いいえ。

まさとの母(はは)：　こちらにどうぞ。すぐに、お茶(ちゃ)をいれますね。

エレナ：　どうぞ、おかまいなく。

まさとの母(はは)：　今(いま)、食事(しょくじ)の用意(ようい)をしていますから、しばらくここでゆっくりしていてくださいね。

エレナ：　ありがとうございます。

[Dinner is ready]

19 まさとの母(はは)：　じゃあ、簡単(かんたん)なものですけど、どうぞ。
20 エレナ：　わあ、おいしそう。いただきます。
(Elena has finished her bowl of rice.)
21 まさとの母(はは)：　エレナさん、おかわりいかがですか？
22 エレナ：　いえ、もうおなかいっぱいです。ごちそうさまでした。
23 まさとの母(はは)：　いいえ、おそまつさまでした。

## 単語(たんご)と表現(ひょうげん) Vocabulary and Expressions (Dialogue)

| | | | | | |
|---|---|---|---|---|---|
| 3 | 母(はは) | One's own mother | 15 | おかまいなく | don't bother |
| 6 | あがる | enter one's house | 16 | 食事(しょくじ) | meal |
| 8 | 長旅(ながたび) | long trip | 16 | 用意(ようい) | preparation |
| 9 | つまらない | boring, trivial | 16 | ゆっくりする | relax |
| 11 | 口(くち)に合(あ)う | suitable for one's taste | 21 | おかわり | another |
| 11 | ～かどうか | whether or not …. | 22 | おなか | stomach |
| 12 | 気(き)をつかう | to take care, worry | 22 | いっぱい | full |
| 23 | おそまつさまでした | It was nothing at all | | | |

### Dialogue in English

**[At Masato's house]**

1 M: I'm home! Mother, this is Elena.
2 MM: Hi. (Welcome home)
3 M: This is my mother.
4 E: How do you do? I'm Elena. Nice to meet you.
5-6 MM: How do you do? I'm Masato's mother. Nice to meet you too. Please enter.
7 E: Thank you.

**[In a Japanese-style room]**

8 MM: You must be tired after such a long trip.
9 E: No, I'm okay. Well, this is a little something… (I've brought for you).
10 MM: Oh, no, such a…(you shouldn't have).
11 E: I don't know if you like it but…
12 MM: Thank you for your consideration.
13 E: No (problem).
14 MM: Please come this way. I'll make some tea.
15 E: Don't bother… (yourself on my account)
16 MM: I'm getting dinner ready, so please relax
17 here for a while.
18 E: Thank you.

**[Dinner is ready]**

MM = Masato's mother

19 MM: We don't have much to offer, but please.
20 E: Wow, it looks delicious! Thank you.
(Elena finishes her bowl of rice.)
21 MM: Elena, would you like another bowl of rice?
22 E: No, thank you. I'm already full. Thank you for the meal.
23 MM: It was nothing at all.

## 文(ぶん)法(ぽう) Grammar

### 1. 〜でしょう

**Formation rule**

〜でしょう is basically used with plain forms of predicates, except for the case of the non-past copula (〜だ). 〜だ drops in this case.

| | Non-past | Past |
|---|---|---|
| Verbs | 食(た)べるでしょう<br>食(た)べないでしょう | 食(た)べたでしょう<br>食(た)べなかったでしょう |
| い-adjectives | 高(たか)いでしょう<br>高(たか)くないでしょう | 高(たか)かったでしょう<br>高(たか)くなかったでしょう |
| Copula な-adj. | 静(しず)かでしょう<br>静(しず)かではないでしょう | 静(しず)かだったでしょう<br>静(しず)かではなかったでしょう |
| Nouns | 学生(がくせい)でしょう<br>学生(がくせい)ではないでしょう | 学生(がくせい)だったでしょう<br>学生(がくせい)ではなかったでしょう |

**1.1. Probability: 'probably, must be'**

〜でしょう indicates the relatively strong belief of the speaker.

(1) あした、雨(あめ)が降(ふ)るでしょう。 It will probably rain tomorrow.

(2) 東京(とうきょう)は、いま、あまり寒(さむ)くないでしょう。 It is probably not so cold in Tokyo now.

(3) 田中(たなか)さんは、たぶんパーティーに行(い)かなかったでしょう。
Tanaka-san probably did not go to the party.

〜でしょう is not normally used towards seniors: It would sound as if the speaker was imposing his/her belief onto the listener. Other expressions such as 〜と思(おも)います are preferably used in such a case.

(4) A: あした、天気(てんき)はどうでしょうか。(What is your opinion about the weather tomorrow?)

B: 雨(あめ)が降(ふ)ると思(おも)います。 I think it will rain.

(?雨(あめ)が降(ふ)るでしょう。It will probably rain. (and you should believe it))

**文法練習 1**

**Look at the following pictures and tell tomorrow's weather and temperature as a meteorologist.**

(例) あした、東京は雨が降るでしょう。気温は１２度ぐらいで、涼しいでしょう。

| | | | | |
|---|---|---|---|---|
| 雨 rain; 雨が降る to rain (literally 'fall rain') | | | 雪 snow; 雪が降る to snow | |
| 晴れ sunny, fine | くもり cloudy | 台風 typhoon | 気温 temperature | |
| 度 degree | 暖かい warm | 暑い hot | 涼しい cool | 寒い cold |

(e.g.) 東京　(1) 札幌

(2) 大阪　(3) 福岡

(4) 広島　(5) 青森

**1.2. Empathy, Seeking agreement: 'You must be …', 'It must be …'**

～でしょう may be used to check if your conversation partner agrees that your understanding is correct. In such a situation, a rising intonation is used and it is often shortened to でしょ. This phrase is used to seek agreement or sometimes show empathy.

(1) 疲れたでしょう。　You must be tired (I suppose).

(2) テスト、たいへんだったでしょう。 The test must have been difficult.

**文法練習(ぶんぽうれんしゅう) 2**

**Make an empathetic comment to the other person in the following situations using 〜でしょう. Make additional phrases, as in the example, wherever possible.**

(例(れい)) [ Your friend has just finished a big test.]

→ <u>お疲(つか)れさまでした。テスト、たいへんだったでしょう。</u>

(1) [ Your friend has just finished his/her hard work. ]

(2) [ Your friend is carrying a heavy box. ]

(3) [ It is very cold outside. Your friend has just come back from work and looks cold. ]

(4) [ It is summer. Your housemate has just come home by foot and is sweaty. ]

(5) [ You found some restaurant that is really good. You suggested it to your friend and she had dinner there last night. You have just met your friend. ]

(6) [ There were sounds of gun shots last night near your friend's house. She is living alone. You have just met your friend. ]

(7) [ Your friend has just come back from her first driving practice. ]

(8) [ Your friend worked over night as she had to complete her long essay by today. ]

**1.3. In polite questions**

〜でしょうか is also used in polite questions:

| | | |
|---|---|---|
| (1) | あの建物(たてもの)は何(なん)でしょうか。 | What is that building? |
| (2) | コンサートは何時(なんじ)でしょうか。 | What time is the concert? |
| (3) | 田中(たなか)さんは学生(がくせい)でしょうか。 | Is Tanaka-san a student? |
| (4) | テストはいつでしょうか。 | When is the test? |
| (5) | お手洗(てあら)いはどこでしょうか。 | Where is the toilet? |

## 2. ～から Reason, cause: '… so, …', 'Since …'

**Formation rule**

～から is used with plain forms of predicates. ～だ appears in the case of the non-past copula.

| | | Non-past | Past |
|---|---|---|---|
| Verbs | | 食べるから<br>食べないから | 食べたから<br>食べなかったから |
| い-adjectives | | 高いから<br>高くないから | 高かったから<br>高くなかったから |
| Copula | な-adj. | 静かだから<br>静かでは(じゃ)ないから | 静かだったから<br>静かでは(じゃ)なかったから |
| | Nouns | 学生だから<br>学生では(じゃ)ないから | 学生だったから<br>学生では(じゃ)なかったから |

**Note:** Polite forms (～ます／～です) may also be used for further polite feeling.

(例) 食べますから； 食べましたから； 食べませんから etc.

(例) 学生ですから； 学生でしたから； 学生ではありませんから etc.

**2.1.** から is used to give the reason for, or the cause of, a situation, a proposal, and so on. から always appears at the end of the 'reason' clause.

| ～ (reason) から、(result, situation, proposal, etc)。 |
|---|

(1) あした、テストがあるから、今日は勉強します。

Because we will have an exam tomorrow, I will study today.

(2) この映画は見たから、あれを見ましょう。

I watched this movie, so let us watch that one.

**Note:** ～から may be attached directly to a noun or the て form for different meaning. Compare each pair:

(例) 3月だから 'Because it's March, …' *vs.* 3月から 'from March'

(例) 食べたから 'Because I have eaten, …' *vs.* 食べてから 'after eating'

## 文法練習 3

**Rewrite the following sentences in Japanese using ～から.**

(例) It is cold, so please close the window. → <u>寒いから、窓を閉めてください。</u>

(1) Because it is Sunday today, I will not go to school.

(2) Because I don't have a car, I will go to Sydney by bus.

(3) I didn't buy the bag, because it was expensive.

(4) It is nice weather today, so let us go to the park.

(5) I like Japanese animation, so I have watched all (of them). (all ぜんぶ)

**2.2.** In speech, the following order is very common and sounds less abrupt.

| (result, situation, proposal, etc)。～ (reason) から。 |
|---|

(1) 車で行きましょう。雨ですから。 Let's go by car. Because it's raining.

(2) こちらへどうぞ。お茶を入れましたから。 Please come in. The tea is ready.

## 文法練習 4

**Rewrite the following sentences in Japanese. Use the から clause as in the example.**

(例) I will not go to the party today. (Because) I have a test tomorrow.

→ <u>きょうはパーティーに行きません。あしたテストですから。</u>

(1) I will eat now. (Because) I am hungry.

(2) I will study tonight at home. (Because) there will be a test soon. (soon もうすぐ)

(3) I will go to the coast (sea). (Because) I am now on holiday.

(4) I will sleep. (Because) I am tired.

## 自然な日本語 Natural Conversation Notes

### 1. Clause omission

It is common in Japanese conversation to leave out parts of a sentence when speaking. A good example of this is the concluding clause which is often omitted. This can also happen when one is making a proposal or request, giving a negative opinion or answer, and so forth, as shown in the examples below.

(1) A: お茶、もし よかったら… Tea, if you like it…(please have some).

B: あ、すみません。じゃあ、いただきます。 Oh, thank you. I'll have it.

(2) A: あした、映画に 行きましょうか。 Shall we go to the movies tomorrow?

B: すみません、あしたは ちょっと…

Sorry, but tomorrow is a bit… (inconvenient for me and so I can't go).

The use of such clause omission is a useful strategy for delivering remarks more softly to the listener: moreover, the speech no longer sounds too imposing, direct or obtrusive.

#### 自然な日本語：練習 1

**Write an appropriate sentence including a clause omission for each situation. Each question has more than one possibility.**

(例) [You want to ask some questions to the listener.] (use ～たい)

→ ちょっと 聞きたいことが あるんですが…

(1) [You are invited to a party tomorrow, but you cannot go.]

(2) [You are invited to a movie on Sunday, but you cannot make it on Sunday.]

(3) [You have made tea and want to offer it to the person you are addressing.]

(4) [You want to return home, and ask for permission.] (use ～たい)

(5) [You are giving a gift to the listener.]

## 2. Exclaimers

あら, あれ, わあ, まあ are used as interjections expressing the speaker's surprise. あら and まあ are in principle used by women. あら, あれ are used for a relatively small surprise and まあ, わあ are used for a more forceful exclamation.

| | | |
|---|---|---|
| (1) | あら、田中(たなか)さん、こんにちは。 | Oh, Tanaka-san! Hello. |
| (2) | あれ、雨(あめ)が降(ふ)っていますよ。 | Oh, it's raining! |
| (3) | わあ、これは重(おも)い！ | Oh, this is heavy! |
| (4) | まあ、すてき！ | Oh, that's wonderful! |

**自然(しぜん)な日本語(にほんご)：練習(れんしゅう) 2**

**Make an appropriate statement for each situation. Include an interjection.**

(例(れい)) [You received chocolates from your friend on your birthday.]

→ わあ、おいしそう！　ありがとう。

(1) [You received beautiful flowers from your friend on your birthday.]

(2) [You happened to see your neighbor, Yamada-san, at a supermarket.]

(3) [You saw a very big apple which looked delicious.]

(4) [You've heard a very big noise.]

(5) [You tasted sake and found it was really nice.]

## 表現(ひょうげん) Expression Notes

### 1 ～ている (Progressive)

**[1]** ☛ [Verb]て form plus いる (polite ています) indicates that an action/event expressed by the verb is in progress (NB. ている may also be used for the 'result' meaning, depending basically on the verb type. Refer to a later lesson for details of this usage.).

(1) 田中さんは 家で 寝ています。 Tanaka-san is sleeping at home.

(2) わたしは 日本語を 勉強しています。 I am studying Japanese.

(3) 山下さんは いま 喫茶店で 友達と 話しています。
Yamashita-san is talking with his friend in the coffee shop now.

**[2]** ☛ Affirmative-negative and past-non-past distinctions are expressed by changing ている.

| | | | |
|---|---|---|---|
| [Present] | Affirmative | 田中さんは ねています。<br>(plain ねている) | Mr. Tanaka **is sleeping.** |
| | Negative | 田中さんは ねていません。<br>(plain ねていない) | Mr. Tanaka **is not sleeping.** |
| [Past] | Affirmative | 田中さんは ねていました。<br>(plain ねていた) | Mr. Tanaka **was sleeping.** |
| | Negative | 田中さんは ねていませんでした。<br>(plain ねていなかった) | Mr. Tanaka **was not sleeping.** |

**[3]** ☛ In response to a question which ends with ～ていますか, you have to repeat the main verb, and not just います.

(1) A: 田中さんは 本を 読んでいますか。 Is Tanaka-san reading a book?

B: はい、読んでいます。／ いいえ、読んでいません。

Yes, (he) is reading (a book). No, (he) is not reading (a book).

## 表現練習 1

**Change the following verbs into ～ています form.**

(例) (読む) 読みます → 読んでいます

(1) (話す) 話します (2) (買う) 買います (3) (待つ) 待ちます

(4) (泳ぐ) 泳ぎます (5) (遊ぶ) 遊びます (6) (走る) 走ります

(7) (書く) 書きます (8) (聞く) 聞きます (9) (食べる) 食べます

(10) (見る) 見ます (11) (勉強する) 勉強します (12) (歩く) 歩きます

## 表現練習 2

(ひょうげん れんしゅう)

**Rewrite the following sentences in Japanese. Use the ～ている form.**

(例) Kimura-san is learning English in London.

→ 木村(きむら)さんは ロンドンで 英語(えいご)を 習(なら)っています。

(1) I am now eating dinner at home.

(2) Tanaka-san is studying in the library now.

(3) Yamada-san is waiting for her friend.

(4) The teacher is writing kanji.

(5) My younger brother is playing in the park.

(6) Okada-san is not drinking coffee now.

(7) Suzuki-san was writing a letter.

(8) Nomura-san was watching TV at home at 10 o'clock last night.

## 2 Various expressions used when visiting one's house

**[1]** ☛ • ごめんください 'Excuse me; Hello' (*lit.* 'Sorry to bother you'); Typical expression used when you visit someone's house alone.

• いらっしゃい； いらっしゃいませ (formal) 'Welcome.'

**[2]** ☛ • つまらないものですが… 'It's a little something but ….' Typical expression used when one offers a gift. The expression in this case is usually incomplete, omitting the rest of the phrase which implies 'take this' or 'please accept this'.

• お口(くち)にあうかどうかわかりませんが… 'I don't know if you like it, but…' This is used when one gives food as a gift. 口(くち)にあう literally means 'suitable for one's mouth'. Of course, even though the giver has carefully chosen the gift, this expression is still used to show humbleness.

**[3]** ☛ • ごちそうさまでした 'It was delicious.' When you have finished your meal.

• おそまつさまでした 'It was a poor meal (Host's typical response to the above).'

**[4]** ☛ These expressions are used as ways to show the speaker's humility. Being humble by belittling oneself or one's gift, meal, and so on is an important part of being polite in Japanese culture.

## 3 ～かどうか 'whether or not ....'

[plain form] ～かどうか nominalises a yes/no question, and may be used with various expressions. The non-past copula ～だ is often dropped in the case of a noun and な-adjective (cf. (4) and (5) below).

(1) 田中さんが来るかどうか、知っていますか。

'Do you know whether or not Tanaka-san will come?'

(2) 田中さんがきょう忙しいかどうか、知りません。

'I don't know whether or not Tanaka-san is busy today'

(3) 田中さんが日本に帰ったかどうか、山田さんに聞いてください。

'Please ask Yamada-san whether or not Tanaka-san has gone back to Japan.'

(4) 松本さんが元気かどうか、教えてください。

'Please tell (*lit.* teach) me whether or not Matsumoto-san is in good health.'

(5) これが 先生の本かどうか、調べました。

'I checked whether or not this was the teacher's book.'

### 表現練習 3

**Rewrite the following sentences in Japanese.**

(例) I am not sure whether or not this book is interesting.

→ <u>この本が おもしろいかどうか、わかりません。</u>

(1) Do you know whether or not John passed the exam?

(2) I am not sure whether or not this is my book.

(3) I don't know whether or not the library is far.

(4) Do you know whether or not we have class next week?

(5) Do you know whether or not Tanaka-san has already had (eaten) lunch?

(6) I will check whether or not there are seats available. (席 seat)

(7) I am not sure if this answer is correct. (正しい correct)

## 4 Kinship terms

| | Someone else's family | Own family | | Someone else's family | Own family |
|---|---|---|---|---|---|
| Father | お父(とう)さん | 父(ちち) | Husband | ご主人(しゅじん) | 主人(しゅじん)／夫(おっと) |
| Mother | お母(かあ)さん | 母(はは) | Wife | 奥(おく)さん | 家内(かない)／妻(つま) |
| Older brother | お兄(にい)さん | 兄(あに) | Grandfather | おじいさん | 祖父(そふ) |
| Older sister | お姉(ねえ)さん | 姉(あね) | Grandmother | おばあさん | 祖母(そぼ) |
| Younger brother | 弟(おとうと)さん | 弟(おとうと) | Grandchild | おまごさん | まご |
| Younger sister | 妹(いもうと)さん | 妹(いもうと) | Child | お子(こ)さん | うちの子(こ) |

### 表現(ひょうげん)練習(れんしゅう)4

**Rewrite the following sentences in Japanese.**

(例(れい)) My father is a bank employee. → 父(ちち)は 銀行員(ぎんこういん)です。

(1) My mother is a public servant.

(2) Where is your wife now?

(3) Which school is your child going to?

(4) My grandmother is watching TV.

(5) What is your elder brother's hobby?

(6) My husband is a company worker.

(7) My grandfather is in London now.

(8) How old is your younger sister?

## 対話 Communicative Exchanges

### 対話練習 1

**Pre-task:** Kinship terms

(i) Let's talk about family members. For the purpose of practice, you can make up information about your own family members, using the role-play card below.

(ii) Fill in the blanks in [Role card A] for your own family members. Use [Role card B] to write down information of your conversation partner's family members.

(ii) In pairs, ask each other about his/her family members, as in the example.

(例) A: お父さんは何歳ですか。

B: 父は５３歳です。

A: そうですか。どこに住んでいますか。

B: 父は中国に住んでいます。 [continued]

**Role card A – Own family**

| | Age | Where they live | Occupation | Hobby |
|---|---|---|---|---|
| Father | (e.g.) 60 | (e.g.) Australia | | |
| Mother | | | | |
| Elder brother | | | | |
| Younger brother | | | | |
| Elder sister | | | | |
| Younger sister | | | | |

**Role card B – Your conversation partner's family**

| | Age | Where they live | Occupation | Hobby |
|---|---|---|---|---|
| Father | (e.g.) 53 | (e.g.) China | | |
| Mother | | | | |
| Elder brother | | | | |
| Younger brother | | | | |
| Elder sister | | | | |
| Younger sister | | | | |

## 対話練習(たいわれんしゅう) 2

**Pre-task: 〜ている**

(i) Randomly give a name to the person in each picture below. You must use the names in the list below. Your conversation partner will do the same, and so will possibly have a different name for the same picture.

(ii) In pairs, find out what name your partner gave to each picture, by asking what each named person is doing, as in the example.

| 山本(やまもと) | 田中(たなか) | 木村(きむら) | 岡田(おかだ) | 野村(のむら) | 山田(やまだ) | 坂田(さかだ) | 鈴木(すずき) | 佐藤(さとう) |
|---|---|---|---|---|---|---|---|---|

(例(れい)) You: 山本(やまもと)さんは いま 何(なに)をしていますか。

Y.P.: 家(いえ)で 寝(ね)ています。

[Write down the name given by you on the left side of '||' and by your partner on the right.]

| | | |
|---|---|---|
| [home]  | [room]  | [home]  |
| \|\| | \|\| | \|\| 山本(やまもと) |
| [pool in town]  | [shopping in town]  | [part-time work in town]  |
| \|\| | \|\| | \|\| |
| [home]  |   [town] | [tennis court in university]  |
| \|\| | \|\| | \|\| |

## 対話練習3

**Pre-task: ～ている**

**Your conversation partner is traveling all over the world. Now, you and your partner are talking on the phone. Practice the conversation as in the example below, changing the underlined parts. Expand your conversation, by making up your own answers.**

(例) A: いま どこに いますか。

B: 日本(にほん)に います。

A; 何(なに)をしていますか。

B: <u>すもうを見(み)ています。</u>

A: <u>わあ、いいですね。</u>

Japan

(1) Canada

(2) Paris

(3) Australia

(4) Tokyo

(5) Hawaii

(6) Egypt

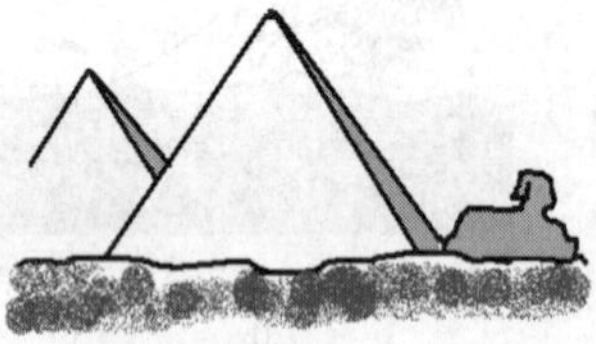

(7) Samoa

(8) Hong Kong

(9)

You decide a place and an activity that you are currently doing.

## 対話作り Comprehensive Exercises

✍ **In pairs, create a dialogue for the given situation. Please feel free to ask the instructor if you have any questions about Japanese expressions for your dialogue.**

**Situation:**

You are invited to the home of a Japanese family. You talk with your host in the following four situations:

[1] At the gate/genkan

[2] At the tea table: You give a gift; the host offers and serves tea.

[3] At the dinner table: You are having a conversation over dinner; include typical expressions in serving dinner, complements, offering another serving of food, and so on. While eating, talk about each other's family.

[4] You are leaving now. Make appropriate closing comments.

If time is not enough to do all, you may concentrate on two above situations.

Please incorporate the following expressions/phenomena in your dialogue:

- ～でしょう／～から／～ている／～かどうか
- Various typical expressions used when visiting one's home
- Clause omission
- Kinship terms
- Exclaimers

**[Sample Dialogue] Sue visits Tanaka's place**

<u>At the gate/genkan</u>

スー： ごめんください。
田中： どなたでしょうか。
スー： あの～、スーと申しますが…。
田中： あ、スーさん。[Open the gate]
どうぞ、お入りください。
スー： こんばんは。[move to the genkan]

<u>At the gate/genkan</u>

S: Excuse me!
T: Who is it?
S: Well… it is Sue.
T: Oh, Sue-san. Please come in.
S: Good evening.

田中(たなか)：　いらっしゃい。さあ、どうぞ、あがってください。

スー：　すみません。おじゃまします。 [enter inside]

わあ、すてきな絵(え)ですね。きれい！

田中(たなか)：　いいえ、そうでもありませんよ。

さあ、ここに座(すわ)ってください。

スー：　すみません。

T: Welcome! Please come in.

S: Thank you. Excuse me.

Wow, what a wonderful painting. It's beautiful!

T: No, it's nothing. Well, please sit here.

S: Thank you.

[Sue gives a gift; Tanaka offers and serves tea] — Omitted (cf. Lesson 11 Dialogue)

<u>At the dinner table</u>

田中(たなか)：　お口(くち)に合(あ)うかどうか分(わ)かりませんが、さあ、どうぞ、食(た)べてください。

スー：　いただきます。まあ、この魚(さかな)、おいしいですね。

田中(たなか)：　そうですか。それはよかった。さあ、これも食(た)べてください。

ところで、スーさんは、何人家族(なんにんかぞく)ですか。

[They are talking about family, hobbies, etc] — Omitted (cf. Lesson 11 Dialogue)

田中(たなか)：　スーさん。おかわり、いかがですか。

スー：　いいえ、もう おなか いっぱいです。

ごちそうさまでした。

田中(たなか)：　おそまつさまでした。コーヒーは、

いかがですか。

スー：　あ、すみません。じゃあ、いただきます。

<u>Leaving</u>

スー：　そろそろ、帰(かえ)らないと…。すっかり

長居(ながい)をしてしまいました。

田中(たなか)：　そうですか。

スー：　きょうは本当(ほんとう)に楽(たの)しかったです。

田中(たなか)：　ええ、わたしも楽(たの)しかったです。

スー：　今度(こんど)、わたしの家(うち)にも遊(あそ)びに来(き)てください。

田中(たなか)：　ありがとうございます。

スー：　お邪魔(じゃま)しました。おやすみなさい。

[leave the gate]

田中(たなか)：　じゃあ、お気(き)をつけて。

<u>At the dinner table</u>

T: I hope you like it. Please begin eating.

S: I will. Wow, this fish is delicious.

T: Really? That's good. Please try this too. By the way, Sue-san, how many family members do you have?

[Talk continues for a while]

T: Sue-san. Would you like to have another bowl of rice?

S: No, thank you. I'm already full. The meal was delicious.

T: It was nothing at all. Would you like to have some coffee?

S: Oh, thank you. I will have some.

<u>Leaving</u>

S: I must go now. I've been here too long.

T: I see.

S: I really had a good time today.

T: Yes, I had a good time too.

S: Please you too visit my place next time.

T: Thank you.

S: Sorry for disturbing you. Good night.

T: Take care.

## 知(し)ってた？ Did you know?

### 日本(にほん)の家(いえ)・たたみの部屋(へや) Japanese house・Tatami-room

#### 調(しら)べましょう Research

**Find the names of the following terms/things, which are commonly found in a traditional Japanese house.**

| Item | Japanese term | Item | Japanese term |
|---|---|---|---|
| Entrance | | Corridor | |
| Garden | | Stairs | |
| Living room | | Japanese-style room | |
| Closet | | Drawing room | |
| Alcove | | Kitchen | |
| Bathroom | | Toilet | |
| Mat in living room | | Heated table | |

#### 話(はな)し合(あ)いましょう Discussions

**List three distinctive features of a Japanese house, compared with houses in your own country.**

(1)

(2)

(3)

**Useful Words/Expressions**

玄関(げんかん)　靴(くつ)をぬぐ　あがってください　スリッパ
かけじく　押(お)し入(い)れ　ふすま　しょうじ　座布団(ざぶとん)

## 新しい単語・表現 New Vocabulary & Expressions

(Basic words/expressions are marked with '*')

| | |
|---|---|
| 上がる* | go up, enter a house |
| アニメ | animation |
| いっぱい* | full |
| 運転 | driving |
| お母さん／母* | mother |
| おかえり(なさい)* | welcome back home |
| おかまいなく | do not bother |
| おかわり | another (cup/bowl/plate etc.) |
| お子さん | child (someone else's) |
| おじいさん／祖父* | grandfather |
| おじゃまします* | excuse me (when entering an office/house) |
| 夫／(ご)主人* | husband |
| お手洗い* | toilet |
| お父さん／父* | father |
| 弟／弟さん* | younger brother |
| おなか* | stomach |
| おばあさん／祖母* | grandmother |
| お孫さん／孫 | grandchildren |
| 科学 | science |
| 家内／奥さん* | wife |
| 気温* | temperature |
| 気を遣う | care about, worry |
| 口に合う | suitable for one's taste |
| くもり | cloudy |
| 歳／才* | counting word for age |
| すっかり* | completely |
| 素敵(な)* | wonderful |
| 相撲 | sumo |
| 全部* | all |
| 外* | outside |
| 祖父／おじいさん* | grandfather |
| 祖母／おばあさん* | grandmother |
| 台風 | typhoon |
| 大変(な)* | big problem, difficult |
| たぶん* | probably, perhaps |
| 疲れる* | get tired |
| 度* | degree |
| 長居 | staying (at place) long |
| 長旅 | long trip |
| ぬぐ* | take off (footwear) |
| 入る* | enter |
| 母／お母さん* | mother |
| 晴れ* | sunny, fine |
| 孫／お孫さん | grandchildren |
| 用意* | preparation |

# 第１２課（だいじゅうにか）

## ハチ公（こう）の前（まえ）だとお伝（つた）えください

## Please tell him to wait in front of *Hachiko*

[Elena is making a phone call to Masato's house]

まさとの母（はは）：　もしもし、山田（やまだ）でございます。

エレナ：　もしもし、エレナです。こんにちは。

まさとの母（はは）：　ああ、エレナさん。こんにちは。お元気（げんき）ですか。

エレナ：　ええ、おかげさまで。あの、まさと君（くん）、いらっしゃいますか。

まさとの母（はは）：　まさとですか。まさとはまだなんですよ。きょうは帰（かえ）りが遅（おそ）いと思（おも）いますよ。１１時（じ）までアルバイトがあるそうですから。

エレナ：　あ、そうですか。

まさとの母（はは）：　すみませんね。何（なに）か伝（つた）えましょうか。

エレナ：　あ、じゃあ、お願（ねが）いします。あしたのことなんですけど…。

まさとの母（はは）：　ええ。

エレナ：　待（ま）ち合（あ）わせは１２時（じ）に渋谷（しぶや）のハチ公（こう）の前（まえ）だとお伝（つた）えください。

まさとの母（はは）：　１２時（じ）に渋谷（しぶや）のハチ公（こう）の前（まえ）ですね。はい、わかりました。そう伝（つた）えますね。

エレナ：　すみません。よろしくお願（ねが）いします。じゃ、失礼（しつれい）します。

まさとの母（はは）：　はい、また。

### 単語（たんご）と表現（ひょうげん）　Vocabulary and Expressions (Dialogue)

| | | | | | |
|---|---|---|---|---|---|
| 1 | もしもし | hello (telephone) | 5 | 遅（おそ）い | late, slow |
| 4 | [name]君（くん） | term for addressing a male; more casual than 〜さん | 6 | まで | till, until |
| | | | 8 | 何（なに）か | something |
| 5 | まだ | still, (not) yet | 8 | 伝（つた）える | to tell, to convey |
| 5 | 帰（かえ）り | return(ing) | 12 | 待（ま）ち合（あ）わせ | meeting up, rendezvous |
| 4 | いらっしゃいますか　(いますか) | is/are in (there)? | | | |

**Dialogue in English**

MM = Masato's mother

| | | |
|---|---|---|
| 1 | MM: | Hello. (This is) Yamada. |
| 2 | E: | Hello, (This is) Elena speaking. Konnichiwa. |
| 3 | MM: | Oh, Elena-san. Konnichiwa. How are you doing? |
| 4 | E: | I'm fine (Thank you for asking). Well, is Masato in (at home)? |
| 5-6 | MM: | Masato? Masato hasn't come home yet. I think he'll come home late today. I heard that (he has) a part-time job till 11pm. |
| 7 | E: | Oh, I see. |
| 8 | MM: | Sorry (about that). Shall I take a message? |
| 9-10 | E: | Oh, then please. It is about tomorrow… |
| 11 | MM: | Yes. |
| 12-13 | E: | Please tell him that (our) meeting-up is at 12 noon in front of Hachiko in Shibuya. |
| 14-15 | MM: | At 12 in front of Hachiko in Shibuya, isn't it? All right, I'll tell him so. |
| 16 | E: | Sorry (to bother you). Thank you for your favour. Bye (Now excuse me). |
| 17 | MM: | Bye (See you again). |

## 文法 Grammar

### 1. [plain]と伝える／思う／書く／言う／聞く

**1.1.** In the above expressions, と marks the contents of telling (〜と伝える), thinking (〜と思う), writing (〜と書く), speaking (〜と言う) and hearing (〜と聞く), etc. The marked content is given in the plainstyle of speech (plain forms of non-past and past).

(1) 私はきょうの夜シドニーに行くと、田中さんに伝えてください。

'Please tell Tanaka-san that I will go to Sydney tonight.

(2) あした雨がふると思います。

'(I) think that it will rain tomorrow.'

(3) 日記に、今日すしを食べたと書きました。

'(I) wrote in my diary that I had eaten sushi today.'

(4) 私の父は、山田さんはあしたシンガポールに行かないと言いました。

'My father said Yamada-san would not go to Singapore tomorrow'

(5) 私は、田中さんが車を買ったと聞きました。

'(I) heard that Tanaka-san had bought a car.'

**1.2.** A part of the marked content can also be a noun and/or an adjective in its plain form. Note that an い-adjective is directly followed by と, while a noun and a な-adjective need to have the plain ending だ before と.

(1) 東京(とうきょう)は、とても大(おお)きいと聞(き)きました。
'(I) heard that Tokyo was very big.'

(2) この車(くるま)は高(たか)かったと聞(き)きました。
'(I) heard that this car was expensive.'

(3) 田中(たなか)さんは、木村(きむら)さんはいい医者(いしゃ)だと言(い)いました。
'Tanaka-san said that Kimura-san was a good doctor.'

(4) 京都(きょうと)はとても静(しず)かだったと、岡田(おかだ)さんに伝(つた)えてください。
'Please tell Okada-san that Kyoto was very quiet.'

### Tense in embedded clauses: Relative tense

In an embedded clause in English, the tense of a predicate coincides with that of the main predicate. In Japanese, the basic rule is whether an event/state expressed by a predicate occurs 'before', 'simultaneously' or 'after' the time reference expressed by the main predicate: た indicates 'before' and ている／る indicates 'simultaneously' or 'after'.

(1) a. わたしは、ご飯(はん)を食(た)べたと言(い)いました。 — I said that I had eaten dinner.
occurred before I said

b. わたしは、ご飯(はん)を食(た)べていると言(い)いました。 — I said that I was eating dinner.
simultaneously occurring at the time I said

c. わたしは、ご飯(はん)を食(た)べると言(い)いました。 — I said that I would have dinner.
occurred/occurs after I said

(2) 今日(きょう)すしを食(た)べたと書(か)きました。 — I wrote that I had eaten sushi today.

(3) この車(くるま)は高(たか)かったと聞(き)きました。 — I heard that this car was expensive.

(4) 田中(たなか)さんは、木村(きむら)さんはいい医者(いしゃ)だと言(い)いました。 — Tanaka-san said that Kimura-san was a good doctor.

(Expressions underlined are predicates in embedded causes; main predicates are highlighted by ▒.)

**文法練習 1**

**Rewrite the following sentences in Japanese, using the quotation marker と. Be careful with the tense in the embedded clauses.**

(例) Suzuki-san said that he had played tennis yesterday.

→ 鈴木さんは、きのうテニスをしたと言いました。

(1) I heard that Honda-san had caught a cold.

(2) I think that Kimura-san's baby is cute.

(3) I wrote in the love letter that I loved Tanaka-san. (use 好きだ)

(4) I heard that Yoshida-san was very kind.

(5) Matsuda-san said that Tokyo was cold.

(6) Please tell Kimura-san that I will not buy a new house.

(7) Please tell Tanaka-san that the meeting will be at 2 o'clock. (meeting 会議)

## 2. [plain] そうだ（そうです） '(hearsay)'

**1.1.** This expression indicates 'hearsay' that the information conveyed is based on what the speaker has heard. A plain form of predicate is used before そうだ and the copula だ for nouns and な-adjectives is retained in the case of the non-past tense.

(1) 加藤さんは、毎日５時前に起きるそうです。
'I heard/Someone says that Katoo-san gets up before 5 o'clock everyday.'

(2) 鈴木さんは、魚を食べないそうです。
'I heard/Someone says that Suzuki-san doesn't eat fish.'

(3) 日本の生活費は、とても高いそうです。 (生活費 living costs)
'I heard/They say that living costs in Japan are very high.'

(4) ジョンさんは、日本語が上手だそうです。 (〜が上手 be good at~)
'I heard/Someone says that John speaks good Japanese.'

(5) ジェニーさんは、英語の先生だそうです。
'I heard/Someone says that Jenny is a teacher of English.'

### 文法練習(ぶんぽうれんしゅう) 2

**Pictures below indicate what the speaker has heard. Look at the pictures and make up sentences using the hearsay ～そうだ. Use polite endings.**

(例(れい)) <u>この車(くるま)は高(たか)いそうです。</u>

(e.g.)

(1)

(2)

(3)

(4)

(5)

### 文法練習(ぶんぽうれんしゅう) 3

**Put the two Japanese sentences (a) and (b) together to make one sentence.**

(例(れい)) (a) 田中(たなか)さんは言(い)いました。 (b) あの車(くるま)は高(たか)いです。

→ <u>田中(たなか)さんは、あの車(くるま)は高(たか)いと言(い)いました。</u>

(1) (a) 岡田(おかだ)さんは言(い)いました。 (b) このケーキはおいしいです。

(2) (a) 私(わたし)は、はがきに書(か)きました。 (b) 先週結婚(せんしゅうけっこん)しました。

(3) (a) ～そうです。 (b) 今日の朝(あさ)、町(まち)で事故(じこ)がありました。 (事故(じこ) accident)

(4) (a) ～そうです。 (b) 木村(きむら)さんは有名(ゆうめい)な作曲家(さっきょくか)です。 (作曲家(さっきょくか)composer )

(5) (a) 山田(やまだ)さんに伝(つた)えてください。 (b) この映画(えいが)はおもしろくありません。

(6) (a) みんなに言(い)ってください。 (b) 私(わたし)はここで待(ま)っています。

(7) (a) 私(わたし)は聞(き)きました。 (b) あしたは雨(あめ)でしょう。

## 自然(しぜん)な日本語(にほんご) Natural Conversation Notes

### Echo question

An echo question is a type of question used in a situation where the speaker repeats (echoes) a part of what the other speaker has said/asked. For example;

エレナ：　まさとくん、いらっしゃいますか。
まさとの母(はは)：　まさとですか。まさとはまだなんです。

By using this type of question, the speaker not only confirms what the other person said/asked, but also makes the conversation coherent by repeating a part of the person's utterance. It also helps to avoid sounding blunt in responding to a question or request.

(1) A: あの、オーストラリアのワイン、ありますか。
B: オーストラリアのワインですか。はい、あります。

(2) A: 先週(せんしゅう)の宿題(しゅくだい)、もうしましたか。
B: 先週(せんしゅう)の宿題(しゅくだい)ですか。ええ、もうしましたよ。

What is repeated depends on the interest/concern of the speaker.

(3) A: あした、富士山(ふじさん)に行(い)きませんか。
B: (a) あしたですか。いいですね。行(い)きましょう。
(b) 富士山(ふじさん)ですか。いいですね。行(い)きましょう。
(c) あした、富士山(ふじさん)ですか。いいですね。行(い)きましょう。

### 自然(しぜん)な日本語(にほんご)：練習(れんしゅう)

**Provide echo questions. There is more than one possibility in some cases. Also provide answers and/or further relevant comments as in the example.**

(例(れい)) あした、富士山(ふじさん)に行(い)きませんか。

→ あしたですか。いいですね。行(い)きましょう。 or
→ あしたですか。あしたはちょっと…。 etc.

(1) 魚、好きですか。

(2) １２時３０分ごろ、いっしょに昼ご飯を食べませんか。

(3) あのカフェで、コーヒー、いかがでしょうか。

(4) 写真をとっていただけませんか。

(5) すみません。トイレはどこでしょうか。 (Use ５階 for answer)

(6) あの、日本語のテストはいつでしょうか。 (Use 来週の木曜日 for answer)

(7) わたし、今、パリでワインを飲んでいます。

(8) わたし、来週、アフリカへ旅行に行きます。

## 表現 Expression Notes

### 1 お〜ください 'Could you please ...?; Please ....'

**[1]** ☛ [お-(ます stem) +ください] is another expression of request. It is more polite than [(て form) +ください].

| Verb | ます stem | お〜ください | 〜てください |
|---|---|---|---|
| 待ちます | 待ち | お待ちください | 待ってください |
| 伝えます | 伝え | お伝えください | 伝えてください |
| 使います | 使い | お使いください | 使ってください |

**[2]** ☛ There are two cases where this construction cannot be used: (i) when the ます stem has only one syllable; and (ii) when a verb has a corresponding honorific verb. In such cases, other alternative expressions are used, e.g. 〜てくださいませんか, 〜ていただけませんか, or [honorific verb-てください] in the case of (ii). ('*' means 'ungrammatical')

| Verb | お〜ください | other request expressions / honorific verb |
|---|---|---|
| 見ます | *お見ください | 見てくださいませんか／ご覧ください |
| 来ます | *お来ください | 来ていただけませんか／いらっしゃってください |
| 食べます | *お食べください | 食べていただけませんか／召し上がってください |
| します | *おしください | していただけませんか／なさってください |

[Details of honorific expressions will be given in Lesson 20.]

## 表現(ひょうげん)練習(れんしゅう)１

**Rewrite the following sentences in Japanese using お～ください. If お～ください cannot be used, use an alternative expression.**

(例(れい)) Please read this instruction manual. (Instruction manual 説明書(せつめいしょ))

→ <u>この説明書(せつめいしょ)をお読(よ)みください。</u>

(1) Please write your name here.

(2) Please wait a moment.

(3) Please speak in Japanese.

(4) This is French wine. Please try some. (try 試(ため)す)

(5) Please eat this apple.

(6) Please come at around 7 pm.

(7) Please look at this.

## 2 Some examples of telephone conversation

**Example 1** Hiroshi Tanaka calls Naomi Sato, who answers the call.

なおみ： はい、もしもし、佐藤(さとう)でございます。

ひろし： 田中(たなか)ですが／田中(たなか)ともうしますが、

なおみさん、おねがいします／なおみさん、いらっしゃいますか。

なおみ： はい、私(わたし)ですが…。

N: Hello, this is Sato.
H: This is Tanaka calling / This is Tanaka. Can I speak to Naomi, please? / Is Naomi in (at home)?
N: Yes, speaking…

**Example 2** Hiroshi Tanaka calls Naomi Sato who is in, but one of her family members (FM) answers.

FM：　はい、もしもし、佐藤(さとう)でございます。

ひろし：　田中(たなか)ですが／田中(たなか)ともうしますが、

なおみさん、おねがいします／なおみさん、いらっしゃいますか。

FM：　はい、しょうしょう　お待(ま)ちください。

なおみ：　お待(ま)たせしました。なおみです。

FM: Hello, this is Sato.
H: This is Tanaka calling / This is Tanaka. Can I speak to Naomi, please? / Is Naomi in (at home)?
FM: Yes, Please wait a moment.
N: Sorry to have kept you waiting. This is Naomi.

**Example 3** Hiroshi Tanaka calls Naomi Sato but she is not in. One of her family members (FM) asks if you want to leave a message, but you don't want to.

FM：　はい、もしもし、佐藤(さとう)でございます。

ひろし：　田中(たなか)ですが／田中(たなか)ともうしますが、

なおみさん、おねがいします／なおみさん、いらっしゃいますか。

FM：　すみません。なおみは出(で)かけておりますが・・・。

ひろし；　あ、そうですか。

FM：　何(なに)か、伝言(でんごん)はございますか。

ひろし：　いいえ、けっこうです。また、

のちほど電話(でんわ)します。

> おります formal expression of います；
> 伝言(でんごん) 'message'；
> ございます formal expression of あります；
> のちほど 'later', more polite than あとで

FM: Hello, this is Sato.
H: This is Tanaka calling / This is Tanaka. Can I speak to Naomi, please? / Is Naomi in (at home)?
FM: Sorry, but Naomi is out ….
H: Oh, I see.
FM: Would you like to leave any message?
H: No, that's alright. I will call her back later.

**表現(ひょうげん) 練習(れんしゅう) 2**

**In pairs, practice the telephone conversations in examples 1, 2 and 3 above. Change the names into your/your partner's name.**

## 3 Reference terms for self and addressees

In Japanese, personal pronouns (such as the English 'I' and 'you') are not the only words available for addressing oneself or an addressee. Various other forms, such as kinship and occupational terms are also frequently used. Their use is determined by various socio-cultural factors, such as gender and social status of the speaker and the listener, the level of formality in a situation, and the relationship between the speaker and the listener.

**Commonly used personal pronouns for oneself**

| | Male speaker | Female speaker |
|---|---|---|
| Formal | わたくし／わたし | わたくし／わたし |
| Informal | 僕 (plain)／俺 (vulgar) | わたし／あたし |

**Commonly used personal pronouns for an addressee**

| | Male speaker | Female speaker |
|---|---|---|
| Male addressee | | |
| higher* | NA** | NA** |
| same | きみ | あなた |
| lower | きみ／おまえ(vulgar) | あなた／きみ |
| Female addressee | | |
| higher | NA** | NA** |
| same | きみ／あなた | あなた |
| lower | きみ | あなた |

* 'Higher', 'same', and 'lower' indicate the relative status of the addressee and the speaker.

** NA — personal pronouns are not normally used.

**あなた** In Japanese, あなた 'you' is used only in limited situations such as when a wife refers to her husband (in this case, its meaning is something like the English 'darling') and between female friends etc. Second person pronouns are not normally used when the addressee is higher in social status than the addresser. In this situation, personal names, kinship terms, occupational terms, and titles are preferred.

**先生** For example, 先生 'teacher' is used to refer not only to a person who is in a teaching position but also more generally, for anyone who demands social respect, such as instructors, doctors, and politicians. It is used as a single word or as a title as in 田中先生.

In a family In a family, younger members normally use kinship terms such as お父(とう)さん 'father' and お兄(にい)さん 'older brother' to refer to older members, although older members do not refer to younger members with kinship terms, but with their names.

Note also that address terms within a family are often absolute ones that are reflected from the position of the youngest generation, rather than an actual relationship between an addresser and the addressee. For example, when a man has a grandchild, he is normally addressed as おじいさん 'grandfather' not only by his grandchild, but also by any members of the family (e.g. by his son, daughter in law and his wife).

Below shows how まさと changes terms to address himself and his addressees, depending on their relationships.

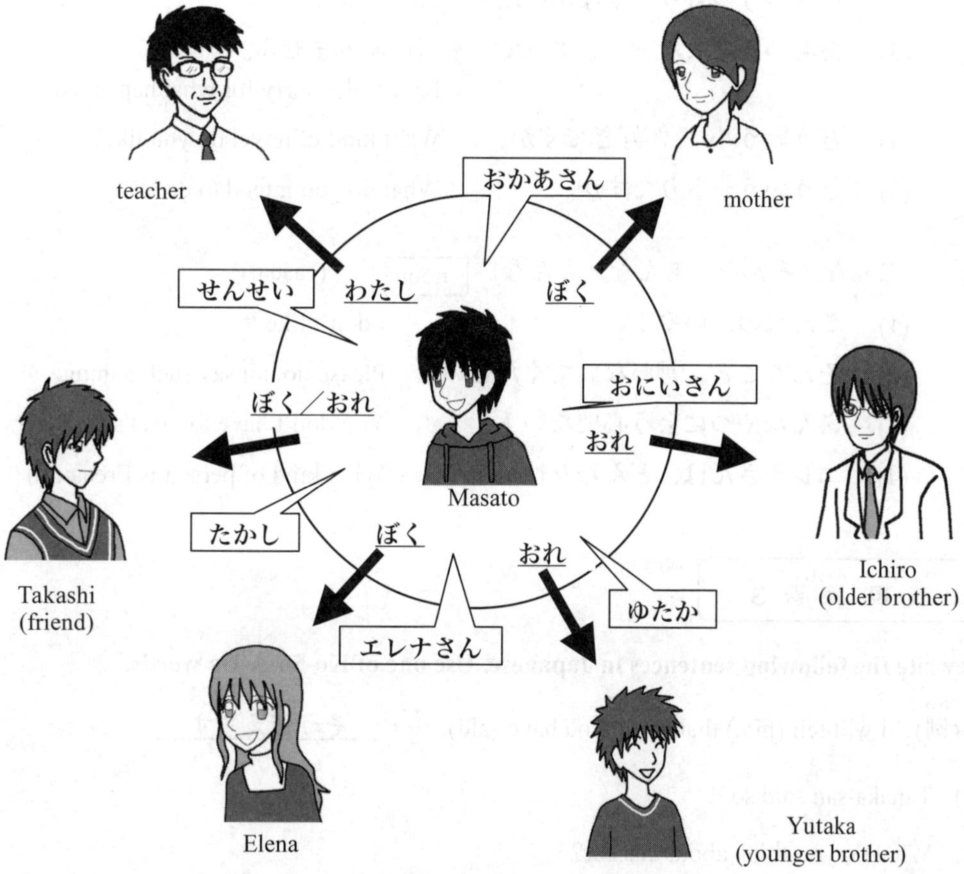


(e.g.) In the case of 'teacher' above, which involve [せんせい] and わたし, Masato uses;

- 'せんせい' to address the teacher: 「せんせい、テストは何時(なんじ)でしょうか」
- 'わたし' to address himself when talking to a teacher: 「わたしは９時(じ)に大学(だいがく)に来(き)ました」

## 4 こう、そう、ああ、どう

**[1]** ☛ These words are used as adverbs .

(1) こうやってください。 Please do like this.

(2) そう伝(つた)えます。 I will tell (him/her) that (what you have said).

(3) いきなり雨(あめ)が降(ふ)り出(だ)しましたが、かさを持(も)っていません。どうしますか。

It's suddenly started raining, but you do not have an umbrella. What will you do?

(4) どうしよう。 What should I do?

**[2]** ☛ [こういう／そういう／ああいう／どういう] – noun

(1) こういう映画(えいが)は始(はじ)めてです。 It is my first time to watch a movie like this.

(2) そういうつもりじゃなかった。 I didn't mean it.

(3) ああいう事(こと)になってしまって、本当(ほんとう)にすみません。

I am really sorry for what happened.

(4) どういう小説(しょうせつ)が好(す)きですか。 What kind of novel do you like?

(5) どういうつもりですか。 What do you intend to do?

**[3]** ☛ [こんな／そんな／あんな／どんな] – noun '(casual)'

(1) こんなの、いや！ I don't like it!

(2) そんなこと、言(い)わないでください。 Please do not say such a thing.

(3) あんなやつに会(あ)う必要(ひつよう)ない！ You don't have to meet such a person!

(4) エレナさんは、どんな女性(じょせい)ですか。 What kind of person is Erena-san?

### 表現(ひょうげん) 練習(れんしゅう) 3

**Rewrite the following sentences in Japanese. Use one of Ko-So-A-Do words.**

(例(れい)) I will tell (him) that (what you have said). → そう伝(つた)えます。

(1) Tanaka-san said so.

(2) What do you think about this car?

(3) I think so too.

(4) What kind of movie is this?

(5) I don't like a movie of this kind.

(6) It's my first time to eat this kind of food.

## 対話 Communicative Exchanges

### 対話練習1

**Pre-task: 〜そうだ '(hearsay)'**

(i) In pairs, make some comment about Tanaka-san based on 'About Tanaka-san' below.
(ii) Your partner will then respond to the comment, using one of cues and 〜そうです '(hearsay)'.

(例) A： 田中さん、泣いていますね。
B： ええ、犬が死んだそうです。
A： あ、そうですか。お気のどくに…　(お気のどくに 'I feel sorry for that.')

About Tanaka-san:

(e.g.) She is crying. (1) She is upset. (2) She is tired. (3) She is smiling.
(4) She didn't come to class yesterday. (5) She didn't come to the party last night.

Cues
She was busy; She was sick; Her dog died; She had visitors from Japan;
She had an exam; She did part-time work for 10 hours; Her car was broken down;
She got a 100 mark in the exam; *You can make up your own cues.

[be broken down 故障する; visitors お客さん]

### 対話練習2

**Pre-task:** Opening of telephone conversation

(i) In pairs, practise the opening conversation on the telephone.
(ii) In responding, you can decide to be either the person with whom the caller wants to talk, as in example (a), or someone else as in (b).

| Person with whom you want to talk | (e.g.) 松田まなぶ | (1) 木村まゆみ | (2) 山田けんじ | (3) 加藤ゆき | (4) 鈴木のぶお |
|---|---|---|---|---|---|
| Receiver | a. 松田まなぶ<br>b. someone else | | | | |

(例) (a) A： もしもし、松田でございます。
B： [your name]と申しますが、まなぶさん、いらっしゃいますか。
A： はい、私ですが…

(b) C： もしもし、松田でございます。
B： [your name]と申しますが、まなぶさん、おねがいします。
C： まなぶですか。はい、しょうしょう お待ちください。
B： はい。ありがとうございます。

## 対話練習(たいわれんしゅう) 3

**Pre-task:** Leaving a message

(i) In pairs, practise a telephone conversation, using role play cues given below.

(ii) While playing a role of caller, the purpose of your call is one of the following. Choose one of them in random order for each time of practice and expand the conversation in an appropriate manner.

I want Naomi Kimura to know:

(e.g.) that the meeting will be held in a cafe, Minato, at 2 p.m. tomorrow.

- that I will wait her in the university library tomorrow.
- that Honda-san will come to school at 10 a.m. tomorrow.
- that I did not meet Yamada-san yesterday.
- that the movie stars at 4 p.m. tomorrow.
- that there will be no exam next week.

(iii) As a receiver, you are playing one of the following roles. Choose one of them in random order for each time of practice and reply and expand the conversation in an appropriate manner, using the given information.

(e.g.) I am Naomi Kimura's grandfather . [Naomi is out now.]

- I am Naomi Kimura's father. [Naomi is not at home; working part time until 10 p.m.]
- I am Naomi Kimura.
- I am Naomi Kimura's younger brother/sister. [Naomi is studying in her room now.]
- I am Naomi Kimura's mother. [Naomi went shopping and has not come back home yet.]
- I am Naomi Kimura's older brother/sister. [Naomi is not at home. I don't know where she is now.]

(例(れい)) You： もしもし、[your name]と申(もう)しますが、直美(なおみ)さん、いらっしゃいますか。

Y.P.： 直美(なおみ)ですか。直美(なおみ)は、いま、出(で)かけています。

You： そうですか。

Y.P.： 何(なに)か伝(つた)えましょうか。

You： あ、はい。会議(かいぎ)のことなんですが、あしたの２時(じ)にカフェ、ミナトだとお伝(つた)えください。

Y.P.： ２時(じ)にカフェ、ミナトですね。わかりました。そう伝(つた)えます。

You： よろしくお願(ねが)いします。では、失礼(しつれい)します。

Y.P.： 失礼(しつれい)します。

## 対話作り Comprehensive Exercises

✍ **In pairs, create a dialogue for the given situation. Please feel free to ask the instructor if you have any questions about Japanese expressions for your dialogue.**

**Situation:**

Speaker A is calling the other person B, and suggesting they do an activity together.

[Examples for activities]

映画を見る ／ 山にのぼる ／ 宿題をする ／ すしを食べる ／ お茶を飲む
町へ買い物に行く ／ カラオケに行く ／ テニスをする ／ CDを聞く　など

At first B does not accept A's suggestion. B explains the reason:

[Reasons for rejection]

高い ／ 好きではない ／ 宿題をする／ アルバイトがある／ 痛い ／ からい
いま忙しい ／ おいしくない ／ おもしろくない ／ 疲れる　など

A and B are negotiating alternative activities and decide the day, time and/or venue to meet:

Please incorporate the following expressions/strategies into your dialogue:

- [plain]と伝える／言う／思う／聞く／書く
- [plain] そうだ
- お～ください
- こう／そう／ああ／どう
- address terms
- Echo question

**[Sample Dialogue]**

| | |
|---|---|
| ゆかの母：もしもし、高田でございます。 | Y.M: Hello. This is Takada. |
| さとる：もしもし、さとると申しますが、ゆかさん、いらっしゃいますか。 | S: Hello. This is Satoru speaking. Is Yuka in (at home)? |
| ゆかの母：ゆかですか。少々、お待ちください。 | Y.M: Yuka? Please wait a moment. |

さとる：　あ、すみません。

ゆか：　はい、電話(でんわ)、替(か)わりました。

さとる：　ゆかさん、おはようございます。さとるです。

ゆか：　あ、さとる君(くん)、おはよう。どうしたんですか、こんなに早(はや)く。

さとる：　あの～、今度(こんど)の土曜日(どようび)に、映画(えいが)に行(い)こうと思(おも)っているんですけど、いっしょに行(い)きませんか。

ゆか：　土曜日(どようび)ですか。

さとる：　ええ。

ゆか：　あ、土曜日(どようび)はちょっと…、アルバイトがあります。

さとる：　そうですか。じゃあ、日曜日(にちようび)はどうですか。

ゆか：　日曜日(にちようび)ですか。日曜日(にちようび)は大丈夫(だいじょうぶ)です。

さとる：　そうですか。あ～、よかった。

ゆか：　どんな映画(えいが)ですか。

さとる：　ラブストーリーという映画(えいが)ですけど…

ゆか：　あ、その映画(えいが)、おもしろいと聞(き)きました。

さとる：　ええ、音楽(おんがく)もとてもいいそうです。

ゆか：　そうですか。

さとる：　ええ。ところで、せっかくですから、映画(えいが)の前(まえ)に食事(しょくじ)でもしましょうか。

ゆか：　食事(しょくじ)ですか。いいですね。じゃあ、どこで会(あ)いましょうか。

さとる：　渋谷駅(しぶやえき)のハチ公(こう)の前(まえ)、１１時半(じはん)はどうですか。

ゆか：　ハチ公(こう)の前(まえ)、１１時半(じはん)ですね。わかりました。ところで、弟(おとうと)と妹(いもうと)を連(つ)れていってもいいですか。

さとる：　えっ、弟(おとうと)さんと妹(いもうと)さんですか。は、はい、いいですよ。そうしてください。

ゆか：　じゃあ、日曜日(にちようび)に。

さとる：　はい、日曜日(にちようび)に。

S: Thank you.

Y: Yes, Yuka speaking. (lit: Yes, (the person on) the phone has changed)

S: Yuka, good morning. It's Satoru.

Y: Oh, Satoru, good morning. What's going on this early in the morning?

S: Well, I'm thinking of going to watch a movie this Saturday. Would you like to go with me?

Y: Saturday?

S: Yes.

Y: Um, Saturday is a little bit… I have a part-time job (to do).

S: I see. Well then, what about Sunday?

Y: Sunday? Sunday is fine.

S: Is it? Oh, that's good.

Y: What sort of movie is it? (What sort of movie are we going to watch?)

S: It is called 'Love Story'….

Y: Oh, I've heard that the movie is interesting.

S: Yes. They say that the music (of the movie) is good as well.

Y: Is that so? I see.

S: Yes. By the way, since we are going to meet, shall we have a meal before watching the movie?

Y: A meal? Sounds good. Where shall we meet?

S: What about (meeting) in front of Hachiko in Shibuya at 11:30?

Y: In front of Hachiko at 11:30, isn't it? All right. By the way, is it all right to bring my younger brother and younger sister?

S: Oh, (your) younger brother and younger sister? Ye, yes, that's fine. Please do so.

Y: Ok, then, (I'll) see you on Sunday.

S: Yes. On Sunday.

## 知(し)ってた？ Did you know?

# 電話(でんわ) Telephone

### 調(しら)べましょう Research

**What is the Japanese for the following words or expressions?**

(例(れい)) telephone 電話(でんわ)

(a) payphone or public phone

(b) mobile phone

(c) phone number

(d) phone book

(e) answering machine

(f) message

(g) make a phone call

(h) receive a phone call

(i) call Kimura-san

(j) line is busy

(k) long distance call

(l) international call

### 練習(れんしゅう)しましょう Exercise

**Read the phone numbers in (a) to (f). Rewrite (g) to (k) in Japanese.**

(例(れい)) （０３）３５１１−６７８９

→ ゼロさんの さんごいちいちの ろくななはちきゅう番(ばん)

('の' and '番(ばん)' may be dropped)

(a) （０３）７４６３−６３９８

(b) （０６）６１２５−３２０５

(c) （０２５）３２３４−１７２５

(d) ０３０４ ５６４６ ４０７９

(e) ８１−３−６３６８−３１３２

(f) ６１−２−３２６５−７７０５

(g) What is your phone number? Please tell (teach) me your phone number.

(h) My phone number is 0401 5453 006.

(i) Do you know the phone number of the fire station?

(j) The phone number of the fire station is 119.

(k) Tanaka-san's phone number is (02) 9547-1234.

## 新しい単語・表現（あたらしいたんご・ひょうげん） New Vocabulary & Expressions

(Basic words/expressions are marked with '*')

| | |
|---|---|
| 赤ちゃん（あかちゃん） | baby |
| あたし | I (informal; female) |
| いらっしゃいますか (=いますか) | is, are in (there)? |
| エアコン | air-conditioner |
| お気のどくに（おきのどくに） | I feel sorry for that |
| 怒る（おこる）* | get upset, get angry |
| 遅い（おそい）* | slow, late |
| おまえ | you (vulgar) |
| おります | formal expression of います |
| 俺（おれ） | I (vulgar; male) |
| 外国（がいこく）* | foreign country |
| 帰り（かえり）* | return(ing) |
| かぜをひく* | catch a cold |
| 替わる（かわる）* | get changed |
| きみ | you (informal) |
| [name]君（くん） | term to address a male; more casual than ～さん |
| 結婚する（けっこんする）* | marry |
| ございます | formal expression of あります |
| 故障する（こしょうする）* | be broken down |
| 作曲家（さっきょくか） | composer |
| 事故（じこ）* | accident |
| 少々（しょうしょう）* | a little |
| 消防署（しょうぼうしょ） | fire station |
| 女性（じょせい）* | woman |
| 生活費（せいかつひ） | living costs |
| 説明書（せつめいしょ） | instruction manual |
| 伝える（つたえる）* | pass (message, thing) |
| 伝言（でんごん） | message |
| 泣く（なく）* | cry |
| 何か（なにか）* | something |
| 何番（なんばん） | what number |
| 日記（にっき） | diary |
| のちほど* | later, more polite than あとで |
| はがき* | postcard |
| はじめて* | first time |
| 番（ばん） | number, turn (e.g. my turn) |
| 必要（ひつよう）* | necessity |
| 百点（ひゃくてん） | 100 marks, full mark |
| 僕（ぼく）* | I (plain; male) |
| まで* | till, until |
| 申す（もうす） | say (formal) |
| もしもし* | hello (telephone) |
| ラブレター | love letter |
| わたくし | I (formal) |

# 第13課（だいじゅうさんか）

## お誕生日（たんじょうび）、おめでとうございます

## Happy birthday!

[Today is Masato's birthday. Elena and Masato meet at a coffee shop]

エレナ：　まさとさん、お誕生日（たんじょうび）、おめでとうございます。
まさと：　どうも ありがとう。
エレナ：　これ、つまらないものですけど…。
まさと：　ええ、そんな。どうも、すみません。
エレナ：　どうぞ、開（あ）けてみてください。
まさと：　いいんですか。じゃあ…うわあ、時計（とけい）。ほしかったんです。
ありがとう！ でも、こんな高価（こうか）なものをもらってもいいんですか。
エレナ：　別（べつ）に高価（こうか）な時計（とけい）じゃないから、気（き）にしないでください。
まさとさんには、お世話（せわ）になっているし、ほんの気持（きも）ちです。

まさと：　本当（ほんとう）に、ありがとう。じゃあ、きょうは誕生日（たんじょうび）だし、
何（なに）かおいしいものでも食（た）べに行（い）きましょうか。
エレナ：　いいですね。
まさと：　何（なに）がいいですか。
エレナ：　私（わたし）は何（なん）でもかまいませんけど。
まさと：　じゃあ、この近（ちか）くに、おいしいタイ料理（りょうり）のレストランがあるから、
そこにいきましょうか。
エレナ：　ええ、そうしましょう。

## 単語(たんご)と表現(ひょうげん) Vocabulary and Expressions (Dialogue)

| | | | | | |
|---|---|---|---|---|---|
| 5 | 開(あ)ける | open | 9 | ほんの | mere |
| 5 | ～てみる | try to… | 9 | 気持(きも)ち | feeling |
| 7 | 高価(こうか)（な） | expensive | 14 | 何(なん)でも | anything |
| 7 | もらう | receive | 14 | かまう | care, mind |
| 8 | 気(き)にする | care about, be concerned | 15 | 近(ちか)く | close, near |
| 9 | 世話(せわ)になる | receive a kindness | | | |

### Dialogue in English

**[Today is Masato's birthday. Elena and Masato meet at a coffee shop.]**

1 E: Masato, happy birthday!
2 M: Thank you.
3 E: This is a little something but (please take it).
4 M: Oh, no. Well, thank you.
5 E: Please open it.
6 M: Is it OK? Then…. Wow! A watch! I wanted a
7 watch. Thank you! But, is it really OK to get such an expensive thing?
8 E: This is not really an expensive watch, so, don't worry.
9 You always help me a lot. So, this is just to express my gratitude.
10 M: Really, thank you. Well, it's my
11 birthday, so shall we go to eat something delicious?
12 E: That sounds good.
13 M: What do you feel like?
14 E: Anything is OK – I don't mind.
15 M: Then, there is a good Thai restaurant
16 near here. Shall we go there?
17 E: Yes, let's do that (go there).

## 文法(ぶんぽう) Grammar

## 1. Various questions (summary)

### 1.1. Two types of questions

There are two types of questions: *Yes-no* questions and *Wh* questions. The former, also called a 'closed question', is a type of question that may be answered with either 'yes' (true) or 'no' (false), while the latter, also called 'open question', generally requires answers with who-when-how type of information, rather than a 'yes' or 'no'.

*Yes-no* questions (Closed questions)

In Japanese, a *yes-no* question is formed simply by adding the question marker か to the end of a descriptive sentence. The intonation normally rises at the end of the question.

(a) 田中(たなか)さんは学生(がくせい)です。 → 田中(たなか)さんは学生(がくせい)ですか。

'Tanaka-san is a student.' → 'Is Tanaka-san a student?'

(b) 木村(きむら)さんはあした東京(とうきょう)に行(い)きます。 → 木村(きむら)さんはあした東京(とうきょう)に行(い)きますか。

'Kimura-san will go to Tokyo tomorrow.' → 'Will Kimura-san go to Tokyo tomorrow?'

(c) テストは難(むずか)しかったです。 → テストは難(むずか)しかったですか。

'The test was difficult.' → 'Was the test difficult?'

*Wh*-questions (Open questions)

A *wh*-question is formed with the 'interrogative' word (which depends on the type of information sought), and placing the marker か at the end of the sentence.

| | |
|---|---|
| なん／なに | 'what' なん is also used with a counting word (or 'quantifier') to form a combined question word: なんじ 'what time', なんにん 'how many people', なんさい 'how old', etc. |
| だれ | 'who' (cf. どなた 'who (formal)'; だれの 'whose') |
| どこ | 'where' |
| どちら | 'which' |
| いつ | 'when' |
| どう | 'how' (cf. いかが 'how (formal)') |
| いくら | 'how much' |
| いくつ | 'how many' |
| なぜ／どうして | 'why' |
| どういう／どんな | 'what sort of' |

Note: (i) Within a sentence, the interrogative word appears in the same position as the sought information (See examples in (d) below).
(ii) The particle は is not used with a question word, i.e. there is no combination as *だれは、*なには、*いつは etc.

(d) 田中(たなか)さんは　あした　シドニーに　いきます。
(who)　(when)　(where)

asking 'who' → だれが　あした　シドニーに　いきますか。

asking 'when' → 田中(たなか)さんは　いつ　シドニーに　いきますか。

asking 'where' → 田中(たなか)さんは　あした　どこに　いきますか。

## 文法練習１

**Fill the brackets [　　] with an appropriate question word. You may need to use a particle as well.**

(例)　今朝、[　なにを　] 食べましたか。　→　トーストを 食べました。

(1)　スミスさんは [　　　　　] 勉強しましたか。→　日本語を勉強しました。

(2)　[　　　　　] 来ましたか。→　友達が来ました。

(3)　[　　　　　] 来ましたか。→　８時に来ました。

(4)　[　　　　　] 見ましたか。→　町で見ました。

(5)　映画は [　　　　　] でしたか。→　おもしろかったです。

(6)　お手洗いは [　　　　　] ですか。→　(お手洗いは) あちらです。

(7)　田中さんは [　　　　　] 来ませんでしたか。→　病気だったからです。

(8)　きのう [　　　　　] しましたか。→　映画を見ました。

## 文法練習２

**Rewrite the following questions in Japanese. Then provide your own answers in Japanese.**

(例)　What time is it now?　→　Q: いま、何時ですか。　A: いま、７時半です。

(1)　What will you do tonight?

(2)　What time did you have breakfast today?

(3)　Who wrote this book?

(4)　Whose car is this?

(5)　When is the exam?

(6)　How was the movie?

(7)　How much is this car?

(8)　Why did you buy a new car?

(9)　When did you meet Kimura-san?

(10)　How many watches does Yamada-san have?

### 1.2. Negative questions

When a *yes-no* question is in the negative style, the way to answer is different in English and Japanese. In English we indicate basically whether the fact involved in the question is true with 'yes' or false with 'no'.

(1) A: Didn't you drink coffee today?
B: Yes, I drank coffee. Yes → [I did]
No, I didn't drink coffee. No → [I didn't]

In Japanese we indicate whether what is said/assumed in the question is correct (はい), or incorrect (いいえ). Thus, in Japanese, an answer with はい usually appears with a negative expression and いいえ with an affirmative expression, as in this case.

(2) A: きょう、コーヒー 飲(の)みませんでしたか。
B: はい、飲(の)みませんでした。 はい → [what you said is correct]
いいえ、飲(の)みました。 いいえ → [what you said is incorrect]

## 文法練習(ぶんぽうれんしゅう) 3

**Answer the following questions in Japanese.**

(例(れい)) ゆうべ、町(まち)に行(い)きませんでしたか。 → はい、行(い)きませんでした。
→ いいえ、行(い)きました。

(1) 鈴木(すずき)さんと映画(えいが)を見(み)ませんでしたか。

(2) 山田(やまだ)さん、きょう学校(がっこう)に来(き)ませんでしたか。

(3) ゆうべ、雨(あめ)、降(ふ)りませんでしたか。

(4) きのう、山田(やまだ)さんに電話(でんわ)しませんでしたか。

(5) 町(まち)で高田(たかだ)さんに会(あ)いませんでしたか。

(6) 映画(えいが)はおもしろくありませんでしたか。

(7) 田中(たなか)さんは学生(がくせい)ではありませんでしたか。

(8) 野村(のむら)さんは、さしみ、食(た)べませんか。

## 2. [plain]んだ／のだ　Explanatory attitude

～んだ／んです, for which the written form is ～のだ／のです, is a sentence ending which indicates that the speaker is (i) offering an explanation or justification for what he/she is talking about, rather than simply stating it as a fact. It connotes the speaker's attitude "…, you see", "that's why", "it is a fact that …' and it is not usually precisely translatable in English. When it is used in a question, it indicates that the speaker (ii) wants the hearer to give an explanation or justification, and often (iii) to seek confirmation about what he/she found surprising, "really!".

As such, ～んだ／んです conveys the speaker's explanatory attitude/feelings, which is 'in addition', to the expression without it: (e.g.) じこが ありました (simple statement) *vs.* じこが あったんです ('you know, that's how I became like this') or パーティーに いきますか (simple statement) *vs.* パーティーに いくんですか (surprise; really!). Due to such an additional attitude/feeling of the speaker, its usage is sometimes seen as conveying 'emphasis'.

**[Formation]** ～んだ／んです is basically attached to a plain form of predicates. In the case of non-past copula for nouns and な-adjectives, な is required.

| | Verb | い-adjective | な-adjective | Noun |
|---|---|---|---|---|
| Non-past | 行くんです | 安いんです | 静かなんです | 先生なんです |
| Past | 行ったんです | 安かったんです | 静かだったんです | 先生だったんです |

(1) A: えっ、雨が降っているんですか。　'Is it raining? (I didn't know and please confirm)'

B: ええ、かなり降っていますよ。　'Yes, it is raining a lot.'

(2) A: きのう、学校に来ませんでしたね。　'You didn't come to school yesterday, did you.'

B: ええ、頭が痛かったんです。　'No (Yes), I had a headache. (that's way I didn't)'

(頭 head; 痛い painful)

## 文法練習 4

**Rewrite the sentences, using 〜んです.**

(例) どうしましたか。 → どうしたんですか。

(1) 今晩、木村さんもいっしょに食事をしますか。

(2) この映画はもう3回見ました。

(3) きのう、頭が痛くて学校に来ませんでした。

(4) ここで、この車が一番速いです。

(5) この町は、ほんとうに賑やかですね。

(6) 田中さんは、とても親切でした。

(7) これは私のテレビです。

(8) あの人は去年、私の先生でした。

## 自然な日本語 Natural Conversation Notes

### Various uses of けど

**1. Clause connective: ‘contrastive’**

けど has variations, けれども, けれど and けども (NB. が has a similar function as けど, but is a more formal expression). It is used to connect two clauses, as in “C1 けど、C2” (‘C1’ and ‘C2’ = ‘Clause 1’ and ‘Clause 2’). Grammatically it belongs to C1 (the preceding subordinate clause). C1 may end with a predicate in either a plain or a polite form, depending on the level of politeness to be expressed (See examples below for illustrations).

It basically indicates that C1 and C2 are in a contrastive relationship.

(a) 私は学生ですけど、田中さんは会社員です。

(b) 私は映画に行きましたけど、田中さんは行きませんでした。

(c) 私の車は赤いけど、木村さんの車は黄色い。

## 2. Various functions in spoken conversation

In spoken conversation, けど may be used for wider functions. It is typically used to indicate introductory (or background) information for an up-coming message (e.g. (d) and (e) below), or parenthetic (additional) information (e.g. (f) and (g)) when it is used in the "C2、C1 けど" construction.

(d) あの人は木村さんだけど、去年日本から来ました。

(e) 映画のチケットが２枚ありますけど、一緒に行きませんか。

(f) このピザ、おいしいですよ。ちょっと高いですけど。

(g) きのうは遅くまで、みんな、あ、田中さんは早く寝たけど、テレビでサッカーを見ていました。

Furthermore, the けど clause, "C1 けど", may be used alone without "C2". The use of such a suspended clause is often interpreted as more polite or softer.

(h) 山田さん、頭はいいですけどね・・・
(implies something negative about Yamada, e.g. 'but, he is not honest')

(i) まさと、いい人だけどね・・・ (implies, for example, 'but, he is lazy')

(j) お茶が入りましたけど・・・ (e.g. 'would you like to have it?' or 'please accept them')

(k) あのー、もう７時ですけど・・・ (e.g. 'May I return home?')

### 自然な日本語：練習

**Rewrite the following sentences in Japanese. Use けど.**

(例) I would like to ask some questions, but …
→ ちょっと聞きたいことがあるんですけど・・・

(1) Last year, Kimura-san was in Japan but his younger brother was not (in Japan).

(2) I met Nomura-san for the first time yesterday and she was very kind.

(3) I bought a new bicycle last week and it was made in Japan. (made in Japan 日本製)

(4) I want to watch this film, but … (e.g. 'would you like to watch it with me?')

(5) Yumi is very cute, but …. (implying something negative)

## 表現 Expression Notes

### 1 Verbs of giving and receiving: ～を　もらう／あげる

[1] ☛ There are three ways of indicating the action of giving and receiving in Japanese: They are あげる, くれる and もらう. While both あげる and くれる are equivalent to 'give', the former is used when 'I' (the speaker) gives to someone else, and the latter when someone else gives to 'me' (the speaker). もらう is basically the same as 'receive'.

あげる ——— give ('I' give to someone else)
くれる ——— give (Someone else gives to 'me')
もらう ——— receive

[2] ☛ Basic sentence patterns that involve the giving and receiving verbs are:

a. [giver] は [receiver] に [thing] を あげる／くれる
b. [receiver] は [giver] に／から [thing] を もらう

[focus on giver] 山田さんは私に、本をくれました。
[focus on receiver] 私は山田さんに、本をもらいました。

[focus on giver] 私は佐藤さんに、CDをあげました。
[focus on receiver] *佐藤さんは私に／から、CDをもらいました。

Note: When 'I' is the giver, the sentence with the focus on the receiver is not normally used.

Between third persons, あげる and もらう are normally used.

[focus on giver] 木村さんは高田さんに、りんごをあげました。
[focus on receiver] 高田さんは木村に／から、りんごをもらいました。

## 表現練習 1

**Look at the pictures and make up sentences that begin with the subject in the box, using the verbs of giving and receiving. Be aware that a receiver cannot be the subject in some situations.**

(例) 山田さんは田中さんに、時計をもらいました。
田中さんは山田さんに、時計をあげました。

(e.g.)

(1)

(2)

(3)

(4)

(5)

> Verbs of giving and receiving are particularly important since they may be used in an expression of appreciation as in ～てあげる／くれる／もらう; (e.g.) 田中さんは 私に 本を 読んでくれた。'Tanaka-san read a book for me.'; 野田さんに 手紙を 書いてもらった 'Noda-san wrote a letter for me.' See Lesson 16 for details.

## 2 ～ないでください 'Please do not …'

☛ [Verb *nai*-form] + で ください is used to ask or instruct someone not to do something.

(1) ここで寝ないでください。 'Please don't sleep here.'

(2) いま、雨が降っているから、外に出ないでください。
'It is raining now, so please don't go outside.'

(3) わたしは大丈夫ですから、心配しないでください。(心配する worry)
'I'm all right, so please don't worry.'

## 表現練習２

**The following pictures involve expressions of notice, caution, and so on. Make up an appropriate sentence for each picture, using ～ないでください. Use given words.**

(例)　ここで たばこを 吸わないでください。

(e.g.)　ここ、たばこ

(1)　ここ、写真

(2)　この公園、野球

(3)　運転中、電話

(4)　ここ、とめる

(5)　絵、さわる

## 表現練習３

**Rewrite the following sentences in Japanese, using ～ないでください.**

(例)　Please don't worry.　→　心配しないでください。

(1)　Don't say that (such a thing).

(2)　Please don't hesitate.　(hesitate 遠慮する)

(3)　Don't cry.　(cry 泣く)

(4)　Please don't go.

(5)　Don't forget to bring your textbook.　(forget 忘れる)

(6)　Don't speak loudly in the library.　(loudly 大きい声で／大声で)

(7)　Don't make a joke.　(make a joke 冗談を言う)

## 3 [Predicate]し、 Listing of activities/events

**[1]** ☛ The basic meaning of [predicate]し indicates that what has been said is followed by the same type of information: ‘and’, ‘and moreover’.

(1) 田中(たなか)さんは頭(あたま)もいいし、スポーツもよく出来(でき)る。

‘Tanaka-san is clever and can play sports well.’

(2) 同窓会(どうそうかい)に田中(たなか)さんも来(き)たし、野村(のむら)さんも来(き)ました。 (同窓会(どうそうかい) reunification)

‘Tanaka-san came to the school reunion and Nomura-san came too.’

**[2]** ☛ It is often used to list events/situations that are cause of something; ‘and so’.

(3) 田中(たなか)さんも来(き)たし、もう時間(じかん)だし、会議(かいぎ)を始(はじ)めましょう。

‘Tanaka-san has come too, and it’s already the time, and so let us start the meeting.’

(4) あしたは休(やす)みだし、今晩(こんばん)は友達(ともだち)と町(まち)で買(か)い物(もの)をするつもりです。

‘Tomorrow is a holiday and I plan to go shopping with my friend in town tonight.’

(5) お金(かね)もないし、食(た)べ物(もの)もないし、ほんとうに大変(たいへん)です。

‘No money and no food, it is really a difficult time.’

### 表現(ひょうげん) 練習(れんしゅう) 4

**Rewrite the following sentences in Japanese, using 〜し.**

(例(れい)) It’s already 7 o’clock and so let us go back home.

→ もう7時(じ)だし、家(うち)に帰(かえ)りましょう。

(1) This is Tanaka-san’s car and that is also Tanaka-san’s.

(2) I drank coffee and also ate a hamburger today.

(3) I went to Tokyo and also went to Kyoto. But I didn’t go to Sapporo.

(4) Today is Sunday, and so please have a good rest. (use ゆっくり休(やす)む ‘have a good rest’)

(5) Yamamoto-san is handsome and also has lots of money, and I really envy him.
(I envy うらやましい)

(6) I am hungry, and so let us have dinner.

(7) We have finished our homework, and so let us watch TV.

## 4 Various expressions for special occasions

[1] ☛ おめでとうございます (おめでとう for casual speech) 'Congratulations!'

This is a general expression to indicate the speaker's feeling of celebrating various occasions.

| | |
|---|---|
| お誕生日(たんじょうび)、おめでとうございます！ | 'Happy birthday!' |
| 合格(ごうかく)、おめでとうございます！ | 'Congratulations on your success in the exam!' |
| ご入学(にゅうがく)、おめでとうございます！ | 'Congratulations on your entrance (to school)!' |
| ご卒業(そつぎょう)、おめでとうございます！ | 'Congratulations on your graduation!' |
| ご就職(しゅうしょく)、おめでとうございます！ | 'Congratulations on your employment!' |
| ご結婚(けっこん)、おめでとうございます！ | 'Congratulations on your marriage!' |

[2] ☛

| | | |
|---|---|---|
| New Year's Day: | あけましておめでとうございます。 | 'A happy New Year.' |
| | 今年(ことし)もよろしくお願(ねが)いします。 | |
| Funeral | このたびはご愁傷様(しゅうしょうさま)でした。 | 'Please accept my condolences.' |
| | お悔(く)やみ、申(もう)し上(あ)げます。 | 'You have my sympathies.' |
| Visiting a sick person | お加減(かげん)、いかがですか。 | 'How do you feel?' |
| | お大事(だいじ)に。 | 'Take care.' |

The phrases above indicate a few basic expressions. There are a number of other conventional expressions that are used on particular occasions. They are often very important in building up and sustaining a good interpersonal relationship with other people.

### 表現練習(ひょうげんれんしゅう) 5

**Make an appropriate comment for each situation.**

(1) When your friend gets a job.

(2) When you say goodbye to a sick person.

(3) When you see someone on New Year's Day.

(4) When you go to a funeral and see the family.

(5) When your friend gets married.

## 対話 Communicative Exchanges

### 対話練習1

Pre-task: Verbs of giving & receiving

(i) In pairs, ask your partner what he/she gave and/or received on the following occasions. You can make up your own sentences, for the purpose of practice.

(ii) In some situations, you can be only either a giver or a receiver (e.g. birthday). In other situations, you can be both (e.g. Christmas Day). In the latter case, you can choose either role.

(iii) Try to expand the conversation further, as in the example.

(例) A: 誕生日に、何をもらいましたか。

B: 兄に時計をもらいました。

A: へえ～、そうですか。どんな時計ですか。

B: とてもきれいな、スイスの時計です。

A: いいですね。

| | Your own answers | Your partner's answers |
|---|---|---|
| (e.g.) Partner's birthday (誕生日) | | A watch from older brother |
| (1) Your own birthday (誕生日) | | |
| (2) Friend's birthday (友達の誕生日) | | |
| (3) School graduation (学校の卒業式) | | |
| (4) Christmas Day (クリスマス) | | |

### 対話練習2

Pre-task: ～んです
～ないでください

(i) First, study the expressions in the boxes below.

(ii) Then in pairs [A] and [B], [A] begins a conversation by asking what happened to [B].

(iii) [B] decides what happened to him/her. Choose one from 〈出来事〉. You can add extra information such as the time when, and place where, it happened/happens.

(iv) [A] makes some comments, as in the example.

(例) A:　どうしたんですか。

B:　きのう、うちの猫が死んだんです。

A:　あ、そうですか。それは…。あまり落ち込まないでください。

〈出来事〉

- 猫が 死んだ
- あした 面接が ある
- ふられた
- あした 大事な試験が ある
- 試験の点数が わるい
- コンピューターが 壊れた
- あした お見合いが ある
- Your own events

〈コメント〉

- 落ち込まない
- 緊張しない
- 泣かない
- 遅くまで勉強しない
- 心配しない
- Your own comments

## 対話作り Comprehensive Exercises

✍ **In pairs, create a dialogue for the given situation. Please feel free to ask the instructor if you have any questions about Japanese expressions for your dialogue.**

**Situation:**

You are celebrating your conversation partner's success, such as in passing an entrance examination or getting a good job. Make your own decision as to what kind of celebration you and your partner will have.

Please incorporate the following expressions/phenomena into your dialogue:

- ～んです　・～けど　・～し、
- ～ないでください
- ～を あげる／くれる／もらう
- Appropriate expression for the given special occasion

**[Sample Dialogue]　You are celebrating your partner's new employment.**

みちこ：　ジョンさん、就職(しゅうしょく)、おめでとうございます。

ジョン：　どうも、ありがとう。

みちこ：　これ、つまらないものですけど、お祝(いわ)いです。

ジョン：　ええ？　そんな…もらってもいいんですか？

みちこ：　もちろん。どうぞ、あけてみてください。

ジョン：　ええ、じゃあ…。うわあ、ネクタイですね。
ほしかったんですよ。ありがとう。

みちこ：　どういたしまして。本当(ほんとう)によかったですね。

ジョン：　ええ、でも、ちょっと不安(ふあん)なんです。

みちこ：　どうして？

ジョン：　会社(かいしゃ)では、日本語(にほんご)を使(つか)うんです。

みちこ：　心配(しんぱい)しないでください。ジョンさんの日本語(にほんご)は
とても上手(じょうず)ですし、大丈夫(だいじょうぶ)ですよ。

ジョン：　いいえ、そんな…まだまだです。

みちこ：　がんばってくださいね。はい、ビール。

ジョン：　ありがとう。

みちこ：　かんぱい。

ジョン：　かんぱい。

M: John, congratulations on your employment.
J: Thank you.
M: This is just a little something, but it's to celebrate.
J: Really? Well, but…can I really take this?
M: Of course. Please open it.
J: Yes, then… Wow! A tie! I really wanted one. Thank you.
M: You're welcome. You really did well, didn't you?
J: Yes, but I'm a bit anxious.
M: Why?
J: In my company, I'll use Japanese.
M: Don't worry. Your Japanese is very good, so it will be no problem.
J: No, it's not…,not yet.
M: Gook luck! Here's a beer.
J: Thank you.
M: Cheers!
J: Cheers!

**知(し)ってた？ Did you know?**

## 贈(おく)り物(もの)の習慣(しゅうかん)　Gift-giving in Japan

Japanese people give gifts on various occasions. Seasonal gifts are traditionally given in the middle of summer and at the end of the year. The gift given in summer is called お中元(ちゅうげん), while the gift at the end of year is called お歳暮(せいぼ). People give gifts to their supervisors, teachers and so on. This custom comes from an old tradition relating to the apprenticeship system used during the Edo period. During that period farmers and merchants sent their children to town as apprentices at stores. It was customary for the children to be given holidays twice a year, at New Year and during *Obon* (which is in the middle of summer). On these occasions, it was customary for the employer to give the children some gifts to take back to their families. In the course of time, it became common practice for everyone to send gifts twice a year to others to express appreciation for any kindness or assistance we have received.

## 練習(れんしゅう)しましょう Exercise

**Refer to the example below and ask three of your classmates what they generally give as a gift to the specified person on the following occasions.**

(例(れい))　A:　Bさんは友達(ともだち)の誕生日(たんじょうび)に、たいてい何(なに)をあげますか。

B:　わたしはチョコレートをあげます。[A] さんは？

A:　わたしはたいてい、ケーキをあげます。

| クラスメートの名前(なまえ) → | | | |
|---|---|---|---|
| (e.g.) 友達(ともだち)の誕生日(たんじょうび)<br>receiver: your friend | | | |
| 母(はは)の日(ひ)<br>receiver: your mother | | | |
| 父(ちち)の日(ひ)<br>receiver: your father | | | |
| クリスマス<br>receiver: your boyfriend/girlfriend | | | |
| バレンタインデー<br>receiver: your boyfriend/girlfriend | | | |

## 話(はな)し合(あ)いましょう Discussions

**In class, discuss when, or on what occasions, people normally give and receive gifts in their various cultures, and what kind of gifts they normally give and receive. Choose 2 or 3 occasions on which people most frequently give and receive gifts.**

| 名前(なまえ) ↓ | Culture/Country | Occasions | Gifts |
|---|---|---|---|
| (e.g.) 田中(たなか) | にほん | Mother's Day<br>Valentine's Day | Carnation<br>Chocolate |
| | | | |
| | | | |
| | | | |

## 新（あたら）しい単語（たんご）・表現（ひょうげん） New Vocabulary & Expressions

(Basic words/expressions are marked with '*')

| | |
|---|---|
| あげる* | (I) give (to someone else) |
| 頭（あたま）* | head |
| うらやましい* | envious |
| 運転中（うんてんちゅう） | in the middle of driving |
| 絵（え）* | drawing, painting |
| 遠慮（えんりょ）する* | hesitate |
| お祝（いわ）い | celebration |
| 大声（おおごえ） | loud voice |
| お悔（く）やみ | condolence |
| お歳暮（せいぼ） | Oseibo (end of year) |
| 落（お）ち込（こ）む | get depressed |
| お中元（ちゅうげん） | Ochuugen |
| お見合（みあ）い | meeting for arranged marriage |
| かまう | care, mind |
| かんぱい | cheers (drink up) |
| 黄色（きいろ）い* | yellow |
| 気（き）にする* | care about, be concerned |
| 気持（きも）ち* | feeling |
| 緊張（きんちょう）する | get nervous |
| クリスマス | Christmas |
| くれる* | (someone) gives (to me) |
| 高価（こうか）(な) | expensive |
| 壊（こわ）れる* | be broken |
| さわる* | touch |
| 就職（しゅうしょく） | getting a job |
| 冗談（じょうだん） | joke |
| 心配（しんぱい）する* | worry |
| セーター* | sweater |
| 世話（せわ）になる* | receive a kindness |
| 大事（だいじ）(な)* | important |
| たばこを すう | smoke |
| 父（ちち）の日（ひ） | Father's Day |
| チョコレート | chocolate |
| 出来事（できごと） | event, happening |
| ～てみる | try to … |
| 点数（てんすう） | score, mark |
| どうして* | how come, why |
| 同窓会（どうそうかい） | reunion |
| とめる* | park (a car) |
| なぜ* | why |
| 何（なん）でも | anything |
| 日本製（にほんせい） | made in Japan |
| 花（はな）* | flower |
| 母（はは）の日（ひ） | Mother's Day |
| バレンタイン・デー | Valentine's Day |
| 不安（ふあん）(な)* | anxious |
| ふられる | get dumped |
| ほんの* | mere |
| まだまだ | not yet, insufficient |
| 面接（めんせつ） | interview |
| もらう* | receive |

# 第14課

# 祖母からもらった椅子なんです

## That's a chair that I got from my grandmother

[フリーマーケットで]

エレナ：　わあ、いろんなものがありますね。
まさと：　うん、そうだね。
エレナ：　わあ、この椅子、すてき！
売り手：　それは私の祖母からもらった椅子なんですよ。
　　　　　５０年前のものです。
エレナ：　へえ～、５０年前ですか。すごいですね。いくらですか？
売り手：　５万円です。いかがですか。
エレナ：　えっ、５万円？ あ、じゃ、けっこうです。

[違う店で品を見ている]

エレナ：　あ、このお皿、いいですね。いくらですか。
売り手：　一枚５００円だよ。
まさと：　５００円ですか。[エレナに] 高いね。ちょっと値切ったら、どう？
エレナ：　そうね。すみません、このお皿、少し安くしていただけませんか。
売り手　　そうだね。４５０円は、どう？
エレナ：　あ、いいですか。じゃあ、このお皿２枚とこの本１冊、ください。
売り手：　はい、じゃあ、全部で１２００円ね。ありがとう。

| ♣ 単語と表現 (たんごとひょうげん) Vocabulary and Expressions (Dialogue) | | | | | |
|---|---|---|---|---|---|
| 1 | いろんな | various, all kinds/sorts of | 9 | お皿 (さら) | dish, plate |
| 3 | すてき(な) | wonderful, nice, fantastic | 10 | ～枚 (まい) | counting word for thin object |
| 4 | 売り手 (うりて) | person who sells | 11 | 値切る (ねぎる) | get a discount |
| 4 | 祖母 (そぼ) | (my) grandmother | 14 | ～冊 (さつ) | counting word for books |
| 4 | 椅子 (いす) | chair | 15 | 全部で (ぜんぶで) | in all, altogether |
| 6 | すごい | great, excellent | | | |
| 8 | 結構(な) (けっこう) | I'm fine; no thank-you | | | |

## Dialogue in English

**[At a flea market]**

1 E: Wow! There are all kinds of things, aren't there?
2 M: Yeah, that's true.
3 E: Wow, this chair, it's great.
4 S: That's a chair that I got from my
5 grandmother. It was made 50 years ago.
6 E: Wow, 50 years! That's great! How much is it?
7 S: It's 50,000 yen. How is that?
8 E: 50,000 yen?! Ah, well then, no, thank you.

**[They are now looking at things in another shop]**

9 E: Oh, this dish is nice, isn't it? How much is it?
10 S: It's 500 yen per plate.
11 M: 500 yen! [to Elena] That's expensive. How about bargaining with the shop staff?
12 E: That sounds good. Excuse me, could you make this dish a little bit cheaper?
13 S: Let me see. How about 450 yen?
14 E: Thank you very much. Well, please give me these two dishes and this book.
15 S: Okay, so that's 1200 yen in all. Thanks.

## 文法 (ぶんぽう) Grammar

### 1. Noun-modifying clause

A clause is like a 'mini sentence' that has the structure of a sentence, but occurs within a sentence. A 'noun-modifying' clause provides detailed or additional information about a noun; for example, in the sentence *This is a chair [which I got from my grandmother]*, the 'which'-clause in [ ] is a noun-modifying clause which modifies (or adds information to) the noun, *chair*.

In Japanese, the following five key points are particularly important.

(i) A modified noun is always preceded by the modifying clause:

| [ ............ *predicate* ] | noun |
|---|---|
| modifying clause | modified noun |

(ii) A predicate within a modifying clause basically ends with a plain form of predicates, except for the case of the non-past copula (for な-adjectives and nouns):

| Verb: | い-adj: | な-adj: | noun: |
|---|---|---|---|
| ～る | ～い | ～な | ～の |
| ～た | ～かった | ～だった | ～だった |

(iii) Unlike English, there is no relative pronoun such as *which*, *when*, *whom*, *that*, etc. in Japanese. Instead, a plain form within a sentence is a clue to a modifying clause:

E: I am watching the TV which I bought yesterday.

J: わたしは、きのう買ったテレビを見ています。

(iv) A whole phrase [modifying clause + modified noun] behaves grammatically as a noun:

(1) [東京から来た田中さん] は 会社員です。 ← subject (topicalised)

(2) わたしは、[東京から来た田中さん] を 知っています。← object

(3) [東京から来た田中さん] に 電話をしました。 ← indirect object

(v) Topic marker は is not normally used within a modifying clause:

(4) [私がきのう読んだ] 本は、おもしろかったです。

## 文法練習 1

**Complete the following sentences by providing an appropriate noun-modifying clause.**

(例) 私があした見る 映画は、スーパーマンです。
The movie which I will see tomorrow is *Superman*.

(1) ______________________________人は、田中さんです。
The person whom I will meet tomorrow is Tanaka-san.

(2) ______________________________所 は、大学の図書館です。
The place where I met Kimura-san is the university library.

(3) ______________________________人は、わたしの母です。
The person who wrote this book is my mother.

(4) ______________________________町に住んでいます。
I live in a town that is far from the university.

(5) ______________________________人は、ゆかさんです。
The person who has long hair (with long hair) is Yuka-san.

live 住む
far 遠い
hair 髪

(6) ＿＿＿＿＿＿＿＿＿＿＿＿＿＿＿＿友達を知っています。

I know a friend who likes Japanese food.

(7) 中村さんは、＿＿＿＿＿＿＿＿＿＿＿＿＿＿＿＿歌手です。

Nakamura-san is a singer who is very famous in Japan. (=a very famous singer in Japan)

(8) きのう、＿＿＿＿＿＿＿＿＿＿岡田さんに会いました。

I met Okada-san who is a doctor yesterday.

(9) ＿＿＿＿＿＿＿＿＿＿＿＿＿＿＿＿＿＿＿＿坂田先生に町で会いました。

I met Sakada-sensei, who was my Japanese teacher last year, in town.

## 文法練習 2

**Rewrite the sentences in Japanese, using noun-modifying clauses.**

(例) I am watching the TV which I bought yesterday.

→ わたしは、きのう買ったテレビを見ています。

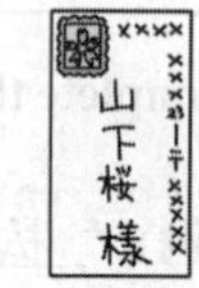


(1) Toda-san is the person whom I met in Sydney.

(2) This is the café I often go to.

(3) The person who is playing the guitar is my friend.

(4) This is the house in which I lived last year.

(5) This is the letter that Suzuki-san wrote.

## 文法練習 3

**Rewrite the following sentence to include the given additional information.**

私は きのう 田中さんと 私の家で お茶を 飲みました。

Additional information:

(i) Tanaka-san came from Sapporo last year.

(ii) My home is in Ueno.

(iii) I bought the tea (*ocha*) in Kyoto.

## 自然な日本語 Natural Conversation Notes

### Interactive particles: Incorporative ね *vs.* monopolistic よ

The interactive particles (also known as 'sentence-final particles') ね and よ are frequently used in Japanese spoken conversation. Their use is particularly important since they indicate the speaker's concern for the conversation partner, which is in turn important for continuously maintaining the interaction between the conversation participants.

**ね** indicates the speaker's willingness to align with the conversation partner with respect to the utterance contents or feeling. Typically, with rising intonation it indicates that the speaker seeks the partner's confirmation or agreement; and with falling intonation it shows the speaker's confirmation, agreement or empathy, i.e. 'I assume that you would understand what I am saying and what I feel'.

(1) A: 日本(にほん)は、いいところですね。

B: そうですね。

(2) A: 私(わたし)の電話番号(でんわばんごう)は、４３１－２９８５です。

B: ４３１－２９８５ですね。

(3) A: 日曜日(にちようび)も仕事(しごと)をしました。

B: えっ、そうですか。たいへんですね。

ね is also used often as a filler within a sentence. It may appear after a phrase. (a) below is an example of formal conversation and (b) of casual conversation.

(4) a. 私(わたし) は ですね、去年(きょねん) ですね、アメリカを旅行(りょこう)したんですけど、…

b. きのう ね、僕(ぼく)が ね、図書館(としょかん)で勉強(べんきょう)していたら ね、ミカが来(き)たんだけど…

**よ** is used when the speaker wishes to enhance his/her position as the deliverer of the utterance contents or feeling toward the conversation partner. Thus, よ is often used when the speaker wants to assure the partner of what he/she says; i.e. 'I assume that you did not know this and I now will tell you, so listen'.

(1) [To a person who is about to go out lightly dressed]

外(そと)、寒(さむ)いですよ。

(2) A: あの人(ひと)は田中(たなか)さんですね。

B: いいえ、違(ちが)いますよ。鈴木(すずき)さんですよ。

(3) A: その本(ほん)を貸(か)してくれませんか？

B: いいですよ。

よ may also be used as a filler within a sentence. However it expresses a very strong tone, indicating the speaker's dominance over the hearer, which is too strong to be used in normal conversation. It may be found, for example, in the speeches of gangsters in TV drama.

(4) おれは よ、そんなことは よ、もう 何回も やったことが あるんだよ。

**自然な日本語：練 習**

**Fill in each space ( ) with the particle ね or よ. In some cases both are possible (but would indicate different attitudes on the part of the speaker).**

(1) A: いい天気です（　）。

B: そうです（　）。

(2) A: すみません。これ、ください。

B: これです（　）。

(3) A: 財布が 落ちました（　）。

B: えっ、あ、ありがとうございます。

(4) A: この水、飲んでもいいですか。

B: あ、大丈夫です（　）。

(5) A: じゃ、今度の土曜日、一緒に食事しませんか。

B: あ、食事ですか。いいです（　）。

(6) A: スーパーマン、面白かった（　）。

B: 本当！ 私も見たい！

(7) A: 日本語って 難しい（　）。

B: え、でも、面白いと思う（　）。

(8) A: この お刺身、おいしい（　）。

B: うん、おいしい（　）。

(9) みちこさん、電話です（　）。早く来てください。

(10) 寒いです（　）。ヒーターを付けましょうか。

## 表　現　Expression Notes

### 1　Suggestion/advice:　～たらどうですか (and its variations) ‘Why don’t you do ….?, How about doing ….?’

[predicate]たら どうですか involves ～たら ‘if you do …’ and どうですか ‘what about?’, which literally means ‘what about, if you do …’. The construction is used when you wish to advise or recommend someone to do something. It differs from ～ませんか or ～ましょうか, which are used to invite the hearer to do something.

This type of expression indicates the speaker’s direct concern/opinion that may be interpreted as threatening the hearer’s ‘face’ or ‘territory’. A wide range of variable expressions are available, reflecting the complexity of interpersonal relationship between the speaker and the hearer, which are often conveyed by different levels of formality, as exemplified by the Japanese expression for ‘How about going to bed early?’ (There are other expressions such as 早くお休みになったらいかがですか, which is more formal than their ～どうですか counterparts.)

早くお休みになったらいかがですか。　[formal]
早く寝たらどうですか。
早く寝たらどう？
早く寝たら？　[casual]

### 2　[noun]でも：　Marginal choice, ‘[noun] or something’

The particle でも indicates the speaker’s marginal feeling “I’ve selected this referent (of the noun), but it does not have to be this”. The phrase is often used with ～ませんか／～ましょうか or ～たらどうですか, since it is useful for softening the tone of the speaker’s declarative, advisory or suggestive attitude, which otherwise tends to be interpreted as imposing the speaker’s opinion directly onto the hearer. In this regard, ‘[noun]でも’ can be seen as more polite than ‘[noun]を’ when used with ～ませんか／～ましょうか／～たらどうですか’.

(1)　いっしょに映画でも見ませんか。

(2)　あした暇だし、野球でも見に行きましょうか。

(3)　お茶でも、いかがですか。

(4)　退屈だろうし、本でも読んだらどうですか。

## 表現練習1

**Give some advice/make a suggestion, using the cues below.**

(例) To your *senpai* (who looks sleepy) / have a cup of coffee or something

→ <u>コーヒーでも飲んだらどうですか。</u>

(1) To your friend / watch TV or something

(2) To your *senpai* / listen to music or something

(3) To your friend / cook or something

(4) To your younger brother / clean his room or something

(5) To your *senpai* / go on a trip or something

## 3 Request: 〜てくれませんか (and its variations) 'Would you please ….?, Can you please ….?'

Similar to the case of 〜たらどうですか, these expressions also directly involve the hearer's face/territory and a wide range of variations are available, again reflecting the complexity of the interpersonal relationship between the speaker and the hearer.

すみません。ペンを貸していただけませんか。 [formal]

あの〜、ペンを貸してくださいませんか。

あの〜、ペンを貸してくれませんか。

ペン、貸してくれない？ [casual]

## 表現練習2

**Look at the following pictures and make sentences using 'request' forms.**

(例)

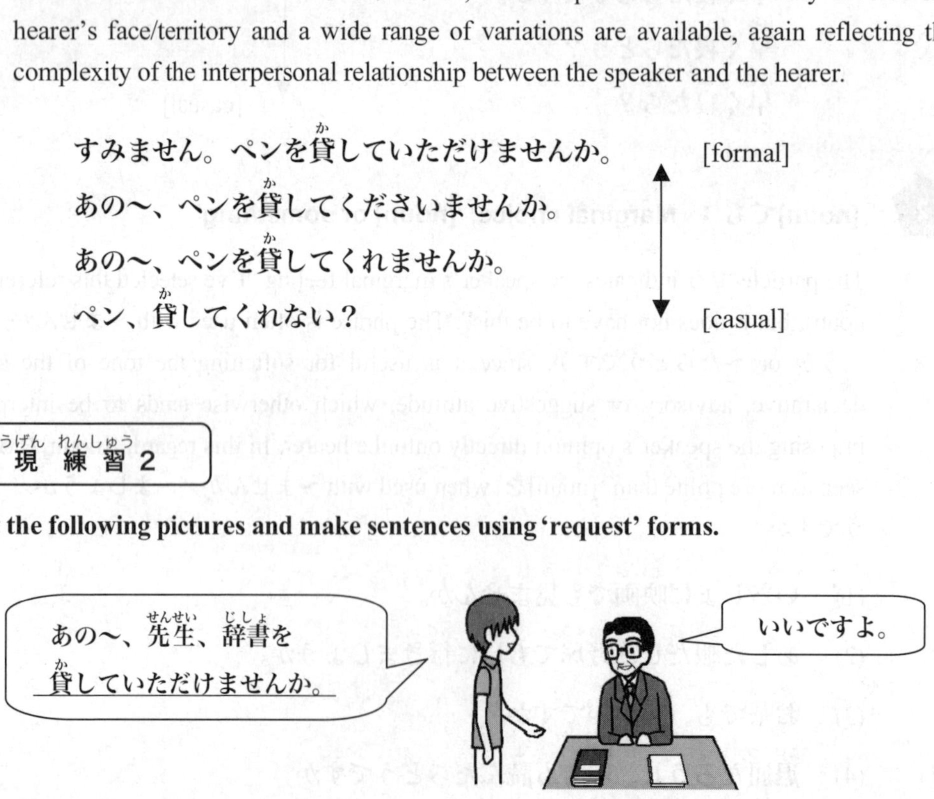
あの〜、先生、辞書を貸していただけませんか。
いいですよ。

(1)

(2)

(3)

(4)

ジャックさん、英語の手紙を
____________________
うん、いいよ。
I cannot read …


## 表現練習３

**Consider the following situations and ask your friend a favour accordingly. Also provide an appropriate response to each request. Suppose you are talking with a close friend.**

(例) You can't read a kanji. → A: ごめん。この漢字、ちょっと教えてくれない？

B: あ、いいよ。 or ごめん。私も分からない。

(1) You cannot read a letter that is written in Japanese.

(2) You want your partner to go to the library with you.

(3) Your conversation partner talks really fast.

(4) You do not have a pen, but you need one to fill out some documents. (use 貸す 'lend')

(5) At the dinner table, you want to use the table salt that is on your partner's side of the table. (use 取る 'take, pass')

(6) You feel it's hot inside. Your partner is near the window.

(7) You feel it's cold inside. Your partner is near the heater.

## 4 Counting objects

**[1]** ☛ Japanese is rich in counting words (or qualifiers/classifiers; e.g. a 'piece' of paper, a 'cup' of coffee). Getting familiar with their use is crucial to indicating the number of target objects properly, since each object has its own unique counting word(s) and the wrong use of those words sound odd, and is sometimes rude.

| | General counting | 冊 for bound volumes | 枚 for thin, flat objects | 本 for long, slender objects | 人 for people | 匹 for small animals |
|---|---|---|---|---|---|---|
| 1 | ひとつ | いっさつ | いちまい | いっぽん | ひとり | いっぴき |
| 2 | ふたつ | にさつ | にまい | にほん | ふたり | にひき |
| 3 | みっつ | さんさつ | さんまい | さんぼん | さんにん | さんびき |
| 4 | よっつ | よんさつ | よんまい | よんほん | よにん | よんひき |
| 5 | いつつ | ごさつ | ごまい | ごほん | ごにん | ごひき |
| 6 | むっつ | ろくさつ | ろくまい | ろっぽん | ろくにん | ろっぴき |
| 7 | ななつ | ななさつ | ななまい | ななほん | ななにん | ななひき |
| 8 | やっつ | はっさつ | はちまい | はちほん | はちにん | はっぴき |
| 9 | ここのつ | きゅうさつ | きゅうまい | きゅうほん | きゅうにん | きゅうひき |
| 10 | とお | じゅっさつ | じゅうまい | じゅっぽん | じゅうにん | じゅっぴき |
| Objects | egg, apple | book, comic, magazine | paper, CD, shirt, towel | pencil, bottle, film (movie) | person | dog, cat, fish |
| Question words | いくつ | なんさつ | なんまい | なんぼん | なんにん | なんびき |

(1) ゆうべ、パーティーに３０人ぐらい来たと思います。

(2) わたしは、犬が２匹、います。

(3) A: きのう、本、何冊 読みましたか。

B: ３冊、読みました。

(4) A: コーラを、何本 、飲みましたか。

B: ２本、飲みました。

Note:
(i) The counting word for books is 冊 and not 本.
(ii) '５本' does not indicate 5 books, but 5 bottles.

**[2]** ☛ [１つ／１枚／１冊, etc]も ～ません 'do not … at all (even one)'

(5) コーラを１本も飲みませんでした。

(6) A: りんごを、いくつ買いましたか。

B: １つも買いませんでした。

表現(ひょうげん) 練習(れんしゅう) 4

**Describe the following pictures, as in the example.**

[younger brother]

× 2

(例(れい)) わたしは、弟(おとうと)が２人(ふたり)います。

(1)

× 3

(2)

× 5

(5)

× 3

and

× 6

(3)

× 23

(4)

× 4

**[3]** ☛ A quantifier (= counting word) may be used in the following three types of phrases:

(i) [noun]-[number-quantifier]-particle

本(ほん)３冊(さつ)を 買(か)いました。／ 友達(ともだち)５人(にん)が 家(うち)に来(き)ました。

(ii) [number-quantifier]-の-[noun]-particle

３冊(さつ)の本(ほん)を 買(か)いました。／ ５人(にん)の友達(ともだち)が 家(うち)に来(き)ました。

(iii) [noun]-particle-[number-quantifier]

本(ほん)を３冊(さつ) 買(か)いました。／ 友達(ともだち)が５人(にん) 家(うち)に来(き)ました。

表現(ひょうげん) 練習(れんしゅう) 5

**Rewrite the following sentences in Japanese. Use a type of phrase given in ( ).**

(例(れい)) I have two younger brothers. ([number-quantifier]-の-[noun]-particle)

→ わたしは、２人(ふたり)の 弟(おとうと) がいます。

(1) I ate 3 apples this morning. ([noun]-[number-quantifier]-particle)

(2) I met 5 friends yesterday. ([number-quantifier]-の-[noun]-particle)

(3) I drank 2 cups of coffee today. ([noun]-particle-[number-quantifier])

(4) Tanaka-san saw 2 movies yesterday. ([noun]-particle-[number-quantifier])

(5) I have 7 cats. ([noun]-[number-quantifier]-particle)

## 対話(たいわ) Communicative Exchanges

### 対話練習(たいわれんしゅう) 1

**Pre-task:** Noun-modifying clauses

**In pairs, ask your partner the following questions in Japanese. You will need question words such as どこ and なん.**

(例(れい)) A: [ B ]さんがよく行(い)くレストランは、どこですか。

B: そうですね。私(わたし)がよく行(い)くレストランは、「レモングラス」です。

**restaurant**
where you often go
You: いおり
Y.P.: レモングラス

**shopping centre**
where you often go shopping
You: ______
Y.P.: ______

**TV program**
which you always watch
You: ______
Y.P.: ______

**sport**
which you often play
You: ______
Y.P.: ______

**food**
which you often cook
You: ______
Y.P.: ______

**coffee shop**
where you always go with your friends
You: ______
Y.P.: ______

**music**
which you often listen to
You: ______
Y.P.: ______

### 対話練習(たいわれんしゅう) 2

**Pre-task:** 〜たらどうですか

(i) First, you consider what advice you will give for each situation stated in the box.

(ii) In pairs, give some advice to your partner for five situations, as in the example. In giving advice, you can make up your own answers.

(例(れい)) A: 日本語(にほんご)の辞書(じしょ)がほしいです。

B: 町(まち)の本屋(ほんや)に行(い)ってみたら、どうですか。

A: あ、そうですね。そうします。

- 日本語(にほんご)の辞書(じしょ)が ほしい！
- おいしい日本料理(にほんりょうり)が 食(た)べたい！
- 宿題(しゅくだい)が 難(むずか)しい！
- 暑(あつ)い！
- 日本人(にほんじん)の彼氏(かれし)／彼女(かのじょ)が ほしい！
- コアラが 見(み)たい！
- 日本語(にほんご)を勉強(べんきょう)したい！
- *Make up your own prompt

## たいわ れんしゅう 対話練習 3

**Pre-task:** Counting objects

**Ask three of your classmates the following questions and write down their answers. If it is necessary, you may add appropriate related words, such as time, place, etc.**

Some further counting words: 〜杯(はい) (cup/glass)　〜回(かい) (frequency)　〜台(だい) (machine, car)

(例(れい)) A:　[ B ]さんはきょう、コーヒーを何杯(なんばい)、飲(の)みましたか。

B:　そうですね。えっと、２杯(にはい)、飲(の)みました。／ １杯(いっぱい)も飲(の)みませんでした。

A:　そうですか。

| Names → | (Yourself) | | | |
|---|---|---|---|---|
| きょう／コーヒー／飲(の)んだ | | | | |
| 日本語(にほんご)の辞書(じしょ)／ある | | | | |
| 兄弟(きょうだい)／いる | | | | |
| 日本(にほん)の歌(うた)の CD／ある | | | | |
| 犬(いぬ)／飼(か)っている | | | | |
| コンピューター／ある | | | | |
| 今月(こんげつ)／映画(えいが)／見(み)た | | | | |

## たいわ づく 対話作り Comprehensive Exercises

✍ **In pairs, create a dialogue for the given situation. Please feel free to ask the instructor if you have any questions about Japanese expressions for your dialogue.**

**Situation:**

You go to an electric shop in Akihabara with your friend and find some goods (e.g. iPod, mobile phone, laptop computer) which you saw in an advertisement on TV. It looks very nice, but there is no price on it. Ask the shop staff for the price, try to get a discount for it, and decide to buy it.

or

You go to a second-hand shop in Osaka with your friend and find some goods (e.g. shoes, shirt, table) which you saw in a magazine. It looks very nice, but the price is 30,000 yen which is too expensive for you. Negotiate the price with the shop staff and decide to buy it.

Please incorporate the following expressions/phenomena into your dialogue:

- Noun-modifying clause
- ね／よ　　・[noun]でも
- ～たらどうですか (or its variations)
- ～てくれませんか (or its variations)
- Counting objects

**[Sample Dialogue]  At a computer shop in Akihabara**

まなぶ：　あ、このコンピューター、いいね。
なおこ：　最近、ソニーが出したコンピューターだよ。すごくいいと聞いたけどね。
まなぶ：　ほんとに？ ほしい。
なおこ：　でも、今、もう１台あるでしょう。
まなぶ：　うん、でも、古いから。
なおこ：　じゃあ、値段、聞いてみたらどう？
まなぶ：　そうだね。あの～、すみません、このコンピューター、いくらですか。
店員：　ああ、それは１４万２８００円です。
まなぶ：　え～、ちょっと高いですね。少し安くしてくれませんか。
店員：　う～ん。じゃあ、１４万はどうですか。
なおこ：　もうちょっと、安くできませんか。
店員：　じゃあ、１３万８０００円はどうですか。
まなぶ：　ありがとうございます。じゃあ、それ、買います。

M: Oh, this computer is nice, isn't it?
N: (It is) the one that Sony has recently produced. I've heard that it's really good.
M: Really? I want (it).
N: But, now you have one already, don't you?
M: Yeah, but (it's) old.
N: Well then, why don't you ask (its) price?
M: Yes. Umm, excuse me, how much is this computer?
SA: Well that one is 142,800yen.
M: What? It's a bit too expensive. Can't you make it a little bit cheaper?
SA: Umm(let me see..). Well, what about 140,000yen?
N: Can't you make it a little cheaper?
SA: Ok, then what about 138,000 yen?
M: Thank you very much. Then, I'll buy it.

**Useful Words/Expressions**

| | | | |
|---|---|---|---|
| 最近 recently | ソニー Sony | 出す release a product | 値段 price |
| もう少し a little bit more | できる you can, it's possible | | 店員 shop staff |
| 服 clothes | たった only | ラップトップ laptop | 広告 advertisement |
| 電気製品 electronic products | 中古品 second-hand goods | | 品物 things, products |

## 知(し)ってた？ Did you know?

## いろいろな店(みせ) Various shops

### 調(しら)べましょう Research

**The followings are the names of some shops and facilities available in a town in Japan. Look up each word in your dictionary and write it down in Japanese.**

| English | Japanese | English | Japanese |
|---|---|---|---|
| Bakery | | Florist | |
| Bank | | Hospital | |
| Book shop | | Pharmacy | |
| Butcher | | Post office | |
| Cake shop | | Police box | |
| Convenience store | | Shoe shop | |
| Coffee shop | | Stationary shop | |
| Deli | | Supermarket | |
| Electric shop | | Sushi shop | |
| Family Restaurant | | Toy shop | |
| Fish shop | | Vegetable shop | |

### 練習(れんしゅう)しましょう Exercise

**Asking-giving directions:**

(i) First study the expressions given in the box below.

Useful Words/Expressions

まっすぐ straight　曲(ま)がる turn　かど corner　信号(しんごう) traffic light

右(みぎ) right　左(ひだり) left　つきあたり T junction　そうすると and then

[counting word]-目(め) (order: １つ目(ひとつめ) the first、３人目(さんにんめ) the third person、２杯目(にはいめ) the second drink)

(ii) In pairs, choose randomly 5 places/shops and ask your partner for directions to the places/shops. Ask for directions to one place/shop, one by one.

(iii) Refer to the map and give the directions in Japanese, as in the example below.

(例(れい)) A: すみません。薬局(やっきょく)はどこでしょうか。

B: 薬局(やっきょく)ですか。まっすぐ行(い)って、1つ目(ひとつめ)の信号(しんごう)を右(みぎ)に曲(ま)がってください。そうすると、左(ひだり)に薬局(やっきょく)があります。

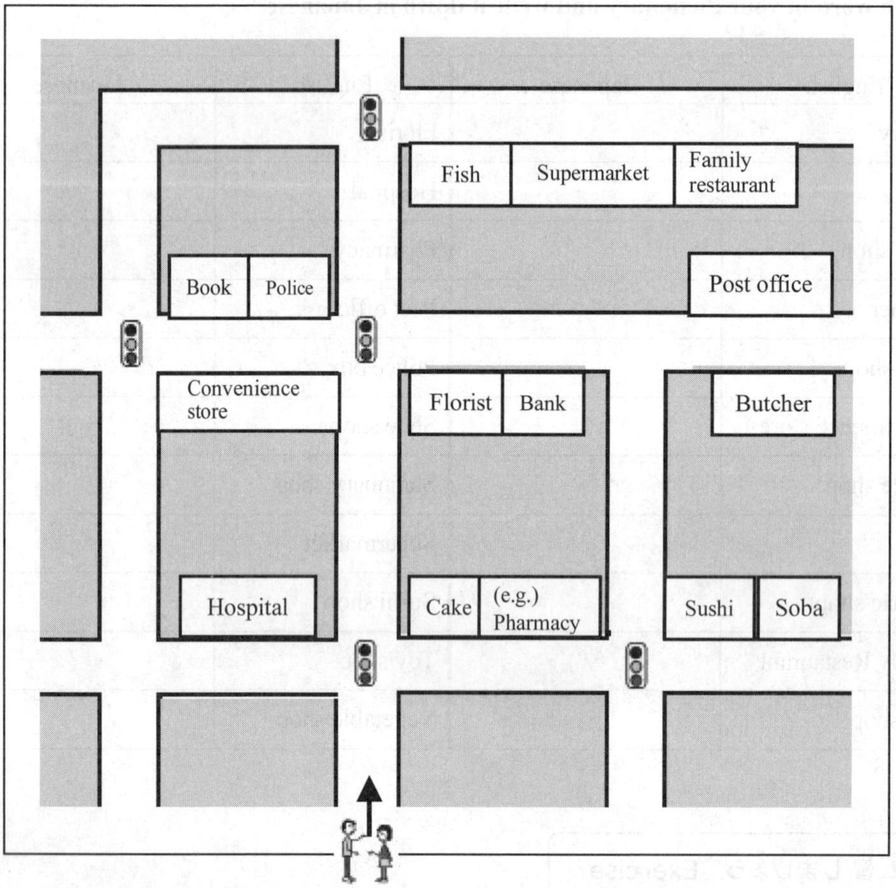

## 新しい単語・表現 New Vocabulary & Expressions

(Basic words/expressions are marked with '*')

| | |
|---|---|
| いろんな* | various |
| 売り手 | person who sells |
| お皿 | plate, dish |
| ～回* | counting word for frequency |
| かど | corner |
| 彼女* | girlfriend |
| 彼氏* | boyfriend |
| ギター | guitar |
| 結構(な) | I'm fine; no thank-you |
| 広告 | advertisement |
| 最近* | recently |
| 財布 | purse, wallet |
| ～冊* | counting word for books |
| 品物 | things, products |
| 食事する* | have a meal |
| 信号 | traffic light |
| スーパーマン | Superman |
| すごい* | great, excellent |
| 先輩* | senpai, senior colleague |
| そうすると | and then |
| ～台 | counting word for machine |
| 出す* | release, produce |
| たった | only |
| 中古品 | second-hand goods |
| つきあたり | T-junction (dead end) |
| できる* | possible |
| デザイン | design |
| テレビ番組* | TV program |
| 電気製品 | electronic products |
| なおす* | fix |
| ～人* | counting word for person |
| 値切る | bargain |
| 値段* | price |
| ～杯* | counting word for drinks in cup/glass |
| ～匹* | counting word for small animals |
| 弾く* | play (musical instrument) |
| 左 * | left |
| ～本* | counting word for long, slender objects |
| ～枚* | counting word for thin material/objects |
| 曲がる* | turn |
| まっすぐ* | straight |
| 右 * | right |
| [counting word]目* | (thing) order |
| もう少し* | a little bit more |
| もらう* | receive |
| ～屋* | kinds of shops/ professions |
| ラップトップ | laptop |

# 第１５課

## 丁寧すぎるよ

## That's too polite

[まさとと エレナが 町を 歩いている]

まさと： おなか すいた？
エレナ： そうですね、少し。
まさと： じゃ、何か食べる？
エレナ： ええ。
まさと： 何 食べたい？
エレナ： 私 は何でもいいですけど…
まさと： じゃ、すしにしようか。
エレナ： いいですね！

[食事の後、すし屋で]

まさと： この店のトロとアナゴ、特においしかったね。
エレナ： ええ、本当においしかったですね。
あ、もう１０時ですね! バスが来るので、帰らなければなりません。
今日は、本当にありがとうございました。
まさと： いえいえ。僕こそ楽しかったよ。
ところでエレナ、僕に「です」や「ます」を使わなくてもいいよ。
エレナの言葉はていねいすぎるよ。
エレナ： ていねいすぎる？
まさと： うん。ふつう、日本人は、親しい人と話すとき、ですます 調 で
話さないんだ。
エレナ： へえ、知らなかった。
まさと： だから、僕たちの会話は、「食べる？」「うん、食べる」でいいんだよ。
エレナ： はい、わかりました。あ、じゃない。わかった！

## 単語(たんご)と表現(ひょうげん)

| | | | | | |
|---|---|---|---|---|---|
| 1 | おなかが すく | become hungry | 15 | 丁寧(ていねい)（な） | polite, courteous |
| 9 | トロ／とろ | toro (a part of a tuna used for Sushi) | 15 | ～すぎる | exceed, too … |
| | | | 17 | ふつう | usually, normally |
| 9 | アナゴ／あなご | eel | 17 | 親(した)しい | close, intimate |
| 9 | 特(とく)に | particularly, especially | 17 | ですます調(ちょう) | *desu-masu* style |
| 14 | ところで | by the way | 19 | 知(し)る | know |
| 14 | 使(つか)う | use | 20 | 僕(ぼく)たち | we |

### ダイアログ（英語(えいご)）

**[Masato and Elena are walking in town]**

1 M: Are you hungry?
2 E: Yes, a little bit.
3 M: Then, shall we eat something?
4 E: Yes.
5 M: What would you like to eat?
6 E: I don't mind what.
7 M: Right, then, shall we have sushi?
8 E: Great!

**[At a sushi restaurant, after eating]**

9 M: The toro and unagi in this restaurant were particularly delicious, weren't they?
10 E: Yes, they were really delicious. Oh, it's already 10
11 o'clock. As a bus is coming, I have to go.
12 Masato, thank you very much for today.
13 M: No, no. I also enjoyed it (It is me who should thank you).
14 By the way Elena, it is all right for you not to use 'desu'
15 or 'masu' to me. Your speech is too polite (courteous).
16 E: Too polite?
17 M: Yeah. Usually Japanese people don't speak in 'desu-masu' style in conversation with people close to them.
19 E: Huh, I didn't know that.
20 M: So it's OK for our conversation to be like 'eat? (*taberu?*)', 'yeah, (I) eat (*un, taberu*)'.
21 E: Yes, 'I understand (*wakarimashita*)'. Oh, no. 'I 've got it! (*wakatta*).

## 文法(ぶんぽう)

## 1. Noun phrases: [Question word] + か、も、でも

### 1.1. [Question word]-か： 'indefinite; something, somewhere, someone'

なにか 'something'; どこか 'somewhere'; だれか 'someone'; いつか 'one day'

(1) 今朝(けさ)、なにかを 食(た)べましたか。 'Did you eat something this morning?'

(2) きのう、どこかに 行(い)きましたか。 'Did you go somewhere yesterday?'

(3) 家(うち)に、だれかが 来(き)ましたか。 'Did anyone come to the house yesterday?'

(4) いつか日本(にほん)に行(い)きたいです。 'I want to go to Japan one day.'

**Note:** (i) In spoken conversation, なにか and どこか tend to become なんか and どっか, respectively: (e.g.) なんか 食べましたか; どっか 行きましたか.

(ii) いつか is not marked by case particles (such as を, に, が).

(iii) In the case of なにか, どこか, だれか, case particles may be omitted as in the examples below.

(1)' 今朝、なにか 食べましたか。 'Did you eat something this morning?'

(2)' きのう、どこか 行きましたか。 'Did you go somewhere yesterday?'

(3)' 家に、だれか 来ましたか。 'Did someone come to your home?'

### 文法練習 1

**Rewrite the following sentences in Japanese. Use polite endings.**

(1) A: Did you buy something at the shop yesterday?
B: Yes, I did.
A: What did you buy?
B: I bought a pen and a CD.

(2) Did you go somewhere during the holiday? (during the holiday 休みの間)

(3) I want to cook something tonight. (cook つくる)

(4) My book is somewhere in this room.

(5) Did you tell the story to someone?

(6) I want to meet Tanaka-san one day.

## 1.2. [Question word]-も 'emphatic denial; any…+ negative'

なにも 'nothing'; どこにも 'nowhere'; だれも 'no one'

(1) 今朝、なにも食べませんでした。 'I didn't eat anything this morning.'

(2) どこにも行きませんでした。 'I didn't go anywhere.'

(3) その本は、どこにもありません。 'The book is not anywhere (I could not find it).'

(4) 家に、だれも来ませんでした。 'No one came (anyone did not come) to my home.'

**Note:** (i) どこもに is ungrammatical (i.e. the order of the particles).

(ii) いつも 'always' is not one of these words.

## 文法練習 2

(ぶんぽうれんしゅう)

**Rewrite the following sentences in Japanese. Use polite endings.**

(1) I did not buy anything (I bought nothing) at the shop yesterday.

(2) I didn't go anywhere during the holiday.

(3) I will not cook anything tonight.

(4) My book is not anywhere in this room.

(5) I don't want to go anywhere.

(6) I didn't tell it to anyone.

(7) I didn't meet anyone yesterday.

### 1.3. [Question word]-でも '…ever (whatever; wherever; …); any…; every…'

なんでも 'whatever'; どこでも 'wherever'; いつでも 'whenever'; だれでも 'whoever'

(1) なんでも いいです。 'Whatever will be fine.'

(2) いつでも どうぞ。 'Please (do, come, etc) anytime.'

## 文法練習 3

(ぶんぽうれんしゅう)

**Rewrite the following sentences in Japanese. Use polite endings.**

(1) A: What would you like to eat?

B: Anything is fine.

(2) A: Where would you like to eat?

B: Anywhere is fine.

(3) A: When would you like to eat?

B: Anytime is fine.

(4) A: With whom would you like to eat?

B: Anyone is fine.

(5) Everything (whatever) is 100-yen.

## 自然な日本語

## カジュアル・スピーチ Expressions in casual conversation in Japanese

In casual conversation, speakers are normally in a close relationship and the key interpersonal relationship underlying their conversational exchanges is intimacy and friendliness, rather than a higher level of politeness and formality. Compared to formal conversation, casual conversation characteristically displays:

(i) less restriction on what speakers may or may not talk about
(ii) a more straightforward and stronger expression of a speaker's feeling and emotions toward the hearer
(iii) stylistically casual endings (as opposed to polite endings)
(iv) frequent use of interactive particles such as *ne*, *yo* and *sa*
(v) frequent occurrence of particle omission

While we have already studied some of the above features in previous lessons, and will study some in later lessons, in this lesson we will first focus on casual endings in various types of sentences.

### 1. Descriptive/declarative sentences

Within descriptive sentences in casual conversation predicates normally have plain endings (cf Lesson 10), with a frequent occurrence of よ／ね and particle omission, in addition to a stronger and more straightforward expression of the speaker's feeling/emotion, compared with formal /polite conversation.

**1.1. Verbs:**

(1) a. 私は、カレーライスを食べます。 (polite)
b. 私、カレーライス、食べるよ。 (casual)

(2) a. 私は行きません。 (polite)
b. 私、行かない！ (casual)

(3) a. きのう、ドイツ語の辞書を買いました。 (polite)
b. きのう、ドイツ語の辞書、買ったよ。 (casual)

**1.2. い-adjectives:**

(1) a. このケーキはおいしいです。 (polite)
b. このケーキ、おいしい！ (casual)

(2) a. きのうのテストは難しかったです。 (polite)
b. きのうのテスト、難しかったよ。 (casual)

**1.3. Copula (for な-adjectives and nouns):**

(1) a. ここは静(しず)かですね。 (polite)
　　b. ここは静(しず)かだね。 (casual)

(2) a. きのうのテストは簡単(かんたん)でした。 (polite)
　　b. きのうのテスト、簡単(かんたん)だったよ。 (casual)

(3) a. 木村(きむら)さんは大学(だいがく)の先生(せんせい)です。 (polite)
　　b. 木村(きむら)さん、大学(だいがく)の先生(せんせい)だよ。 (casual)

(4) a. きのう、田中(たなか)さんの誕生日(たんじょうび)でした。 (polite)
　　b. きのう、田中(たなか)さんの誕生日(たんじょうび)だったよ。 (casual)

**2. Interrogative sentences**

In questions

The interrogative marker か is not normally used (it may be heard in muscular speech) and intonation plays an important role in distinguishing a question (rising) from a descriptive sentence (falling). In writing, a question mark '？' is often added to questions. For な-adjectives and nouns in the case of the non-past tense, the copula だ is dropped and the stem of the adjective or the noun itself is used.

| | Verbs | い-adjectives | な-adjectives | Nouns |
|---|---|---|---|---|
| Non-past | 食(た)べる？ | 高(たか)い？ | 静(しず)か？ | 学生(がくせい)？ |
| Past | 食(た)べた？ | 高(たか)かった？ | 静(しず)かだった？ | 学生(がくせい)だった？ |

In answers

はい and いいえ are hardly used. うん (falling) 'yes' and ううん (falling-rising) 'no' are normally used instead.

(1) A: 今晩(こんばん)、コンサートに行(い)く？
　　B. うん、行(い)くよ。 ／ ううん、行(い)かない。

(2) A: きのう、田中(たなか)さんに会(あ)った？
　　B: うん、会(あ)ったよ。 ／ ううん、会(あ)わなかったよ。

(3) 映画(えいが)、おもしろかった？

(4) 日本(にほん)の歌(うた)、好(す)き？

(5) これ、たかし君(くん)の本(ほん)？

(6) ちょっと、聞(き)きたいことがあるんだけど、今(いま)、いそがしい？

**The interactive marker の**

This may further be added (なの in the case of the non-past な-adjective and noun) in casual conversation:

| | Verbs | い-adjectives | な-adjectives | Nouns |
|---|---|---|---|---|
| Non-past | 食べるの？ | 高いの？ | 静かなの？ | 学生なの？ |
| Past | 食べたの？ | 高かったの？ | 静かだったの？ | 学生だったの？ |

While the question without の (e.g. 行く？) indicates that the speaker 'unilaterally' requests the hearer to provide an answer, the question with the marker (e.g. 行くの？) indicates the speaker's attitude, 'I wish to continue this conversation with you, so please tell/explain me' (this is similar to ～んですか in polite conversation).

A sentence with this marker often more strongly expresses the speaker's (i) intimacy toward the hearer, and/or often reveals the speaker's (ii) feeling/emotion that is related to the given context (e.g. surprise).

(7) a. どうする？ 歩いていく？ [simple question]
　　b. どうする？ 歩いていくの？ [stronger expression of intimacy]
　　c. えっ、雨なのに、歩いていくの？ [surprise; wonder]

**Question word -ですか**

becomes [ Question word ? ], i.e. only the question word is used without ですか: (e.g.) 何？, どこ？, 何時？ (何なの？, どこなの？, 何時なの？, respectively, with the marker の (なの in this case) for a stronger expression of the speaker's emotion, feeling and/or intimacy).

(8) これ、何？ ／ これ、何なの？

(9) たかし君、今 どこ？ ／ たかし君、今 どこなの？

### 3. Other types of sentences: ～(よ)う and ～ない

Volitional (～ましょう) and negative (～ません) expressions are ～(よ)う and ～ない, respectively.

(1) 7時に晩ご飯を食べよう。(食べましょう)

(2) あした、いっしょに買い物に行こう。(行きましょう)

(3) 今度の土曜日、いっしょに映画でも見ようか。(見ましょうか)

(4) コーヒーでも飲もうか。(飲みましょうか)

(5) その車、高いから買わなかったよ。(買いませんでした)

(6) テスト、あまり難しくなかったね。(難しくありませんでした)

## 自然(しぜん)な日本語(にほんご)：練習(れんしゅう)

**Rewrite the following sentences in their casual counterpart expressions. Incorporate the features of casual conversation (e.g. particle omission, ね／よ) in an appropriate manner.**

(例(れい)) A: 何(なに)を食(た)べますか。　　<u>何(なに) 食(た)べる？</u>

B: 私(わたし)は何(なん)でもいいです。　　<u>私(わたし)は 何(なん)でも いいよ。</u>

(1) A: きょう、学校(がっこう)に行(い)きますか。

B: はい、行(い)きます。

(2) A: いい 天気(てんき)ですね。

B: そうですね。

(3) A: いま 何時(なんじ)ですか。

B: いまですか。３時(じ)です。

(4) A: ゆうべ、田中(たなか)さんに会(あ)いましたか。

B: 田中(たなか)さんですか。はい、会(あ)いました。

(5) A: 日本(にほん)に行(い)ったこと、ありますか。

B: いいえ、ありません。

(6) A: さしみ、好(す)きですか。

B: あ、食(た)べますけど、あまり好(す)きではありません。

(7) A: 映画(えいが)、どうでしたか。

B: とてもおもしろかったです。

(8) A: あの人(ひと)は誰(だれ)ですか。

B: たかし君(くん)のお父(とう)さんです。

(9) A: あの建物(たてもの)は何(なん)ですか。

B: あれですか？ あれは図書館(としょかん)です。

(10) A: あした、いっしょに勉強(べんきょう)しましょう。

B: はい、そうしましょう。

(11) A: 日本(にほん)にいる田中(たなか)さんに、手紙(てがみ)を書(か)きましょうか。

B: いいですね。

## 表現

## 1 ～すぎる 'to do (something) excessively', 'to be ... excessive', 'too much'

[1] ☛ 過ぎる means 'to pass', 'to go beyond a certain limit' when used as a main verb, as in もう 3時を 過ぎた 'It has already passed 3 o'clock'. It often forms a compound with a verb or an adjective. When it forms a compound, the *masu*-stem of the verb (both 5-base and 1-base verbs) or the stem of the adjective (both い-adjectives and な-adjectives) is required before すぎる. It does not form a compound with nouns.

| Verbs | い-adjectives | な-adjectives |
|---|---|---|
| 読みます → 読みすぎる | 小さい → 小さすぎる | 静かな→ 静かすぎる |
| 見ます → 見すぎる | 高い → 高すぎる | 簡単な→ 簡単すぎる |

[2] ☛ When used in a compound, it expresses the feeling that someone or something does something excessively, or is in a particular state to an excessive degree.

(1) 私の 弟 は、まんがを読みすぎる。

(2) このぼうしは、私 に小さすぎますね。

(3) 今回のテスト、簡単すぎたね。

(4) おいしくて、食べすぎました。

[3] ☛ The *masu*-stem of the compound, i.e. ～すぎ, is often used as a noun.

(5) 飲みすぎ、食べすぎは健康によくない。　（健康　health）

(6) A: 目と 頭 が痛い。

B: コンピューター・ゲームのしすぎだよ。

### 表現練習 1

**Make up a sentence which describes the feeling/situation in each picture, using ～すぎる and other key expressions given. Use polite endings. Include 私に 'to me' if it is possible.**

(e.g.) この服

(例) この服は、古すぎます。

(1) このシャツ

(2) この宝石(ほうせき)

(3) このケーキ

(4)

(5) このテスト

(6) ゆうべ

(7) このごろ

(8) この電車(でんしゃ)

(9) きょう

## 2 Xこそ 'It is indeed [X] that …'

☞ This indicates the speaker's feeling that it is indeed [X] that is whatever has been mentioned. 'こちらこそ' may be used for the same meaning as (and is more polite than) 私(わたし)こそ.

(1) A: いろいろと、すみません。 I am sorry for many things.

B: いいえ、こちらこそ（私(わたし)こそ）、本当(ほんとう)にすみません。

No, it's indeed me who should be sorry.

(2) [After finishing hard work together]

山田(やまだ): お疲(つか)れ様(さま)でした。 Good work (You must be tired).

鈴木(すずき): いいえ、山田(やまだ)さんこそ、お疲(つか)れ様(さま)でした。

No, it should be you, Yamada-san, who has worked hard (has got tired).

(3) [After having tried to see Tanaka-san without success for the past several days.]

きょうこそ、ぜったいに田中(たなか)さんに会(あ)います。

I absolutely must meet Tanaka-san today.

## 3 ～に する '(given possible choices) I select ...'

☛ This basically indicates the speaker's choice among a number of given possibilities. It sometimes simply conveys the speaker's decision to do something (selected the option mentally before he/she states it) as in (4).

(1) [At a restaurant]

A: わたしは、カレーライスを食(た)べます。 B-さんは？

B: じゃ、私(わたし)もカレーライスにします。

(2) A: 赤(あか)いネクタイと茶色(ちゃいろ)いネクタイがあるのですが、どちらにしますか。

B: 私(わたし)は赤(あか)いネクタイにします。

(3) 何(なに)にしましょうか。／ いつにしましょうか。／ どこにしましょうか。

すしにしましょう。／ 木曜日(もくようび)にしましょう。／ 町(まち)の喫茶店(きっさてん)にしましょう。

(4) おなかすいたし、昼(ひる)ご飯(はん)にしましょう。

### 表現(ひょうげん) 練習(れんしゅう) 2

**Provide appropriate replies to the questions, using ～に する, as in the example. Choose one from the expressions in the box.**

(例(れい)) 映画(えいが)、いつに しましょうか。

→ 映画(えいが)ですか。じゃあ、今週(こんしゅう)の土曜日(どようび)にしましょうか。

(1) 食事(しょくじ)、何(なに)に しましょうか。

(2) 映画(えいが)、何(なに)に しましょうか。

(3) ピクニック、どこに しましょうか。

(4) ピクニック、いつに しましょうか。

(5) あしたの約束(やくそく)、何時(なんじ)に しましょうか。

(6) あしたの約束(やくそく)、どこに しましょうか。

| | | | | |
|---|---|---|---|---|
| 今週(こんしゅう)の土曜日(どようび) | 来週(らいしゅう)の日曜日(にちようび) | ハンバーガー | 『ラブストーリー』 | 『００７』 |
| 湖(みずうみ)の近(ちか)くの公園(こうえん) | 図書館(としょかん)の前(まえ) | しあさって | 夜(よる)８時(じ) | 月曜日(げつようび)５時(じ) |

## 4 [reason (plain form)] ので '..., and so ...'

☛ ので is used to give the reason for the situation similar to から. However, ので sounds more polite than から. ので follows the plain form of predicates and it is ～な-ので in the case of the non-past tense for な-adjective and a noun.

| | Verbs | い-adjectives | な-adjectives | Nouns |
|---|---|---|---|---|
| Non-past | 食(た)べるので | 高(たか)いので | 静(しず)かなので | 学生(がくせい)なので |
| Past | 食(た)べたので | 高(たか)かったので | 静(しず)かだったので | 学生(がくせい)だったので |

(1) 宿題(しゅくだい)がたくさんあるので、今日(きょう)はパーティーに行(い)きません。

(2) ゆうべ、遅(おそ)くまで起(お)きていたので、眠(ねむ)たいです。

(3) 今日(きょう)は暑(あつ)いので、アイスクリームを食(た)べたいです。

(4) あのレストランは有名(ゆうめい)なので、いつも満席(まんせき)です。 (満席(まんせき) full house)

(5) 退屈(たいくつ)だったので、DVD を見(み)ました。

(6) 今日(きょう)は雨(あめ)なので、外(そと)に出(で)たくありません。

(7) この映画(えいが)、おもしろいので、3回(かい)、見(み)ました。

## 5 ～なければならない 'have to ...; must ...'

[1] ☛ ～なければならない involves the combination of the negative expression ～ない (its ば form) and ならない (negative of なる) 'it is no good'. The phrase literally means 'It would be no good, if one does not do...'. It indicates an obligatory or compulsory meaning, 'it is necessary to do; must...; have to ...'. Needless to say, the ない form of predicates is required to form the phrase, and なりません is the polite form of ならない.

(1) バスが来(く)るので、行(い)かなければなりません。

(2) あした、朝(あさ)、早(はや)く起(お)きなければなりません。

(3) あした、テストなので、今晩(こんばん)、勉強(べんきょう)しなければなりません。

(4) 子供(こども)のおもちゃは、安全(あんぜん)でなければなりません。(安全(あんぜん)な safe)

(5) 映画(えいが)はおもしろくなければならないと思(おも)います。

[2] ☛ ～なければならない tends to become ～なきゃ in casual conversation.

(6) 田中(たなか)さんに 電話(でんわ)しなきゃ。

(7) もう遅(おそ)いから、家(うち)に帰(かえ)らなきゃ。

### 表現練習 3

**Make up sentences using given cues, ～ので and ～なければなりません, as in the example. Refer to expressions in the box below for ～なければなりません. Feel free to include additional expressions such as time, location, etc.**

(例) 病気でした

→ 病気だったので、きょうは、学校を休まなければなりませんでした。

(1) あした、テストです

(2) 雨が降っています

(3) 来年、旅行したいです

(4) お金がありません

(5) あした、友達が家に来ます

(6) あした、朝が早いです

(7) 車が故障しました

| | | | | |
|---|---|---|---|---|
| 学校を 休む | 勉強する | アルバイトを する | 家を そうじする | 車で 学校に 行く |
| たくさん お金を 稼ぐ | 早く 寝る | 学校に 歩いて 行く | [*Your own expression] | |

[稼ぐ earn]

## 対話

### 対話練習 1

**Pre-task:** [Question word] か、も、でも

**Ask three of your classmates about their breakfast, weekend and summer holiday, as in the examples. Feel free to ask further questions such as だれと行きましたか, どうでしたか.**

(例)

A: 朝ご飯、何か食べましたか。

B: はい、食べました。

(or いいえ、何も食べませんでした。)

A: そうですか。何を食べましたか。

B: コーヒーとトーストを食べました。

A: 週末／夏休みに、どこかに 行きましたか。

B: はい、行きました。

(or いいえ、どこにも 行きませんでした。)

A: どこに 行きましたか。

B: 家族と いっしょに 海に 行ってきました。

|  | (e.g.) B-さん | yourself |  |  |  |
|---|---|---|---|---|---|
| 朝ご飯 | Yes; Coffee and toast |  |  |  |  |
| 週末 | No: Stayed home |  |  |  |  |
| 夏休み | Yes: Coast with family |  |  |  |  |

## 対話練習 2

**Pre-task:** casual speech

**In pairs, convert the following polite dialogue between Satoshi and Mari into a casual one and practise this casual style of conversation with your conversation partner.**

ダイアログ

さとし： きょうは、どこに行きますか。
まり： 私は、どこでもいいですけど…。
さとし： そうですか。じゃあ、原宿にでも行きましょうか。
まり： いいですね。ここから原宿までどのくらいかかりますか。
さとし： 電車で1時間半ぐらいかかると思います。
まり： ずいぶん遠いですね。
さとし： はい。でも、とても楽しいと思いますよ。

[原宿で]
まり： うわー、いろんなお店がありますね。
さとし： そうですね。まりさん、おなかが空きましたか。
まり： はい。少し空きました。
さとし： じゃ、何か食べませんか。
まり： そうですね。
さとし： 何にしましょうか。
まり： そうですね、私は何でもいいですけど…。
さとし： じゃあ、せっかく原宿にいるのでクレープにしませんか。
まり： あ、いいですね。そうしましょう。

[クレープの店で]
さとし： まりさん、よく食べますね。
まり： とても おいしいです。
さとし： でも、もう5枚目ですよ。
まり： まだ 大丈夫ですよ。
さとし： …

クレープ 'crêpe'　5枚目 '5th slice'

## 対話作り

✍ **In pairs, create a dialogue for the given situation. Please feel free to ask the instructor if you have any questions about Japanese expressions for your dialogue.**

**Situation:**

You and your friend have just finished a big exam, and want to do something special tonight. Discuss with your friend what to do. You may choose one of the following:

(i) Watching a movie: Discuss what movie you would like to watch and where (which movie theatre) you would like to go.

(ii) Going out for dinner: Discuss what (e.g. Thai food or Japanese food) and where (which restaurant) you would like to eat.

(iii) Something else: You can decide on your own activity; discuss things such as what you would like to do and where you would like to go.

Please incorporate the following expressions/phenomena into your dialogue:

- [Question words]-か／でも／も
- ～すぎる
- ～こそ
- ～に する
- ～ので／から
- ～なければならない／～なきゃ

### サンプル・ダイアログ

けん：テストが終わったから、何か一緒にしようか。
みか：あ、いいね。映画でも見る？
けん：いいねえ。みかは、何、見たいの？
みか：そうねえ、私は何でもいいけど。けんは？
けん：そうだねえ、「パニックルーム」は、どう？
みか：ええ～、怖すぎるよ。
けん：そう？ じゃあ、「バットマン」は？
みか：いいね。おもしろそう。
けん：映画館は どこにしようか？
みか：どこでも いいけど・・。渋谷の映画館は、どう？
けん：うん、じゃ、渋谷にしよう。映画の後、食事でもしようか。
みか：あ、ごめん。私、夜、アルバイトがあるから、6時までに家に帰らなきゃ。
けん：あ、ほんとう？ じゃあ、食事は、今度にしよう。

K: Since the test has finished, shall we do something together?
M: Oh, that's a good idea. Why don't we watch a movie or something?
K: Sounds good! What do you want to watch?
M: Well…, any kind is ok with me. What about you, Ken?
K: Well, what about "Panic Room"?
M: Mmmm, it's too scary.
K: Is that so? Well, what about "Batman" then?
M: That's good. Sounds interesting.
K: Which cinema shall we go to?
M: Any cinema is fine, but… What about one in Shibuya?
K: Ok, let's go to the Shibuya one. Shall we have meal after the movie?
M: Ah…sorry but I have to go home by 6 o'clock because I have a part-time job to do at night.
K: Oh, really? Well, let's have a meal next time then.

## 知(し)ってた？　食事処(しょくじどころ)のいろいろ　Eating places

Japan is rich in a diversity of restaurants from western style to Asian styles, as well as well-developed traditional Japanese style. There are also many fusion style restaurants. Having a variety of foods and cuisines is one of the most important and pleasant experiences while visiting different cultures. Let us first be familiar with basic Japanese eating places and typical cuisines.

## 調(しら)べましょう

**Research the eating places and foods/cuisines below. If you can access the internet, have a look at the photographs.**

ファミリーレストラン　居酒屋(いざかや)　寿司屋(すしや)　回転寿司(かいてんずし)　ラーメン屋(や)　そば屋(や)　焼きとり屋(や)
焼き肉屋(やにくや)　和食(わしょく)　洋食(ようしょく)　中華(ちゅうか)　ステーキ　定食(ていしょく)　どんぶり　麺(めん)（そば、うどん）　イタ飯(めし)

## 練習(れんしゅう)しましょう　レストランで注文(ちゅうもん)しましょう：

(i) First study the names of the foods/drinks in the menu below.

### メニュー

〈サラダ〉

| | |
|---|---|
| グリーンサラダ | ３００円 |
| 豆腐(とうふ)サラダ | ３５０円 |

〈ドリンク〉

| | |
|---|---|
| コーヒー（ホット・アイス） | ３００円 |
| 紅茶(こうちゃ)（ホット・アイス） | ３００円 |
| オレンジジュース | ３００円 |
| アップルジュース | ３００円 |
| 生(なま)ビール | |
| 大(だい) | ６００円 |
| 中(ちゅう) | ４５０円 |
| 小(しょう) | ３００円 |
| ワイン（グラス） | |
| 白(しろ)／赤(あか) | ６００円 |

〈メイン〉

| | |
|---|---|
| ハンバーグステーキ | ７００円 |
| ビーフステーキ | ８００円 |
| シーフードカレー | ６５０円 |
| ミートスパゲティ | ７００円 |
| 親子丼(おやこどん) | ５５０円 |
| 牛丼(ぎゅうどん) | ５５０円 |
| カツ丼(どん) | ５５０円 |
| うどん | ４５０円 |
| そば | ４５０円 |
| セット（ごはん・味噌汁(みそしる)・お新香(しんこう)付(つき)） | |
| てんぷらセット | ７００円 |
| とんかつセット | ７００円 |
| 刺身盛り合わせ(さしみもあ)セット | ９００円 |
| 唐揚(からあ)げセット | ７００円 |

(ii) In pairs, refer to the menu above and discuss what to order, as in the example below.

(例(れい)) 田中(たなか)： 佐々木(ささき)さんは、何(なに)にしますか。

佐々木(ささき)： えっと～、そうですね。私(わたし)は、カツ丼(どん)にしようかな。田中(たなか)さんは？

田中(たなか)： そうですね。私(わたし)は、てんぷらセットにします。飲(の)み物(もの)は何(なに)にしますか。

佐々木(ささき)： あ、オレンジジュースにします。

田中(たなか)： じゃあ、私(わたし)も。

佐々木(ささき)： [ウェイターに] すみません。カツ丼(どん)とてんぷらセット、ください。
あと、オレンジジュースを２つ、おねがいします。

> When ordering drinks, １つ(ひとつ) (２つ(ふたつ)、３つ(みっつ)…) is normally used instead of １杯(いっぱい) (２杯(にはい)、３杯(さんばい)…).

## 新(あたら)しい単語(たんご)・表現(ひょうげん)

(Basic words/expressions are marked with '*')

| | | | |
|---|---|---|---|
| アイスクリーム | ice cream | 知(し)る* | know |
| 間(あいだ)* | between, during | ずいぶん* | a lot, many, much |
| 味(あじ)* | taste, flavour | スープ | soup |
| アナゴ／あなご | eel | 好(す)き(な)* | like, be fond of |
| 安全(あんぜん)(な)* | safe | ～すぎる | exceed, too … |
| オーケー | O.K. | すく* | become empty |
| おなか* | stomach, tummy | 絶対(ぜったい)に | absolutely |
| おなかが すく* | become hungry | 茶色(ちゃいろ)い* | brown |
| おもちゃ | toy | 作(つく)る* | make, cook |
| 会話(かいわ) | conversation | 丁寧(ていねい)(な) | polite, courteous |
| 稼(かせ)ぐ | earn | ですます調(ちょう) | *desu-masu* style |
| クレープ | crêpe | 出(で)る* | go out |
| ゲーム | game | とりあえず | for the present |
| 子供(こども)* | child | トロ／とろ | toro (part of tuna) |
| 親(した)しい* | close, intimate | 眠(ねむ)たい* | sleepy |
| 渋谷(しぶや) | Shibuya (a central city in Tokyo) | 働(はたら)く* | work |
| | | 話(はなし)* | talk, story |

| | |
|---|---|
| ピクニック | picnic |
| 普通（ふつう）* | usually, normally |
| 宝石（ほうせき） | jewellery |
| 僕（ぼく）たち | we (male) |
| 本棚（ほんだな） | bookshelf |
| ～枚目（まいめ） | …th slice |
| 満席（まんせき） | full house |
| 約束（やくそく）* | promise, appointment |
| 休（やす）み* | day-off, break, holiday |

# 第16課

## 卒業より入学の方が難しい

## Entering (university) is more difficult than graduating

[まさとの大学で]

エレナ：　いい大学だね。広くてきれいで…。

まさと：　まあね。でも、エレナの大学ほどじゃないよ。エレナの大学の方がずっと広いよ。

エレナ：　そうかな。それは、たぶん、大きい建物がないからだと思う。

まさと：　あ、そうか。

エレナ：　勉強は大変？

まさと：　そうでもないよ。大学に入る前は大変だけど。

エレナ：　ああ、そう。じゃ、まさと君も受験勉強、大変だった？

まさと：　そりゃもう、すっごく大変だったよ。毎日、学校の後、塾に行って夜遅くまで勉強したよ。

エレナ：　うわー、大変そう。

まさと：　うん。日本の大学は、卒業より入学の方が難しいからね。

エレナ：　そうか。

まさと：　入学したら、その後は勉強以外のことを楽しむ学生が多いよ。サークルとか、飲み会とか、アルバイトとか。

エレナ：　なるほどね。日本は、先輩と後輩の関係が厳しいって聞いたけど。

まさと：　うん、普段はそうでもないけど、サークルとかに入るとね。

エレナ：　そうか。

## 単語(たんご)と表現(ひょうげん)

| | | |
|---|---|---|
| 2 | まあね | sort of, kind of, well |
| 2 | ほど | as [adj.] as |
| 3 | ずっと | more [adj.] |
| 4 | たぶん | perhaps |
| 6 | 大変(たいへん)(な) | hard |
| 9 | 受験勉強(じゅけんべんきょう) | study for the entrance examination |
| 10 | そりゃ | (＝それは) |
| 10 | そりゃもう | It definitely … |
| 11 | 塾(じゅく) | cram school |
| 15 | 以外(いがい) | except, besides |
| 15 | 楽(たの)しむ | enjoy |
| 16 | サークル | group activities |
| 16 | 飲(の)み会(かい) | drinking party |
| 17 | なるほど | I see; well understood |
| 17 | 先輩(せんぱい) | senior colleague/student |
| 17 | 後輩(こうはい) | junior colleague/student |
| 17 | 厳(きび)しい | strict |
| 17 | 〜って | (＝〜と、〜という) |

### ダイアログ(英語(えいご))

**[At Masato's university]**

1 E: It's a good university, isn't it? It's big, beautiful…
2-3 M: Well, sort of. But, it is not as big as your university. Your university is much bigger.
4 E: I wonder. That's probably because it does not have big buildings.
5 M: Oh, I see.
6 E: Is studying hard for you?
7-8 M: Not really. It's hard before entering university though.
9 E: Oh, I see. So, was it hard for you to study for the entrance examination?
10-11 M: It was extremely hard. Everyday after school I went to cram school and studied until late.
12 E: Wow!! It sounds hard.
13 M: In Japan, entering university is harder than graduating from it.
14 E: I see.
15 M: There are a lot of students who enjoy something besides studying after entering university,
16 for example, group activities, drinking parties, part-time jobs, etc.
17 E: Understood. I heard that the relationship between senior and junior students is strict in Japan.
18 M: Yeah. It is not usually like that but, when you join group activities or something, you know.
19 E: I see.

## 文法(ぶんぽう)

### 1. Provisional/conditional expressions: 〜たら／ば／と／なら

There are several ways to render the English 'if' in Japanese. Some also overlap with 'when':

Uncertain *if vs.* definite *when*

- If John comes, please give him this. (uncertain whether or not he comes)
- When John comes, please give him this. (definite)

Japanese often overlooks this difference between 'uncertain' and 'definite'. Use of もし makes the status of 'if' clear in Japanese. On the other hand, in Japanese 〜たら／と／ば／なら distinguishes in terms of the type of relationship between clauses.

### 1.1. ～たら

In {X-たら, Y}, X is typically a single, specific event, which has been completed or exists before Y. It connotes '(On a particular occasion), if X happened/happens, then Y would/will follow'. Focus on Y: 'Given X, what Y ensues?'.

(1)　田中さんが来たら、会議を始めましょう。

(2)　この本読んだら、私に貸してください。

### 1.2. ～ば

Necessary condition for outcome: In {X-ば, Y}, provided that X, if and only if X'. Focus on X: 'What condition is necessary to produce outcome Y?'.

(3)　この薬を飲めば、なおります。（飲まなければ、なおりません）

(4)　話せば、わかります。

### 1.3. ～と

Chiefly generic, habitual: In {X と、Y}, 'if/whenever X, Y naturally follows'. Present tense in both X and Y. (In written Japanese, {X と、Y-た} is common in narrative, etc., indicating a natural, immediate consequence.)

(5)　このスイッチを押すと、歌が始まります。

(6)　春になると、花がさく。

### 1.4. ～なら

In {X なら、Y}, 'if (as you say, as is evidently so, etc.) X is the case', 'if it is true that X'. It can follow present or past and the preceding だ disappears (日本人だ＋なら　日本人なら).

(7)　加藤さんは日本で有名な歌手なので、日本人なら、みんな知っています。

(8)　宿題が多いなら、今晩パーティーに行くのをやめましょう。

**1.5.** In some cases, more than one expression may be possible, but with different nuances:

(9)　この道をまっすぐ行ったら、駅の前に出ます。

When you will have completed the action of going straight to this road, you will see the train station.

(10)　この道をまっすぐ行けば、駅の前に出ます。

Provided that you go straight to this road, you will see the train station.

(11)　この道をまっすぐ行くと、駅の前に出ます。

If you go straight to this road, you will naturally see the train station.

## 文法練習(ぶんぽうれんしゅう) 1

**Complete the formation table:**

| | ～たら | ～と | ～ば | ～なら |
|---|---|---|---|---|
| 行(い)く | ________ | ________ | ________ | ________ |
| 行(い)かない | ________ | ________ | ________ | ________ |
| 食(た)べる | ________ | ________ | ________ | ________ |
| する | ________ | ________ | ________ | ________ |
| 来(く)る | ________ | ________ | ________ | ________ |
| 高(たか)い | ________ | ________ | ________ | ________ |
| 静(しず)かな | ________ | ________ | ________ | ________ |
| 学生(がくせい)だ | ________ | ________ | ________ | ________ |

- ◆ ～たら： [た form + ら] for all predicates
- ◆ ～と： [plain]-と／[～だ]-と for non-past な-adj/Noun
- ◆ ～ば： [5-base-*e*]-ば、[1-base stem]-れ-ば／[い-adj stem]-けれ-ば／[な-adj stem/Noun]-であれ-ば
- ◆ ～なら： [plain]-なら／[な-adj stem/Noun]-なら

## 文法練習(ぶんぽうれんしゅう) 2

**Provide the most appropriate conditional expression for the given situation. Use the word in [ ].**

(1) 今晩(こんばん)、シドニーに________________、すぐ電話(でんわ)します。 [着(つ)く]

(2) ３に２を________________、５になる。 [足(た)す]

(3) ________________ このレストランがいい。 [日本料理(にほんりょうり)]

(4) ゆっくり________________、わかります。 [話(はな)す]

(5) あした テストが________________、映画(えいが)に行(い)きましょう。 [終(お)わる]

(6) 授業(じゅぎょう)が________________、いつも町(まち)に行(い)きます。 [終(お)わる]

(7) A: パソコンを買(か)いたいのですが。

B: パソコンを________________、いい店(みせ)を教(おし)えてあげますよ。 [買(か)う]

自然(しぜん)な日本語(にほんご)

## Expressions of appreciation: ～てあげる／くれる／もらう

あげる ---- give ('I' give to someone else)
くれる ---- give (Someone else gives to 'me')
もらう ---- receive

**1. Giving-receiving acts:** Giving-receiving verbs, あげる, くれる and もらう may be used to refer to a situation that involves not only giving-receiving things but also 'giving-receiving acts'. This is very important for indicating the speaker's appreciative attitude (cf. Section 3 below), and hence for natural conversation in Japanese.

The basic patterns in the case of 'giving-receiving acts' are the same as in the case of giving-receiving things. The major difference between the two is whether they involve a thing (verb), which is typically marked by the objective particle を, or an act (verb), which is indicated in て form. For example, (i-b) below is interpreted as 'I gave Kimura-san an act of reading a book; I read a book for Kimura-san'.

| | | | |
|---|---|---|---|
| (i) | a. | giver は receiver に noun を あげる。 | 私(わたし) は 木村(きむら)さんに 本(ほん)を あげました。 |
| | b. | giver は receiver に verb て あげる。 | 私(わたし) は 木村(きむら)さんに 本(ほん)を読(よ)んで あげました。 |
| (ii) | a. | giver は receiver に noun を くれる。 | 高田(たかだ)さんは 私(わたし) に 本(ほん)を くれました。 |
| | b. | giver は receiver に verb て くれる。 | 高田(たかだ)さんは 私(わたし) に 本(ほん)を読(よ)んで くれました。 |
| (iii) | a. | receiver は giver に noun を もらう。 | 私(わたし) は 高田(たかだ)さんに 本(ほん)を もらいました。 |
| | b. | receiver は giver に verb て もらう。 | 私(わたし) は 高田(たかだ)さんに 本(ほん)を読(よ)んで もらいました。 |

**2. くれる *vs.* もらう**

As can be seen above, the use of くれる and もらう depends on whether the focus is given to the giver (高田(たかだ) for くれる, as in (ii)) or to the receiver ( 私(わたし) for もらう, as in (iii)).

**3. With and without ～てあげる／くれる／もらう:**

～てあげる／くれる／もらう basically indicates that the act is something to be appreciated.

(1) 私(わたし) は、手紙(てがみ)を読(よ)みました。[simple statement]
私(わたし) は、手紙(てがみ)を読(よ)んであげました。[read a letter for someone's sake]

(2) 高田(たかだ)さんがメルボルンに行(い)きました。[simple statement]
高田(たかだ)さんがメルボルンに行(い)ってくれました。 [For example, I was supposed to go to Melbourne, but was sick and Takada-san went there for me instead.]

**自然(しぜん)な日本語(にほんご)：練習(れんしゅう)**

**Complete the following sentences, using ～てあげる／くれる／もらう, and the words in the box below. Be careful with the particles. There are more than two possibilities for different meanings in some cases.**

(例(れい)) スミスさんは日本語(にほんご)がわからないので、 私(わたし)が手紙(てがみ)を書(か)いてあげました。

(1) 寒(さむ)かったので、田中(たなか)さんにヒーターを＿＿＿＿＿＿＿＿＿＿＿＿＿＿＿＿

(2) （私(わたし)は）漢字(かんじ)がわからなくて困(こま)っていましたが、伊藤(いとう)さんが

＿＿＿＿＿＿＿＿＿＿＿＿＿＿＿＿＿＿＿＿＿＿

(3) テレビが壊(こわ)れたので、山田(やまだ)さんに＿＿＿＿＿＿＿＿＿＿＿＿＿＿＿＿

(4) (私(わたし)の)誕生日(たんじょうび)に、母(はは)は私(わたし)に新(あたら)しい靴(くつ)を＿＿＿＿＿＿＿＿＿＿＿＿＿＿＿＿

(5) (私(わたし)の)誕生日(たんじょうび)に、私(わたし)は母(はは)に新(あたら)しい靴(くつ)を＿＿＿＿＿＿＿＿＿＿＿＿＿＿＿＿

書(か)く　行(い)く　買(か)う　つける　なおす　教(おし)える　貸(か)す　借(か)りる

**4. Honorific expressions for giving-receiving acts**

The expressions ～てくれる／もらう may indicate a higher level of formality, by using the honorific counterparts of くれる and もらう.

くれる ---- くださる

もらう ---- いただく

> In modern Japanese くださる has a special pattern of conjugation. It behaves as a 5-base verb, except for:
> - Masu-form: くださいます
> - Imperative: ください

(3) 高田(たかだ)さんがメルボルンに行(い)ってくださいました。

(4) 私(わたし)は高田(たかだ)さんに本(ほん)を読(よ)んでいただきました。

Further, ～てくださる and ～ていただく may be used to indicate the speaker's polite request of the hearer in a formal situation.

(5) 3時(じ)に私(わたし)の家(うち)に来(き)て(neutral)／来(き)てくれ (male)。

(6) 3時(じ)に私(わたし)の家(うち)に来(き)てください。

(7) 3時(じ)に私(わたし)の家(うち)に来(き)てくださいませんか。

(8) 3時(じ)に私(わたし)の家(うち)に来(き)ていただきたいのですが。

(9) 3時(じ)に私(わたし)の家(うち)に来(き)ていただけないでしょうか。

casual ↕ formal

> くれ in (5) is the imperative form of くれる.

## 表現

### 1 Comparison: [noun X] の ほうが [noun Y]より～です 'X is more than Y'

[1] ☛ This phrase is a typical expression for comparing two items

(1) わたしは、京都の方が東京より好きです。 'I like Kyoto more than Tokyo.'

(2) 車の方が自転車より、もっと速いです。 'A car is faster than a bicycle.'

N.B. Adverbs such as もっと 'more' or ずっと 'way more' may be added for clearer and emphasized expression of the comparison, as shown in (2).

### 表現練習 1

**Look at the pictures and describe them using 'X のほうが Y より～です'.**

(例) （私は）りんごのほうがなしより好きです。

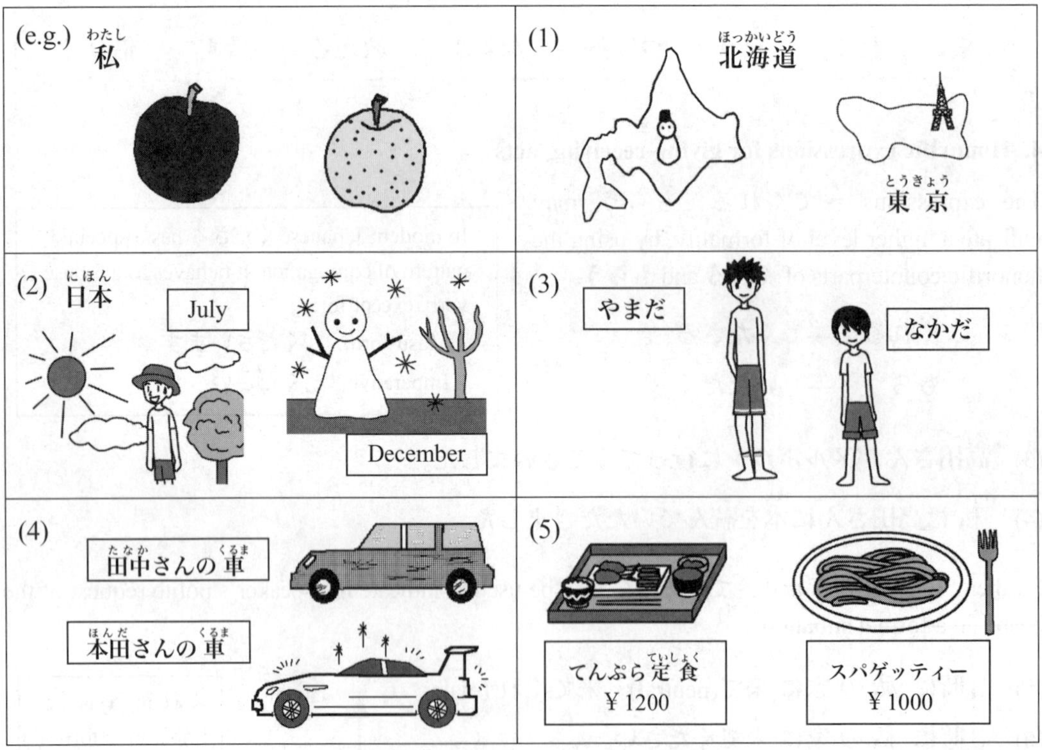


[2] ☛ The phrase 'の ほう' in '[noun X] の ほうが' is often omitted:

(3) わたしは、京都が東京より好きです。

(4) 車が自転車より、もっと速いです。

**[3]** ☛ '[noun X] の ほうが' and '[noun Y]より' often appear in the reverse order:

(5) **わたしは、東京より京都の方が好きです。**

(6) **自転車より車の方が、もっと速いです。**

**[4]** ☛ **Question:** [noun X] と [noun Y] と どちらの方が ～か（どちらが ～か）
'Which one between X and Y is more …. ?':

(7) **京都と東京と、どちらの方が好きですか。**

(8) **てんぷら定食とスパゲッティーと、どちらが高いですか。**

N.B. どちら often becomes どっち in casual speech: e.g. どっちの方が好き？

**[5]** ☛ **[verb-の]**, where の is a nominaliser, may occur instead of [noun X] or [noun Y].

(9) A: **泳ぐのとテニスをするのと、どちらの方が好きですか。**

B: **泳ぐ方が好きです。**

> The nominaliser の is not needed here, since 方 itself is a noun; i.e. 泳ぐの方 is wrong.

**表現練習 2**

**Look at the pictures and make up questions and then answer them as in the example.**

(例) Q: **沖縄と北海道と、どちらが暑いですか。**

A: **沖縄のほうが北海道より、ずっと暑いです。**

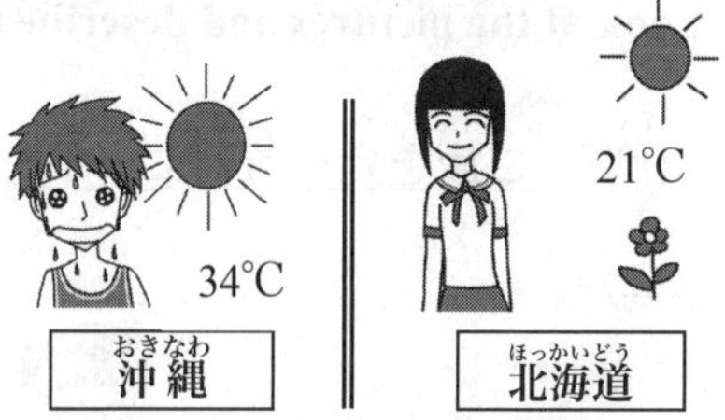


(1)

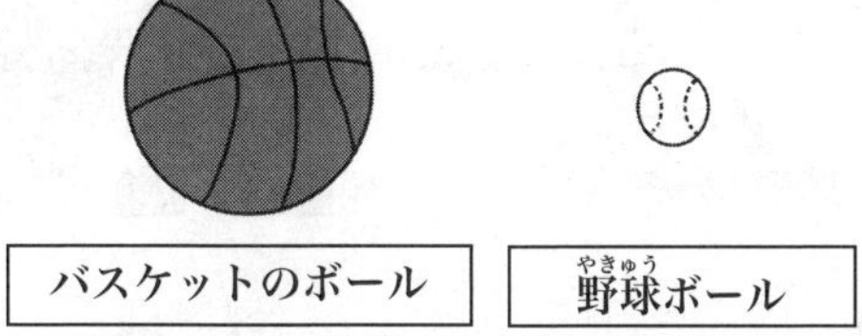


(2)

(3)

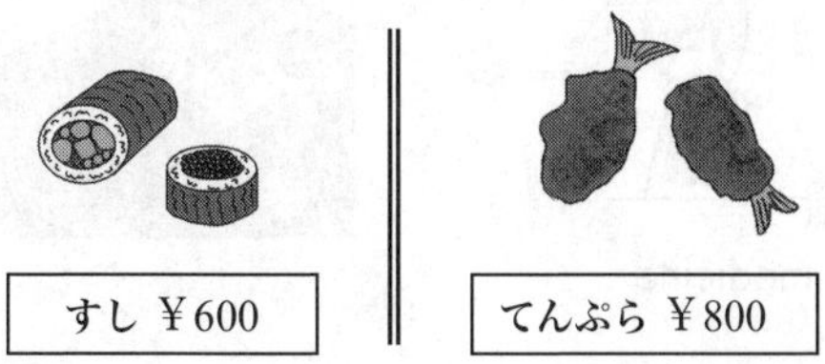


(4)

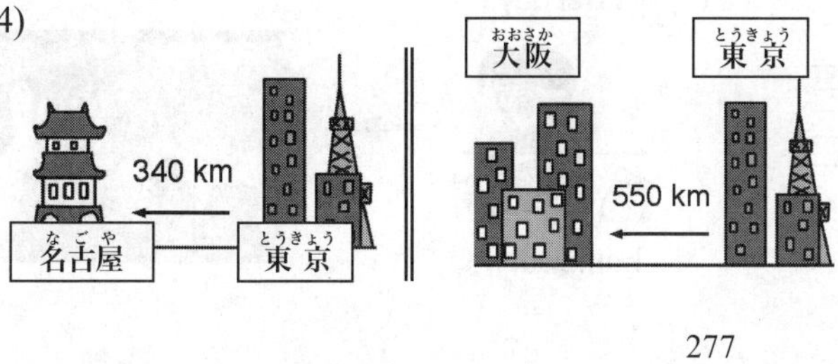


(5)

## 2 ～る前(に) 'before doing …'；～た後(で) 'after doing …'

**[1]** ☛ A verb before 前 is always in the る form (= 'plain non-past' or 'dictionary' form) and before 後 is always in the た form (= 'plain past' form). The particle に in 前に, and で in 後で, are often omitted (cf. (2) and (4) below).

(1) **食事をする前に、手を洗ってください。**

(2) **田中さんはいつも寝る前、シャワーをあびます。**

(3) **大学を卒業した後で、1年間、旅行したいです。**

(4) **野村さんはいつも、起きた後、すぐ新聞を読みます。**

**[2]** ☛ ～前(に) and ～後(で) may indicate the same situation.

(5) **食事をする前に、手を洗ってください。**

(6) **手を洗った後で、食事をしてください。**

### 表現練習3

**Look at the pictures and describe the situations using '～前、and ～後, as in the example.**

**(例)** ご飯を食べる前に、手を洗います。　　手を洗った後、ご飯を食べます。

(e.g.)

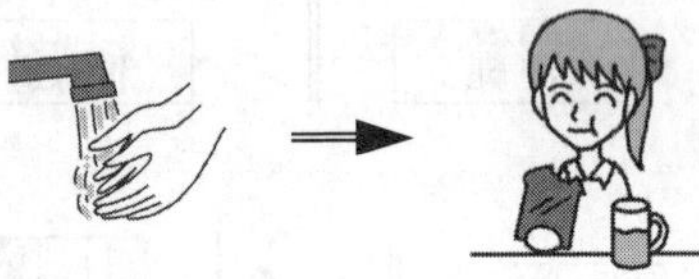

(1)

(2)

(3)

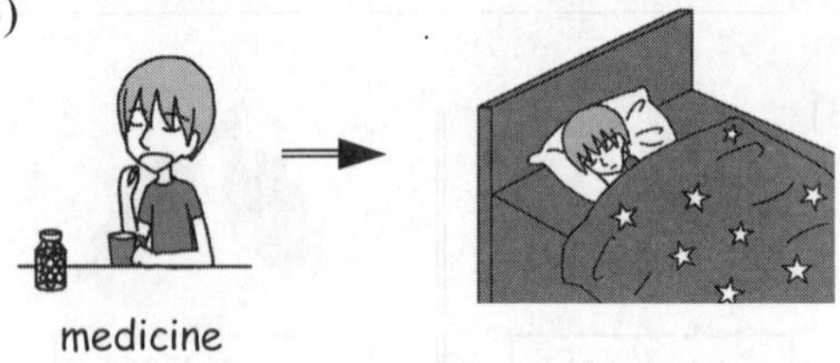


(4)

(5) yesterday

## 3 〜って（＝〜と、〜と聞(き)いた）

[1] ☛ This is used in spoken conversation basically for the same function as the quotation marker と, but with a casual nuance, compared to と. While it is used with most verbs that are related to the transfer of the message, it is not normally used with 思(おも)う.

(1) 日本(にほん)は、先輩(せんぱい)と後輩(こうはい)の関係(かんけい)が厳(きび)しいって聞(き)きました。

(2) あした田中(たなか)さんは東京(とうきょう)に行(い)くって言(い)いました。

(3) 木村(きむら)さんに、わたしは行(い)かないって伝(つた)えてください。

(4) 田中(たなか)さんはいつも寝(ね)る前(まえ)にシャワーをあびるって聞(き)いたよ。

[2] ☛ In casual conversation, 〜って often occurs in the end of a sentence and indicates 〜と聞(き)いた／〜と言(い)った.

(5) あした雨(あめ)だって。 I heard that it would rain tomorrow.

(6) 山田(やまだ)さん、きのう夜(よる)１１時(じ)まで勉強(べんきょう)したって。
Yamada-san said that he studied until 11 o'clock last night.

Note: 〜って may be used for further different meanings such as 〜という, 〜というの, etc. In this lesson, we focus on its use equivalent to 〜と and 〜と聞(き)いた.

### 表現(ひょうげん)練習(れんしゅう)４

**Rewrite the following sentences in Japanese, using 〜って.**

(例(れい)) 日本(にほん)は、先輩(せんぱい)と後輩(こうはい)の関係(かんけい)が厳(きび)しいって聞(き)きました。

(e.g.) I heard that the relationship between senior and junior students is strict in Japan.

(1) I heard that Masato-san went to cram school and studied until late everyday.

(2) I wrote that Japanese is not difficult (to learn).

(3) Okada-san said that this movie is interesting.

(4) Nomura-san said that it rained in Tokyo yesterday.

(5) Please tell Hanako-san that I am busy today. (use 伝(つた)える)

(6) I heard that this computer was cheap. (in casual speech)

(7) I heard that Tanaka-san will go to Indonesia next Monday. (in casual speech)

## 4 ～とか　'(list of things/events as examples)'

☛ ～とか is used to list two or more items, actions or states as non-exhaustive examples. Normally, noun and verb (plain non-past form) occurs before ～とか.

(1) 私は休みの間、奈良とか、京都とかに行きました。

(2) 私は果物が好きです。みかんとか、りんごとか。

(3) 日曜日は、そうじをするとか、本を読むとかします。

(4) ゆうべ、寝る前にいろいろなことをしました。テレビを見るとか、友達に手紙を書くとか。

### 表現練習5

**Make up sentences, using～とか, as in the example. Use your own items.**

(例) 動物　好きだ　→　私は動物が好きです。犬とか、猫とか。

(1) 日本料理　よく食べる

(2) アニメ　よく見る

(3) きのう　友達に会う

(4) いろんな国　行きたい

(5) 週末　いろいろする

(6) 休みの間　いろいろする予定だ

## 対話

### 対話練習1

Pre-task: ～前；～後

**Ask three classmates what they do/did at the time that are stated in the prompts.**

(例) A: ゆうべ、晩ご飯の後、何をしましたか。

B: 晩ご飯の後、テレビを見ました。

| | You | Classmate 1 | Classmate 2 | Classmate 3 |
|---|---|---|---|---|
| (1) After eating dinner last night | | (e.g.) Watched TV | | |
| (2) Before going to bed last night | | | | |
| (3) Before coming to this class | | | | |
| (4) After finishing this class | | | | |

## 対話練習(たいわれんしゅう) 2

**Pre-task:** casual expressions

(i) Using the cues given below, make up appropriate questions. Questions may be closed ones (yes-no questions) or open ones (*wh*-questions). They could also relate to the past, present or future.

(ii) Ask your partner the questions. Use casual expressions.

(例(れい)) A: きのう、友達(ともだち)に電話(でんわ)した？

B: うん、したよ。 ／ ううん、しなかったよ。

| | | |
|---|---|---|
| (e.g.) 電話(でんわ)する | (1) 学校(がっこう)に来(く)る | (2) 洗濯(せんたく)する |
| (3) 部屋(へや)をそうじする | (4) イーメールを書(か)く | (5) 友達(ともだち)に会(あ)う |
| (6) 起(お)きる | (7) 寝(ね)る | (8) 食(た)べる |
| (9) 見(み)る | (10) 行(い)く | (11) 買(か)う |

## 対話練習(たいわれんしゅう) 3

**Pre-task:** どちら～；～より

**In pairs, ask your partner his/her preference using the prompts and the question word どちら. Feel free to use もっと and also to include a further question どうして.**

(例(れい)) A: りんごと オレンジと、どちらが好(す)きですか。

B: りんごよりオレンジのほうが、もっと好(す)きです。

A: そうですか。どうしてオレンジのほうが、もっと好(す)きですか。

B: あまいからです。

| | You | Your partner |
|---|---|---|
| (e.g.) りんご；オレンジ | りんご | オレンジ |
| (1) 夏(なつ)；冬(ふゆ) | | |
| (2) 山(やま)；海(うみ) | | |
| (3) 犬(いぬ)；猫(ねこ) | | |
| (4) ドライブをする；家(うち)で DVD を見(み)る | | |
| (5) 買(か)い物(もの)をする；映画(えいが)を見(み)る | | |

## 対話作り（たいわづくり）

✍ **In pairs, create a dialogue for the given situation. Please feel free to ask the instructor if you have any questions about Japanese expressions for your dialogue.**

> **Situation:**
>
> You and your partner are talking about your and his/her time in high school. You may include the following topics in your dialogue:
>
> (i) what subject you and your partner liked the most;
>
> (ii) what club activity (extra curricular activity) you and your partner did; and
>
> (iii) a teacher (or teachers) you and your partner liked.

Please incorporate the following expressions/phenomena into your dialogue:

- Expressions of comparison: どちら、～より、もっと
- ～てあげる／くれる／もらう
- ～る前（まえ）／～た後（あと）
- ～って
- ～とか

### サンプル・ダイアログ

スー：　まなぶは高校生（こうこうせい）のとき、どうだった？

まなぶ：　毎日（まいにち）、楽（たの）しかったよ。昼時間（ひるじかん）に友達（ともだち）とおしゃべりしたり、放課後（ほうかご）、クラブ活動（かつどう）したり。

スー：　何（なん）のクラブだったの？

まなぶ：　テニス部（ぶ）。

スー：　へえ。どうだった？

まなぶ：　練習（れんしゅう）はきつかったけど、楽（たの）しかった。プロのコーチに教（おし）えてもらったんだよ。

スー：　わぁ、すごいね。

まなぶ：　うん。すごいでしょう。

スー：　勉強（べんきょう）はどうだった？

まなぶ：　大変（たいへん）だった。たくさんテストがあったから。

スー：　私（わたし）の高校（こうこう）もテストがたくさんあったよ。毎（まい）タームが終（お）わる前（まえ）に、大（おお）きい試験（しけん）があった。

まなぶ：　うん、僕（ぼく）の高校（こうこう）もそうだったよ。

S: How was it when you were in high school?

M: It was fun everyday, doing such things as chatting with my friend(s) during lunch time and some club activity after school, etc.

S: What club did you belong to?

M: The tennis club.

S: Oh, how was it?

M: Practice was tough but I enjoyed it. A professional coach taught (us).

S: Wow, that's great.

M: Yes, it was great, wasn't it?

S: How was (your) study?

M: It was hard, because we had lots of tests.

S: My high school had lots of test too. There was a big exam before finishing each term.

M: Yeah, our school was like that too.

スー：　一番好きな科目は何だったの？
まなぶ：　物理が一番好きだった。スーはどうだった？物理、勉強した？
スー：　うん、勉強したよ。
まなぶ：　ほんとうに？物理と数学と、どっちが好きだった？
スー：　私は数学がもっと好きだった。数学の先生が、とてもいい先生だったから。
まなぶ：　へえ。そうだったんだ。

S: What subject did you like the most?
M: I liked Physics the most. What about you, Sue? Did you study Physics?
S: Yeah, I studied that.
M: Really? Between Physics and Mathematics, which one did you like more?
S: I liked Mathematics more. The Math teacher was a very good one, so…
M: Oh, that was the reason.

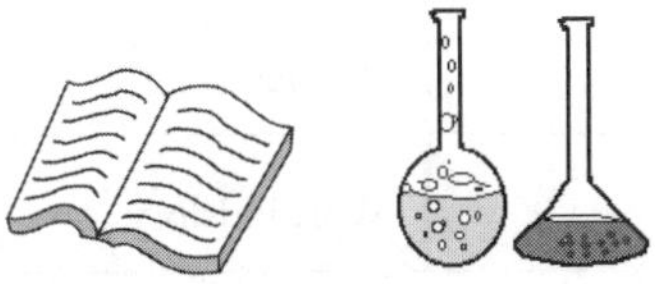

## 知ってた？　学校システム School system

**調べましょう**

**1. Let us be familiar with the school system in Japan. Research the name of each school level in Japanese and fill in the table below. Also, find the school year of each level.**

| 英語 | 日本語 | 学年 |
|---|---|---|
| Kindergarten | | 年少・年中・年長* |
| Primary school | | （ 1 ）年生 〜（　　）年生 |
| Junior high school | | （　　）年生 〜（　　）年生 |
| Senior high school | | （　　）年生 〜（　　）年生 |
| University (undergraduate) | | （　　）年生 〜（　　）年生 |
| Postgraduate (M.A.) | | 1年目、2年目 |
| Postgraduate (PhD) | | 1年目、2年目、3年目 |

（*幼稚園は普通，1年生、2年生、3年生と呼ばない。）

2. **The followings are the names of some of the major subjects in school. Look up each word in your dictionary and write it down in Japanese.**

| 英語(えいご) | 日本語(にほんご) | 英語(えいご) | 日本語(にほんご) |
|---|---|---|---|
| Art | | Japanese history | |
| Chemistry | | Mathematics | |
| English | | Music | |
| Ethics | | Physical education | |
| Geography | | Physics | |
| Home economics | | Politics | |
| Japanese as a national language | | World history | |

## 新(あたら)しい単語(たんご)・表現(ひょうげん)

(Basic words/expressions are marked with '*')

| | |
|---|---|
| ～以外(いがい) | except for, besides |
| おしゃべり | chat |
| 押(お)す* | push |
| オレンジ | orange |
| 学年(がくねん) | school year |
| 課題(かだい) | assignment, task |
| 活動(かつどう) | activity, movement |
| 科目(かもく) | school subject(s) |
| 関係(かんけい)* | relationship |
| 薬(くすり)* | medicine |
| げらげら | guffaw |
| 後輩(こうはい) | one's junior student(s) |
| コーチ | coach |
| サークル | group activities |
| 塾(じゅく) | cram school |
| 受験勉強(じゅけんべんきょう) | study for entrance exam |
| スイッチ* | switch |
| 数学(すうがく)* | Mathematics |
| すごく* | very |
| スパゲッティ | spaghetti |
| ターム | (school) term |
| だから* | so |
| 足(た)す* | add |
| 楽(たの)しむ* | enjoy |
| ～たら* | (provisional, conditional) |
| ～って | ＝～と, ～という, etc. |
| 定食(ていしょく) | regular set menu |
| てんぷら | tempura |

| | |
|---|---|
| ～と* | (provisional, conditional) |
| なし | pear |
| ～なら* | (provisional, conditional) |
| なるほど | I see, I understand |
| 入学（にゅうがく） | entering school |
| 飲（の）み会（かい） | drinking party |
| ～ば* | if (provisional, conditional) |
| バスケットボール | basketball |
| 久（ひさ）しぶりに* | after a long time |
| ～部（ぶ） | … Section, … Club |
| 普段（ふだん）* | usually, normally |
| 物理（ぶつり） | Physics, physics |
| プロ | professional |
| 放課後（ほうかご） | after school time |
| ボール* | ball |
| まあね | sort of, kind of, well |
| みかん | mandarin |
| みんな* | everyone, all |
| やめる* | quit, stop |
| 練習（れんしゅう）* | practice, exercise |
| 笑（わら）う* | laugh |

# 第１７課

## ゆっくり休んだ方がいいですよ
## It's better for you to have a good rest

[エレナ、調子がよくない]

まさと：　エレナ、どうしたの？元気ないね。

エレナ：　うん、頭がずきずきするの。

まさと：　大丈夫？ 少し寝たほうがいいよ。

エレナ：　そうね。ちょっと寒気もするし。

まさと：　本当？ 熱、計ってみたら。はい、体温計。

エレナ：　うん。ありがとう。 ああ、３９度もある。

まさと：　ええ！ ３９度？ 病院に行ったほうがいいよ。

[エレナが医者にみてもらっている]

医者：　どうしましたか。

エレナ：　ちょっと頭が痛くて、寒気もするんです。喉も少しひりひりするし。

医者：　そうですか。ちょっとみてみましょう。う～ん、かぜをひいたようですね。

エレナ：　かぜですか。

医者：　ええ。薬を出しますから、毎食後に飲んでください。２、３日はゆっくり休んだ方がいいですよ。

エレナ：　はい、わかりました。ありがとうございました。

医者：　お大事に。

[医者にみてもらった後]

まさと：　どうだった？

エレナ：　かぜだって。

まさと：　やっぱり。じゃあ、あたたかくして、ゆっくり休んで、しばらく外出しない方がいいよ。

エレナ：　うん、そうね。

## 単語(たんご)と表現(ひょうげん)

| | | | | | |
|---|---|---|---|---|---|
| 2 | 頭(あたま) | head | 9 | 喉(のど) | throat |
| 2 | ずきずきする | throbbing | 9 | ひりひりする | irritating |
| 4 | 寒気(さむけ) | chilly feeling | 10 | かぜを ひく | catch cold |
| 4 | 寒気(さむけ)が する | feel a chill, feel cold | 13 | 薬(くすり) を 出(だ)す | give medicine (prescribe) |
| 5 | 熱(ねつ) | temperature, fever | 13 | 毎食後(まいしょくご) | after every (each) meal |
| 5 | 計(はか)る | measure | 16 | お大事(だいじ)に | take care (saying goodbye to a patient) |
| 5 | 体温計(たいおんけい) | (clinical) thermometer | | | |
| 9 | 痛(いた)い | aching, painful | 20 | 外出(がいしゅつ)する | go out |

## ダイアログ（英語(えいご)）

**[Elena is unwell]**

1 M: Elena, what's wrong? You don't look well.
2 E: I have a bad headache (My head is throbbing with pain).
3 M: Are you all right? I think you should sleep a little while.
4 E: You are right (I think so). I also feel a little bit chilly.
5 M: Really. I think you'd better check your temperature. Here is a thermometer.
6 E: Yes, thank you. Oh it reaches 39 degrees.
7 M: What? 39 degrees! You'd better go to the hospital.

**[Elena is seeing a doctor]**

8 Doc: What brought you here today?
9 E: I have a slight headache and also feel chilly. My throat is also irritating.
10 Doc: I see. Let me check. Umm, it seems you
11 have a cold.
12 E: A cold?
13 Doc: Yes. I will give (prescribe for) you
14 some medicine, so take it after every meal. You'd better have a good rest for at least 2 or 3 days.
15 E: Yes, I understand. Thank you very much.
16 Doc: Please take care (of yourself).

**[After seeing the doctor]**

17 M: How was it?
18 E: (The doctor said) it's a cold.
19 M: That's what I thought. Well then you
20 should keep warm, have a good rest and you should not go out for a while.
21 E: Yes, I think so.

## 文法(ぶんぽう)

### Tense and Aspect

(i) Tense: A grammatical category which refers to different time locations; 'past', 'present' and 'future' are basic time locations in an absolute tense; る *vs.* た.

(ii) Aspect: A grammatical category which involves the internal structure of time; in Japanese 'progressive (action in progress)' and 'resultative (temporal result)' have important aspectual meanings; る *vs.* ている.

(iii) Perfect: Expression which refers to whether or not an action/event has been completed; た.

## 1. Tense

**1.1.** た forms: The past is specifically expressed by the た form (for any type of predicates).

(1) a. 私はきのう、家でご飯を食べました。

b. 私は夕べ、田中さんに会いました。

c. 木村さんは買い物に行かなかった。

d. 私は去年、ずっと日本にいたよ。

e. きのうの映画、おもしろかったね。

**1.2.** る forms: る may express the present or future. Whether a given verb is stative or dynamic is important.

Stative verbs: いる 'be (animate)', ある 'be (inanimate)', 要る 'be necessary', (〜することが) 出来る 'be able to (do)')

Their る form indicates the present or the future.

(2) a. 田中さんは、いま学校にいます。

b. 私はあしたも、ここにいます。

c. その本は机の上にある。

Dynamic verbs: All other (the majority of) verbs.

Their る form indicates the future.

(3) a. 私はあした、日本に帰ります。

b. いま、行きます。 (near future)

c. じゃ、後で電話するね。

NB. Their present tense is expressed by the ている form or other expressions (cf. the next section).

(4) a. 田中さんは、いま、家でテレビを見ています。

b. 私は、いま、カフェでコーヒーを飲んでいます。

**1.3.** Summary: Past た *vs.* Non-past る

As such, the Japanese tense system presents an opposition between Past (た) and Non-past (る, present or future).

**2. Aspect:**

ている (ていた for past) indicates an action/event in progress or a result of the action/event. Whether it indicates a progression or a result is basically dependent on the type of verb that is used with ている. Japanese verbs can be divided into the following 5 groups, depending on the aspectual meaning of their ている form.

**2.1.** Progressive verbs: Their ている form basically indicates that the action/event is in progress.

書く　食べる　見る　話す　電話する　飲む　寝る　歩く　泳ぐ

(1) a. 木村さんは、いま、手紙を書いています。

b. 私は、きのうの3時頃、家でテレビを見ていました。

**2.2.** Resultative verbs: Their ている form normally indicates the result of an action/event. English- speaking learners need to pay special attention to the ている form of this group of verbs since its meaning often differs from the meaning of 'be –ing'.

死ぬ　行く　来る　帰る　落ちる　倒れる　乗る　着く　結婚する

(2) a. 田中さんは今、日本に行っています。(Tanaka-san has gone to and is still in Japan.)

b. 道ばたに、犬が死んでいる。(What is observed is a result of 死ぬ, i.e. the death.)

Different expressions are used to indicate the progressive meaning of the action/event in this group.

(3) a. 田中さんは、いま、日本に行く途中です。　(～途中 'in the middle of…')

b. 死にかけている。　([Masu-stem]-かけている 'in the middle of …', 'about to …')

**2.3.** Change verbs: Their ている form may indicate an action/event in progress or the result of an action/event, depending on the context.

溶ける　（服を）着る　（めがねを）かける

(4) a. 氷が、全部、溶けている。　'The ice has all melted.'

b. 氷が、だんだん溶けている。　'The ice is gradually melting.'

**2.4.** *Teiru* verbs: They are always used in the ている form, and indicate a state.

似る　隣り合う　そびえる

(5) a. 木村さんは、お父さんによく似ている。

b. 田中さんの家は、木村さんの家と隣り合っている。

**2.5.** Stative verbs: They are always used in the る form; they indicate a state.

ある　いる　（～することが）出来る　要る

(6) a. オペラハウスは、シドニーにあります。

b. 私は日本語を話すことが出来ます。

c. 私は、いま、新しい車が要ります。

### 文法練習1

**Make up a sentence using the given words.**

(例) 田中さんは、いま、家で山田さんとテレビを見ています。

(e.g.) いま　テレビ　見る　(1) きのう　ひとりで　(2) 先週　日本から

(3) いま　町　ともだち　(4) 来年　勉強する　(5) いま　鈴木さん

(6) 戸田さん　ここ　来る　(7) いま　行く　(8) 山田さん　似る

## 3. Relative tense

While the tense discussed above is based on the time of the utterance, in an embedded clause different rules apply. The basic rule is whether an event/state expressed by a predicate occurs 'before', 'simultaneously' or 'after' the time reference expressed by the main predicate: た indicates 'before' and ている／る indicates 'simultaneously' or 'after'. In this regard, a speaker returns to the original tense in a direct quotation in Japanese.

(1) *Direct quotation* → *Indirect quotation*

a. E: I said, "Yumi is eating dinner". → I said that Yumi was eating dinner.

J: 『ユミはご飯を食べている』と言った。→ ユミはご飯を食べていると言った。

occurs at the same time as "I said"

b. 私は『ユミはご飯を食べた』と言った。→ 私は、ユミはご飯を食べたと言った。

occurs before "I said"

c. 私は『ユミはご飯を食べる』と言った。→ 私は、ユミはご飯を食べると言った。

occurs after "I said"

d. 『きのう木村さんに会いました』と書いた。→ きのう木村さんに会ったと書いた。

occurs before "I wrote"

e. 『映画（えいが）はおもしろい』と言（い）った。→ 映画（えいが）はおもしろいと言（い）った。
feeling at the same time as "I said"

f. 『映画（えいが）はおもしろかった』と言（い）った。→ 映画（えいが）はおもしろかったと言（い）った。
what he felt before "I said"

**4. Perfect**

The た form and the ている form may be used to indicate whether an action/event has been completed (た form) or not (ている form). This is particularly well indicated when used with adverbs もう (completion; 'already') or まだ (incompletion; 'not yet').

(1) 朝（あさ）ご飯（はん）、もう食（た）べましたか。→ はい、もう食（た）べました。 or
→ いいえ、まだ食（た）べていません。
(「いいえ、まだ食（た）べませんでした」sounds odd.)

(2) （もう）終（お）わりましたか。 → はい、（もう）終（お）わりました。 or
→ いいえ、（まだ）終（お）わっていません。

When a question contains a word that indicates the action/event happened in the past, it is a simple past tense. In this case, the answers are also simply given in a past tense (i.e. た form rather than ている form) in both affirmative and negative answers.

(3) きのう、田中（たなか）さんに会（あ）いましたか。→ はい、会（あ）いました。 or
→ いいえ、会（あ）いませんでした。

**文法練習（ぶんぽうれんしゅう）2**

**Answer the questions. For the purpose of practice, provide both positive and negative answers.**

(例（れい）) 朝（あさ）ご飯（はん）、もう食（た）べましたか。→ はい、もう、食（た）べました。
→ いいえ、まだ、食（た）べていません。

(1) この本（ほん）、もう読（よ）みましたか。
(2) 宿題（しゅくだい）、もう終（お）わりましたか。
(3) このCD、もう聞（き）きましたか。
(4) 田中（たなか）さんに、もう電話（でんわ）しましたか。
(5) この映画（えいが）、見（み）ましたか。
(6) 花子（はなこ）に、イーメールを送（おく）りましたか。
(7) リナさんに、会（あ）いましたか。
(8) あの新（あたら）しいレストラン、行（い）きましたか。

## 自然(しぜん)な日本語(にほんご)

## 擬態語(ぎたいご)・擬声語(ぎせいご) Onomatopoeia (Sound-symbolic words, mimetic words)

Japanese is very rich in words that represent the sounds/movement of various things, animals and phenomena. They are not a compulsory component for the sentence in many cases. However, their use adds a higher degree of reality and vividness to the expression, and is very important for the 'naturalness' of expressions in Japanese.

They often do not have equivalent words in English, and are not clearly translatable. Many of these words involve the repetition of the same sound sequence. They are sometimes written in katakana for special visual effect.

(1)
- a. ざあざあ　　ざあざあ雨(あめ)が降(ふ)る
- b. げらげら　　げらげら笑(わら)う。
- c. にこにこ　　にこにこ笑(わら)う。　いつも、にこにこしている。
- d. くるくる　　椅子(いす)をくるくる回(まわ)す。
- e. ぺこぺこ　　おなかがペコペコだ。
- f. からから　　喉(のど)が、からからだ。
- g. ぶつぶつ　　ぶつぶつしゃべる。　ぶつぶつ文句(もんく)を言(い)う。(文句(もんく) complaints)
- h. わんわん　　犬(いぬ)がわんわん吠(ほ)える。　(吠(ほ)える bark)
- i. ぺらぺら　　ペラペラしゃべる。　英語(えいご)がぺらぺらだ。

Some of these words do not involve a repetition.

(2)
- a. ぽきん　　木(き)が、ぽきんと折(お)れる。
- b. そっと　　そっと歩(ある)く。
- c. のんびり　　のんびり暮(く)らす。
- d. ぴたっ　　水漏(みずも)れが、ぴたっと止(と)まった。

### 自然(しぜん)な日本語(にほんご)：練習(れんしゅう) 1

**Match the related two words, by linking them with a line.**

| (1) | | | (2) | |
|---|---|---|---|---|
| | いぬ | カーカー | のど | ぺらぺら |
| | ねこ | モーモー | 雨(あめ) | ぶつぶつ |
| | からす | わんわん | 日本語(にほんご) | からから |
| | うし | ニャーニャー | 文句(もんく) | ぺこぺこ |
| | ぶた | ブーブー | おなか | ざあざあ |

## 自然な日本語：練 習 2

**Make up sentences, using onomatopoeia. Use polite endings.**

(例) The dog saw me and barked. → <u>その犬は、私を見てわんわんと吠えました。</u>

(1) I am so thirsty now. Please give me some water.

(2) It is raining a lot outside. (outside そと)

(3) I was hungry, so I had dinner alone.

(4) Yamada-san can speak French very well.

(5) It was so funny and I laughed a lot. (funny おかしい)

## 表 現

### 1 Useful expressions when you feel ill

☛ Various expressions are use to describe a symptom of a certain sickness or how you feel. Usually, a certain symptom goes with a particular verb and/or is expressed/described by an adjective. The following are some examples.

- I have / feel a chill. 寒気がします
- I have diarrhea. 下痢をしています
- I have a fever. 熱があります
- I feel very sick. 気分がとても悪いです
- I have a cough. せきが出ます
- I feel dizzy. 目まいがします
- I feel nauseous. 吐き気がします

[part of body] が 痛いです／痛みます ‘sore/ache [part of body]’

- I have pain here. ここが痛いです
- I have sore throat. のどが痛いです
- I have a sore eye. 目が痛いです
- I have a toothache. 歯が痛いです
- I have a stomach ache. 胃が痛いです
- I have a headache. 頭が痛いです

Other related words:

- 病院 hospital
- 看護士 nurse
- 医者 doctor
- 入院 hospitalization
- 怪我 wound
- 手術 surgery
- 患者 patient
- お見舞い visit patient

## 表現練習１

**Look at the pictures and express/describe each symptom.**

(例) 頭が痛いです。

(e.g.)

(1)

(2)

(3)

(4)

(5)

## 2 ～方がいい 'You had better…' 'It's better for you (him/her etc) to…', etc.

**[1]** ☛ This expression is useful for making a suggestion or offering advice. Normally, [affirmative-た] of verb is used.

(1) もっと野菜を食べた方がいいですよ。　(野菜 vegetable)

(2) すぐタバコを止めた方がいいですよ。

(3) A: 日本語の本をたくさん読んだ方がいいですよ。

B: そうですね。じゃあ、そうします。

(4) A: もう少し運動した方がいいと思いますよ。

B: そうですね。

(5) A: あした、田中さんに会った方がいいですよ。

B: あしたですか。忙しいので、あしたはちょっと…。

(6) A: 熱もあるし、頭が痛くて…。

B: じゃあ、病院に行った方がいいと思いますよ。

A: そうですね。行ってみます。

## 表現練習 2

**Respond to the following statements with the appropriate advice/suggestions, as given in the box below.**

(例) 本を忘れました。 → [d] じゃあ、ともだちに（本を）借りた方がいいですよ。

（忘れる forget/leave something somewhere; 借りる borrow）

(1) 財布をなくしました。（なくす lose）

(2) 道が分かりません 。

(3) おなかが、すごく痛いです。

(4) 日本語が話したいです。

(5) 今日は、とても疲れました。

(6) あした、テストがあります。

(7) タバコを吸いすぎて、のどが痛いです。

(8) きょう、寒いですね。

| | |
|---|---|
| (a) 警察署に行く (警察署 police station) | (b) 学校で習う |
| (c) 地図をみる （地図 map） | ~~(d)~~ ともだちに借りる |
| (e) 早く寝る | (f) 病 院 に行く |
| (g) 禁煙する （禁煙する quit smoking） | (h) 今晩、勉 強 する |
| (i) 厚着にする | (j) [ your own answer ] |

**[2]** ☛ [〜ない方がいい] is used when a recommendation has the negative form

(1) コーヒーを飲まない方がいいですよ。

(2) 出来れば、学校を休まない方がいいですよ。 （出来れば if it is possible）

## 表現練習 3

**Rewrite the following sentences in Japanese, using 〜ない方がいい.**

(例) You'd better not sleep here. → ここで寝ない方がいいですよ。

(1) You had better not smoke inside restaurants.

(2) Since he is having a nap, it's better not to go to Suzuki-san's room. (have a nap 昼寝をする)

(3) Since this water is old, you should not drink it.

(4) You had better not exercise too much. (exercise too much 運動しすぎる)

(5) You should not sleep too much.

## 3 [Quantifier]も '(enough)'；[Quantifier]は '(at least)'

**[1]** ☛ When も is used with [quantifier], it indicates the speaker's feeling that the amount or duration expressed by the quantifier is sufficient, too much, too long.

(1) パーティーに、５０人も来ました。

(2) 休温が、38.5度もあります。

**[2]** ☛ In contrast, しか indicates the insufficient feeling of 'only'. It is always accompanied by a negative expression. だけしか may be used to emphasize a feeling of insufficiency.

(3) パーティーに、１０人しか来ませんでした。
（１０人だけしか来ませんでした）

(4) コーヒーを飲みたいですが、いま、１００円しかありません。

(5) 田中さんしかその映画を見ていません。

**[3]** ☛ は with a quantifier indicates the speaker's feeling of 'at least'.

(6) パーティーに、２０人は来ると思います。

(7) このかばん、2万円はすると思います。

### 表現練習４

**Make up sentences using the given key words.**

(例) パーティー　[quantifier]も　→ <u>きのうのパーティーに、１００人も来ました。</u>

(1) 猫　7匹も

(2) あした　テスト　5時間も

(3) 田中さん　背丈　[quantifier]も　（背丈 height）

(4) 野村さん　１７５センチは

(5) この車　[quantifier] は

(6) パーティー　5人しか

(7) コーヒー　～しか

(8) 朝　ミルク　～しか

## 対話(たいわ)

### 対話練習(たいわれんしゅう) 1

**Pre-task: ～方(ほう)がいい**

**In pairs, state the situation below in random order. The other speaker then makes an appropriate suggestion or offers advice using ～方(ほう)がいいですよ.**

(例(れい)) A: クラスに遅(おく)れています。
B: 学校(がっこう)に、タクシーで行(い)った方(ほう)がいいですよ。
A: そうですね。そうします。

- I am late for class
- I lost my wallet
- I have an oral test in Japanese tomorrow
- I have a fever
- I feel cold
- I want to speak Japanese fluently

fluently りゅうちょうに

### 対話練習(たいわれんしゅう) 2

**Pre-task: ～ない方(ほう)がいい**

**In pairs, state the situation below in random order. The other speaker then makes an appropriate suggestion or offers advice using ～ない方(ほう)がいいですよ.**

(例(れい)) A: のどが痛(いた)いです。
B: タバコを吸(す)いすぎない方(ほう)がいいですよ。
A: そうですね。そうします。

- I have a sore throat
- I drank too much (wine) yesterday
- I watched TV too much, so my eyes are tired
- I have a hangover
- I am so tired
- I have no money in my bank account

bank account 銀行口座(ぎんこうこうざ)

## 対話練習3

**Pre-task: もう〜た／まだ〜てない**

**In pairs, ask your partner if he/she has done the things illustrated in the pictures. Use the casual style. You can ask the questions in random order.**

(例) A: もう9時だけど、朝ご飯、もう食べた？
B: 朝ご飯？うん、もう食べたよ。 or 朝ご飯？ううん、まだ食べていない。
A: あ、ほんとう。

(e.g.) 9:00 am

[ have eaten breakfast? ]

(1) tomorrow; exam

[ have studied? ]

(2) this movie, looks interesting

[ have watched the movie? ]

(3) today; your mother's birthday

[ have bought a present?]

(4) heard; hard to get a driving licence

[ have got a licence? ]

(5) next week; departure

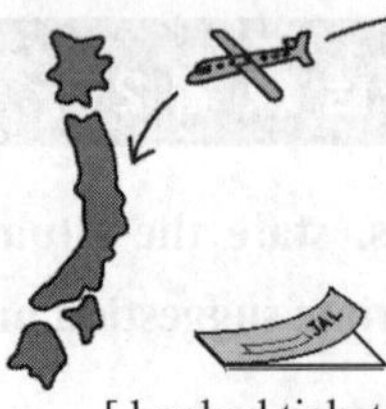

[ booked tickets? ]

departure 出発；book 予約する；get a driving licence 運転免許を取る

(6) today; your father's birthday

[ have called your father in Kyoto? ]

(7) dinner soon

[ have cooked dinner? ]

(8)

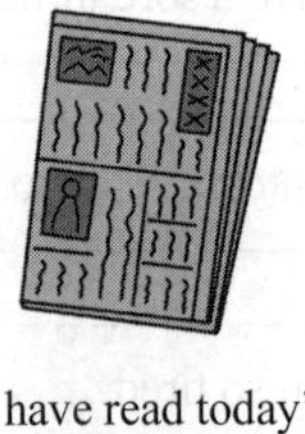

[ have read today's newspaper?]

## 対話(たいわ)作(づく)り

✍ **In pairs, create a dialogue for the given situation. Please feel free to ask the instructor if you have any questions about Japanese expressions for your dialogue.**

**Situation:**

You and your partner are talking in one of the following situations. Express how you feel and/or offer some appropriate suggestions/advice.

(i) Your partner is unwell. ([a part of body] sore; e.g. headache, throat sore, etc.)
(ii) Your partner has lost his/her wallet.
(iii) Your partner is thinking of traveling abroad.

Please incorporate the following expressions/phenomena into your dialogue:

- ～た方(ほう)がいい／～ない方(ほう)がいい
- part of body
- もう　～した？
- まだ　～ていない
- onomatopoeia
- [quantifier] も／は
- ～しか

### サンプル・ダイアログ

まゆみ：　どうしたの？
つよし：　うん、ちょっと頭(あたま)が痛(いた)くて…
まゆみ：　ほんとう！とても痛(いた)いの？
つよし：　うん、頭(あたま)がガンガンするし、ちょっと寒気(さむけ)もするんだ。
まゆみ：　熱(ねつ)はどう？
つよし：　さっき計(はか)ったら、３８度(ど)だった。
まゆみ：　えっ！３８度(ど)もあるの。それは大変(たいへん)！何(なに)か、食(た)べた？
つよし：　ううん、朝(あさ)から水(みず)しか飲(の)んでいない。
まゆみ：　そうだね。今(いま)は何(なに)も食(た)べない方(ほう)がいいと思(おも)う。
つよし：　お腹(なか)がペコペコだけど、あまり食(た)べたくないから。
まゆみ：　かぜをひいたようね。薬(くすり)、もう飲(の)んだ？
つよし：　ううん、まだ飲(の)んでない。
まゆみ：　薬(くすり)、飲(の)んで、ゆっくり休(やす)んだ方(ほう)がいいよ。
つよし：　そうだね。そうするよ。

M: What happen?
T: Well, I have a headache…
M: Really! Does it hurt badly?
T: Yeah, my head's very painful and I also feel cold.
M: What about a fever?
T: I measured it before and it was 38 degrees.
M: Oh, 38 degrees! That's a problem! Have you eaten something?
T: No, I have only drunk some water since this morning.
M: That's good. I think you'd better not eat anything for the moment.
T: I am hungry, but I do not want to eat anything, so…
M: It seems that you have caught a cold. Have you already taken medicine?
T: No, I have not yet.
M: You'd better take some medicine, and have a good rest.
T: You're right. I will do so.

## 知(し)ってた？

### 調(しら)べましょう

**Provide the Japanese words for these parts of the body. Choose one from the list in the box.**

(1)

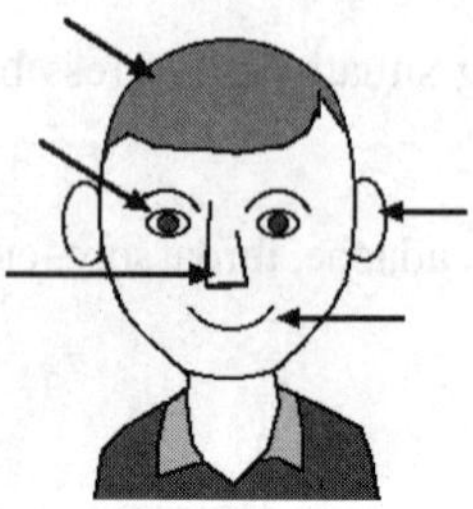

[others]

head: face: forehead:

eyelash: eyelid: eyebrow:

cheek: chin: tongue:

teeth: lips: neck:

| | | | | | | | | |
|---|---|---|---|---|---|---|---|---|
| 頭(あたま) | 髪(かみ)の毛(け) | 顔(かお) | 額(ひたい)(おでこ) | 目(め) | 眉毛(まゆげ) | まつ毛(げ) | まぶた | |
| 耳(みみ) | 鼻(はな) | 頬(ほお)(ほっぺた) | 唇(くちびる) | 口(くち) | 歯(は) | 舌(した) | あご | 首(くび) |

(2)

[others] chest:

shoulder: finger(s):

thighs: heel:

ankle: toe:

| | | | | | | |
|---|---|---|---|---|---|---|
| お尻(しり) | 肩(かた) | おなか | 肘(ひじ) | 胸(むね) | 太(ふと)もも | 腕(うで) |
| 手(て) | 指(ゆび) | 膝(ひざ) | 足(あし) | 足首(あしくび) | つま先(さき) | かかと |

### 練習(れんしゅう)しましょう

**Write an appropriate part of the body in each space between the brackets [　].**

顔(かお)の真(ま)ん中(なか)には [　　　] があり、その上(うえ)には二(ふた)つの[　　　]があります。私(わたし)たちは、[　　　]で、匂(にお)いをかいで、[　　　]で物(もの)を見(み)ます。[　　　]で音(おと)を聞(き)きます。また、[　　　]では、物(もの)を食(た)べたり、話(はな)したりします。

[　　　]で、物(もの)を運(はこ)んだり、道具(どうぐ)を使(つか)ったりします。[　　　]では歩(ある)いたり、走(はし)ったり、物(もの)を蹴(け)ったりします。

## 新(あたら)しい単語(たんご)・表現(ひょうげん)

(Basic words/expressions are marked with '*')

| | |
|---|---|
| 頭(あたま)* | head |
| 厚着(あつぎ)にする | wear many clothes |
| 胃(い) | stomach |
| 椅子(いす)* | chair |
| 以前(いぜん) | before, used to |
| 痛(いた)む* | get sore |
| 要(い)る* | need |
| 運転免許(うんてんめんきょ) | driving licence |
| 運動(うんどう)* | sport |
| おかしい* | funny, strange |
| お見舞(みま)い | visit patient |
| 折(お)れる* | be cut, break |
| 外出(がいしゅつ)する* | go out |
| かぐ* | smell |
| かける* | put on, hang on, call |
| 肩(かた) | shoulder |
| 髪(かみ)* | hair (on head) |
| 看護師(かんごし)* | nurse |
| 患者(かんじゃ)* | patient |
| 木(き)* | tree |
| 気分(きぶん)* | feeling |
| 禁煙(きんえん)する | quit smoking |
| 薬(くすり)を出(だ)す | to give medicine |
| 暮(く)らす* | spend (time), live |
| 警察署(けいさつしょ) | police station |
| 怪我(けが)* | wound |
| 下痢(げり) | diarrhea |
| 蹴(け)る | kick |
| 口座(こうざ) | (bank) account |
| 氷(こおり)* | ice |
| 寒気(さむけ) | chilly feeling |
| 寒気(さむけ)がする | feel a chill, feel cold |
| 死(し)にかける | nearly die |
| しゃべる* | chat, speak |
| 手術(しゅじゅつ) | surgery |
| ずきずきする | throbbing |
| せき | cough |
| 背丈(せたけ) | height |
| そびえる | (big objects) rise high |
| 体温計(たいおんけい) | (clinical) thermometer |
| だんだん* | gradually |
| 地図(ちず) | map |
| 着(つ)く* | arrive |
| 出来(でき)れば* | if it is possible |
| 道具(どうぐ) | tool, instrument |
| 溶(と)ける | melt |
| 途中(とちゅう)* | in the middle of |
| 隣(とな)り合(あ)う | be next to each other |
| 止(と)まる* | stop |
| 匂(にお)い* | smell |
| 入院(にゅういん) | hospitalization |
| 似(に)る* | get similar |
| 熱(ねつ)* | temperature, fever, heat |
| 喉(のど)* | throat |
| 計(はか)る* | measure |
| 吐(は)き気(け)がする | be nauseous |
| 運(はこ)ぶ* | carry |
| 病院(びょういん)* | hospital |

| | |
|---|---|
| ひりひりする | irritating |
| 昼寝（ひるね） | nap |
| 服（ふく）* | clothes |
| 豚（ぶた） | pig |
| 二日酔い（ふつかよい） | hangover |
| 吠える（ほえる） | bark |
| 毎食後（まいしょくご） | after every (each) meal |
| まだ* | (not) yet |
| 回す（まわす）* | turn |
| 真ん中（まんなか）* | centre, middle |
| 水漏れ（みずもれ） | water drip, leak |
| 道ばた（みちばた）* | roadside, wayside |
| 目まい（めまい） | dizzy |
| もう* | already |
| 文句（もんく） | complaints |
| 流暢に（りゅうちょうに） | fluently |

# 第（だいじゅうはっか）18課

## 舞妓（まいこ）さんに会（あ）えるなんて、感激（かんげき）！

## It is amazing that I am seeing maiko

[まさととエレナ、京都（きょうと）の金閣寺（きんかくじ）に来（き）ている]

**エレナ：** ああ、ここが有名（ゆうめい）な金閣寺（きんかくじ）。ほんとに全部（ぜんぶ）、金色（きんいろ）なんだね。きれい！

**まさと：** うん、そうだね。

**エレナ：** ところで、平日（へいじつ）なのに、どうしてこんなに中学生（ちゅうがくせい）や高校生（こうこうせい）が多（おお）いの？

**まさと：** 修学旅行（しゅうがくりょこう）でここに来（き）ているんだよ。

**エレナ：** 修学旅行（しゅうがくりょこう）？修学旅行（しゅうがくりょこう）って何（なに）？

**まさと：** School excursion trip だよ。

**エレナ：** ああ、なるほど。

[京都（きょうと）の町（まち）を見物（けんぶつ）している]

**エレナ：** この辺（へん）には、まだ古（ふる）い建物（たてもの）やお寺（てら）がたくさんあるんだね。いいねえ。

**まさと：** うん、いいね。

**エレナ：** あ、あそこ見（み）て！あの人（ひと）たち、舞妓（まいこ）さん？

**まさと：** あ、ほんとうだ。きれいな着物（きもの）、着（き）てるね。

**エレナ：** 舞妓（まいこ）さんに会（あ）えるなんて、感激（かんげき）！

**まさと：** そうだね。この頃（ごろ）は、日本人（にほんじん）でもなかなか直接（ちょくせつ）見（み）るチャンスがないから、ラッキーだね。

**エレナ：** へえ、そうなんだ。

**まさと：** じゃあ、もう暗（くら）くなってきたし、そろそろ帰（かえ）ろうか。

**エレナ：** そうだね。おなかもすいてきたしね。でも、ほんと楽（たの）しかったね。

## ♣ 単語(たんご)と表現(ひょうげん)

| | | | | | |
|---|---|---|---|---|---|
| 1 | 金閣寺(きんかくじ) | the Kinkaku Temple | 13 | 着(き)る | wear |
| 1 | 金色(きんいろ) | golden colour | 14 | 感激(かんげき) | emotionally moving, stirring |
| 3 | 平日(へいじつ) | weekdays | | | |
| 5 | 修学旅行(しゅうがくりょこう) | school excursion trip | 15 | この頃(ごろ) | these days |
| 8 | なるほど | I see | 15 | なかなか | hardly, rarely |
| 9 | この辺(へん) | around here | 15 | 直接(ちょくせつ) | directly |
| 9 | 建物(たてもの) | building | 15 | チャンス | chance, opportunity |
| 9 | お寺(てら) | temple | 16 | ラッキー | lucky |
| 12 | 舞妓(まいこ) | maiko (traditional young female dancer) | 18 | 暗(くら)い | dark |
| | | | 18 | そろそろ | sooner or later |
| 13 | 着物(きもの) | kimono | | | |

### ダイアログ（英語(えいご)）

**[Masato and Elena are in the Kinkaku Temple in Kyoto]**

1 E: Oh, this is the famous Kinkaku Temple. It's really all in golden colour. It's beautiful!

2 M: Yeah, that's true.

3-4 E: By the way, it is a weekday; why are there so many middle school and high school students?

5 M: They are here for '*Shuugaku Ryokoo*'.

6 E: '*Shuugaku Ryokoo*'? What's '*Shuugaku Ryokoo*'?

7 M: It's a school excursion trip.

8 E: Oh, I see.

**[They are on sightseeing of towns in Kyoto]**

9 E: There are still many old buildings and
10 temples remaining around here. Very good.

11 M: Yeah, it's good.

12 E: Oh, look over there! Are they maiko-san?

13 M: Oh, you're right. They are wearing beautiful kimono.

14 E: It's amazing that I am seeing maiko-san!

15 M: That's right. Even Japanese people rarely
16 have an opportunity to see them in person these days. We're lucky.

17 E: Oh, is that so?

18 M: Well, it has become dark, so (it's time to) let's go home now.

19 E: You're right. I am getting hungry as well. But, it was really good.

### 文法(ぶんぽう)

## 1. Verb phrases: ～てくる／ていく／てしまう／てみる／ておく／てある

The て form of a verb may form a phrase with various supplementary (or auxiliary) verbs, and indicates the diverse phases or aspects of an action/event that the verb conveys. They are normally written in hiragana.

### 1.1. ～てくる

This indicates that someone, something, some state, message, etc. moves towards 'here' and/or 'now'. It is often not translated clearly in English.

(1) 私(わたし)の部屋(へや)に田中(たなか)さんが入(はい)ってきました。

(2) 暗(くら)くなってきました。

(3) となりの部屋(へや)から声(こえ)が聞(き)こえてきました。

(4) 田中(たなか)さんが電話(でんわ)してきました／電話(でんわ)をかけてきました。

It sometimes indicates the 'onset of some feeling/process' ((5) and (6)), or some errand 'go and do (and come back)' ((7) and (8)).

(5) 日本(にほん)のアニメに興味(きょうみ)が出(で)てきました。

(6) 日本語(にほんご)がだんだんおもしろくなってきた。

(7) 去年(きょねん)、日本(にほん)に行(い)ってきました。

(8) ちょっと、ミルク買(か)ってきます。

### 1.2. ～ていく

This indicates that someone, something, some state, message, etc. is moving away from 'here' and/or 'now'.

(1) 部屋(へや)から田中(たなか)さんが出(で)ていきました。

(2) これからだんだん寒(さむ)くなっていきますね。

(3) 船(ふね)は港(みなと)から遠(とお)ざかっていった。　(遠(とお)ざかる disappear from view)

#### 文法練習(ぶんぽうれんしゅう) 1

**Make up a sentence using the given expressions. Use polite endings.**

(例(れい)) 東京(とうきょう)　～てくる　→　先週(せんしゅう)、一人(ひとり)で東京(とうきょう)に行(い)ってきました。

(1) だいぶ　寒(さむ)い　～てくる

(2) 山田(やまだ)さん　訪(たず)ねる　～てくる

(3) 町(まち)　中村(なかむら)さん　～てくる

(4) 猫(ねこ)　三浦(みうら)さん　～ていく

(5) 鈴木(すずき)さん　車(くるま)　遠(とお)ざかる　～ていく

## 1.3. ～てしまう（～ちゃう）

This phrase indicates that an action/event has been completed ((1) below), and/or is often accompanied by the speaker's regretful feeling that it is an undesirable happening, outside his/her control ((2) and (3)). In casual conversation, it is often contracted to ～ちゃう.

(1) もう宿題を全部やってしまった。(やっちゃった)

(2) どうしよう。コンピューターが壊れてしまった。(壊れちゃった)

(3) 田中さんが一人でお金を全部使ってしまった。(使っちゃった)

## 1.4. ～てみる

This means 'do and find/see what happens or what it looks like; have a go at doing something'.

(1) このオレンジ、おいしいかどうか、食べてみてください。

(2) 田中さん、家にいるかどうか、電話してみました。

(3) 何か大きい声が聞こえたので外を見てみましたが、誰もいませんでした。

## 1.5. ～ておく（～とく）

This means 'do it and get it done; do for now; do for future purpose' (e.g. (1), (2) and (3)); and sometimes indicates 'leave as it is' (e.g. (4)). It is often contracted to ～とく.

(1) そこに置いておいてください。(置いといて)

(2) あした忙しいから、宿題は今やっておきましょう。

(3) 今晩パーティーがあるから、飲み物をたくさん買っておきました。

(4) A: 窓を閉めましょうか。

B: いいえ、開けておいてください。

## 1.6. ～てある

This phrase is basically used with a volitional (and transitive) verb only, and conveys a state as a result of the action/event which has purposefully been undertaken. Its meaning is similar to ～ておく and is often interchangeable with it. The focus is on the state (with an indication that it is done purposefully) with ～てある, while the focus is on the purposeful action itself with ～ておく.

(1) A: 部屋、煙でいっぱいですね。窓は開けてありますか。

B: はい、開けてあります。

(2) 今晩パーティーがあるから、飲み物をたくさん買ってあります。

**文法練習 2**

**Make up a sentence using the given expressions. Use polite endings.**

(1) 高田さん　ご飯　～てしまう

(2) 会いたくない　道で　人　会う　～てしまう

(3) 疲れる　いつの間にか　～てしまう

(4) 前田さん　～かどうか　パーティー　電話する　～てみる

(5) となり　うるさい　開ける　～てみる

(6) おいしい　味見　～かどうか　～てみる　(味見をする test taste)

(7) 今晩　映画　宿題　～ておく

(8) 暑いから　窓　～ておく

(9) 野村さん　いない　メッセージを残す　～ておく

(10) 食べ物　すでに　～てある

## 2. Potential forms: 'can; be able to'

### 2.1. Meaning

The potential form is a grammatical form of verbs, which indicates the capacity, ability or possibility of doing something. The capacity or ability could be a result of learning processes (e.g. 日本語が話せます 'I (learnt Japanese and) can speak it') or something permitted by situation or environment (e.g. ここでは泳げません '(The water is so dirty that) you cannot swim here). Adjectives and copula do not have a potential form.

### 2.2. Formation

| 5-base verbs: Replace the final *-u* with *-e* る | 1-base verbs: Replace -る with -られる |
|---|---|
| a. 書く kak**u** → 書ける kak**eru**<br>b. 話す hanas**u** → 話せる hanas**eru** | a. 食べる → 食べ**られる**<br>b. 見る → 見**られる** |

Irregular verbs: a. する → できる

b. 来る → 来られる

**2.3. Conjugation:** Potential verbs are all 1-base verbs.

| *Base* | *ない-form* | *ます-form* | *て-form* | *ば-form* |
|---|---|---|---|---|
| 書ける | 書けない | 書けます | 書けて | 書ければ |
| 見られる | 見られない | 見られます | 見られて | 見られれば |
| できる | できない | できます | できて | できれば |
| 来られる | 来られない | 来られます | 来られて | 来られれば |

## 文法練習 3

**Provide the missing forms of given verbs.** ([1]= 1-base verb; [5]= 5-base verb)

| | Base | Potential base | Potential ます form | Potential ない form |
|---|---|---|---|---|
| (例) | 話す[5] | 話せる | 話せます | 話せない |
| (1) | 読む [5] | ______ | ______ | ______ |
| (2) | 言う [5] | ______ | ______ | ______ |
| (3) | 信じる [1] | ______ | ______ | ______ |
| (4) | 泳ぐ [5] | ______ | ______ | ______ |
| (5) | 寝る [1] | ______ | ______ | ______ |
| (6) | 勉強する | ______ | ______ | ______ |
| (7) | 来る | ______ | ______ | ______ |

**2.4. Particles (object; subject)**

With a potential verb, the objective marker を becomes が. However, を may also be heard in contemporary Japanese.

(1) a. 日本語を 話します → 日本語が 話せます／日本語を 話せます

b. ピアノを ひきます → ピアノが ひけません／ピアノを ひけません

c. 窓を 開けます → 窓が 開けられますか／窓を 開けられますか

This is due to the dual aspects of the verb phrase in this case: On the one hand, the original verb is transitive and thus the object may be marked by を; and on the other hand, the potential verb is intransitive in nature (and thus が may be used). Other particles, such as は, に, may also be used, depending on the context or the intended meaning of the speaker.

## 文法練習4

**Rewrite the following sentences in Japanese. Use polite endings.**

(例) Can you speak Chinese? Yes, I can. / No, I cannot.
中国語が話せますか。 はい、話せます。／ いいえ、話せません。

(1) Can you read Japanese books? Yes, I can. / No, I cannot.

(2) Can you ride a bicycle? Yes, I can. / No, I cannot.

(3) I cannot write a letter in Japanese.

(4) Tanaka-san is busy and so I cannot meet him.

(5) The car was expensive and so I was not able to buy it.

(6) Kimura-san can play golf, but cannot play tennis.

(7) Nakao-san can speak French, but cannot speak English.

---

**Shortened form:** 〜られる tends to be 〜れる in spoken conversation.

a. ここではさしみが食べられます。→ ここではさしみが食べれます。

b. 朝、早く起きられますか。→ 朝、早く起きれますか。

c. あした７時に、大学に来られますか。→ あした７時に、大学に来れますか。

---

### 2.5. [〜る]ことが出来る

This expression is similar to the potential form in terms of its meaning; it is a different way of expressing the potential meaning.

(3) a. スミスさんは、日本語を話すことが出来ます。

b. ピアノをひくことが出来ます。

c. ここで泳ぐことは出来ません。

### 2.6. [Dynamic noun] が出来る

出来る can be used directly with a noun that has the dynamic feature (i.e. movement), typically languages and sports.

(4) a. スミスさんは日本語が出来ます。

b. ゴルフは出来ますが、サッカーは出来ません。

## 文法練習 5

**Rewrite the following sentences in Japanese. Use ～ことが出来ます or [dynamic noun]が出来ます.**

(例) I can speak Chinese. → 私は中国語が出来ます。

(1) Can you speak Indonesian? Yes, I can. / No, I cannot.

(2) Can you play baseball? Yes, I can. / No, I cannot.

(3) Kimura-san cannot swim.

(4) You are not allowed to enter this room.

(5) Tanaka-san can play hockey, but cannot play tennis.

(6) I can speak English, but cannot speak Spanish.

## 自然な日本語

### なんて Expressions of the speaker's feeling/emotion

In colloquial Japanese, there are various expressions which convey the speaker's emotional attitude towards the contents of the utterance or towards the listener. '[X]なんて～' is one of them. [X]なんて is followed by expressions which convey the speaker's evaluative and/or emotional attitude, such as surprise, envy, pleasure and contempt, towards the preceding phrase, [X]. For [X], plain forms (だ for the non-past な-adjective and nouns) are used before なんて.

(1) 家族でハワイ旅行だなんて、うらやましい！

(2) ここで美穂さんに会うなんて、びっくりしたよ。

(3) スピーチコンテストで優勝するなんて、すご～い！ (優勝する win the victory)

(4) 田中さんが会社を辞めたなんて、信じられません。 (信じられない unbelievable)

When なんて is directly attached to a noun, the following expressions tend to be somewhat contemptuous and/or abusive.

(5) 戦争なんて、ばかげている！

(6) たけし君なんて、大嫌い！

**自然な日本語：練習**

**Make up the first half of these phrases which are followed by なんて〜.**

(1) ________________________________________なんて、うれしいです。

(2) ________________________________________なんて、信じられない。

(3) ________________________________________なんて、いいなあ！

(4) ________________________________________なんて、嫌ですよ。

(5) ________________________________________なんて、ひどい。

(6) ________________________________________なんて、うらやましい。

(7) ________________________________________なんて、びっくりした。

(8) ________________________________________なんて、ばかばかしい。

(ばかばかしい stupid, silly, ridiculous)

## Others

There are a number of words, expressions and phenomena which play an important role in conveying the speaker's feeling/emotion: for example, なんか, だって; particle omission; interactive particles (e.g. ね, よ); etc.

(1) 私なんか、いつも失敗ばかりで…。 'I always make mistakes, and ...'

(2) テストなんか、どうでもいいよ。 'I don't care about the exam.'

(3) A: なんで、昨日来なかったの？ 'Why didn't you come yesterday?'

B: だって、あんなに雨が降っていたから… ''Cause, it was raining a lot, so ...'

(4) ３時に、図書館に来てくださいね。 'Please come to the library at 3 o'clock.'

| | |
|---|---|
| なんか | This expression is used with a noun, and indicates the speaker's attitude/feeling to put the referent of the noun down. |
| だって | This is a sentence connective, which includes the speaker's unsatisfactory or unhappy feeling in stating the up-coming event/state; 'but, yet, because'. |
| ね／よ | These indicate the speaker's friendly feeling towards the hearer whereby the speaker's declarative, commanding tone is softened, when used in a request or imperative expression. |

Needless to say, the speaker's body/face expressions and prosodic features which include intonation, prominence, volume of voice, are also very important for appropriately indicating the speaker's intended diverse aspects of feeling/emotion.

## 表 現

### 1 ～のに 'however; on the contrary; despite…' (unexpected consequence)

☛ [Xのに、Y] indicates that what happens, [Y], is not something expected from what is stated in the preceding element, [X]. Plain forms (and ～な(のに) in the case of な-adjectives and nouns) are used before のに.

(1) この映画はもう３回も見たのに、まだ見たい。

(2) このテレビ、まだ新しいのに、壊れてしまった。

(3) 寒いのに、どうしてヒーターを付けないんですか。

(4) 病気なのに、休めない。

(5) あしたは日曜日なのに、会社に行かなければなりません。

#### 表 現 練 習 1

**Provide the other half of the sentence. Provide your own expressions.**

(例) 田中さんは日本人なのに、漢字が書けません。

(1) もう４月なのに、________________________________

(2) １０時間も寝たのに、________________________________

(3) あしたテストがあるのに、________________________________

(4) この映画、おもしろくないのに、________________________________

(5) ________________________________のに、学校に行きました。

(6) ________________________________のに、働かなければならない。

(7) ________________________________のに、窓を閉めなかった。

### 2 ～ても／でも ～する 'do… although, even though'

(1) 雨が降っても、予定どおりピクニックをします。

(2) 何回聞いても、歌の意味が分かりません。

(3) 疲(つか)れているので、何(なに)をしても楽(たの)しくありません。

(4) いくら勉強(べんきょう)しても、日本語(にほんご)が上手(じょうず)になりません。

(5) いくら何(なん)でも、それはないでしょう。 (いくら何(なん)でも whatever the reasons are)

(6) 先生(せんせい)でも、分(わ)からないことがあります。

(7) 貧(まず)しい人(ひと)でも、幸(しあわ)せな人(ひと)は多(おお)い。 (貧(まず)しい poor)

(8) 男(おとこ)でも泣(な)く時(とき)があります。

**表現練習(ひょうげんれんしゅう) 2**

**Rewrite the following sentences in Japanese, using 〜ても／でも 'even though'.**

(例(れい)) No matter how many times I listen, I do not understand the meaning of this song.

→ 何回聞(なんかいき)いても、この歌(うた)の意味(いみ)が分(わ)かりません。

(1) Even though he is busy, Tanaka-san goes swimming everyday after work.

(2) Although it will rain tomorrow, I will go fishing.

(3) No matter how much she eats, Nomura-san does not gain weight. (太(ふと)る gain weight)

(4) No matter how cold it is, Suzuki-san does not wear socks.

(5) That is easy. Even a primary school student knows it.

### 3 〜く／になる 'become ..., get...'

☛ This phrase involves a combination between a noun, verb or adjective and なる 'become', and indicates some change in a thing or state.

[noun/な-adj]に-なる [い-adj]く-なる [verb]ことに-なる

(1) いつの間(ま)にか、１２月(がつ)になりましたね。

(2) 学校(がっこう)を卒業(そつぎょう)したら、日本語(にほんご)の教師(きょうし)になりたいです。

(3) だいぶ寒(さむ)くなりましたね。

(4) 来週(らいしゅう)から授業(じゅぎょう)が始(はじ)まるので、もっと忙(いそが)しくなります。

(5) 日(ひ)が沈(しず)んで暗(くら)くなったら、周(まわ)りが静(しず)かになりました。

(6) お金(かね)が貯(た)まったので、やっと来年(らいねん)２月(がつ)に日本(にほん)へ行(い)くことになりました。

### 表現練習 3

**Look at the pictures and make up a sentence using 〜なる. Use polite endings.**

(例)　木が大きくなりました。

(e.g.)

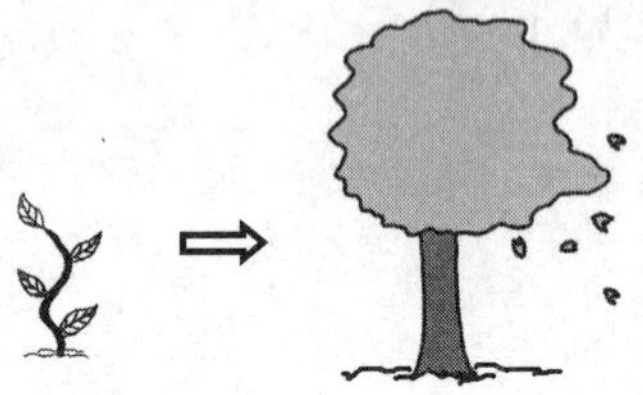

(1)

(2)

(3)

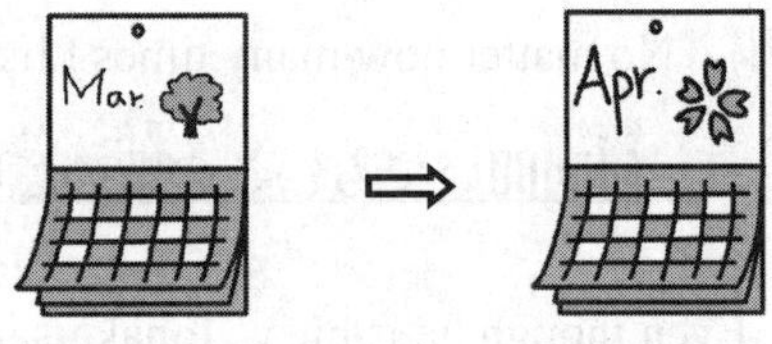


(4)

(5)

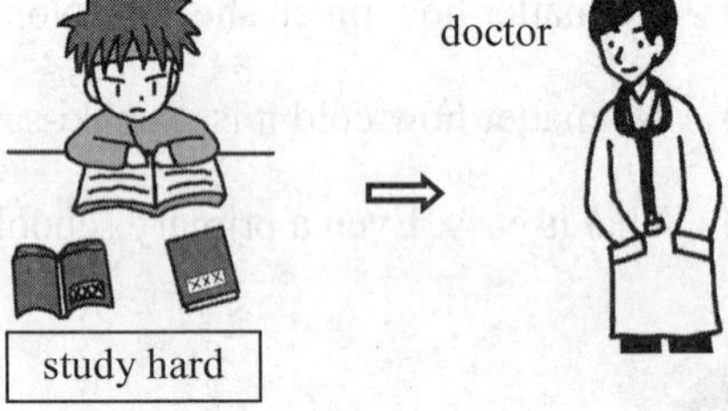


(6)

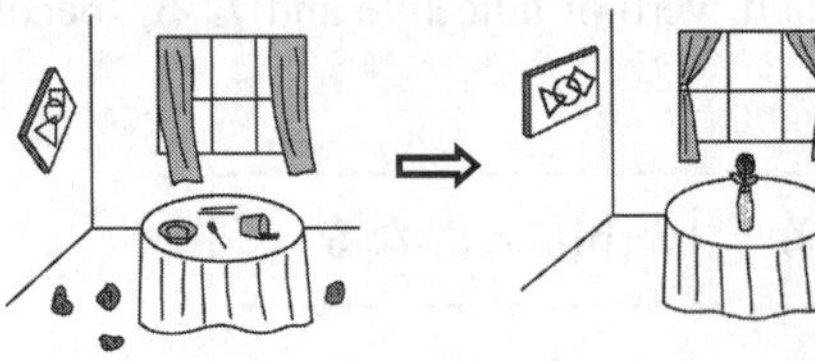

(7)

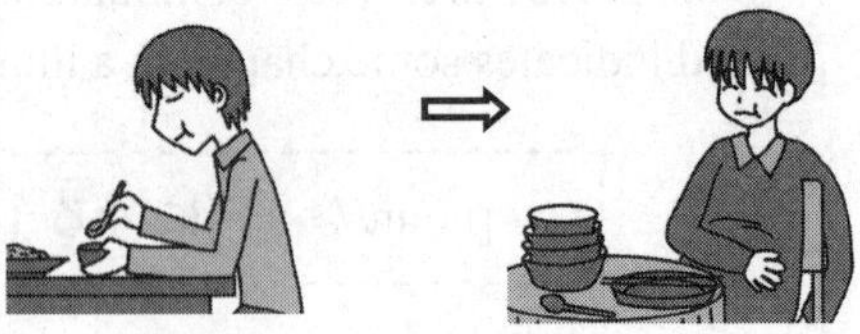

(8)

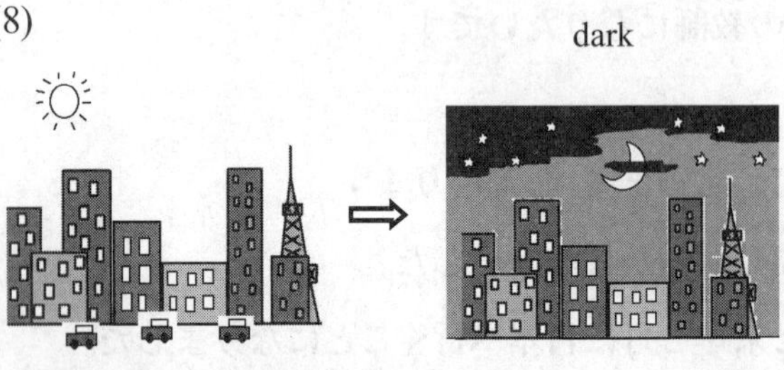


(9)

## 4 なかなか 'relatively, rarely'； そろそろ 'it's about time to do…'

**[1]** ☛ These are adverbs that add various meanings and nuances to what is expressed by the predicate. In an affirmative sentence なかなか is normally used with adjectives which convey the speaker's assessment, and indicates that the speaker's assessment is relatively good/high, although it is not best/highest. In a negative sentence, it is used with only limited expressions, typically ない and potentials, and indicates that the event/state is not easily achieved.

(1) **この映画は、なかなかおもしろいですよ。**

(2) **今回のテストは、なかなか難しかったね。**

(3) **考え事で、なかなか眠れなかった。**

(4) **最近は日本人でもなかなか舞妓さんを直接見るチャンスがない。**

**[2]** ☛ そろそろ indicates that it is nearly the time to do some action/event.

(5) **そろそろ家に帰る時間ですね。**

(6) **じゃあ、私はこの辺でそろそろ失礼します。**

(7) **もう8時だし、そろそろ食事にしましょう。**

(8) **もう8時半だし、そろそろ学校に行かなければなりません。**

### 表現練習 4

**Make up a sentence using the given words, and なかなか or そろそろ. Use polite endings.**

(例) この映画、なかなかおもしろいですよ。 or
そろそろ映画が始まる時間ですね。

(e.g.) 映画

(1) 授業
(2) レストラン
(3) 鈴木さん　来る
(4) ジョンさん　日本語　上手だ
(5) 遅い　帰る
(6) ピアノ　上手に　ひく
(7) 疲れる　寝る
(8) テスト
(9) 歌
(10) 携帯電話

## 対話

### 対話練習１

Pre-task: potential expression; 出来る

**Ask five of your classmates about their abilities of speaking languages, playing sports and other things, as in the examples. Refer to the lists below. Choose randomly.**

(例) A: [B]さんは、スペイン語が出来ますか。

B: スペイン語ですか。はい、出来ます／少し出来ます／いいえ、出来ません。

A: あ、そうですか。じゃあ、中国語は出来ますか。

: :

A: 自転車に乗れますか。

B: いいえ、自転車には乗れません。

| [Ask two languages] | [Ask two sports] | [Ask two things] |
|---|---|---|
| Chinese | baseball | driving a car |
| English | cricket | eating nattou |
| French | hockey | playing the piano |
| Indonesian | karate | playing the guitar |
| Korean | rugby | singing songs |
| Spanish | soccer | riding a bicycle |
| Thai | swimming | writing email in Japanese |
| Vietnamese | tennis | dancing |
| (your own choice) | (your own choice) | (your own choice) |

### 対話練習２

Pre-task: ～なんて

(i) First, work on the expressions of the prompts.

(ii) In pairs, practise as in the example, using ～って and ～なんて.

Prompts

- 田中さんがあした結婚する
- 田中さんが学生だ
- 田中さんがきのう喧嘩した
- 田中さんが歌手になった
- 田中さんがテストで１００点をとった
- こんなセーターが５０万円だ
- ゆうべ、町で大きい火事があった
- 日本がワールドカップで優勝した
- 田中さんがテレビに出た
- [your own event: something surprising]

(例) A: [B]さん、話、聞いた？

B: うん？何？

A: 田中さん、あした結婚するんだって。

B: えっ、本当！田中さんがあした結婚するなんて、信じられない！

A: ねえ。

| | | | | |
|---|---|---|---|---|
| 信じられない | うらやましい | 感激 | すばらしい | うそ |
| すごい | たいへん | すてき | ばかばかしい | びっくりした |

## 対話練習3

**Pre-task: ～のに**

(i) First, work on the Japanese expressions of the prompts.

(ii) In pairs, practise as in the example, using ～のに and other expressions. Provide relevant comments in an appropriate manner.

(iii) When you have finished the role of [A] or [B], swap roles.

(例) A: [B]さん、熱があるのに大学に行くんですか。休んだ方がいいですよ。

B: ええ。でも、大切な試験があるんです。

A: そうですか。大変ですね。じゃあ、試験、頑張ってください。

B: はい、ありがとうございます。

Prompts for [A]

(例) 熱がある ／ 大学に行く

- 暖かい ／ コートを着る
- あしたテストがある ／ パーティーに行く
- お金がない ／ 新しいかばんを買う
- 土曜日だ ／ 勉強する
- 朝2時だ ／ テレビを見ている

Prompts for [B]

(例) 大切な試験がある

- かぜを引く
- 十分勉強した
- 本当にほしい
- 月曜日に発表がある
- 寝られない

仕方ない 'cannot help, no other options'　十分(な) 'enough, sufficient'

発表 'presentation'

## 対話作り

✍ **In pairs, create a dialogue for the given situation. Please feel free to ask the instructor if you have any questions about Japanese expressions for your dialogue.**

**Situation:**

You are discussing places for sightseeing with your friend. You may pick up one or two of the following places as your destination(s).

アジア　　アフリカ　　南アメリカ　　ヨーロッパ　　南極

Please incorporate the following expressions/phenomena into your dialogue:

- 〜のに
- potential expressions 〜出来る／〜(ら)れる
- 〜なんて／なんか／だって
- 〜く／になる
- 〜ても／でも
- 〜てしまう／てくる／ていく／てみる／ておく／てある

### サンプル・ダイアログ

武夫：１２月の休みの間、何するの？
真理：まだ予定はないけど。
武夫：旅行でもしようか。
真理：旅行？あ、いいね。どこに行く？
武夫：そうだね。僕、札幌に行きたいな。
真理：えっ、去年，行ったのに、また行きたいの？
　　　ちょっと違うところに行こうよ。
武夫：違うところ？
真理：うん、例えば、アフリカはどう？
武夫：えっ、アフリカなんて、遠すぎるよ。
真理：でも、ライオンや象とかも見られるし、
　　　いいと思うけど。
武夫：うん、でも、飛行機代とか高いと思うよ。
　　　特に１２月には高くなるし。
真理：高くても行きたい。
武夫：わかった。じゃあ、旅行会社に電話してみるよ。

T: What will you do during the holiday in December?
M: I don't have a plan yet.
T: Shall we go on a trip or something?
M: Trip? Oh, that sounds good. Where are we going?
T: Let me see. I would like to go to Sapporo.
M: What?! We went there last year and you want to go again? Let's go to a different place.
T: Different place?
M: Yeah, for example, what about Africa?
T: Oh, Africa is too far (from here).
M: But, we can see lions and elephants, so I think it is good.
T: Yeah, but I think the airfare (and other things) is expensive. It will particularly become more expensive in December.
M: I still want to go even if it is expensive.
T: I see. Well then, I will call the travel agency.

## 知ってた？

## 日本の伝統劇・芸能 Traditional plays/entertainment

### 調べましょう

インターネットで「歌舞伎」「能」「文楽」「落語」「漫才」の写真と動画を探して、それぞれどういうものなのか、調べてみてください。

### やってみましょう

**Circle the correct one in { }.**

**歌舞伎**

(i) １６０３年ごろ始まった。

(ii) 俳優たちの化粧や衣装はユニークで、舞台もとてもきれいで鮮やかである。

(iii) 歌舞伎俳優は全員 { 男性　女性 } である。つまり、{ 男性　女性 } だけが歌舞伎を演ずることが出来る。

(iv) 女性の役を演ずる男性の俳優を { 女形　女優 } という。

**能**

(i) 最も古いミュージカル劇で、１４世紀から発展してきた。

(ii) { 面　化粧 } を使う。

(iii) 歴史的に、能は { 侍　庶民 }のためのもので、歌舞伎、文楽は { 侍　庶民 }のためのものだった。

**文楽**

(i) 明治時代(1868-1912)の終わり頃から、今のような名前で知られるようになった。{ 面　人形 } を使う。

(ii) 音楽には { 三味線　琴 } を使う。

**落語**

(i) 落語は、{ 1人で　2人で } 演じる。

(ii) 落語家の舞台のことを { 高座　座席 } という。

(iii) 主に2つの道具を使う。{ 扇子　手ぬぐい　傘 } である。

**漫才**

(i) 漫才は日本の{ 関西　関東 } 地方で発達した話芸である。

(ii) 演者は主に { 1人　2人　3人 } である。

(iii) ボケ役とツッコミ役がいることが特徴である。

## 新(あたら)しい単語(たんご)・表現(ひょうげん)

(Basic words/expressions are marked with '*')

| | |
|---|---|
| 鮮(あざ)やか(な)* | clear, beautiful, vivid |
| アジア | Asia |
| 味見(あじみ)をする | test taste |
| 衣装(いしょう) | costume |
| いつの間(ま)にか* | suddenly, without notice |
| 意味(いみ)* | meaning |
| 嫌(いや)(な)* | dislike, awful |
| うそ* | lie |
| 演(えん)じる | perform |
| お寺(てら)* | temple |
| 男(おとこ)* | man |
| 主(おも)に* | mainly, generally |
| 火事(かじ) | fire (accidental) |
| 考(かんが)え事(ごと) | things to think about |
| 感激(かんげき) | emotionally moving, stirring |
| 関西(かんさい) | Kansai (West) area |
| 関東(かんとう) | Kanto (East) area |
| 聞(き)こえる* | hear, can hear |
| 興味(きょうみ)* | interests |
| 金色(きんいろ) | golden colour |
| 金閣寺(きんかくじ) | the Kinkaku Temple |
| 化粧(けしょう) | makeup |
| 煙(けむり) | smoke |
| 喧嘩(けんか) | fight |
| 琴(こと) | koto (musical instrument; string) |
| この頃(ごろ)* | these days |
| この辺(へん) | around here |
| 侍(さむらい) | samurai |
| 幸(しあわ)せ(な)* | happy |
| 仕方(しかた)ない* | cannot help |
| 沈(しず)む* | sink |
| 失敗(しっぱい)* | failure |
| 三味線(しゃみせん) | shamisen (musical instrument; string) |
| 修学旅行(しゅうがくりょこう) | school excursion trip |
| 十分(じゅうぶん)(な)* | enough, sufficient |
| 庶民(しょみん) | ordinary people |
| すでに* | already |
| すばらしい* | wonderful, excellent |
| 世紀(せいき) | century |
| 扇子(せんす) | fan |
| 戦争(せんそう) | war |
| 象(ぞう) | elephant |
| そろそろ* | sooner or later |
| 大嫌(だいきら)い* | dislike a lot, hate |
| だいぶ* | considerably, very |
| 訪(たず)ねる* | visit |
| 例(たと)えば* | for example |
| 貯(た)まる | be saved |
| 男性(だんせい)* | male |
| 違(ちが)う* | differ |
| チャンス | chance, opportunity |
| 直接(ちょくせつ)* | directly |
| 手(て)ぬぐい | towel |
| 動画(どうが) | movie clips |
| 遠(とお)ざかる | disappear from view |

| | |
|---|---|
| なかなか* | relatively, hardly, rarely |
| 南極（なんきょく） | Antarctica |
| 人形（にんぎょう）* | doll, puppet |
| 眠る（ねむ）* | have a sleep |
| 残す（のこ）* | leave (something/ someone somewhere) |
| ばかげている | ridiculous |
| ばかばかしい | stupid, silly, ridiculous |
| ばかり* | only |
| 発展する（はってん）* | develop |
| 発表（はっぴょう） | presentation |
| 日（ひ）* | sun, day |
| 日が沈む（ひ　しず） | sunset |
| 飛行機代（ひこうきだい） | airfare |
| びっくりする* | get surprised |
| 舞台（ぶたい） | theatre stage |
| 太る（ふと）* | gain weight |
| 船（ふね）* | ship, boat |
| 平日（へいじつ） | weekdays |
| 舞妓（まいこ） | maiko (traditional young female dancer) |
| 貧しい（まず）* | poor |
| 周り（まわ）* | around |
| 漫才（まんざい） | manzai performance |
| 南アメリカ（みなみ） | South America |
| ミュージカル劇（げき） | musical play |
| 明治時代（めいじじだい） | Meiji period |
| 面（めん） | mask |
| 役（やく）* | role |
| 辞める（や）* | resign, quit |
| 優勝する（ゆうしょう） | win the victory |
| ヨーロッパ | Europe |
| 予定通り（よていどお）* | as planned, as scheduled |
| ライオン | lion |
| 落語（らくご） | rakugo performance |
| ラッキー | lucky |
| 歴史的に（れきしてき） | historically |
| ワールドカップ | World Cup |

だいじゅうきゅうか
# 第１９課

こ　　　　　　　みち
## 混んでるね、道

## The road is busy, isn't it

[正人（まさと）とエレナが今日何（きょうなに）をするか、計画（けいかく）を立（た）てている]

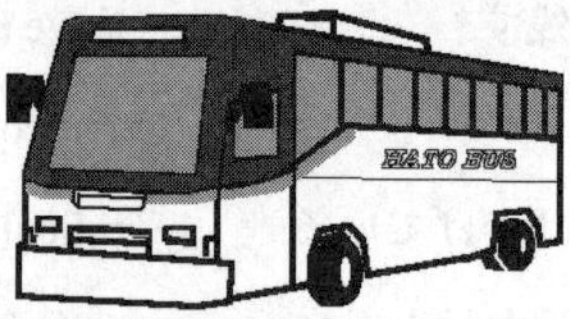


正人（まさと）：　今日（きょう）は天気（てんき）もいいし、東京見物（とうきょうけんぶつ）でもしようか。

エレナ：　あ、それ、いい。どんなところに行（い）くの？

正人（まさと）：　そうだなあ。エレナ、はとバス、乗（の）ったことある？

エレナ：　はとバス？

正人（まさと）：　東京（とうきょう）の観光（かんこう）バスだよ。いろんなとこ行（い）くよ。
国会議事堂（こっかいぎじどう）とか、東京（とうきょう）タワーとか、浅草（あさくさ）とか。

エレナ：　へえ、おもしろそう。乗（の）りたい。

正人（まさと）：　オッケー。

[はとバスの中（なか）]

エレナ：　混（こ）んでるね、道（みち）。

正人（まさと）：　まあ、たいていそうだよ、都内（とない）は。
人（ひと）も車（くるま）も多（おお）すぎるんだよ、東京（とうきょう）は。

エレナ：　あ、あの建物（たてもの）は？

正人（まさと）：　ああ、あれは歌舞伎座（かぶきざ）。見（み）たことある？　歌舞伎（かぶき）。

エレナ：　歌舞伎（かぶき）？　ううん、ない。

正人（まさと）：　じゃ、今度一緒（こんどいっしょ）に見（み）に行（い）こうか。

エレナ：　うん、行（い）こう行（い）こう。

[夜（よる）、二人（ふたり）で高層（こうそう）ビルのレストランで食事（しょくじ）をしている]

エレナ：　食事（しょくじ）をしながら夜景（やけい）が見（み）られるなんて、最高（さいこう）！

正人（まさと）：　うん、そうだね。

エレナ：　あれ！　外（そと）、雨（あめ）みたい。

正人（まさと）：　雨（あめ）？　あ、本当（ほんとう）だ。いつの間（ま）にか、雨（あめ）が降（ふ）り出（だ）してきたんだね。

エレナ：　さっきまで、あんなに天気（てんき）、よかったのに。

正人（まさと）：　うん。最近（さいきん）は雨（あめ）ばかりだね。

エレナ：　うん、そうだね。でも、私（わたし）たちが見物（けんぶつ）してる間（あいだ）、雨（あめ）に降（ふ）られなくてよかったね。

正人（まさと）：　そうだね。

## ♣ 単語（たんご）と表現（ひょうげん）

| | | | | | |
|---|---|---|---|---|---|
| | 計画（けいかく）を立（た）てる | make a plan | 10 | 都内（となnext） | Tokyo metropolitan area |
| 1 | 見物（けんぶつ） | sightseeing | 13 | 歌舞伎座（かぶきざ） | the Kabuki Theatre |
| 3 | はとバス | the Hato Bus | 13 | 歌舞伎（かぶき） | kabuki |
| 5 | 観光（かんこう） | tourism, sightseeing | | 高層（こうそう）ビル | tall building |
| 5 | いろんな | ＝いろいろな various | 17 | ～ながら | while doing … |
| 5 | とこ | ＝ところ place | 17 | 夜景（やけい） | night view |
| 6 | 国会議事堂（こっかいぎじどう） | Parliament House | 17 | 最高（さいこう） | best, wonderful |
| 6 | 東京（とうきょう）タワー | the Tokyo Tower | 21 | さっき | before |
| 8 | オッケー | O.K. | 22 | ばかり | only |
| 9 | 混（こ）む | get crowded | 23 | 降（ふ）られる | get rained on |

## ダイアログ（英語（えいご））

**[Masato and Elena are making a plan about what they are doing today]**

1 M: It is nice weather today, so shall we go to Tokyo sightseeing (or something)?
2 E: Oh, that's good. Where (what kind of places) are we going?
3 M: Let me see. Elena, have you been on the Hato Bus?
4 E: Hato Bus?
5 M: It's a tourist bus in Tokyo. It goes to various
6 places, such as the Parliament House, Tokyo Tower, Asakusa, etc.
7 E: Wow, it sounds fun. I want to go on it.
8 M: O.K.

**[In the Hato Bus]**

9 E: The road is busy.
10 M: Well, it is usually like this in Tokyo
11 metropolitan area. There are too many people and cars in Tokyo.
12 E: Oh, what is that building over there?
13 M: Oh, that's the Kabuki Theatre. Have you ever seen kabuki?
14 E: Kabuki? No, I haven't.
15 M: Then, shall we go together to see it next time?
16 E: Yeah, let's go, let's go.

**[At night, they are having dinner at a restaurant in a tall building]**

17 E: It is wonderful that we can see a night view while we are having dinner.
18 M: Yeah, that's right.
19 E: Oh! It seems it is raining outside.
20 M: Rain? Oh, that's true. It has suddenly begun raining.
21 E: It was such good weather before.
22 M: Yeah. It is always raining these days.
23 E: Yeah, that's right. But, it was fortunate
24 that it did not rain while we were going sightseeing.
25 M: Indeed.

## 文法

## 1. Modal expressions (summary): ～かもしれない／～そうだ／～らしい／～ようだ／～みたいだ／～はずだ

(i) Modality is a grammatical category which refers to the speaker's judgment on certainty (how certain he/she is) or evidentiality (what kind of evidence the statement is based upon) about the proposition (who-where-what-how type of information).

(ii) In Japanese, the modal expressions are attached to the main predicate (verbs, い-adjectives and copula).

(iii) Basically the plain forms of predicates are used with modal expressions; But, in the case of the copula (for nouns or な-adjectives), its non-past expression, i.e. ～だ, may be sustained, omitted, or replaced with の or な — the variety is pre-determined for a particular modal expression and we need to become familiar with each case.

### 1.1. ～かもしれない　no commitment to truth by the speaker: 'might, maybe'

Plain forms: ～だ is omitted in the case of non-past な-adjectives and nouns. In casual speech, しれない is sometimes omitted, leaving the phrase～かも. (cf. (4) below)

| | | | | |
|---|---|---|---|---|
| Non-p. | 書くかもしれない | 安いかもしれない | 静かかもしれない | 学生かもしれない |
| Past | 書いたかもしれない | 安かったかもしれない | 静かだったかもしれない | 学生だったかもしれない |

(1) 田中さんは、この映画、もう見たかもしれません。

(2) 田中さんは今日、忙しいので、今晩、映画に行かないかもしれません。

(3) この車、思ったより安いかもしれない。

(4) 今日、日曜日だし、マキさん、いま家にいるかも。

### 1.2. ～そうだ [1]　based on second-hand audio evidence: 'I heard, they say'

Plain forms: ～だ is sustained in the case of non-past な-adjectives and nouns.

| | | | | |
|---|---|---|---|---|
| Non-p. | 書くそうだ | 安いそうだ | 静かだそうだ | 学生だそうだ |
| Past | 書いたそうだ | 安かったそうだ | 静かだったそうだ | 学生だったそうだ |

(1) 田中さんは、映画に行かないそうです。

(2) 田中さんは、この映画、もう見たそうです。

(3) あの店の料理は、おいしくて安いそうだ。

(4) テレビの天気予報によると、あしたは雨が降るそうだ。

### 1.3. ～そうだ [2]  based on visual evidence: 'looks like'

This phrase is attached to the Masu-stem of verbs and a stem of adjectives. Nouns are not used with this phrase. When it is attached to ない and いい, it becomes ～なさそうだ and よさそうだ, respectively. It has a couple of varieties for negative expressions; ～そうもない, ～そうにない.

| | | | | |
|---|---|---|---|---|
| Non-p. | 書きそうだ | 安そうだ | 静かそうだ | --------------- |
| Past | 書きそうだった | 安そうだった | 静かそうだった | --------------- |

(1) 雨が降りそうです。

(2) 山田さんは明日テストなので、映画に行きそうにない。

(3) この車は、あまり高くなさそうだ。

(4) あしたも天気がよさそうだね。

(5) 空は晴れていて、全然雨が降りそうもありません。

### 1.4. ～らしい  the speaker guesses as he/she has indirect evidence only: 'apparently'

Plain forms: ～だ is omitted in the case of non-past な-adjectives and nouns.

| | | | | |
|---|---|---|---|---|
| Non-p. | 書くらしい | 安いらしい | 静からしい | 学生らしい |
| Past | 書いたらしい | 安かったらしい | 静かだったらしい | 学生だったらしい |

(1) 田中さんは、新しい車を買うらしいです。

(2) 見る人も多くないし、どうもこの映画はあまりおもしろくないらしい。

(3) あの人は、アメリカ英語のアクセントも強いし、どうもアメリカ人らしい。

### 文法練習 1

**Add the elements indicated to the sentences given, and translate the result into English. Use polite endings, unless specified.**

(例) スミスさんは、アメリカ人です。 (そうだ '(hearsay)')

→ スミスさんは、アメリカ人だそうです。 I heard that Smith-san is an American.

(1) もうすぐ、雨が降りますね。 (そうだ 'looks like')

(2) 日本は、きのう雨が降りましたね。 (そうだ '(hearsay)')

(3) このかばんは高いから、買いません。 (かもしれない)

(4) 最近、雨が全然降っていません。 （そうだ '(hearsay)'）

(5) 私は忙しいから、今夜パーティーに行けません。 （かもしれない）

(6) あしたの天気は、雪です。 （そうだ '(hearsay)'）

(7) あしたの天気は、雪です。 （らしい）

(8) 鈴木さんはもう朝ご飯を食べた。 （らしい; in casual speech）

(9) これは加藤さんの車だよ。 （かもしれない; in casual speech）

(10) どこにも行かないで、家で休んだ方が楽だ。 （かもしれない; in casual speech）

**1.5. 〜ようだ** judging from a variety of available evidence: 'seem, likely'

Plain forms: 〜だ is replaced with 〜な in the case of non-past な-adjectives and with 〜の in the case of non-past nouns.

| | | | | |
|---|---|---|---|---|
| Non-p. | 書くようだ | 安いようだ | 静かなようだ | 学生のようだ |
| Past | 書いたようだ | 安かったようだ | 静かだったようだ | 学生だったようだ |

(1) 田中さんは来週大きいテストがあるので、今週はとても忙しいようです。

(2) この手紙は岡田さんが書いたようです。

(3) 武志は、奈津子のことがとても好きなようです。

(4) 木村さんは学生のようです。

**1.6. 〜みたいだ** basically the same as 〜ようだ, but more casual: 'seem, likely' (more casual)

Plain forms: 〜だ is omitted in the case of non-past な-adjectives and nouns. 〜みたいだ is な-adjective and often ends without だ, i.e. 〜みたい.

| | | | | |
|---|---|---|---|---|
| Non-p. | 書くみたいだ | 安いみたいだ | 静かみたいだ | 学生みたいだ |
| Past | 書いたみたいだ | 安かったみたいだ | 静かだったみたいだ | 学生だったみたいだ |

(1) 田中さんは病気で、今日、休むみたいです。

(2) あの人の名前は誰も知らないみたいです。

(3) みんな、この映画が好きみたい。

(4) 天気予報によると、あしたは雨みたい。

(5) バカみたい！

**1.7. 〜はずだ** judging on the basis of normal expectations: 'be supposed to, it is expected that …'

Plain forms: 〜だ is replaced with 〜な in the case of non-past な-adjectives and with 〜の in the case of non-past nouns. There are a couple of ways for negative expressions: 〜はずがない and 〜ないはずだ.

| | | | | |
|---|---|---|---|---|
| Non-p. | 書くはずだ | 安いはずだ | 静かなはずだ | 学生のはずだ |
| Past | 書いたはずだ | 安かったはずだ | 静かだったはずだ | 学生だったはずだ |

(1) 今日は月曜日だから、野村さんは今、会社で仕事しているはずです。

(2) 山田さんには言っていないから、これについて山田さんは知らないはずです。

(3) この携帯にはいろんな機能が付いているから、あれよりもっと高いはずです。

(4) 田中さんが真由美さんは髪が長いと言ったから、あの人が真由美さんのはずです。

**文法練習 2**

**Add the elements indicated to the sentences given, and translate the result into English. Use polite endings, unless specified.**

(1) 鈴木さんは、まじめな学生ですね。 (ようだ)

(2) 映画は８時に始まる。 (ようだ)

(3) 今度のテストは難しいです。 (みたいだ)

(4) 田中さんは忙しくて会議に行けない。 (みたいだ; in casual speech)

(5) 鈴木さんはお金持ちだよ。 (みたいだ; in casual speech)

(6) 田中さんは日本人だから、この漢字が読めます。 (はずだ)

(7) 今日は休みだから、木村さんは今、家にいます。 (はずだ)

## 2. Passive

The same situation may be expressed in many different ways. In passive sentences the focus (or viewpoint) is given to the object, while the focus is on the doer in active sentences.

Focus on the doer → active sentence

ユキさんは 手紙を 書きました。

Focus on the object → passive sentence

その手紙は ユキさんによって 書かれました。

### 2.1. Forms

| 5-base verbs: -*u* → -*a*れる | 1-base verbs: -る → -られる |
|---|---|
| 書く → 書かれる<br>kak**u** kak**a** れる<br>話す → 話される<br>言う → 言われる (〜う → 〜われる) | 食べる → 食べられる<br>見る → 見られる<br><br>(N.B. same as the potential form) |

| Irregular verbs: | する → される | 来る → 来られる |
|---|---|---|

### 2.2. Two types of passive in Japanese

In Japanese, there are two types of passive constructions: pure passive and adversative passive.

**Pure passive**

Basically it is the same as the passive in English. Pure passive may be constructed with transitive verbs only. 'Original doer' is marked by 〜によって(creative verbs) or 〜に (non-creative).

(1) この本は、たくさんの若者に読まれている。 [N.B. 読む is not a creative verb.]

(2) このペンは、日本で広く使われている。[N.B. Generic/general doers are often not specified.]

(3) このロボットは佐藤さんによって作られた。 [N.B. 作る is a creative verb.]

**Adversative passive**

In Japanese a passive construction tends to be used to describe actions and events done by others which are felt as adversely affecting the speaker (or someone whose viewpoint the speaker adopts): i.e. (a) somebody does something and (b) this is felt as inconveniencing.

Adversative passive may be constructed with intransitive verbs as well. The 'perpetrator' may be a person, thing or natural phenomenon. There is no general equivalent in English (but cf. the use of *on* in *They told on me*, *They walked out on me*) and it takes time to become familiar with this type of passive expression.

| Victim (Subject) | Perpetrator | Event |
|---|---|---|
| Nが<br>(often omitted) | Nに／から | Nを<br>Nで<br>etc. } *Verb*-passive |

(N = noun)

(1) 高田さんに、残ったご飯を全部食べられてしまった。

(2) 赤ちゃんに泣かれて全然寝られなかった。

(3) 屋根が風で飛ばされてしまった。

(4) 雨に降られた。

(5) 泥棒にテレビを盗まれてしまった。

## 文法練習3

**Re-phrase the following sentences, using the passive construction. In particular, be careful with the use of particles for (4)-(8) which involve the speaker's adversative feeling.**

(例)　田中さんはその本を書いた。 → その本は田中さんによって書かれた。

(1)　木村さんがこの船を作りました。

(2)　日本人はこの歌をよく知っている。

(3)　このカメラはたくさんの人が使っています。

(4)　遅く起きたので、父が（私を）叱りました。

(5)　みんなが（私を）馬鹿にしました。

(6)　そんなことを言ったら、人が笑いますよ。

(7)　田中先生が（私に）、『静かにしなさい』と言いました。

(8)　となりの人が、一晩中うるさくしました。

## 自然な日本語

### Flexible word order

In Japanese, a predicate (verb, adjective or copula) in principle occurs in the end of a sentence; (e.g.) subject-object-verb, subject-destination-verb, subject-adjective/copula. However, the word order is often flexible, particularly in colloquial conversation, and a predicate (and related elements; e.g. particle, adverbs, object, destination, etc) may be placed in a non-final position in a sentence.

(1) 道、混んでるね。 → 混んでるね、道。

(2) このラーメン、本当においしいね。 → 本当においしいね、このラーメン。

(3) （はとバスは）国会議事堂とか、東京タワーとか、浅草とか、いろんなとこ行くよ。

→ いろんなとこ行くよ、国会議事堂とか、東京タワーとか、浅草とか。

(4) 東京は、人も車も多すぎるんだよ。 → 人も車も多すぎるんだよ、東京は。

The effect of the flexible word order is that prominence is given to the component that is placed in the beginning of the sentence; for example, in (1) above, the 'crowdedness' of the road is more strongly indicated in the second sentence, compared to the first that uses the normal word order.

## 自然な日本語：練習

**Rewrite the following sentences in Japanese, using flexible word order. Prominence is to be given to the underlined part of the sentence. Use polite endings unless specified.**

(例) I studied Japanese at the library. → (私は) 勉強しました、日本語を、図書館で。

(1) I eat lunch with Mr Tanaka.

(2) I've seen that movie. (casual)

(3) Kimura-san is not a university student.

(4) Please look at this picture.

(5) Is this bag Tanaka-san's?

(6) Did you meet Ms Yamashita last weekend?

(7) What did you do last night? (casual)

(8) I really like Japanese.

(9) Have you ever been to Japan? (casual)

(10) Kanji is difficult, isn't it? (casual)

## 表現

### 1 〜(よ)う '(volitional; hortative)'

[1] ☛ 〜(よ)う 'Let's ~' may be used to propose an action, or to make a suggestion to do something, together with one or more others in casual conversation.

| 5-base verbs: Replace the final *-u* with *-o* う | 1-base verbs: Replace -る with -よう |
|---|---|
| a. 書く kak**u** → 書こう kak**oo**<br>b. 話す hanas**u** → 話そう hanas**oo** | a. 食べる → 食べよう<br>b. 見る → 見よう |

| Irregular verbs: | a. する → しよう | b. 来る → 来よう |
|---|---|---|

[2] ☛ いっしょに 'together (with)' is often used with this expression. While this is equivalent to 〜ましょう of the polite style, 〜(よ)うか 'shall we…' is equivalent to 〜ましょうか.

(1) 今晩、いっしょに食事をしよう。

(2) A: あした、いっしょに東京見物に行こうか。

B: あ、いいね。行こう。

## 表現練習(ひょうげんれんしゅう) 1

**Provide ～(よ)う forms.**

| | | | | | |
|---|---|---|---|---|---|
| (例(れい)) | 見(み)る | → | 見(み)よう | | |
| (1) | 読(よ)む | → | ______ | | |
| (2) | 歩(ある)く | → | ______ | | |
| (3) | 起(お)きる | → | ______ | | |
| (4) | 買(か)う | → | ______ | | |
| (5) | 帰(かえ)る | → | ______ | | |
| (6) | 開(あ)ける | → | ______ | | |
| (7) | 勉強(べんきょう)する | → | ______ | | |

## 表現練習(ひょうげんれんしゅう) 2

**Make up sentences which propose or suggest doing something illustrated in the pictures together with your friend, as in the example. Use ～(よ)う.**

(例(れい)) 土曜日(どようび)にいっしょに映画(えいが)を見(み)よう。

(e.g.)

(1)

(2)

(3)

(4)

(5)

(6)

(7)

(8)

[3] ☛ 〜(よ)うと思(おも)っている 'I am thinking that I intend to do…'; 〜(よ)うとする 'try to do…, is about to do…'; 〜(よ)うとしている 'is trying to do…'.

(1) 私(わたし)は来年(らいねん)の3月(がつ)にアフリカに行(い)こうと思(おも)っています。
(2) 私(わたし)は木村(きむら)さんにEメールを送(おく)ろうと思(おも)っています。
(3) 田中(たなか)さんは、今(いま)、自分(じぶん)の部屋(へや)でコーヒーを飲(の)もうとしている。
(4) 今(いま)、ちょうど、電話(でんわ)をしようとしていた。
(5) 暗(くら)くて寒(さむ)かったから，誰(だれ)も外(そと)に出(で)ようとしなかった。

## 表現(ひょうげん)練習(れんしゅう)3

**Make up sentences, using the given words and 〜(よ)うと思(おも)う／する／しない／している. Use polite endings.**

(例(れい)) 今(いま)テレビを見(み)ようとしていました。

(e.g.) 今(いま)　テレビ
(1) 木村(きむら)さん　家(うち)　今(いま)　コーヒー
(2) 図書館(としょかん)　山田(やまだ)さん
(3) 田中(たなか)さん　ちょうど　電話(でんわ)する
(4) 靴下(くつした)　履(は)く
(5) ちょうど　出(で)かける
(6) 高(たか)い　誰(だれ)も　買(か)う
(7) 疲(つか)れる　動(うご)く　(動(うご)く move)

## 2 [Masu-stem]-ながら 'while …'

[1] ☛ [Masu-stem]-ながら indicates that two actions/events occur simultaneously. Note that these actions/events are done by one person.

(1) 田中(たなか)さんはいつもテレビを見(み)ながら、朝(あさ)ご飯(はん)を食(た)べます。
(2) 私(わたし)は、シャワーを浴(あ)びながら、歌(うた)を歌(うた)います。
(3) 映画(えいが)を見(み)ながら泣(な)いている。
(4) 太田(おおた)さんは子供(こども)を育(そだ)てながら、仕事(しごと)をしています。

[2] ☛ Different expressions are used to indicate two actions/events that occur simultaneously but are done by different persons.

(1) 田中(たなか)さんがテレビを見(み)ている間(あいだ)、木村(きむら)さんは朝(あさ)ご飯(はん)を食(た)べています。
(2) 私(わたし)が歌(うた)を歌(うた)っている時(とき)、鈴木(すずき)さんはシャワーを浴(あ)びていました。

## 表現練習４

**Make up sentences, using the information given in the pictures below and ～ながら. Use polite endings.**

(例)　戸田さんは、音楽を聞きながらそうじをしています。

(e.g.) 戸田

(1) 野村

(2) 山田

(3) 黒田

(4) 田中

(5) 本田

### 3　[Masu-stem]-出す／始める／終わる／やすい／にくい '(compounds)'

**[1]** ☛ [Masu-stem]-出す indicates that the action/event expressed by the stem has suddenly begun.

(1) 田中さんはお母さんからの手紙を読んで、いきなり泣き出しました。

(2) 道を歩いていたら、いきなり雨が降り出した。

**[2]** ☛ [Masu-stem]-始める／[Masu-stem]-続ける／[Masu-stem]-終わる indicate that the action/event expressed by the stem begins, continues and ends, respectively.

(3) 私は今年２月から日本語を勉強し始めました。

(4) じゃあ、そろそろ食べ始めましょうか。

(5) 木村さんは同じことを何回も黒板に書き続けました。

(6) 高田さんは、１０時間もずっと寝続けている。

(7) この本、１週間も読み続けて、きのうやっと読み終わりました。

(8) この手紙、5時までには書き終わりたい。

**[3]** ☛ [Masu-stem]-やすい／[Masu-stem]-にくい indicate that the action/event expressed by the stem is easy to do, or is hard to do, respectively.

(9) このペンは書(か)きやすいですね。

(10) 田中(たなか)さんの説明(せつめい)は分(わ)かりやすかった。

(11) この肉(にく)は噛(か)みにくい。

(12) この小説(しょうせつ)は難(むずか)しくて分(わ)かりにくいですね。

## 4 ばかり ‘have just done…; only …’

**[1]** ☛ [〜た-ばかり] indicates that an action/event expressed by the verb has just been done.

(1) 私(わたし)はいま起(お)きたばかりです。

(2) A: 朝(あさ)ご飯(はん)、もう食(た)べましたか。

B: あ、いま食(た)べたばかりです。

**[2]** ☛ When ばかり is attached to a verb 〜ている or a noun, it means ‘only’, and indicates that only what is expressed by the verb/noun occurs ‘continuously’ and/or ‘repeatedly’.

(3) 最近(さいきん)は雨(あめ)ばかりですね。(＝最近(さいきん)は雨(あめ)ばかり降(ふ)っていますね。)

(4) 今日(きょう)は暑(あつ)かったので、一日中(いちにちじゅう)、水(みず)ばかり飲(の)みました。

(5) 高田(たかだ)さんは寝(ね)ているばかりで、仕事(しごと)をしようとしない。

(6) ビデオゲームをやっているばかりで、本(ほん)は読(よ)もうとしなかった。

### 表現(ひょうげん)練習(れんしゅう) 5

**Make up sentences, using the given words and 〜ばかり. Use polite endings.**

(例(れい)) 新(あたら)しいパソコンを買(か)ったばかりです。 or

田中(たなか)さんはパソコンばかりやって、ご飯(はん)を食(た)べようとしない。

(e.g.) パソコン

(1) 京都駅(きょうとえき)　着(つ)く

(2) 木村(きむら)さん　手紙(てがみ)　書(か)き始(はじ)める

(3) 日本語(にほんご)　勉強(べんきょう)し始(はじ)める　まだ

(4) 遊(あそ)ぶ　勉強(べんきょう)

(5) 肉(にく)　野菜(やさい)

(6) アルバイト　帰(かえ)る

(7) 会議(かいぎ)

## 対話(たいわ)

### 対話練習(たいわれんしゅう) 1

**Pre-task: 〜(よ)う、〜(よ)うか**

**Refer to the prompts in the table below and make an offer to two of your classmates. Feel free to expand the conversation by adding further questions (e.g. what, where, when, by what, etc), as in the example.**

(例(れい)) A: 土曜日(どようび)に、いっしょに映画(えいが)、見(み)ようか。

B: 映画(えいが)？ あ、いいね。何(なに)見(み)ようか？ or B: ごめん、土曜日(どようび)はちょっと忙(いそが)しくて…。

A: スーパーマンはどう。 ‖ A: あ、ほんとう？

B: いいね。そうしよう。 ‖ B: ごめん。今度(こんど)ね。

| いつ | 何(なに)を | 友達(ともだち)の名前(なまえ)／答(こた)え | |
|---|---|---|---|
| | | 名前(なまえ)： | 名前(なまえ)： |
| 土曜日(どようび) | 映画(えいが) | | |
| あした | 晩(ばん)ご飯(はん) | | |
| 週末(しゅうまつ) | 海(うみ) | | |
| 日曜日(にちようび) | ドライブ | | |
| (make your own prompt) | (make your own prompt) | | |

### 対話練習(たいわれんしゅう) 2

**Pre-task: 〜ながら**

**Refer to the prompts below and ask three of your classmates whether or not they simultaneously do the two things indicated in the prompts, as in the example.**

(例(れい)) A: [ B ] さんは、シャワーを浴(あ)びながら、よく歌(うた)を歌(うた)いますか。

B: はい、よく歌(うた)いますよ。 (or いいえ、あまり歌(うた)いません。)

A: そうですか。

(e.g.) シャワー 歌(うた)

(1) 勉強(べんきょう) 音楽(おんがく)

(2) 晩(ばん)ご飯(はん) テレビ

(3) 道(みち)を歩(ある)く ものを食(た)べる

(4) (悲(かな)しい) 映画(えいが) 泣(な)く

(5) コーヒやお茶(ちゃ) チョコレート

(6) 寝(ね)る いびきをかく

(7) (make your own prompts)

## 対話練習 3

**Pre-task: ～られたことがある**

**Ask three of your classmates whether or not they have experienced the things stated in the table below. Feel free to expand the conversation by adding further relevant questions (e.g. what, when, who, where, etc.).**

(例) A: [B]さん、何か盗まれたこと、ありますか。

B: ああ、あります。
A: え、本当ですか。何を盗まれたんですか。
B: 自転車を盗まれました。
A: そうですか。いつ，どこでですか。
B: えっと、3年前に町でです。

or

B: 幸いなことに、ありません。
A: そうですか。
B: ええ、運がよかったと思います。

| | 友達の名前／答え | | |
|---|---|---|---|
| | 名前： | 名前： | 名前： |
| 何か盗まれた？ | | | |
| ペットに死なれた？ | | | |
| いきなり雨に降られた？ | | | |
| 誰かに叱られた？ | | | |
| 勝手にものを使われた？ | | | |

## 対話作り

**In pairs, create a dialogue for the given situation. Please feel free to ask the instructor if you have any questions about Japanese expressions for your dialogue.**

**Situation:**
You have a visitor(s) who has recently come from another country/city. You take him/her around places in your city/town. You explain about the places, which include what people can do there, what the places are famous for, etc. You may also want to talk about some special features of your city/town.

Please incorporate the following expressions/phenomena into your dialogue:

- Modal expressions: ～かもしれない／ようだ／みたいだ／らしい／そうだ／はずだ
- Passive (～(ら)れる)
- Flexible word order
- ～(よ)う
- ～ながら
- ～し出す／始める／続ける／終わる／にくい／やすい
- ばかり

## サンプル・ダイアログ

信夫：　ここが、僕が住んでいる町なんだ。
理恵：　へえ、緑が多いね。湖もあるし。
信夫：　うん。湖の周りには公園もあるから、週末にはたくさんの人がバーベキューをしたりしてるんだ。
理恵：　いいね。とても住みやすそうな町だね。
信夫：　うん、僕もそう思う。
理恵：　あ、タワーがあるね、あの山の上に。
信夫：　あ、あれはテレコムタワーっていうんだけど、一番上には展望台もあるよ。
理恵：　へえ、そうなんだ。町全体を見ることが出来るね。
信夫：　うん。展望台にはレストランもあって、食事をしながら町が見られるよ。
理恵：　いいね。
信夫：　特に夜景はとてもきれいなんだ。今晩行ってみようか。
理恵：　今晩？いいけど、でも、天気、大丈夫かな。
信夫：　うん、テレビで、晴れって言ってたから、大丈夫なはずだよ。
理恵：　ほんと？じゃあ、楽しみだね。あ、あの建物は何？
信夫：　あ、あれは、国立博物館だよ。
理恵：　国立博物館？
信夫：　うん。昔、ここに住んでいた先祖の服や使ってた道具などが展示されているんだ。
理恵：　へえ、おもしろそう。
信夫：　週末に行ってみようか。
理恵：　うん、行こう行こう。

N: This is the town I live in.
R: Oh, it has a lot of green (trees and plants). It also has a lake.
N: Yeah. There are parks around the lake, and many people have BBQs (and other things) on weekends.
R: That's good. It (the town) looks like it's easy to live in.
N: Yeah, I think so too.
R: Oh, there is a tower, on top of that mountain over there.
N: It (the tower) is called the Telecom Tower, and it has an observatory on top of it as well.
R: Oh, is that so? (You/We) can see the town as a whole.
N: Yeah. The observatory has a restaurant, and (you/we) can see the town while having a meal.
R: Sounds good.
N: Especially the night view (from there) is very beautiful. Shall we go and take a look there tonight?
R: Tonight? Sounds good! But, will the weather be ok?
N: Yes. The weather forecast said it would be fine, so it should be ok.
R: Really? Well then, I'm looking forward to it. Oh, what's that building?
N: That's the National Museum.
R: The National Museum?
N: Yeah. Clothes, tools and other things that (our) ancestors who lived here used are exhibited.
R: Oh, it sounds interesting.
N: Shall we go and have a look?
R: Yeah! Let's go, let's go.

## 知ってた？

### 電車 Train

**Following is a summary of some train lines in and around Tokyo, and some words related to trains. Research the destination of each line. For the words, study their meanings.**

電車　地下鉄　山手線　中央線　～行き（品川行き）　～方面（中野方面）
駅　(number)番線　(number)つ目（４つ目の駅）　乗る　降りる　乗り換える

## 練習しましょう

**First refer to the map below and decide where (which stations) you would like to go. In pairs, then ask your partner how to get there, as in the example.**

(例) A: あの～、すみません。目白駅に行きたいんですけど…。

B: 目白駅ですか。えっと、じゃあ、新宿駅で山手線に乗り換えてください。

A: 山手線ですね。

B: はい。新宿駅で、新大久保方面に行って、3つ目の駅です。

A: 分かりました。どうも、ありがとうございました。

| Current location | Your destinations | Your partner's destinations | Current location | Your destinations | Your partner's destinations |
|---|---|---|---|---|---|
| (e.g.) 中野駅 | 大塚駅 | 目白駅 | 御茶ノ水駅 | | |
| 中野駅 | | | 御茶ノ水駅 | | |
| 中野駅 | | | 御茶ノ水駅 | | |

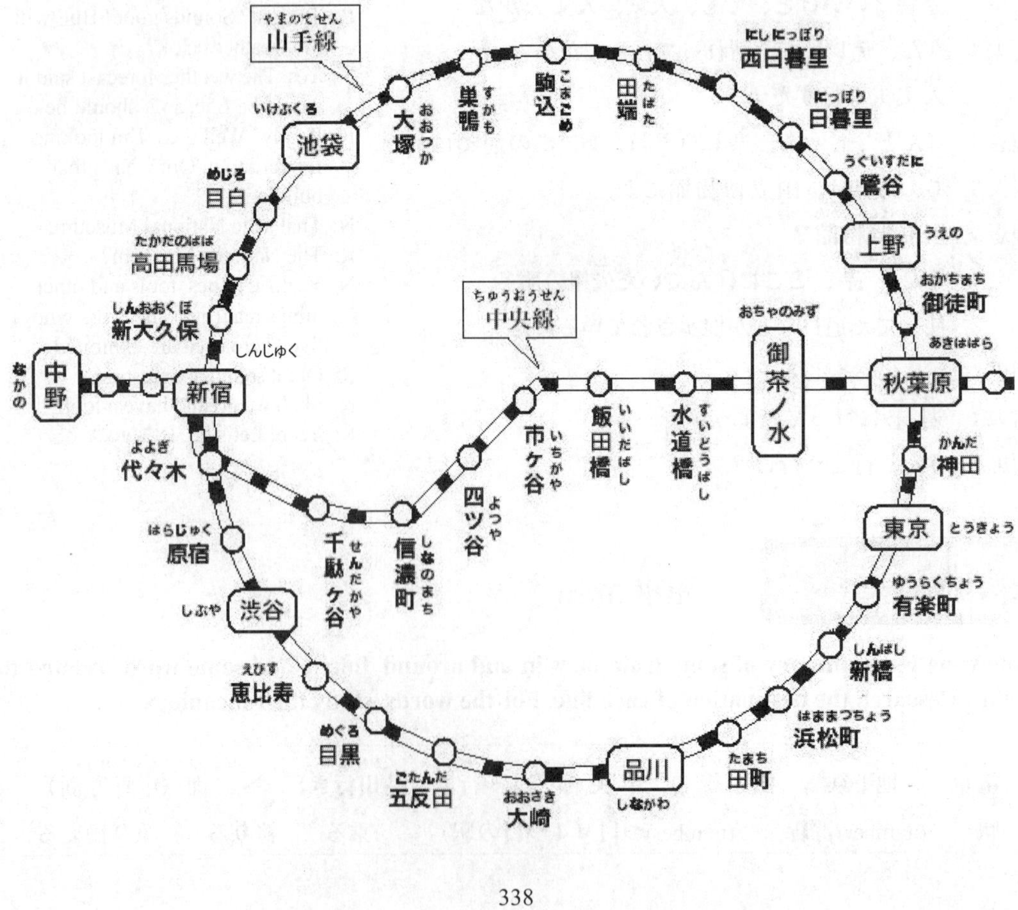

## 新(あたら)しい単語(たんご)・表現(ひょうげん)

(Basic words/expressions are marked with '*')

| | |
|---|---|
| いきなり* | suddenly |
| いびきを かく | snore |
| 動(うご)く* | move |
| 運(うん)が いい | lucky |
| オッケー | O.K. （オーケー is standard） |
| 同(おな)じ* | same, identical |
| 思(おも)ったより | more than I thought |
| 勝手(かって)(な) | one's own way, selfish |
| 歌舞伎(かぶき) | kabuki |
| 歌舞伎座(かぶきざ) | the Kabuki Theatre |
| 噛(か)む* | bite, chew |
| 観光(かんこう) | tourism, sightseeing |
| 機能(きのう) | function |
| 計画(けいかく)を立(た)てる* | make a plan |
| 見物(けんぶつ) | sightseeing |
| 高層(こうそう)ビル | skyscraper |
| 黒板(こくばん) | blackboard |
| 国立博物館(こくりつはくぶつかん) | national museum |
| 答(こた)え* | answer, reply |
| 混(こ)む | get crowded |
| 最高(さいこう) | best, wonderful |
| 幸(さいわ)い(な)* | fortunate, lucky |
| さっき* | before, short while ago, just now |
| 叱(しか)る | scold |
| 先祖(せんぞ) | ancestors |
| 育(そだ)てる | bring up, raise (person) |
| 地下鉄(ちかてつ) | subway |
| 中央線(ちゅうおうせん) | the Chuo Line |
| テレコムタワー | Telecom Tower |
| 天気予報(てんきよほう) | weather forecast |
| 展示(てんじ)する | display |
| 展望台(てんぼうだい) | observatory |
| 東京(とうきょう)タワー | the Tokyo Tower |
| 道具(どうぐ) | tools, instrument |
| とこ* | (＝ところ) place |
| 都内(とない) | Tokyo metropolitan area |
| 飛(と)ばす | make (something) fly |
| 泥棒(どろぼう)* | robber |
| 盗(ぬす)む* | steal |
| 乗(の)り換(か)える | transfer, change |
| 馬鹿(ばか)* | idiot |
| 馬鹿(ばか)にする* | make a fool of |
| パソコン | personal computer, PC |
| はとバス | the Hato Bus |
| 一晩中(ひとばんじゅう)* | all night |
| (中野(なかの)) 方面(ほうめん) | the direction of (Nakano) |
| 緑(みどり) | green |
| 昔(むかし) | old time, ancient times |
| 夜景(やけい) | night view |
| やっと* | at last, with difficulty, somehow |
| 屋根(やね) | roof |
| 山手線(やまのてせん) | the Yamanote Line |
| (品川(しながわ)) 行(ゆ)き | [train] for (Shinagawa) |
| ロボット | robot |
| 若者(わかもの) | young people, youth |

# 第20課

## 本当にお世話になりました
## Thank you very much for having taken care of me

[正人の家]

エレナ：　正人君のお父さん、お母さん、本当にお世話になりました。
正人の母：　いえいえ、とんでもない。でも、さびしくなるわ。
正人の父：　本当だね。でも、また来てくださいね。
エレナ：　はい、ありがとうございます。お二人もぜひオーストラリアに遊びに来てください。
正人の母：　ありがとう。エレナさんも、また遊びに来てくださいね。
正人：　お母さん。実はエレナ、来年、交換留学で、また日本に来ることになっているんだ。
正人の母：　あら、そうなの。じゃあ、また会えるのね。
エレナ：　ええ、また来年、お会い出来るのを楽しみにしています。
正人：　エレナ、そろそろ空港に行かないと。
エレナ：　ええ。じゃあ、お元気で。
正人の父と母：　エレナさんもお元気で。

[空港で]

エレナ：　正人、本当にいろいろと、ありがとう。
正人：　ううん、僕の方こそ、エレナのおかげで楽しかったよ。
エレナ：　じゃ、これからも、またよろしくね。
正人：　こちらこそ。じゃあ、そろそろ出発の時間だよ。
エレナ：　ええ。あっ、そうだ、私、図書館の本、借りたままなの。返してほしいんだけど。
正人：　あ、ほんと。大丈夫だよ。忘れないで、明日、ちゃんと返すから。

# 第20課

## 本当にお世話になりました
## Thank you very much for having taken care of me

[正人の家]

エレナ：　正人君のお父さん、お母さん、本当にお世話になりました。
正人の母：　いえいえ、とんでもない。でも、さびしくなるわ。
正人の父：　本当だね。でも、また来てくださいね。
エレナ：　はい、ありがとうございます。お二人もぜひオーストラリアに遊びに来てください。
正人の母：　ありがとう。エレナさんも、また遊びに来てくださいね。
正人：　お母さん。実はエレナ、来年、交換留学で、また日本に来ることになっているんだ。
正人の母：　あら、そうなの。じゃあ、また会えるのね。
エレナ：　ええ、また来年、お会い出来るのを楽しみにしています。
正人：　エレナ、そろそろ空港に行かないと。
エレナ：　ええ。じゃあ、お元気で。
正人の父と母：　エレナさんもお元気で。

[空港で]

エレナ：　正人、本当にいろいろと、ありがとう。
正人：　ううん、僕の方こそ、エレナのおかげで楽しかったよ。
エレナ：　じゃ、これからも、またよろしくね。
正人：　こちらこそ。じゃあ、そろそろ出発の時間だよ。
エレナ：　ええ。あっ、そうだ、私、図書館の本、借りたままなの。返してほしいんだけど。
正人：　あ、ほんと。大丈夫だよ。忘れないで、明日、ちゃんと返すから。



### サンプル・ダイアログ

| | |
|---|---|
| 信夫：　ここが、僕が住んでいる町なんだ。 | N: This is the town I live in. |
| 理恵：　へえ、緑が多いね。湖もあるし。 | R: Oh, it has a lot of green (trees and plants). It also has a lake. |
| 信夫：　うん。湖の周りには公園もあるから、週末にはたくさんの人がバーベキューをしたりしてるんだ。 | N: Yeah. There are parks around the lake, and many people have BBQs (and other things) on weekends. |
| 理恵：　いいね。とても住みやすそうな町だね。 | R: That's good. It (the town) looks like it's easy to live in. |
| 信夫：　うん、僕もそう思う。 | N: Yeah, I think so too. |
| 理恵：　あ、タワーがあるね、あの山の上に。 | R: Oh, there is a tower, on top of that mountain over there. |
| 信夫：　あ、あれはテレコムタワーっていうんだけど、一番上には展望台もあるよ。 | N: It (the tower) is called the Telecom Tower, and it has an observatory on top of it as well. |
| 理恵：　へえ、そうなんだ。町全体を見ることが出来るね。 | R: Oh, is that so? (You/We) can see the town as a whole. |
| 信夫：　うん。展望台にはレストランもあって、食事をしながら町が見られるよ。 | N: Yeah. The observatory has a restaurant, and (you/we) can see the town while having a meal. |
| 理恵：　いいね。 | R: Sounds good. |
| 信夫：　特に夜景はとてもきれいなんだ。今晩行ってみようか。 | N: Especially the night view (from there) is very beautiful. Shall we go and take a look there tonight? |
| 理恵：　今晩？いいけど、でも、天気、大丈夫かな。 | R: Tonight? Sounds good! But, will the weather be ok? |
| 信夫：　うん、テレビで、晴れって言ってたから、大丈夫なはずだよ。 | N: Yes. The weather forecast said it would be fine, so it should be ok. |
| 理恵：　ほんと？じゃあ、楽しみだね。あ、あの建物は何？ | R: Really? Well then, I'm looking forward to it. Oh, what's that building? |
| 信夫：　あ、あれは、国立博物館だよ。 | N: That's the National Museum. |
| 理恵：　国立博物館？ | R: The National Museum? |
| 信夫：　うん。昔、ここに住んでいた先祖の服や使ってた道具などが展示されているんだ。 | N: Yeah. Clothes, tools and other things that (our) ancestors who lived here used are exhibited. |
| 理恵：　へえ、おもしろそう。 | R: Oh, it sounds interesting. |
| 信夫：　週末に行ってみようか。 | N: Shall we go and have a look? |
| 理恵：　うん、行こう行こう。 | R: Yeah! Let's go, let's go. |

### 知ってた？　電車 Train

**Following is a summary of some train lines in and around Tokyo, and some words related to trains. Research the destination of each line. For the words, study their meanings.**

| | | | | | |
|---|---|---|---|---|---|
| 電車 | 地下鉄 | 山手線 | 中央線 | 〜行き（品川行き） | 〜方面（中野方面） |
| 駅 | (number)番線 | (number)つ目（4つ目の駅） | 乗る | 降りる | 乗り換える |

## 練習しましょう

**First refer to the map below and decide where (which stations) you would like to go. In pairs, then ask your partner how to get there, as in the example.**

(例) A: あの〜、すみません。目白駅に行きたいんですけど…。
B: 目白駅ですか。えっと、じゃあ、新宿駅で山手線に乗り換えてください。
A: 山手線ですね。
B: はい。新宿駅で、新大久保方面に行って、3つ目の駅です。
A: 分かりました。どうも、ありがとうございました。

| Current location | Your destinations | Your partner's destinations | Current location | Your destinations | Your partner's destinations |
|---|---|---|---|---|---|
| (e.g.) 中野駅 | 大塚駅 | 目白駅 | 御茶ノ水駅 | | |
| 中野駅 | | | 御茶ノ水駅 | | |
| 中野駅 | | | 御茶ノ水駅 | | |

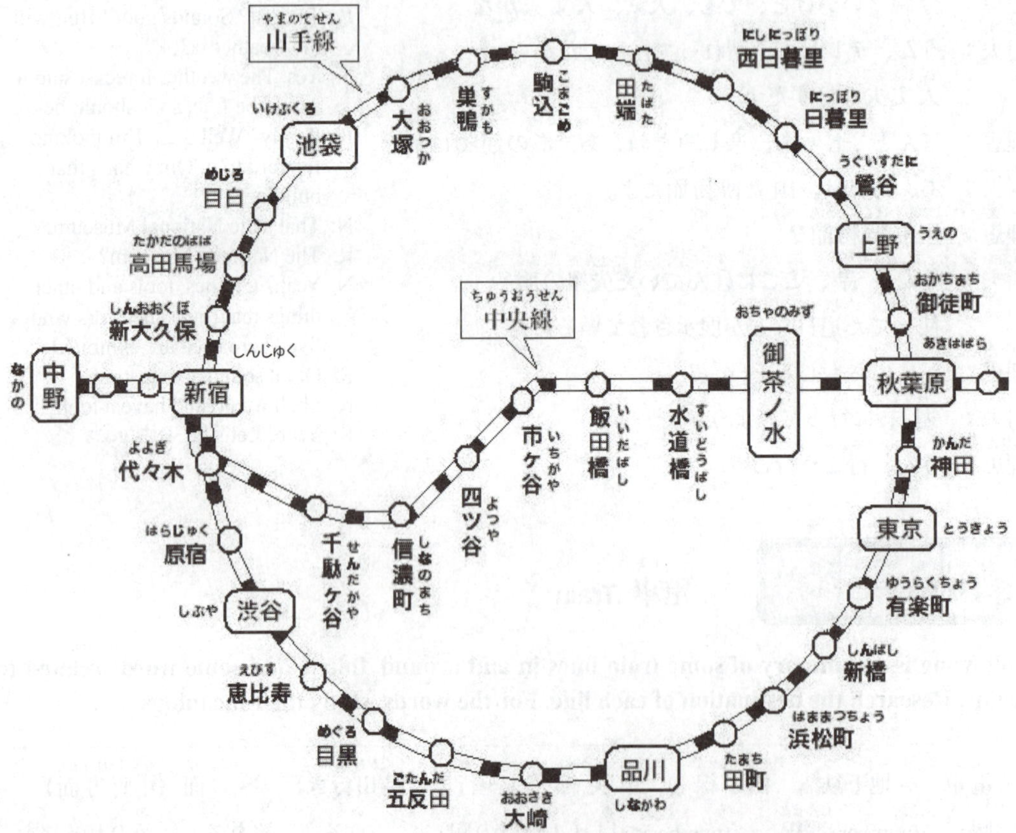




## 新しい単語・表現

(Basic words/expressions are marked with '*')

| | |
|---|---|
| いきなり* | suddenly |
| いびきを かく | snore |
| 動く* | move |
| 運が いい | lucky |
| オッケー | O.K. (オーケー is standard) |
| 同じ* | same, identical |
| 思ったより | more than I thought |
| 勝手(な) | one's own way, selfish |
| 歌舞伎 | kabuki |
| 歌舞伎座 | the Kabuki Theatre |
| 噛む* | bite, chew |
| 観光 | tourism, sightseeing |
| 機能 | function |
| 計画を立てる* | make a plan |
| 見物 | sightseeing |
| 高層ビル | skyscraper |
| 黒板 | blackboard |
| 国立博物館 | national museum |
| 答え* | answer, reply |
| 混む | get crowded |
| 最高 | best, wonderful |
| 幸い(な)* | fortunate, lucky |
| さっき* | before, short while ago, just now |
| 叱る | scold |
| 先祖 | ancestors |
| 育てる | bring up, raise (person) |
| 地下鉄 | subway |
| 中央線 | the Chuo Line |

| | |
|---|---|
| テレコムタワー | Telecom Tower |
| 天気予報 | weather forecast |
| 展示する | display |
| 展望台 | observatory |
| 東京タワー | the Tokyo Tower |
| 道具 | tools, instrument |
| とこ* | (=ところ) place |
| 都内 | Tokyo metropolitan ar |
| 飛ばす | make (something) fly |
| 泥棒* | robber |
| 盗む* | steal |
| 乗り換える | transfer, change |
| 馬鹿* | idiot |
| 馬鹿にする* | make a fool of |
| パソコン | personal computer, PC |
| はとバス | the Hato Bus |
| 一晩中* | all night |
| (中野)方面 | the direction of (Nakano) |
| 緑 | green |
| 昔 | old time, ancient times |
| 夜景 | night view |
| やっと* | at last, with difficulty, somehow |
| 屋根 | roof |
| 山手線 | the Yamanote Line |
| (品川)行き | [train] for (Shinagawa) |
| ロボット | robot |
| 若者 | young people, youth |

21 エレナ：　ありがとう。元気(げんき)でね。オーストラリアから連絡(れんらく)するね。

22 正人(まさと)：　エレナも 元気(げんき)でね。僕(ぼく)も電話(でんわ)するよ。

23 エレナ：　うん。じゃ、またね。

24 正人(まさと)：　うん。気(き)を付(つ)けてね。

## 単語(たんご)と表現(ひょうげん)

| | | | | | |
|---|---|---|---|---|---|
| 2 | とんでもない | not at all | 17 | 出発(しゅっぱつ) | departure |
| 2 | さびしい | lonely | 18 | ～まま | without change |
| 4 | ぜひ | definitely | 19 | 返(かえ)す | return (thing) |
| 7 | 実(じつ)は | as a matter of fact | 19 | ～てほしい | I want you to … |
| 7 | 交換留学(こうかんりゅうがく) | exchange program | 20 | 忘(わす)れる | forget |
| 8 | ～ことになっている | it is decided to … | 20 | 明日(あす) | (＝あした) tomorrow |
| 10 | 楽(たの)しみにする | look forward to | 20 | ちゃんと | promptly, without failure |
| 15 | おかげで | thank you for your consideration for me | 21 | 連絡(れんらく)する | contact |
| | | | 24 | 気(き)を付(つ)ける | take care, be careful |

## ダイアログ（英語(えいご)）

MM=Masato's mother; MF=Masato's father

**[Masato's home]**

1 E: Masato's father and mother, thank you very much for having taken care of me.
2 MM: No, not at all. We will miss you, though.
3 MF: That's true. Please come (back to Japan) again.
4-5 E: Yes. Thank you very much. You two as well, please come to visit Australia.
6 MM: Thank you. Elena, please come and visit us too.
7-8 M: Mum, actually, it has been decided that Elena is coming to Japan again next year on an exchange program.
9 MM: Oh, is that so? Well then, we can see each other again.
10 E: Yes. I look forward to seeing you again next year.
11 M: Elena, it's about time to go to the airport.
12 E: Yes. Well, please take care (to Masato's parents).
13 MF and MM: Elena, you too. Please take care.

**[At the airport]**

14 E: Masato, thanks for everything.
15 M: No, thank you too. I had fun, thanks to you.
16 E: Well, let's keep in touch.
17 M: Same here. Well, it's about time for (your) departure.
18 E: Yes. Oh, that's right. I have borrowed a library book (and haven't returned it). I would like you to return it…
20 M: Oh really? That's all right. I won't forget to return it tomorrow.
21 E: Thanks. Take care. I'll call you from Australia.
22 M: You too, Elena. I'll call you too.
23 E: Yes. Well, see you.
24 M: Yes. Take care.

## 文法

# Honorification and stylisation　敬語（尊敬／謙譲）と待遇表現

(i) Honorification: Different expressions determined by 'whom you are talking about; who is the subject'; Respectful expressions *vs*. humble expressions.

(ii) Stylisation: Different expressions determined by 'whom you are talking to; who is the hearer'; Plain style *vs*. polite style.

## 1. Honorification

Basically two sub-categories: Respectful expressions and humble expressions

### 1.1. Respectful expressions: Used when the subject is someone else other than the speaker.

#### 1.1.1. Nouns/adjectives

Use お (basically for native Japanese) or ご (basically for Sino-Japanese)

(1) お仕事　お国　お返事　お誕生日　ご趣味　ご出身　ご両親　ご家族

(Limited use for adjectives: e.g. お忙しい　ご多忙中)

**美化語**

The use of お in some words (related to foods and drinks, in particular) is not to express the speaker's respectful attitude towards any specific person. Rather, its use is to indicate the speaker's 'general thankful feeling' towards the objects themselves (or towards God), and may be used even for objects that belong to the speaker.

(e.g.) お弁当　お箸　お寿司　お刺身　お酒　おビール　お金

#### 1.1.2. Verbs

The following three are major ways that may be used to indicate the speaker's respectful attitude towards the subject of a sentence.

**(i)** 'お-[Masu stem]に なる' construction

(e.g.) 書く → お書きになる　　話す → お話しになる

(cf. (社長が) お書きになります／お書きになりました／お書きになって, etc)

(1) この手紙は、社長が3年前にお書きになりました。

(2) 社長はいつも、新聞をお読みになってから、朝食を召し上がります。

(3) さあ、早くバスにお乗りになってください。

**(ii)** ‘(ら)れる’ form

(e.g.) 5-base verbs: 書く → 書かれる　　話す → 話される

1-base verbs: 食べる → 食べられる　　起きる → 起きられる

Irregular verbs: する → される　　来る → 来られる

(1) この手紙は、社長が3年前に書かれました。

(2) 社長はもう起きられたのでしょうか。

(3) きのう、先生は、何時に京都へ行かれましたか。

**(iii)** Respectful verbs

These verbs lexically convey the speaker’s respectful feeling.

(e.g.) いらっしゃる（＝いる、来る or 行く, depending on the context)

おっしゃる（＝言う）　くださる（＝くれる）　召し上がる（＝食べる）

なさる（＝する）　ご覧になる（＝見る）

> Note: ‘お-[Masu stem]に なる’ construction is not used for those verbs which have a ‘respectful verb’ counterpart. But, ‘(ら)れる’ forms may be used in this case.
>
> (e.g.) ?お言いになる → We have おっしゃる for 言う and thus お言いになる is not used, while 言われる may be.

## 文法練習 1

**Rewrite the given sentences in the respectful expression, using the お-[Masu-stem]になる construction.**

(例) この本は中村先生が書きました。→ この本は中村先生がお書きになりました。

(1) 社長が話しました。

(2) その寿司は、課長の奥さんがつくりました。

(3) 鈴木先生はたいてい6時に家に帰ります。

(4) 山田先生は手紙を書きませんでした。

(5) 先生もこのペンを使ったよ。

(6) 社長は車に乗らなかった。

**文法練習(ぶんぽうれんしゅう) 2**

**Rewrite the given sentences in the respectful expression, using either the (ら)れる form or respectful verbs if applicable.**

(例(れい)) この本(ほん)は中村先生(なかむらせんせい)が書(か)きました。 → <u>この本(ほん)は中村先生(なかむらせんせい)が書(か)かれました。</u>

(1) 社長(しゃちょう)も会議(かいぎ)に行(い)きました。

(2) 課長(かちょう)がそう言(い)いました。

(3) 鈴木先生(すずきせんせい)は週末(しゅうまつ)にたいてい何(なに)をしますか。

(4) この映画(えいが)、もう見(み)ましたか。

(5) 山田先生(やまだせんせい)は朝(あさ)ご飯(はん)を食(た)べません。

(6) 山田先生(やまだせんせい)は今(いま)、どこにいますか。

(7) 山田先生(やまだせんせい)は部屋(へや)で手紙(てがみ)を書(か)いています。

**1.2. Humble expressions:** Used when the doer is the speaker. These are much simpler, compared to the case of respectful expressions.

**1.2.1. Verbs**

**(i)** <u>'お-[Masu stem] する' construction</u>

(e.g.) 書(か)く → お書(か)きする　　話(はな)す → お話(はな)しする　　願(ねが)う → お願(ねが)いする

( cf. (私(わたし)が) お書(か)きします／お書(か)きしました／お書(か)きしています, etc.)

(1) 私(わたし)が手紙(てがみ)をお書(か)きします。

(2) その手紙(てがみ)、私(わたし)がお送(おく)りします。

(3) すみません。お待(ま)たせしました。　(待(ま)たせる make someone wait)

(4) 私(わたし)が先生(せんせい)にお話(はな)ししました。

**(ii)** <u>Humble verbs</u>

These verbs lexically convey the speaker's humble attitude.

(e.g.) 申(もう)し上(あ)げる（＝言(い)う）　いたす（＝する）　差(さ)し上(あ)げる（＝あげる）

いただく（＝もらう）　うかがう（＝聞(き)く、訪(たず)ねる）　拝見(はいけん)する（＝見(み)る）

(1) 私が先生に申し上げました。

(2) では、あした9時にうかがいます。

(3) 誕生日に、社長にプレゼントをいただきました。

> Note: いたす may replace する in the construction (i) above, i.e. お-[Masu stem] いたす, to further increase the degree of humbleness.
>
> (e.g.) 私がお書きいたします。 お願いいたします。

**文法練習 3**

**Rewrite the given sentences in the humble expression, using either the お-[Masu-stem]する construction or humble verbs if applicable.**

(例) 私が書きます。 → <u>私がお書きします。</u>

(1) そのかばん、私が持ちます。

(2) この英語のチェック、願います。

(3) ちょっと先生に言いたいことがあるのですが…。

(4) それは、私がします。

(5) じゃ、お返事、待っています。

## 2. Stylisation

There are basically three styles: plain style, polite style and extra-polite style.

**2.1.** Casual style (plain endings/forms)

Typically used to indicate the speaker's equal or superior social status towards the hearer. They may also be used to indicate the speaker's intimacy with or friendliness to the hearer.

(1) [to a close friend] 朝ご飯、食べた？ この映画、おもしろかったよ。

(2) [to a young boy whom the speaker meets for the first time] なぜここで泣いているの？

**2.2.** Polite style (*Desu-masu* endings/forms)

Typically used to indicate the speaker's polite/formal attitude towards or a certain degree of social distance from the hearer. They may be used when the hearer is socially equal or superior.

(3) [to a colleague] 朝ご飯、食べましたか。 この映画、おもしろかったですよ。

**2.3.** Extra-polite style (*Gozaimasu* endings/forms)

The use of ございます is not really productive in modern Japanese and is used in limited phrases and expressions which involve a high level of formality. It is basically equivalent to あります.

(4) [to a customer] 靴売(くつう)り場(ば)は５階(かい)にございます。（＝にあります）

エレベーターはあちらでございます。（＝であります＝です）

There are several formulation rules for a situation where it is used with い-adjectives (e.g. those the base form of which ends with ～たい becomes ～とう before ございます: see (e.g.) below); but these rules are not provided here since their use is no longer productive.

(5) [to a customer] 毎度(まいど)、ありがとうございます。（← ありがたい＋ございます）

---

**When the hearer is the doer of the sentence (honorific-polite style)**

Japanese people tend to be very polite and express their highest level of formality when the hearer is a respected person and their expressions directly concern the hearer, e.g. questions about the hearer, requests, etc. Honorifics are often used and the expressions tend to be indirect in such a case.

(1) 社長(しゃちょう)、今日(きょう)は，何時(なんじ)に事務所(じむしょ)にいらっしゃいましたか。

(2) 推薦状(すいせんじょう)を書(か)いていただけないでしょうか。

(3) 今晩(こんばん)、町(まち)のレストランで、お食事(しょくじ)をなさってはいかがですか。

---

### 文法練習(ぶんぽうれんしゅう) 4

**Rewrite the given sentences as specified in [ ].**

(例(れい)) きのう、田中(たなか)さんに会(あ)いました。[in plain ending] → きのう、田中(たなか)さんに会(あ)った。

(1) レストランは７階(かい)にあります。 [in extra-polite style (*Gozaimasu* ending)]

(2) 質問(しつもん)はありませんか。 [in extra-polite style (*Gozaimasu* ending)]

(3) 木村社長(きむらしゃちょう)はあの方(かた)です。 [in extra-polite style (*Gozaimasu* ending)]

(4) きのうのパーティー、人(ひと)がたくさん来(き)たね。 [in polite style]

(5) 山田先生(やまだせんせい)は部屋(へや)で手紙(てがみ)を書(か)いていらっしゃいますよ。 [in casual style]

(6) ８時(じ)にテレビを見(み)てください。 [in honorific-polite style]

(7) これは、先生(せんせい)が書(か)いた本(ほん)ですか。 [in honorific-polite style]

**自然な日本語**

# 対人関係と言語表現　Managing interpersonal relationships

## 1. Interpersonal relationship

One of the most important functions of language is to indicate the interpersonal relationship between the speaker and the hearer: Some related expressions are 'social distance', 'intimacy', 'friendliness', 'politeness, and 'formality'. Expressing the interpersonal relationship is a rather complicated process that involves a variety of factors.

**1.1.** Expressing an interpersonal relationship

The interpersonal relationship is expressed not only by linguistic means, but also by a wide range of non-linguistic means, such as facial expressions, tone, contents of the utterance, and so forth. In fact, non-linguistic means have a great influence on the expression of a different range of interpersonal relationships. For example, although the words used may convey a high level of honorific expression, it would not be so polite if they were used with an angry tone.

(1) そんなことおっしゃらないで、早く質問にお答えください！

(2) 部長には、今日で辞めていただきますが、よろしいですね。

**1.2.** Situational context and social status

Expressing an interpersonal relationship is often influenced by the situational context at the time (e.g. public *vs*. private; asking a favour *vs*. fighting) as well as by the permanent social status (between close friends *vs*. between strangers; employer *vs*. employee; shop keeper *vs*. customer). For example, it is socially expected that casual speech with plain endings is in principle used between close friends. However, a person tends to use more polite expressions (and sometimes with *desu-masu* endings — but perhaps with a friendly tone) in some situations, especially when he/she asks a favour.

(3) 私あした、行けないからね。私の代わりに、よろしくお願いしますね。

**1.3.** Sensitive to culture

What we consider as an 'ideal' interpersonal relationship may vary from culture to culture. For example, in some situations such as purchase-conversations between shopkeeper and customer, the hierarchical relationship with an extra-polite attitude is normally expected in some cultures while an equal relationship with a friendly attitude is preferred in some other cultures. Age difference is regarded as important in some cultures while gender difference may be regarded as more important in others.

Such differences may be reflected in the use of different language expressions and attitudes of communicators. Thus, an understanding of the value of various factors (such as age, gender, social status) in a particular culture is important for successful communication in that language.

## 2. Conversation settings

**2.1.** Formal setting: Polite endings (*-desu/-masu*, *-gozaimasu*); honorifics; polite attitude; logical (indirect expression of feelings and emotions); restrictions on what you can say; great social distance.

(e.g.) Formal meeting, public speech, formal job interview, between strangers

**2.2.** Semi-formal setting: Basically polite endings with a mixed use of casual endings; polite and yet friendly; relatively direct expression of feelings/emotions.

(e.g.) With a senior colleague (talking about private matters at the pub after work)

**2.3.** Casual setting: Casual endings (plain forms); intimacy/friendly attitude; emotional (more direct expression of feelings and emotions); close social distance.

(e.g.) Between close friends (talking about their girl friends, their camping trip, etc)

(1) a. [formal] あした3時に、もう一度、お電話いただけないでしょうか。

b. [semi] あした3時に、もう一度、電話くださいね。待ってます。

c. [casual] あした さ、3時に、もう一度、電話くれる？ 待ってるからね。

(2) a. [formal] 田中さんはきのう、学校に来ませんでした。病気だったようです。

b. [semi] 田中さんきのう、学校に来ませんでしたよ。病気だったみたいですけど。

c. [casual] 田中さん、きのう、学校、来なかったよ。なんか、病気だったみたい。

### 自然な日本語：練習

**Rewrite the following semi-formal sentences into those in formal and casual conversation settings.**

(例) 食事はどうでしたか。おいしかったですか。

[formal] <u>食事は、いかがでしたか。</u>

[casual] <u>食事、どうだった？ おいしかった？</u>

> N.B. In [formal] setting,「おいしかったですか」may be omitted as it requires the hearer to indicate his/her personal desire too directly.

(1) 田中さんに会えてよかったですね。

(2) では、あした午後4時頃、電話しますね。

(3) ここで、待っています。

(4) 魚料理、好きですか。

(5) ここではタバコを吸わないでくださいね。

## 表現

### 1 [Verb plain form]-ことにする（した）／ことになる（なった）

[1] ☛ ことにする expresses personal decisions — that is, the speaker's volitional decision; therefore, if the speaker perceives a given decision to be his/her own, then he/she should use ことにする.

(1) 夏休みには、ハワイに行くことにします／ことにしました。
(*Lit.* 'I decide to go to Hawaii for summer holidays / (have) decided to go to …')

(2) たばこを止めることにする／ことにした。
(*Lit.* 'I decide to quit smoking / I (have) decided to quit smoking')

[2] ☛ ことにする is often used to indicate the speaker's volitional decision which is made at the very moment he/she states it as his/her future plan, as shown in (3), whereas ことにした is used to express the speaker's decision which has already been made to be carried out, as shown in (4).

(3) A: 夏休み、どこに行くか、決めた？
B: まだ決めてない。
A: ハワイはとてもいいらしいよ。
B: そう。よし！ じゃあ、今年はハワイに行くことにするよ。

(4) A: 夏休み、どこに行くか、決めた？
B: うん。今年はハワイに行くことにしたよ。
A: そう。それはいいね。

[3] ☛ ことになる indicates that an impersonal decision or an arrangement will be made by some unspecified agent or factor(s), but not solely by the speaker. The speaker should use this if he/she does not perceive a given decision or arrangement to be completely his/her own. The non-past form ことになる is normally used to indicate that a given decision or an arrangement will take place if the situation requires it. Its past tense form ことになった usually expresses that it has been made and will be credibly carried out under normal circumstances.

(5) もしこの車が壊れたら、新しい車を買うことになります。
(*Lit.* 'If this car breaks down, (it will be decided that) I will buy a new car.')

(6) 結局、田中さんは今晩入院することになった。
(*Lit.* 'As a result, it has been decided that Tanaka-san will be hospitalised tonight.')

(7) 来年、大阪へ転勤することになりました。
(*Lit.* 'It has been decided that I will move to the Osaka office from next year.')

## 表現練習1

**Look at the pictures below and write what decisions you have made or what arrangements have been made for you, using 〜ことにした or 〜ことになった. Use polite endings.**

**(例1)　ミカさんに手紙を書くことにしました。**

**(例2)　休みの間、レストランでアルバイトをすることになりました。**

(e.g.1)

to Mika

your decision

(e.g.2)

during holiday

arrangement for you

(1) have coffee with Hanako tonight

your decision

(2) go to movie with Yuka on the weekend

your decision

(3) go to China

during holiday

arrangement for you

(4) from next year

arrangement for you

(5) everyday, after class

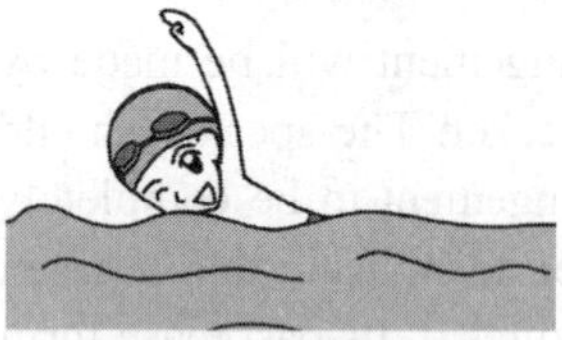

your decision

(6)

go to Japan to study Japanese next year

arrangement for you

(7) go to Mt. Fuji on the weekend

your decision

(8)

quit drinking

your decision

(9) go shopping tomorrow

arrangement for you

(10) go to Kyoto by Shinkansen

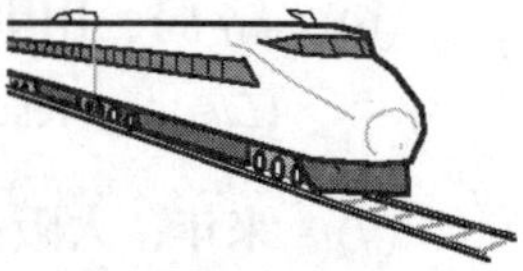

arrangement for you

## 2 〜てほしい　'(I) want (someone) to do…'

[1] ☛ This phrase indicates the speaker's desire or wish that 'someone' does something. When '(someone)' appears in a sentence, it is normally marked by に.

(1) 田中(たなか)さんに来(き)てほしいです。

(2) （あなたに）８時(じ)には家(うち)に帰(かえ)ってほしい。

[2] ☛ It may also be used to indicate the speaker's request in casual speech. When used as a request, it normally has the form of 〜てほしいんだ.

(3) この手紙(てがみ)、ちょっと読(よ)んでほしいんだけど、いい？

[3] ☛ 〜てもらいたい (〜てもらう＋たい) is similar to 〜てほしい, and is interchangeable in many cases. Its humble expressions, 〜ていただきたい or 〜ていただけないでしょうか, etc., are used in formal situations.

(4) 田中(たなか)さんに来(き)てもらいたいです。

(5) （あなたに）８時(じ)には家(うち)に帰(かえ)ってもらいたい。

(6) あしたもう一度(いちど)、来(き)ていただきたいのですが、大丈夫(だいじょうぶ)でしょうか。

(7) この本(ほん)を買(か)っていただけないでしょうか。

### 表現(ひょうげん)練習(れんしゅう)２

**Rewrite the following English in Japanese, using 〜てほしい. Use polite endings unless specified.**

(例(れい)) I want Yuka-san to come to my home on Sunday.

→ 由香(ゆか)さんに、日曜日(にちようび)に家(うち)へ来(き)てほしいです。

(1) I would like Satoo-sensei to read my essay.

(2) I want my dad to buy a car (for me).

(3) I want Jenny to teach me English.

(4) I want (you) to help me with my homework.

(5) I want Katoo-san to eat sushi which I have cooked.

(6) A: I want (you) to return this book to the library, but is it okay? [casual setting]
B: That's all right.

(7) A: I would like (you) to check this document. [casual setting] (document 書類(しょるい))
B: Sorry, I am a little busy now.

## 3 ～(た)まま '(with a state being left unchanged …)'

☛ This phrase indicates that the state expressed by ～た is left unchanged while doing some other thing.

(1) テレビを付けたまま、寝てしまいました。

(2) パジャマを着たまま、出かけた。

### 表現練習3

**Look at the pictures and describe each situation, using ～たまま, as in the example.**

(例) テレビを付けたまま、寝ました。

(e.g.)

(1)

(2)

(3)

(4)

(5)

## 4 ～ないで／～ずに 'without doing …'

☛ ～ないで is used only with a verb. It can be replaced with ～ずに, which is an old form of negative expression: The *Nai*-stem is required before ～ずに (読ま-ずに；食べ-ずに) and する becomes せ before ずに (i.e. 勉強する → 勉強せずに).

(1) 忘れないで、必ず図書館に本を返します。

(2) 夕べは疲れていたので、服も着替えないで寝てしまった。

(3) 今朝、遅く起きたので、朝ご飯も食べずに学校に行きました。

(4) 勉強せずにテストを受けました。

## 表現練習4

**Rewrite the following English in Japanese, using 〜ないで. Use polite endings.**

(例) Yamada-san went to school without eating breakfast.

→ 山田さんは朝ご飯を食べないで学校に行きました。

(1) I was so tired that I went to bed without having a shower.

(2) Tanaka-san went back home without telling me anything.

(3) Please answer my questions without looking at the book. (important 重要(な))

(4) I have an important exam soon, so I studied for 10 hours without sleeping.

(5) I went to see a baseball game yesterday. However, the tickets were sold out, so I had to come back home without watching the game. (be sold out 売り切れる)

# 対話

## 対話練習1

**Pre-task: 〜予定です／〜にする／〜になる**

(i) Make your plans for the up-coming weekend (今度の週末) and summer holiday (夏休み). Write them down in the table below (私).

(ii) Ask three of your classmates about their plans for the weekend and summer holiday, using 何をする予定ですか 'What is your plan?'. In answering the questions, try to use 〜ことにする or 〜ことになる in an appropriate manner. Use polite endings.

(例) A: [B] さん、今度の週末に、何をする予定ですか。
B: 週末ですか。ええと、直子さんと図書館で日本語を勉強することにしました。
A: そうですか。じゃあ、夏休みには何をする予定ですか。
B: 夏休みには旅行に行くことになりました。台湾と香港に行くと思います。
A: そうですか。いいですね。

| 名前 | 今度の週末の予定 | 夏休みの予定 |
|---|---|---|
| 私： | | |
| さん： | | |
| さん： | | |
| さん： | | |

## 対話練習 2

**Pre-task: 〜てほしい**

(i) What is stated in the box is something you would like to ask your friend as a favour. First, study the given expressions and provide your own decisions/answers for the underline, '_____'.

(ii) In pairs, ask your friend a favour, as in the example. Practise with one more friend.

(例) A: [B] さん、この本、ちょっと図書館に返してほしいんだけど。
B: 本？ うん、いいよ。いつまでに返してほしいの？
A: あしたまでなんだけど…。
B: あしたね。オーケー。大丈夫だよ。
A: あ、ほんと？ ありがとう。助かるよ。

| | | |
|---|---|---|
| (e.g.) [この本] 図書館に返す<br>By when? → I need to return it by ___tomorrow___. | [鉛筆] 貸す<br>How many? → I need ___ pencil(s) | [買い物] 一緒に行く<br>When? → I plan to go on ________. |
| [日本語の作文] チェックする<br>By when? → I need to submit it by ________. | 買い物に行ってくる<br>What (to buy)? → I need ________. | あしたの朝、起こす<br>What time? → I need to wake up at ________. |

## 対話練習 3

**Pre-task: 〜まま；〜ないで／ずに**

**Ask your friends whether or not they have experienced the things stated in the prompts below.**

(例) A: [B] さんはテレビを付けたまま寝たことがありますか。
B: はい、あります。[A] さんは、どうですか。
A: はい、私も（テレビを付けたまま寝たことが）あります。
B: そうですか。じゃあ、窓を開けたまま出かけたことがありますか。
.... [continued]

| Prompts | 私 | 友達 1 | 友達 2 | 友達 3 |
|---|---|---|---|---|
| テレビを付けたまま寝る | (e.g.) ○ | | | |
| 窓を開けたまま出かける | | | | |
| ポケットに携帯を入れたまま洗濯する | | | | |
| 朝ご飯を食べないで学校に行く | | | | |
| 休まずに 10時間テレビや DVD を見続ける | | | | |

## 対話作り

✍ **In pairs, create a dialogue for the given situation. Please feel free to ask the instructor if you have any questions about Japanese expressions for your dialogue.**

**Situation:**

You and your friend are talking about your plans for next year in connection with your future. You may want to focus on one or two of the following.

(a) What is your future plan — what would you like to become; in what area would you like to work; etc.?

(b) How do you think you will be able to achieve your plan?

(c) What have you decided to do or what has been arranged/decided for next year (e.g. going overseas, taking some courses, etc)?

(d) Is there anything you wish someone (e.g. your family members, friends and/or instructors) to do for it?

Please try to incorporate the following expressions into your talk:

- Honorific and humble expressions
- [Noun] and/or [Adjective]＋なる
- ～ことにする（した）／ことになる（なった）
- ～てほしい

### サンプル・ダイアログ

信夫：エミは来年、何の授業とるの？

エミ：えっと、私は、前期に日本語と日本史のコースをとって、後期から1年間、日本に留学することにした。

信夫：へえ～、すごいね。留学のために、日本語の試験とかあるの？

エミ：ううん、試験はないけど、日本語のエッセイを提出したあと、日本語で面接があるんだ。

信夫：へえ。

エミ：ねえ、信夫。今度、日本語の面接、手伝ってほしいんだけど、時間ある？

信夫：うん、あるけど、何してほしいの？

エミ：日本語で、いろいろ質問してほしいんだ。

信夫：あ、大丈夫だよ。

N: Emi. What courses will you take next year?

E: Well, I will take Japanese language and Japanese history in the first semester and from second semester, I have decided to go to Japan to study for one year.

N: Wow, that's great. Do you need to sit for any Japanese exam for that?

E: No, I don't, but I need to submit a Japanese essay and have an interview in Japanese.

N: Wow.

E: Nobuo. I hope you can help me with the Japanese interview, but do you have time?

N: Yes, I have, but what do you want me to do?

E: I want you to ask various questions in Japanese.

N: Oh, no problem.

E: Thank you. Oh, that's right. I need recommendation letters from two teachers. Who do you think I need to ask for that?

N: What about Smith-sensei and Tanaka-sensei? I think they will surely write good letters for you.

E: I agree.

エミ：ありがと。あ、そうだ。二人の先生の推薦状も必要なんだけど、どの先生にお願いしたらいいと思う？

信夫：スミス先生と田中先生に書いていただいたらどう？きっといい推薦状書いてくださると思うよ。

エミ：そうね。

## 知ってた？　俳句 Haiku

Haiku (俳句) is a form of Japanese poetry, which expresses a thought, feeling or mood. Haiku generally consists of five morae, seven morae and five morae (NB. '1 mora' is basically the same as '1 hiragana'):

| 古池や | 蛙飛び込む | 水の音 |
|---|---|---|
| fu/ru/i/ke/ya | ka/wa/zu/to/bi/ko/mu | mi/zu/no/o/to |
| (5 morae) | (7 morae) | (5 morae) |

'Old pond, a frog jumps, the sound of water'

(松尾 芭蕉 1644-1694)

Haiku traditionally contains kigo (季語 'season word') which symbolises or imitates the season in which the poem is set (e.g. 蛙 かわず 'frog' — spring).

### 調べましょう

**Research the meaning and season of the following kigo (季語), for example on the internet or in dictionaries.**

| 季語 | 意味 | 季節 | 季語 | 意味 | 季節 |
|---|---|---|---|---|---|
| 蛙 | frog | 春 | 初雪 | | |
| 花火 | | | 蛍 | | |
| 月 | | | 枯れる | | |
| 桜 | | | 鈴虫 | | |
| 書初 | | | かき氷 | | |
| 秋刀魚 | | | 五月晴 | | |

### 作りましょう

(i) Think about what thoughts or feelings you would like to express in 俳句.

(ii) Create a 俳句, using one of 季語 given above. Make sure that your 俳句 has the 5-7-5 structure.

(iii) Share 俳句 in class.

# 新(あたら)しい単語(たんご)・表現(ひょうげん)

(Basic words/expressions are marked with '*')

| | |
|---|---|
| 明日(あす) | (=あした) tomorrow |
| いたす* | (=する) do [humble] |
| いただく* | (=もらう) receive [humble] |
| いらっしゃる* | (=いる exist／行(い)く go／来(く)る come) [honorific] |
| うかがう | (=聞(き)く ask, listen／訪(たず)ねる visit) [humble] |
| (テストを) 受(う)ける | sit for a test |
| 売(う)り切(き)れる | be sold out |
| 売(う)り場(ば) | sales section |
| エレベーター | elevator |
| おかげで | thank you for your consideration for me |
| 起(お)こす | wake (someone) up |
| おっしゃる* | (=言(い)う) say [honorific] |
| お箸(はし)* | chopsticks |
| お弁当(べんとう)* | box lunch |
| ～階(かい)* | -th floor |
| ～方(かた)* | (=人(ひと)) person [honorific] |
| 課長(かちょう) | section chief |
| 必(かなら)ず* | surely, by all means |
| 蛙(かわず) | (classic word of 蛙(かえる)) frog |
| 代(か)わりに* | instead, on behalf |
| 着替(きが)える | change clothes |
| 季語(きご) | season words (in haiku) |
| 決(き)める* | decide, make up one's mind |
| 気(き)を付(つ)ける* | take care, be careful |
| くださる* | (=くれる) give (to me) [honorific] |
| 結局(けっきょく)* | eventually, as a result |
| 交換留学(こうかんりゅうがく) | exchange program |
| 後期(こうき) | second semester |
| 答(こた)える* | answer |
| ご覧(らん)になる* | (=見(み)る) see [honorific] |
| 作文(さくぶん) | composition |
| 差(さ)し上(あ)げる | (=あげる) give [humble] |
| さびしい* | lonely |
| 実(じつ)は* | as a matter of fact |
| 事務所(じむしょ) | office |
| 社長(しゃちょう) | president (of a company) |
| 重要(じゅうよう)(な)* | important |
| 出発(しゅっぱつ) | departure |
| 書類(しょるい) | document |
| 新幹線(しんかんせん)* | Shinkansen |
| 前期(ぜんき) | first semester |
| 対人関係(たいじんかんけい) | interpersonal relationship |
| 台湾(たいわん) | Taiwan |
| 楽(たの)しみにする* | look forward to |
| (ご)多忙中(たぼうちゅう) | while you are busy |
| チェック | check |
| ちゃんと* | promptly, without failure |
| 朝食(ちょうしょく) | breakfast (formal) |
| 付(つ)ける* | turn on, switch on |
| 提出(ていしゅつ)する* | submit |
| 転勤(てんきん)する | transfer (to another branch) |
| 飛(と)び込(こ)む | jump into |
| とんでもない* | not at all (unreasonable) |
| なさる* | (=する) do [honorific] |

| | |
|---|---|
| 日本史 | Japanese history |
| 入院する | be hospitalised |
| 俳句 | haiku (a form of Japanese poetry) |
| 拝見する | (=見る) see [humble] |
| 履く* | wear (shoes, socks, etc) |
| パジャマ | pajama |
| 必要(な)* | necessary |
| 表現* | expression |
| 部長 | division chief |
| 古池 | old pond |
| 返事* | reply, response |
| (〜て) ほしい* | I want someone to … |
| 毎度 | every time |
| 待たせる* | make someone wait |
| 〜まま* | without change |
| 召し上がる | (=食べる) eat [honorific] |
| 申し上げる* | (=言う) say [humble] |
| よし！ | good!, all right! |
| 予定* | plan, schedule |
| よろしい | (=いい) good [honorific] |
| 留学* | study abroad |
| 連絡する* | contact |

## Appendixes

Appendix 1: List of countries, occupations, hobbies and majors/subjects

Appendix 2: Summary of grammatical forms: Conjugation chart

Appendix 3: Summary of modal expressions

# Appendix 1

| Countries | *In Roman script* | *Gloss* |
|---|---|---|
| アメリカ | Amerika | America |
| イギリス | Igirisu | England |
| イタリア | Itaria | Italy |
| インド | Indo | India |
| インドネシア | Indoneshia | Indonesia |
| オーストラリア | Oosutoraria | Australia |
| オランダ | Oranda | Holland / Netherland |
| カナダ | Kanada | Canada |
| シンガポール | Shingapooru | Singapore |
| スウェーデン | Suweeden | Sweden |
| スペイン | Supein | Spain |
| タイ | Tai | Thai |
| デンマーク | Denmaaku | Denmark |
| ドイツ | Doitsu | Germany |
| ニュージーランド | Nyuujiirando | New Zealand |
| ノルウェー | Noruwee | Norway |
| フィンランド | Finrando | Finland |
| ブラジル | Burajiru | Brazil |
| フランス | Furansu | France |
| ベトナム | Betonamu | Vietnam |
| マレーシア | Mareeshia | Malaysia |
| メキシコ | Mekishiko | Mexico |
| モンゴル | Mongoru | Mongolia |
| ロシア | Roshia | Russia |
| 韓国（かんこく） | Kankoku | Korea |
| 香港（ほんこん） | Honkon | Hong Kong |
| 台湾（たいわん） | Taiwan | Taiwan |
| 中国（ちゅうごく） | Chuugoku | China |
| 日本（にほん・にっぽん） | Nihon *or* Nippon | Japan |

**Occupations**

| | | |
|---|---|---|
| 医者（いしゃ） | isha | doctor |
| 会社員（かいしゃいん） | kaishain | office worker |
| 歌手（かしゅ） | kashu | singer |
| 看護師（かんごし） | kangoshi | nurse |

| | | |
|---|---|---|
| 教師（きょうし） | kyooshi | teacher |
| 銀行員（ぎんこういん） | ginkooin | bank employee |
| 警察官（けいさつかん） | keisatsukan | policeman |
| 建築家（けんちくか） | kenchikuka | architect |
| 公務員（こうむいん） | koomuin | public servant |
| 作曲家（さっきょくか） | sakkyokuka | composer |
| 主婦（しゅふ） | shufu | housewife |
| 政治家（せいじか） | seijika | politician |
| セールスマン | seerusuman | salesperson |
| 俳優（はいゆう） | haiyuu | actor |
| パイロット | pairotto | pilot |
| 販売員（はんばいいん） | hanbaiin | salesperson |
| 秘書（ひしょ） | hisho | secretary |
| フライト・アテンダント（=客室乗務員） | furaito atendanto (kyakushitujoomuin) | flight attendant |
| 弁護士（べんごし） | bengoshi | lawyer |
| 漫画家（まんがか） | mangaka | cartoonist |

**Hobbies**

| | | |
|---|---|---|
| 映画鑑賞（えいがかんしょう） | eiga kanshoo | watching movie |
| 音楽鑑賞（おんがくかんしょう） | ongaku kanshoo | listening to music |
| ガーデニング | gaadeningu | gardening |
| かいもの | kaimono | shopping |
| ゴルフ | gorufu | golf |
| コンピューターゲーム | konpyuutaa geemu | computer game |
| サーフィン | saafin | surfing |
| サイクリング | saikuringu | cycling |
| ジョギング | jogingu | jogging |
| 水泳（すいえい） | suiei | swimming |
| ダンス | dansu | dance |
| 釣り（つり） | tsuri | fishing |
| テニス | tenisu | tennis |
| 読書（どくしょ） | dokusho | reading books |
| ピアノ | piano | playing the piano |
| 山登り（やまのぼり） | yamanobori | climbing mountains |
| 料理（りょうり） | ryoori | cooking |
| 旅行（りょこう） | ryokoo | travel |

**Majors / subjects**

| | | |
|---|---|---|
| アジア学（アジアがく） | Ajiagaku | Asian Studies |
| 医学（いがく） | Igaku | Medical Science |
| 音楽（おんがく） | Ongaku | Music |
| 化学（かがく） | Kagaku | Chemistry |
| 海洋学（かいようがく） | Kaiyoogaku | Oceanography |
| 環境科学（かんきょうかがく） | Kankyookagaku | Environmental Studies |
| 観光学（かんこうがく） | Kankoogaku | Tourism Studies |
| 教育学（きょういくがく） | Kyooikugaku | Education |
| 経営学（けいえいがく）（ビジネス） | Keiei (Bijinesu) | Business Administration |
| 経済学（けいざいがく） | Keizaigaku | Economics |
| 建築学（けんちくがく） | Kenchikugaku | Architecture |
| 言語学（げんごがく） | Gengogaku | Linguistics |
| 考古学（こうこがく） | Kookogaku | Archaeology |
| 国際関係学（こくさいかんけいがく） | Kokusaikankeigaku | International Relations |
| 社会学（しゃかいがく） | Shakaigaku | Sociology |
| 商学（しょうがく） | Shoogaku | Commerce |
| 心理学（しんりがく） | Shinrigaku | Psychology |
| 人類学（じんるいがく） | Jinruigaku | Anthropology |
| 数学（すうがく） | Suugaku | Mathematics |
| 政治学（せいじがく） | Seijigaku | Politics |
| 生物学（せいぶつがく） | Seibutsugaku | Biology |
| 哲学（てつがく） | Tetsugaku | Philosophy |
| 日本語（にほんご） | Nihongo | Japanese |
| 物理学（ぶつりがく） | Butsurigaku | Physics |
| 文学（ぶんがく） | Bungaku | Literature |
| 法律学（ほうりつがく） | Hooritsugaku | Law |
| 薬学（やくがく） | Yakugaku | Pharmacology |
| 歴史学（れきしがく） | Rekishigaku | History |

# Appendix 2

## Summary of grammatical forms: Conjugation chart

| | Base form | *Nai*-form | *Masu/Desu*-form | *Te*-form [1] | *Ta*-form | *Ba*-form | *(Yo)o*-form |
|---|---|---|---|---|---|---|---|
| **5-base verbs** (*U*-verbs; Group I verbs) | [end in -*u*] | [-~~*u*~~ → -*a* + ない] | [-~~*u*~~ → -*i* + ます] | [various forms] | [replace て → た] | [-~~*u*~~ → -*e* + ば] | [-~~*u*~~ → -o + う] |
| | 買う 'buy' | かわない | かいます | かって | かった | かえば | かおう |
| | 書く 'write' | かかない | かきます | かいて | かいた | かけば | かこう |
| | 泳ぐ 'swim' | およがない | およぎます | およいで | およいだ | およげば | およごう |
| | 話す 'speak' | はなさない | はなします | はなして | はなした | はなせば | はなそう |
| | 待つ 'wait' | またない | まちます | まって | まった | まてば | まとう |
| | 死ぬ 'die' | しなない | しにます | しんで | しんだ | しねば | しのう |
| | 遊ぶ 'play' | あそばない | あそびます | あそんで | あそんだ | あそべば | あそぼう |
| | 飲む 'drink' | のまない | のみます | のんで | のんだ | のめば | のもう |
| | 売る 'sell' | うらない | うります | うって | うった | うれば | うろう |
| **1-base verbs** (*Ru*-verbs; Group II verbs) | [end in -{*e,i*}る] | [~~る~~ → ない] | [~~る~~ → ます] | [~~る~~ → て] | [~~る~~ → た] | [~~る~~ → れ + ば] | [~~る~~ → よ + う] |
| | 食べる 'eat' | たべない | たべます | たべて | たべた | たべれば | たべよう |
| | 見る 'see' | みない | みます | みて | みた | みれば | みよう |
| **Irregular verbs** | する 'do' | しない | します | して | した | すれば | しよう |
| | 来る 'come' | こない | きます | きて | きた | くれば | こよう |
| ***I*-adjectives** | [end in -い] | [-~~い~~ → -く+ない] | [-い + です] | [-~~い~~ → -く+て] | [-~~い~~ → -かっ+た] | [-~~い~~ → -けれ+ば] | |
| | 安い 'cheap' | やすくない | やすいです | やすくて | やすくない | やすければ | --------- |
| | いい 'good' | よくない | いいです | よくて | よくない | よければ | |
| | ない 'absent/*neg.*' | なくない | ないです | なくて | なくない | なければ | |
| **Copula** (for ***Na*-adj**. and **Nouns**) | [-だ] | [-~~だ~~ → -で+ない[2]] | [-~~だ~~ → -です] | [-~~だ~~ → -で] | [-~~だ~~ → -だっ + た] | [-~~だ~~ → -であれ+ば[3]] | |
| | 静かだ 'quiet' | しずかでない | しずかです | しずかで | しずかだった | しずかであれば | --------- |
| | 学生だ 'student' | がくせいでない | がくせいです | がくせいで | がくせいだった | がくせいであれば | |

[1] 行く 'go' → 行って [2] ～では(underlined)ない(emphasis of negative feeling) → ～じゃ(underlined)ない (colloquial) [3] ～であれば (←～である [long form of ～だ]; written)

## Summary of modal expressions

(i) Modality is a grammatical category which refers to the speaker's judgement on certainty (how certain he/she is) or evidentiality (what kind of evidence he/she is based upon) about the propositional (who-where-what-how type) information.

(ii) In Japanese, the modal expressions are attached to the main predicate (verbs, i-adjectives, and copula).

(iii) Basically plain forms of the main predicate are used for modal expressions; But, in the case of the copular (for nouns or *Na*-adjectives), its non-past expression, i.e. –だ, may be sustained, omitted, or replaced with の or な — The variety is pre-determined for a particular modal expression and we need to get familiar with each case.

### Some modal expressions

| Modal expressions | Tense | Verbs 書(か)く 'write' | I-adjectives 安(やす)い 'cheap' | Na-adjectives 静(しず)かだ 'quiet' | Nouns 学生(がくせい)だ 'student' |
|---|---|---|---|---|---|
| ～だろう (presumptive) | Non-past | 書(か)くだろう | 安(やす)いだろう | 静(しず)かだろう | 学生(がくせい)だろう |
| | Past | 書(か)いただろう | 安(やす)かっただろう | 静(しず)かだっただろう | 学生(がくせい)だっただろう |
| ～かも知れない 'might' | Non-past | 書(か)くかも知(し)れない | 安(やす)いかも知(し)れない | 静(しず)かかも知(し)れない | 学生(がくせい)かも知(し)れない |
| | Past | 書(か)いたかも知(し)れない | 安(やす)かったかも知(し)れない | 静(しず)かだったかも知(し)れない | 学生(がくせい)だったかも知(し)れない |
| ～そうだ(1) 'look' (visual) | Non-past | 書(か)きそうだ | 安(やす)そうだ | 静(しず)かそうだ | —— |
| | Past | 書(か)きそうだった | 安(やす)そうだった | 静(しず)かそうだった | —— |
| ～そうだ(2) (hearsay) | Non-past | 書(か)くそうだ | 安(やす)いそうだ | 静(しず)かだそうだ | 学生(がくせい)だそうだ |
| | Past | 書(か)いたそうだ | 安(やす)かったそうだ | 静(しず)かだったそうだ | 学生(がくせい)だったそうだ |
| ～ようだ 'likely, seem' | Non-past | 書(か)くようだ | 安(やす)いようだ | 静(しず)かなようだ | 学生(がくせい)のようだ |
| | Past | 書(か)いたようだ | 安(やす)かったようだ | 静(しず)かだったようだ | 学生(がくせい)だったようだ |
| ～はずだ 'be supposed to' | Non-past | 書(か)くはずだ | 安(やす)いはずだ | 静(しず)かなはずだ | 学生(がくせい)のはずだ |
| | Past | 書(か)いたはずだ | 安(やす)かったはずだ | 静(しず)かだったはずだ | 学生(がくせい)だったはずだ |
| ～らしい 'appently' | Non-past | 書(か)くらしい | 安(やす)いらしい | 静(しず)からしい | 学生(がくせい)らしい |
| | Past | 書(か)いたらしい | 安(やす)かったらしい | 静(しず)かだったらしい | 学生(がくせい)だったらしい |

# Index

| あ | | Lesson |
|---|---|---|
| あ | | 1 |
| アイスクリーム | | 15 |
| あいだ | 間 | 9 |
| あいます(あう) | 会います | 4 |
| あう | 会う | 7 |
| あおい | 青い | 6 |
| あかい | 赤い | 6 |
| あかちゃん | 赤ちゃん | 12 |
| あがる | 上がる | 11 |
| あかるい | 明るい | 9 |
| あき | 秋 | 7 |
| あける | 開ける | 7 |
| あげる | | 13 |
| あご | 顎 | 17 |
| あさ | 朝 | 4 |
| あさごはん | 朝ごはん | 4 |
| あさって | | 7 |
| あざやか(な) | 鮮やか(な) | 18 |
| あし | 足 | 6 |
| あじ | 味 | 15 |
| アジア | | 18 |
| あしくび | 足首 | 17 |
| あした | 明日 | 3 |
| あじみ | 味見 | 18 |
| あじみする | 味見する | 18 |
| あす | 明日 | 20 |
| あそこ | | 3 |
| あそぶ | 遊ぶ | 7 |
| あたし | | 12 |
| あたたかい | 暖かい | 6 |
| あたま | 頭 | 2 |
| あたまがいい | 頭がいい | 9 |
| あたらしい | 新しい | 6 |
| あつい | 暑い | 5 |
| あつぎにする | 厚着にする | 17 |
| あと | 後 | 4 |
| あなた | | 2 |
| あに | 兄 | 4 |
| アニメ | | 11 |
| あね | 姉 | 7 |
| あの | | 2 |
| あの～ | | 3 |
| あびます（あびる） | 浴びます | 4 |
| あびる | 浴びる | 8 |
| アフリカ | | 4 |
| あまい | 甘い | 9 |
| あまり | | 6 |
| あめ | 雨 | 10 |
| アメリカ | | 1 |
| あります（ある） | | 3 |
| あるく | 歩く | 8 |
| アルバイト | | 3 |
| あれ | | 2 |
| あんぜん(な) | 安全(な) | 15 |
| あんないじょう | 案内嬢 | 6 |

| い | | Lesson |
|---|---|---|
| い | 胃 | 17 |
| いい | | 5 |
| いいえ | | 1 |
| イーメール | | 9 |
| いえ | 家 | 1 |
| ～いがい | ～以外 | 16 |
| いきなり | | 19 |
| いきます（いく） | 行きます | 4 |
| イギリス | | 1 |
| いく | 行く | 7 |
| いくら | | 6 |
| いしゃ | 医者 | 1 |
| いじゅうしゃ | 移住者 | 10 |
| いしょう | 衣装 | 18 |
| いす | 椅子 | 14 |
| いぜんは | 以前は | 17 |
| いそがしい | 忙しい | 5 |
| いそぐ | 急ぐ | 8 |
| いたい | 痛い | 6 |
| いたす | | 20 |
| いただく | | 20 |
| いたむ | 痛む | 17 |
| いちばん | 一番 | 10 |
| いつ | | 4 |
| いっしょに | 一緒に | 5 |
| いつのまにか | いつの間にか | 18 |
| いっぱい | | 11 |
| いつも | | 4 |
| いぬ | 犬 | 3 |
| いびきをかく | | 19 |
| いま | 今 | 2 |
| いま | 居間 | 11 |
| います（いる） | | 3 |
| いみ | 意味 | 18 |
| いもうと | 妹 | 10 |
| いもうとさん | 妹さん | 3 |
| いや(な) | 嫌(な) | 18 |
| いらっしゃいますか | | 12 |
| いらっしゃる | | 20 |
| いりぐち | 入口 | 11 |
| いる | | 7 |
| いる | 要る | 17 |
| いれる | 入れる | 8 |
| いろいろ(な) | | 6 |
| いろんな | | 14 |

| う | | Lesson |
|---|---|---|
| うえ | 上 | 3 |
| うかがう | | 20 |
| (テストを) うける | (テストを)受ける | 20 |
| うごく | 動く | 19 |
| うしろ | 後ろ | 3 |

| | | |
|---|---|---|
| うそ | 嘘 | 18 |
| うた | 歌 | 4 |
| うち | 家 | 4 |
| うで | 腕 | 2 |
| うなぎ | | 15 |
| うみ | 海 | 2 |
| うらやましい | | 13 |
| うりきれる | 売り切れる | 20 |
| うりて | 売り手 | 14 |
| うりば | 売り場 | 6, 20 |
| うる | 売る | 8 |
| うるさい | | 8 |
| うれしい | 嬉しい | 6 |
| うんがいい | 運がいい | 19 |
| うんてん | 運転 | 11 |
| うんてんちゅう | 運転中 | 13 |
| うんてんめんきょ | 運転免許 | 17 |
| うんどう | 運動 | 17 |
| うんどうかい | 運動会 | 7 |
| **え** | | **Lesson** |
| え | 絵 | 13 |
| エアコン | | 12 |
| エアロビクス | | 9 |
| えいが | 映画 | 2 |
| えいがかん | 映画館 | 5 |
| えいご | 英語 | 1 |
| ええ | | 1 |
| ええと | | 4 |
| エジプト | | 3 |
| えっと | | 3 |
| エスカレーター | | 6 |
| エレベーター | | 6, 20 |
| えんじる | 演じる | 18 |
| えんりょする | 遠慮する | 13 |
| **お** | | **Lesson** |
| おいしい | | 5 |
| おいわい | お祝い | 13 |
| おおい | 多い | 9 |
| おおきい | 大きい | 6 |
| オーケー | | 15 |
| おおごえ | 大声 | 13 |
| おおさか | 大阪 | 5 |
| オーストラリア | | 1 |
| おかあさん | お母さん | 11 |
| おかえり(なさい) | | 11 |
| おかげで | | 20 |
| おかしい | | 17 |
| おかね | お金 | 3 |
| おかまいなく | | 11 |
| おかわり | | 11 |
| おきのどくに | お気の毒に | 12 |
| おきます（おきる） | 起きます | 4 |
| おきゃくさん | お客さん | 6 |
| おきる | 起きる | 7 |
| おくさま | 奥様 | 20 |
| おくさん | 奥さん | 1 |
| おくやみ | お悔やみ | 13 |
| おくる | 送る | 8 |
| おこさん | お子さん | 11 |
| おこす | 起こす | 20 |
| おこる | 怒る | 12 |
| おさけ | お酒 | 8 |
| おさら | お皿 | 14 |
| おじいさん | | 11 |
| おしいれ | 押し入れ | 11 |
| おしえる | 教える | 8 |
| おじぎ | お辞儀 | 1 |
| おしゃべり | | 16 |
| おじゃまします(おじゃまする) | | 11 |
| おしょうがつ | お正月 | 9 |
| おしり | お尻 | 17 |
| おす | 押す | 16 |
| おせいぼ | お歳暮 | 13 |
| おそい | 遅い | 12 |
| おちこむ | 落ち込む | 13 |
| おちゃ | お茶 | 5 |
| おちゅうげん | お中元 | 13 |
| おちる | 落ちる | 7 |
| オッケー | | 19 |
| おっしゃる | | 20 |
| おっと | 夫 | 11 |
| おてあらい | お手洗い | 6, 11 |
| おでこ | | 17 |
| おてら | お寺 | 18 |
| おと | 音 | 7 |
| おとうさん | お父さん | 11 |
| おとうと | 弟 | 11 |
| おとこ | 男 | 18 |
| おととい | | 5 |
| おなか | お腹 | 2 |
| おなかがすく | お腹が空く | 15 |
| おなじ | 同じ | 19 |
| おにいさん | お兄さん | 3 |
| おねえさん | お姉さん | 3 |
| おばあさん | | 11 |
| おはし | お箸 | 20 |
| オフィス | | 3 |
| オペラハウス | | 3 |
| おべんとう | お弁当 | 20 |
| おべんとうや | お弁当屋 | 14 |
| おぼん | お盆 | 9 |
| おまえ | お前 | 12 |
| おみあい | お見合い | 13 |
| おみまい | お見舞い | 17 |
| おもい | 重い | 6 |
| おもう | 思う | 10 |
| おもしろい | 面白い | 6 |
| おもちゃ | | 15 |

| | | |
|---|---|---|
| おもちゃや | おもちゃ屋 | 14 |
| おもったより | 思ったより | 19 |
| おもに | 主に | 18 |
| およぎます（およぐ） | 泳ぎます | 4 |
| およぐ | 泳ぐ | 7 |
| おります（おる） | 居ります | 12 |
| おれ | 俺 | 12 |
| おれる | 折れる | 17 |
| オレンジ | | 16 |
| おんがく | 音楽 | 4 |
| か | | Lesson |
| ～かい | ～階 | 6, 20 |
| ～かい | ～回 | 14 |
| かいぎ | 会議 | 8 |
| がいこく | 外国 | 12 |
| かいしゃ | 会社 | 5 |
| かいしゃいん | 会社員 | 1 |
| がいしゅつする | 外出する | 17 |
| かいだん | 階段 | 6, 11 |
| かいます（かう） | 買います | 4 |
| かいもの | 買い物 | 4 |
| かいわ | 会話 | 15 |
| かう | 買う | 7 |
| かう | 飼う | 8 |
| かえす | 返す | 10 |
| かえり | 帰り | 12 |
| かえります（かえる） | 帰ります | 4 |
| かえる | 変える | 7 |
| かえる | 帰る | 10 |
| かお | 顔 | 2 |
| かがく | 化学 | 16 |
| かがく | 科学 | 11 |
| かがくしゃ | 科学者 | 10 |
| かかと | | 17 |
| かきごおり | かき氷 | 20 |
| かきぞめ | 書初め | 20 |
| かきます（かく） | 書きます | 4 |
| かく | 書く | 7 |
| かぐ | 家具 | 6 |
| かぐ | 嗅ぐ | 17 |
| がくせい | 学生 | 1 |
| がくねん | 学年 | 16 |
| かけじく | 掛け軸 | 11 |
| かける | | 17 |
| かさ | 傘 | 2 |
| かじ | 火事 | 18 |
| かしゅ | 歌手 | 6 |
| かす | 貸す | 8 |
| かぜ | 風 | 6 |
| かせぐ | 稼ぐ | 15 |
| かぜをひく | 風邪を引く | 12 |
| かぞく | 家族 | 9 |
| ガソリン | | 5 |
| かた | 肩 | 17 |
| ～かた | ～方 | 20 |
| かだい | 課題 | 16 |
| かちょう | 課長 | 20 |
| がっこう | 学校 | 3 |
| かって(な) | 勝手(な) | 19 |
| かつどう | 活動 | 16 |
| カップ | | 3 |
| かていか | 家庭科 | 16 |
| かど | 角 | 14 |
| かない | 家内 | 11 |
| かなしい | 悲しい | 6 |
| かならず | 必ず | 20 |
| かのじょ | 彼女 | 14 |
| かばん | | 2 |
| かぶき | 歌舞伎 | 19 |
| かぶきざ | 歌舞伎座 | 19 |
| かまう | 構う | 13 |
| かみ | 髪 | 17 |
| かみのけ | 髪の毛 | 6 |
| かむ | 噛む | 19 |
| カメラ | | 2 |
| かもく | 科目 | 16 |
| かようび | 火曜日 | 4 |
| [noun] から | | 10 |
| カラオケ | | 10 |
| かりる | 借りる | 7 |
| かるい | 軽い | 9 |
| カレー | | 4 |
| カレーライス | | 10 |
| かれし | 彼氏 | 14 |
| かれる | 枯れる | 20 |
| かわ | 川 | 10 |
| かわいい | | 6 |
| かわいそう(な) | | 6 |
| かわず | 蛙 | 20 |
| かわりに | 代わりに | 20 |
| かわる | 替わる | 12 |
| かんがえごと | 考え事 | 18 |
| かんがえる | 考える | 7 |
| かんけい | 関係 | 16 |
| かんげき | 感激 | 18 |
| かんこう | 観光 | 19 |
| かんこく | 韓国 | 1 |
| かんこくご | 韓国語 | 4 |
| かんこくりょうり | 韓国料理 | 4 |
| かんごし | 看護師 | 17 |
| かんさい | 関西 | 18 |
| かんじゃ | 患者 | 17 |
| かんじょう | 勘定 | 9 |
| かんたん(な) | 簡単(な) | 6 |
| かんとう | 関東 | 18 |
| かんぱい | 乾杯 | 13 |
| き | | Lesson |
| き | 木 | 17 |

| | | |
|---|---|---|
| きいろい | 黄色い | 6, 13 |
| きおん | 気温 | 11 |
| きがえる | 着替える | 20 |
| ききます（きく） | 聞きます | 4 |
| きく | 聞く | 7 |
| きご | 季語 | 20 |
| きこえる | 聞こえる | 18 |
| ギター | | 14 |
| きたない | 汚い | 9 |
| きっさてん | 喫茶店 | 3 |
| きって | 切手 | 8 |
| きっぷ | 切符 | 4 |
| きにする | 気にする | 13 |
| きのう | 昨日 | 5 |
| きのう | 機能 | 19 |
| きびしい | 厳しい | 6 |
| きぶん | 気分 | 17 |
| きます（くる） | 来ます | 4 |
| きみ | 君 | 12 |
| きめる | 決める | 20 |
| きもち | 気持ち | 13 |
| きもちがいい | 気持ちがいい | 6 |
| きもの | 着物 | 7 |
| キャンプ | | 9 |
| キャンベラ | | 3 |
| きゅうきゅうしゃ | 救急車 | 8 |
| きょう | 今日 | 3 |
| きょうかしょ | 教科書 | 8 |
| きょうしつ | 教室 | 4 |
| きょうだい | 兄弟 | 3 |
| きょうと | 京都 | 3 |
| きょうみ | 興味 | 18 |
| きる | 着る | 7 |
| きる | 切る | 7 |
| きれい(な) | | 6 |
| キロ | | 10 |
| きをつかう | 気を 遣う | 11 |
| きをつける | 気を付ける | 20 |
| きんいろ | 金色 | 18 |
| きんえんする | 禁煙する | 17 |
| きんかくじ | 金閣寺 | 18 |
| ぎんこういん | 銀行員 | 1 |
| きんちょうする | 緊張する | 13 |
| きんようび | 金曜日 | 4 |
| く | | Lesson |
| くすり | 薬 | 16 |
| くすりや | 薬屋 | 14 |
| くすりをだす | 薬を出す | 17 |
| くださる | | 20 |
| くち | 口 | 17 |
| くちにあう | 口に合う | 11 |
| くちびる | 唇 | 17 |
| くつ | 靴 | 2 |
| くつや | 靴屋 | 3 |

| | | |
|---|---|---|
| くに | 国 | 10 |
| くび | 首 | 17 |
| くもり | 曇り | 11 |
| くもる | 曇る | 10 |
| くらい | 暗い | 9 |
| くらい／ぐらい | | 10 |
| クラス | | 10 |
| くらす | 暮らす | 17 |
| クリスマス | | 13 |
| くる | 来る | 7 |
| くるま | 車 | 1 |
| クレープ | | 15 |
| くれる | | 13 |
| くろい | 黒い | 6 |
| ～くん | [name]君 | 12 |
| け | | Lesson |
| け | 毛 | 17 |
| けいかくをたてる | 計画を立てる | 19 |
| けいざいがく | 経済学 | 9 |
| けいさつしょ | 警察署 | 17 |
| けいたいでんわ | 携帯電話 | 3 |
| ケーキ | | 4 |
| ケーキや | ケーキ屋 | 14 |
| ゲーム | | 15 |
| けが | 怪我 | 17 |
| けしき | 景色 | 8 |
| けしょう | 化粧 | 18 |
| けしょうひん | 化粧品 | 6 |
| けっきょく | 結局 | 20 |
| けっこう(な) | 結構(な) | 14 |
| けっこんしき | 結婚式 | 7 |
| けっこんする | 結婚する | 12 |
| げつようび | 月曜日 | 4 |
| けむり | 煙 | 18 |
| げらげら | | 16 |
| げり | 下痢 | 17 |
| ける | 蹴る | 17 |
| けんか | 喧嘩 | 18 |
| げんかん | 玄関 | 11 |
| げんきな | 元気な | 6 |
| けんこう | 健康 | 9 |
| げんごがく | 言語学 | 2 |
| けんぶつ | 見物 | 19 |
| こ | | Lesson |
| [country] ご | 語 | 1 |
| こうえん | 公園 | 3 |
| こうか(な) | 高価(な) | 13 |
| こうかんりゅうがく | 交換留学 | 20 |
| こうき | 後期 | 20 |
| こうこう | 高校 | 5 |
| こうこく | 広告 | 14 |
| こうざ | 口座 | 17 |
| こうしきげんご | 公式言語 | 10 |
| こうしゅうでんわ | 公衆電話 | 12 |

| | | |
|---|---|---|
| こうそうビル | 高層ビル | 19 |
| こうはい | 後輩 | 16 |
| こうばん | 交番 | 14 |
| こうよう | 紅葉 | 7 |
| こえ | 声 | 10 |
| コースト | | 9 |
| コーチ | | 16 |
| コーヒー | | 4 |
| こおり | 氷 | 17 |
| ゴールデンウィーク | | 9 |
| こくご | 国語 | 16 |
| こくさいでんわ | 国際電話 | 12 |
| こくばん | 黒板 | 19 |
| こくりつ | 国立 | 8 |
| こくりつはくぶつかん | 国立博物館 | 19 |
| ここ | | 3 |
| ごご | 午後 | 2 |
| ございます | | 6, 12 |
| こしょうする | 故障する | 12 |
| ごぜん | 午前 | 2 |
| こたえ | 答え | 19 |
| こたえる | 答える | 20 |
| こたつ | | 11 |
| こっか | 国花 | 10 |
| こっかいぎじどう | 国会議事堂 | 3 |
| こと | 琴 | 18 |
| こども | 子供 | 15 |
| この | | 2 |
| このあたり | | 7 |
| このごろ | この頃 | 18 |
| このへん | この辺 | 18 |
| ごはん | ご飯 | 10 |
| こむ | 混む | 19 |
| ごらんになる | ご覧になる | 20 |
| これ | | 2 |
| ～ごろ | ～頃 | 4 |
| こわい | 怖い | 6 |
| こわれる | 壊れる | 13 |
| こんがっき | 今学期 | 7 |
| コンサート | | 2 |
| こんしゅう | 今週 | 5 |
| こんど | 今度 | 3 |
| こんばん | 今晩 | 3 |
| コンビニエンスストア | | 14 |
| コンピューター | | 3 |
| **さ** | | **Lesson** |
| サークル | | 16 |
| サーフィン | | 9 |
| さい | 歳 | 11 |
| さいきん | 最近 | 14 |
| サイクリング | | 9 |
| さいこう | 最高 | 19 |
| さいふ | 財布 | 14 |
| さいわい(な) | 幸い(な) | 19 |

| | | |
|---|---|---|
| さかな | 魚 | 10 |
| さかなや | 魚屋 | 14 |
| さくぶん | 作文 | 20 |
| さくら | 桜 | 6 |
| さけぶ | 叫ぶ | 10 |
| さしあげる | 差し上げる | 20 |
| さしみ | | 5 |
| ～さつ | ～冊 | 14 |
| サッカー | | 4 |
| さっき | | 19 |
| さつきばれ | 五月晴れ | 20 |
| さっきょくか | 作曲家 | 12 |
| ざっし | 雑誌 | 2 |
| さつじん | 殺人 | 7 |
| さっぽろ | 札幌 | 3 |
| さびしい | 寂しい | 20 |
| ざぶとん | 座布団 | 11 |
| さむい | 寒い | 5 |
| さむけ | 寒気 | 17 |
| さむけがする | 寒気がする | 17 |
| さむらい | 侍 | 18 |
| サラダ | | 4 |
| さわる | 触る | 13 |
| ～さん | | 1 |
| さんま | 秋刀魚 | 20 |
| **し** | | **Lesson** |
| しあわせ(な) | 幸せ(な) | 18 |
| しお | | 8 |
| しかたない | 仕方ない | 18 |
| しかる | 叱る | 19 |
| じかん | 時間 | 3 |
| しき | 四季 | 7 |
| しけん | 試験 | 5 |
| じこ | 事故 | 12 |
| しごと | 仕事 | 2 |
| じしょ | 辞書 | 1 |
| しずか(な) | 静か(な) | 6 |
| しずむ | 沈む | 18 |
| した | 下 | 3 |
| した | 舌 | 17 |
| じだいげき | 時代劇 | 10 |
| したしい | 親しい | 15 |
| じっか | 実家 | 9 |
| じつは | 実は | 20 |
| しっぱい | 失敗 | 18 |
| しつもん | 質問 | 8 |
| しつれいする | 失礼する | 8 |
| じてんしゃ | 自転車 | 2 |
| シドニー | | 2 |
| しなもの | 品物 | 14 |
| しにかける | 死にかける | 17 |
| しぬ | 死ぬ | 7 |
| しぶや | 渋谷 | 15 |
| ～します（～する） | | 4 |

| | | |
|---|---|---|
| じみ(な) | 地味(な) | 9 |
| じむしょ | 事務所 | 20 |
| しめる | 閉める | 7 |
| じゃあ | | 2 |
| しゃかい | 社会 | 10 |
| ジャケット | | 6 |
| しゃしん | 写真 | 6 |
| しゃちょう | 社長 | 20 |
| シャツ | | 6 |
| しゃべる | | 17 |
| しゃみせん | 三味線 | 18 |
| シャワー | | 4 |
| しゅうがくりょこう | 修学旅行 | 18 |
| しゅうし | 修士 | 16 |
| しゅうしょく | 就職 | 13 |
| ジュース | | 4 |
| じゅうぶん(な) | 十分(な) | 18 |
| しゅうまつ | 週末 | 3 |
| じゅうよう(な) | 重要(な) | 20 |
| じゅぎょう | 授業 | 2 |
| じゅく | 塾 | 16 |
| しゅくだい | 宿題 | 4 |
| じゅけんべんきょう | 受験勉強 | 16 |
| しゅじゅつ | 手術 | 17 |
| しゅっしん | 出身 | 2 |
| しゅっぱつ | 出発 | 20 |
| しゅと | 首都 | 10 |
| しゅみ | 趣味 | 2 |
| しょうがっこう | 小学校 | 16 |
| しょうじ | 障子 | 11 |
| しょうしょう | 少々 | 12 |
| じょうず(な) | 上手(な) | 6 |
| しょうせつ | 小説 | 10 |
| じょうだん | 冗談 | 13 |
| しょうぼうしょ | 消防署 | 12 |
| ジョギング | | 9 |
| しょくじ | 食事 | 6 |
| しょくじする | 食事する | 14 |
| しょくりょうひん | 食料品 | 6 |
| じょせい | 女性 | 12 |
| しょみん | 庶民 | 18 |
| しょるい | 書類 | 20 |
| しる | 知る | 15 |
| しろい | 白い | 6 |
| [country] じん | 人 | 1 |
| シンガポール | | 3 |
| しんかんせん | 新幹線 | 20 |
| しんごう | 信号 | 14 |
| じんこう | 人口 | 10 |
| しんしふく | 紳士服 | 6 |
| しんじる | 信じる | 7 |
| しんせつ(な) | 親切(な) | 6 |
| しんねん | 新年 | 7 |
| しんぱいする | 心配する | 13 |
| しんぶん | 新聞 | 2 |

| す | | Lesson |
|---|---|---|
| すいえい | 水泳 | 2 |
| すいせんじょう | 推薦状 | 8 |
| スイッチ | | 16 |
| ずいぶん | 随分 | 15 |
| すいようび | 水曜日 | 4 |
| すうがく | 数学 | 16 |
| スーパー | スーパー | 14 |
| スーパーマン | | 14 |
| スープ | | 15 |
| スカート | | 6 |
| すき(な) | 好き(な) | 15 |
| ずきずきする | | 17 |
| すきです | 好きです | 5 |
| ～すぎる | ～過ぎる | 15 |
| すく | 空く | 15 |
| すぐに | | 9 |
| すごい | | 14 |
| すしや | 寿司屋 | 14 |
| すずしい | 涼しい | 9 |
| すずむし | 鈴虫 | 20 |
| すっかり | | 11 |
| すてき(な) | 素敵(な) | 11 |
| すでに | 既に | 18 |
| スパゲッティ | | 16 |
| すばらしい | 素晴らしい | 18 |
| すべる | 滑る | 7 |
| スポーツ | | 4 |
| すまい | 住まい | 2 |
| すもう | 相撲 | 11 |
| すわる | 座る | 8 |

| せ | | Lesson |
|---|---|---|
| せいかつひ | 生活費 | 12 |
| せいき | 世紀 | 18 |
| せいじ | 政治 | 16 |
| セーター | | 13 |
| せかいし | 世界史 | 16 |
| せがたかい | 背が高い | 6 |
| せがひくい | 背が低い | 10 |
| せき | 咳 | 17 |
| せたけ | 背丈 | 17 |
| ぜったいに | 絶対に | 15 |
| せつめいしょ | 説明書 | 12 |
| ぜひ | 是非 | 7 |
| せまい | 狭い | 9 |
| せわになる | 世話になる | 13 |
| ぜんき | 前期 | 20 |
| せんこう | 専攻 | 1 |
| せんしゅう | 先週 | 5 |
| せんす | 扇子 | 18 |
| せんせい | 先生 | 1 |
| ぜんぜん | 全然 | 9 |
| せんぞ | 先祖 | 19 |

| | | |
|---|---|---|
| せんそう | 戦争 | 18 |
| せんたくき | 洗濯機 | 8 |
| せんたくする | 洗濯する | 9 |
| せんぱい | 先輩 | 14 |
| ぜんぶ | 全部 | 11 |
| ぜんぶで | 全部で | 14 |

| そ | | Lesson |
|---|---|---|
| そう | | 1 |
| ぞう | 象 | 18 |
| そうじします | 掃除します | 5 |
| そうじする | 掃除する | 9 |
| そうすると | | 14 |
| そこ | | 3 |
| そだてる | 育てる | 19 |
| そつぎょう | 卒業 | 7 |
| そつぎょうしき | 卒業式 | 7 |
| そと | 外 | 11 |
| その | | 2 |
| そのた | その他 | 10 |
| そば | 側 | 3 |
| そびえる | | 17 |
| そふ | 祖父 | 11 |
| ソファ | | 3 |
| そぼ | 祖母 | 11 |
| そら | 空 | 9 |
| それ | | 2 |
| それから | | 4 |
| そろそろ | | 18 |
| そんなに | | 10 |

| た | | Lesson |
|---|---|---|
| ターム | | 16 |
| タイ | | 3 |
| ～だい | ～台 | 14 |
| たいいく | 体育 | 16 |
| たいいくかん | 体育館 | 5 |
| たいおんけい | 体温計 | 17 |
| だいがく | 大学 | 1 |
| だいがくせい | 大学生 | 1 |
| だいきらい | 大嫌い | 18 |
| たいくつ(な) | 退屈(な) | 6 |
| だいじ(な) | 大事(な) | 13 |
| だいじょうぶ(な) | 大丈夫(な) | 6 |
| たいじんかんけい | 対人関係 | 20 |
| だいすきな | 大好き(な) | 10 |
| たいてい | | 4 |
| だいどころ | 台所 | 11 |
| だいぶ | 大分 | 18 |
| たいふう | 台風 | 7 |
| たいへん(な) | 大変(な) | 11 |
| タイりょうり | タイ料理 | 7 |
| たいわん | 台湾 | 20 |
| たかい | 高い | 5 |
| だから | | 16 |
| たくさん | | 9 |
| タクシー | | 4 |
| たす | 足す | 16 |
| だす | 出す | 8 |
| たすかる | 助かる | 9 |
| たずねる | 訪ねる | 18 |
| たたみ | 畳 | 11 |
| たつ | 立つ | 8 |
| たった | | 14 |
| たてもの | 建物 | 3 |
| たとえば | 例えば | 18 |
| たのしい | 楽しい | 6 |
| たのしそう(な) | 楽しそう(な) | 4 |
| たのしみにする | 楽しみにする | 20 |
| たのしむ | 楽しむ | 16 |
| たばこをすう | たばこを吸う | 13 |
| たぶん | 多分 | 11 |
| たべます（たべる） | 食べます | 4 |
| たべる | 食べる | 7 |
| (ご)たぼうちゅう | (ご)多忙中 | 20 |
| たまご | 卵 | 4 |
| たまに | | 4 |
| たまる | 貯まる | 18 |
| ～たら | | 16 |
| タワー | | 8 |
| たんじょうび | 誕生日 | 7 |
| ダンス | | 9 |
| だんせい | 男性 | 18 |
| だんだん | 段々 | 17 |

| ち | | Lesson |
|---|---|---|
| ちいさい | 小さい | 6 |
| チーズ | | 8 |
| チェック | | 20 |
| ちか | 地下 | 6 |
| ちかい | 近い | 6 |
| ちがう | 違う | 18 |
| ちかてつ | 地下鉄 | 19 |
| ちず | 地図 | 17 |
| ちち | 父 | 5 |
| ちちのひ | 父の日 | 13 |
| ちゃいろい | 茶色い | 15 |
| チャンス | | 18 |
| ちゃんと | | 20 |
| ちゅうおうせん | 中央線 | 19 |
| ちゅうがっこう | 中学校 | 16 |
| ちゅうかりょうり | 中華料理 | 4 |
| ちゅうごく | 中国 | 1 |
| ちゅうこひん | 中古品 | 14 |
| ちゅうしゃじょう | 駐車場 | 6 |
| ちゅうもん | 注文 | 9 |
| ちょうきょりでんわ | 長距離電話 | 12 |
| ちょうじょう | 頂上 | 8 |
| ちょうしょく | 朝食 | 20 |
| ちょうど | | 6 |
| ちょくせつ | 直接 | 18 |

| | | |
|---|---|---|
| チョコレート | | 13 |
| ちょっと | | 5 |
| ちらし | | 6 |
| ちり | 地理 | 16 |
| **つ** | | **Lesson** |
| つかう | 使う | 8 |
| つかれる | 疲れる | 11 |
| つき | 月 | 20 |
| つきあたり | 突き当たり | 14 |
| つく | 着く | 17 |
| つくえ | 机 | 3 |
| つくりかた | 作り方 | 10 |
| つくる | 作る | 15 |
| つける | 付ける | 20 |
| つたえる | 伝える | 12 |
| ～って | | 16 |
| つまさき | つま先 | 17 |
| つまらない | | 9 |
| つゆ | 梅雨 | 7 |
| つよい | 強い | 6 |
| つり | 釣り | 2 |
| つれていく | 連れていく | 8 |
| **て** | | **Lesson** |
| て | 手 | 10 |
| ていしゅつする | 提出する | 20 |
| ていしょく | 定食 | 16 |
| ていねい(な) | 丁寧(な) | 15 |
| デート | | 2 |
| テーブル | | 3 |
| でかける | 出かける | 7 |
| てがみ | 手紙 | 2 |
| できごと | 出来事 | 13 |
| できる | 出来る | 14 |
| できれば | 出来れば | 17 |
| デザイン | | 14 |
| テスト | | 3 |
| ですますちょう | ですます調 | 15 |
| てつだう | 手伝う | 9 |
| てぬぐい | 手ぬぐい | 18 |
| てのひら | 手のひら | 17 |
| デパート | | 3 |
| ～でも | | 5 |
| でる | 出る | 15 |
| テレコムタワー | | 19 |
| テレビ | | 3 |
| テレビばんぐみ | テレビ番組 | 14 |
| てんき | 天気 | 5 |
| でんきせいひん | 電気製品 | 6, 14 |
| でんきや | 電気屋 | 14 |
| てんきよほう | 天気予報 | 19 |
| てんきんする | 転勤する | 20 |
| でんごん | 伝言 | 12 |
| てんじする | 展示する | 19 |
| でんしゃ | 電車 | 2 |

| | | |
|---|---|---|
| てんすう | 点数 | 13 |
| てんぷら | | 16 |
| てんぼうだい | 展望台 | 19 |
| でんわ | 電話 | 3 |
| でんわちょう | 電話帳 | 12 |
| でんわばんごう | 電話番号 | 12 |
| でんわをかける | 電話をかける | 8 |
| **と** | | **Lesson** |
| ど | 度 | 11 |
| ～と | | 16 |
| ドイツ | | 4 |
| トイレ | | 6, 11 |
| どう | | 6 |
| どうが | 動画 | 18 |
| とうきょう | 東京 | 1 |
| とうきょうタワー | 東京タワー | 19 |
| どうぐ | 道具 | 17 |
| どうして | | 13 |
| どうそうかい | 同窓会 | 13 |
| どうやって | | 4 |
| とおい | 遠い | 6 |
| とおざかる | 遠ざかる | 18 |
| トースト | | 9 |
| ときどき | | 4 |
| どくしょ | 読書 | 2 |
| とくちょう | 特徴 | 6 |
| とけい | 時計 | 2 |
| とける | 溶ける | 17 |
| とこ | | 19 |
| どこ | | 2 |
| とこのま | 床の間 | 11 |
| とこや | 床屋 | 10 |
| ところ | 所 | 6 |
| ところで | | 5 |
| とし | 都市 | 10 |
| としょかん | 図書館 | 2 |
| とちゅう | 途中 | 17 |
| どちら | | 2 |
| とても | | 6 |
| とない | 都内 | 19 |
| となり | 隣 | 3 |
| となりあう | 隣り合う | 17 |
| とばす | 飛ばす | 19 |
| とびこむ | 飛び込む | 20 |
| とぶ | 飛ぶ | 8 |
| とまる | 止まる | 17 |
| とめる | 止める | 13 |
| ともだち | 友達 | 1 |
| どようび | 土曜日 | 4 |
| とりあえず | | 15 |
| とります（とる） | 撮ります | 6 |
| とる | 取る | 7 |
| とろ | | 15 |
| どろぼう | 泥棒 | 19 |

| | | |
|---|---|---|
| とんでもない | | 20 |
| **な** | | **Lesson** |
| なおす | | 14 |
| なか | 中 | 3 |
| ながい | 長い | 6 |
| ながい | 長居 | 11 |
| ながたび | 長旅 | 11 |
| なかなか | | 18 |
| なく | 泣く | 12 |
| なくす | | 17 |
| なさる | | 20 |
| なし | | 16 |
| なぜ | | 13 |
| なつ | 夏 | 7 |
| なつやすみ | 夏休み | 5 |
| なに（なん） | 何 | 4 |
| なにか | 何か | 12 |
| なまえ | 名前 | 2 |
| ～なら | | 16 |
| なるほど | | 16 |
| なん (なに) | 何 | 2 |
| なんきょく | 南極 | 18 |
| なんでも | 何でも | 13 |
| なんばん | 何番 | 12 |
| **に** | | **Lesson** |
| におい | 匂い | 17 |
| にがい | 苦い | 9 |
| にぎやかな | 賑やか(な) | 6 |
| にくじゃが | 肉じゃが | 10 |
| にくや | 肉屋 | 14 |
| にちようび | 日曜日 | 4 |
| にっき | 日記 | 12 |
| にど | ２度 | 9 |
| にほん | 日本 | 1 |
| にほんし | 日本史 | 20 |
| にほんせい | 日本製 | 13 |
| にほんちゃ | 日本茶 | 4 |
| にゅういん | 入院 | 17 |
| にゅういんする | 入院する | 20 |
| にゅうがく | 入学 | 16 |
| にゅうがくしき | 入学式 | 7 |
| ニュース | | 7 |
| にる | 似る | 17 |
| にわ | 庭 | 11 |
| ～にん | ～人 | 14 |
| にんぎょう | 人形 | 18 |
| **ぬ** | | **Lesson** |
| ぬぐ | 脱ぐ | 11 |
| ぬすむ | 盗む | 19 |
| **ね** | | **Lesson** |
| ねぎる | 値切る | 14 |
| ねこ | 猫 | 3 |
| ねだん | 値段 | 14 |
| ねつ | 熱 | 17 |
| ねます（ねる） | 寝ます | 4 |
| ねむたい | 眠たい | 15 |
| ねむる | 眠る | 18 |
| ねる | 寝る | 8 |
| ねんちゅうぎょうじ | 年中行事 | 9 |
| **の** | | **Lesson** |
| のこす | 残す | 18 |
| のちほど | | 12 |
| のど | 喉 | 17 |
| のみかい | 飲み会 | 16 |
| のみます（のむ） | 飲みます | 4 |
| のみもの | 飲み物 | 7 |
| のむ | 飲む | 7 |
| のりかえる | 乗り換える | 19 |
| のります（のる） | 乗ります | 4 |
| のる | 乗る | 10 |
| **は** | | **Lesson** |
| は | 歯 | 10 |
| ～ば | | 16 |
| パーティー | | 2 |
| バーベキュー | | 4 |
| はい | | 1 |
| ～はい | ～杯 | 14 |
| はいく | 俳句 | 20 |
| はいけんする | 拝見する | 20 |
| はいる | 入る | 11 |
| ばか | 馬鹿 | 19 |
| はがき | 葉書 | 4 |
| ばかげている | | 18 |
| はかせ | 博士 | 16 |
| ばかにする | 馬鹿にする | 19 |
| ばかばかしい | | 18 |
| ばかり | | 18 |
| はかる | 計る | 17 |
| はきけがする | 吐き気がする | 17 |
| はく | | 20 |
| はこ | 箱 | 3 |
| はこぶ | 運ぶ | 17 |
| はじまる | 始まる | 7 |
| はじめて | 初めて | 12 |
| はじめまして | | 1 |
| はじめる | 始める | 8 |
| パジャマ | | 20 |
| ばしょ | 場所 | 7 |
| はしる | 走る | 7 |
| バス | | 4 |
| バスケットボール | | 16 |
| パスタ | | 4 |
| バスてい | バス停 | 3 |
| パソコン | | 19 |
| はたらく | 働く | 15 |
| はってんする | 発展する | 18 |
| はっぴょう | 発表 | 18 |
| はつゆき | 初雪 | 20 |

| | | |
|---|---|---|
| はで(な) | 派手(な) | 9 |
| はとバス | | 19 |
| バドミントン | | 5 |
| はな | 鼻 | 6 |
| はな | 花 | 13 |
| はなし | 話 | 15 |
| はなしちゅう | 話し中 | 12 |
| はなび | 花火 | 7 |
| はなみ | 花見 | 7 |
| はなや | 花屋 | 14 |
| はは | 母 | 11 |
| ははのひ | 母の日 | 13 |
| はやい | 早い・速い | 4 |
| はる | 春 | 7 |
| はれ | 晴れ | 11 |
| はれる | 晴れる | 10 |
| バレンタイン・デー | | 13 |
| ハワイ | | 10 |
| ばん | 番 | 12 |
| パン | | 4 |
| ばんごはん | 晩ごはん | 4 |
| ハンバーガー | | 9 |
| パンや | パン屋 | 14 |
| ばんりのちょうじょう | 万里の長城 | 8 |
| **ひ** | | **Lesson** |
| ひ | 日 | 18 |
| ビーチ | | 6 |
| ビール | | 6 |
| ひがしずむ | 日が沈む | 18 |
| ～ひき | ～匹 | 14 |
| ひく | 弾く | 14 |
| ピクニック | | 15 |
| ひこうき | 飛行機 | 2 |
| ひこうきだい | 飛行機代 | 18 |
| ひざ | 膝 | 17 |
| ひさしぶりに | 久しぶりに | 16 |
| ひじ | 肘 | 17 |
| びじゅつ | 美術 | 16 |
| びじゅつかん | 美術館 | 8 |
| ひたい | 額 | 17 |
| ひだり | 左 | 6, 14 |
| びっくりする | | 18 |
| ひつよう | 必要 | 12 |
| ひつよう(な) | 必要(な) | 20 |
| ひと | 人 | 2 |
| ひとばんじゅう | 一晩中 | 19 |
| ひま(な) | 暇(な) | 9 |
| ひゃくてん | 100 点 | 12 |
| びょういん | 病院 | 17 |
| びょうき | 病気 | 9 |
| ひょうげん | 表現 | 20 |
| ピラミッド | | 3 |
| ひりひりする | | 17 |
| ひるごはん | 昼ごはん | 4 |
| ひるね | 昼寝 | 17 |
| ひろい | 広い | 6 |
| **ふ** | | **Lesson** |
| ～ぶ | ～部 | 16 |
| ファックス | | 8 |
| ファミリーレストラン | | 14 |
| ふあん(な) | 不安(な) | 13 |
| プール | | 5 |
| ふく | 服 | 17 |
| ふじさん | 富士山 | 6 |
| ふじんふく | 婦人服 | 6 |
| ふすま | 襖 | 11 |
| ぶた | 豚 | 17 |
| ぶたい | 舞台 | 18 |
| ふだん | 普段 | 16 |
| ぶちょう | 部長 | 20 |
| ふつう | 普通 | 15 |
| ふつかよい | 二日酔い | 17 |
| ぶつり | 物理 | 16 |
| ふともも | 太もも | 17 |
| ふとる | 太る | 18 |
| ふね | 船 | 18 |
| ふゆ | 冬 | 7 |
| ふられる | 振られる | 13 |
| フランス | | 1 |
| ブリスベン | | 3 |
| ふる | 降る | 10 |
| ふるい | 古い | 6 |
| ふるいけ | 古池 | 20 |
| プレゼント | | 7 |
| ふろ | 風呂 | 11 |
| プロ | | 16 |
| ふんすい | 噴水 | 7 |
| ぶんぼうぐ | 文法具 | 6 |
| ぶんぼうぐや | 文房具屋 | 14 |
| **へ** | | **Lesson** |
| へいじつ | 平日 | 18 |
| ペット | | 8 |
| へや | 部屋 | 3 |
| ペン | | 2 |
| べんきょうします | 勉強します | 4 |
| べんきょうする | 勉強する | 7 |
| べんごし | 弁護士 | 1 |
| へんじ | 返事 | 20 |
| **ほ** | | **Lesson** |
| ぼう | 棒 | 10 |
| ほうかご | 放課後 | 16 |
| ぼうし | 帽子 | 2 |
| ほうせき | 宝石 | 15 |
| ほうめん | (中野) 方面 | 19 |
| ほえる | 吠える | 17 |
| ほお | 頬 | 17 |
| ボール | | 16 |
| ぼく | 僕 | 12 |

| | | |
|---|---|---|
| ぼくたち | 僕たち | 15 |
| (〜て) ほしい | | 20 |
| ほたる | 蛍 | 20 |
| ほっかいどう | 北海道 | 5 |
| ほっぺた | | 17 |
| ほら | | 8 |
| ほん | 本 | 1 |
| 〜ほん | 〜本 | 14 |
| ほんこん | 香港 | 8 |
| ほんだな | 本棚 | 15 |
| ほんとう | 本当 | 7 |
| ほんとうに | 本当に | 5 |
| ほんの | | 13 |
| ほんや | 本屋 | 3 |

| ま | | Lesson |
|---|---|---|
| まあね | | 16 |
| 〜まい | 〜枚 | 14 |
| まいあさ | 毎朝 | 8 |
| まいこ | 舞妓 | 18 |
| まいしゅう | 毎週 | 4 |
| まいしょくご | 毎食後 | 17 |
| まいつき | 毎月 | 4 |
| まいど | 毎度 | 20 |
| まいにち | 毎日 | 4 |
| まいばん | 毎晩 | 8 |
| 〜まいめ | 〜枚目 | 15 |
| まえ | 前 | 3 |
| まがる | 曲がる | 14 |
| まご | 孫 | 11 |
| まじめ(な) | 真面目(な) | 10 |
| まずい | | 9 |
| まずしい | 貧しい | 18 |
| また | | 6 |
| まだ | | 7 |
| またせる | 待たせる | 20 |
| まだまだ | | 13 |
| まち | 街 | 5 |
| まちあわせ | 待ち合わせ | 12 |
| まちあわせる | 待ち合わせる | 7 |
| まつ | 待つ | 7 |
| まつげ | まつ毛 | 17 |
| まっすぐ | | 14 |
| まつり | 祭り | 6 |
| まで | | 12 |
| まど | 窓 | 8 |
| まぶた | | 17 |
| 〜まま | | 20 |
| まゆげ | 眉毛 | 17 |
| まわす | 回す | 17 |
| まわり | 周り | 18 |
| まんが | 漫画 | 3 |
| まんざい | 漫才 | 18 |
| まんせき | 満席 | 15 |
| まんなか | 真ん中 | 17 |

| み | | Lesson |
|---|---|---|
| ミートパイ | | 9 |
| みがく | 磨く | 10 |
| みかん | | 16 |
| みぎ | 右 | 6, 14 |
| みずうみ | 湖 | 7 |
| みずもれ | 水漏れ | 17 |
| みせ | 店 | 10 |
| みちばた | 道ばた | 17 |
| みどり | 緑 | 19 |
| みなみアメリカ | 南アメリカ | 18 |
| みます（みる） | 見ます | 4 |
| みみ | 耳 | 2 |
| ミュージカルげき | ミュージカル劇 | 18 |
| みょうじ | 苗字 | 2 |
| みる | 見る | 7 |
| みんな | | 16 |

| む | | Lesson |
|---|---|---|
| むかし | 昔 | 19 |
| むずかしい | 難しい | 5 |
| むね | 胸 | 17 |

| め | | Lesson |
|---|---|---|
| め | 目 | 2 |
| 〜め | 〜目 | 14 |
| めいじじだい | 明治時代 | 18 |
| めいしょ | 名所 | 8 |
| めがね | 眼鏡 | 3 |
| めしあがる | 召し上がる | 20 |
| めまい | 目まい | 17 |
| メルボルン | | 3 |
| めん | 面 | 18 |
| めんせき | 面積 | 10 |
| めんせつ | 面接 | 13 |

| も | | Lesson |
|---|---|---|
| もう | | 17 |
| もういちど | もう一度 | 2 |
| もうしあげる | 申し上げる | 20 |
| もうす | 申す | 12 |
| もうすぐ | | 9 |
| もうすこし | もう少し | 14 |
| もくようび | 木曜日 | 4 |
| もしもし | | 12 |
| もちろん | | 7 |
| もつ | 持つ | 10 |
| もっていく | 持っていく | 7 |
| もっと | | 6 |
| もの | 物 | 6 |
| もらう | | 13 |
| もんく | 文句 | 17 |
| もんだい | 問題 | 5 |

| や | | Lesson |
|---|---|---|
| 〜や | 〜屋 | 14 |
| やおや | 八百屋 | 14 |
| やきにく | 焼き肉 | 6 |

| | | |
|---|---|---|
| やきゅう | 野球 | 2 |
| やく | 役 | 18 |
| やくそく | 約束 | 15 |
| やけい | 夜景 | 19 |
| やさい | 野菜 | 8 |
| やすい | 安い | 6 |
| やすみ | 休み | 15 |
| やすむ | 休む | 7 |
| やっと | | 19 |
| やね | 屋根 | 19 |
| やま | 山 | 2 |
| やまのてせん | 山手線 | 19 |
| やまのぼり | 山登り | 9 |
| やめる | 止める | 16 |
| やめる | 辞める | 18 |

| ゆ | | Lesson |
|---|---|---|
| ゆうしょうする | 優勝する | 18 |
| ゆうびんきょく | 郵便局 | 3 |
| ゆうべ | 夕べ | 5 |
| ゆうめい(な) | 有名(な) | 6 |
| ～ゆき | (品川) 行き | 19 |
| ゆきだるま | 雪だるま | 7 |
| ゆきまつり | 雪祭り | 8 |
| ゆっくり | | 2 |
| ゆび | 指 | 17 |

| よ | | Lesson |
|---|---|---|
| ようい | 用意 | 11 |
| ようじ | 用事 | 8 |
| ようちえん | 幼稚園 | 16 |
| ヨーロッパ | | 18 |
| よかったら | | 5 |
| よく | | 4 |
| よこ | 横 | 6 |
| よこはま | 横浜 | 10 |
| よし | | 20 |
| よてい | 予定 | 20 |
| よていどおり | 予定通り | 18 |
| よぶ | 呼ぶ | 8 |
| よみます（よむ） | 読みます | 4 |
| よむ | 読む | 7 |
| よる | 夜 | 4 |
| よろしい | | 20 |
| よろしく | | 1 |

| ら | | Lesson |
|---|---|---|
| ライオン | | 18 |
| らいしゅう | 来週 | 5 |
| らいねん | 来年 | 6 |
| らく(な) | 楽(な) | 6 |
| らくご | 落語 | 18 |
| ラグビー | | 4 |
| ラジオ | | 3 |
| ラッキー | | 18 |
| ラップトップ | | 14 |
| ラブレター | | 12 |

| り | | Lesson |
|---|---|---|
| りっぱ(な) | 立派(な) | 9 |
| りゅうがく | 留学 | 20 |
| りゅうがくせい | 留学生 | 1 |
| りゅうちょうに | 流暢に | 17 |
| りょう | 寮 | 9 |
| りょうしん | 両親 | 5 |
| りょうり | 料理 | 8 |
| りょこう | 旅行 | 6 |
| りんご | | 3 |
| りんり | 倫理 | 16 |

| る | | Lesson |
|---|---|---|
| るすばんでんわ | 留守番電話 | 12 |

| れ | | Lesson |
|---|---|---|
| れきしてきに | 歴史的に | 18 |
| レストラン | | 3 |
| れんきゅう | 連休 | 9 |
| れんしゅう | 練習 | 16 |
| れんらくする | 連絡する | 20 |

| ろ | | Lesson |
|---|---|---|
| ろうか | 廊下 | 11 |
| ロボット | | 19 |
| ロンドン | | 4 |

| わ | | Lesson |
|---|---|---|
| ワールドカップ | | 18 |
| ワイン | | 4 |
| わかもの | 若者 | 19 |
| わかります（わかる） | 分かります | 4 |
| わかる | 分かる | 7 |
| わしつ | 和室 | 11 |
| わすれる | 忘れる | 9 |
| わたくし | | 12 |
| わたし | 私 | 1 |
| わらいます（わらう） | 笑います | 4 |
| わらう | 笑う | 8 |

**Duck-Young Lee**

He earned his M.A. in Area Studies specialised in Teaching Japanese as a Foreign Language at the University Tsukuba, and his Ph.D. in Asian Linguistics at the Australian National University (ANU). Duck-Young has been teaching elementary Japanese at the ANU for twenty-five years. His recent publications include 'Japanese studies in south Korea' (book chapter), 'Contrastive studies: past, present and future' (Journal of Japanese Language), 'Involvement and the Japanese interactive particles ne and yo' (Journal of Pragmatics), 'The use of the zero particle in Japanese conversation' (Journal of Pragmatics), and 'Japanese education in the Australian context' (Japanese Linguistics and Literature).

**Naomi Ogi**

She earned her Graduate Diploma in Education at the University of Canberra, M.A. and Ph.D. in Japanese Applied Linguistics at the ANU. Naomi has been teaching Japanese at the ANU for fifteen years. Her recent publications include 'Involvement and Attitude in Japanese Discourse: Interactive Markers' (John Benjamins) and 'Language and an expression of identities: Japanese sentence-final particles ne and na' (Journal of Pragmatics).

**Masahiro Toma**

He earned his M.A. in Translation and Interpreting at Macquarie University, Graduate Diploma in TESOL at University of Ulster, and Graduate Diploma in Japanese Applied Linguistics at the ANU. He has taught Japanese at the ANU and the Akita International University, and is currently teaching at International College of Liberal Arts, Yamanashi Gakuin University. His research interests include pragmatics, linguistic patterns in various situations, and second language acquisition. His recent publication includes 'An Introduction to SLA for Japanese Language Teachers' in *A Practical Approach to Japanese Language Teaching* (Bonjinsha) .

**Yoko Yonezawa**

She earned her Graduate Diploma in Education at the University of Canberra, Master of Education at Charles Darwin University, M.A. and Ph.D. in Japanese Applied Linguistics at the ANU. Yoko has taught Japanese in Australian secondary schools, and is currently teaching at the ANU. Her research interests include spoken discourse, the socio-cultural aspects of the use of language and language teaching. Her recent publications include 'Native speaker's perceptions of the second person pronoun anata 'you' in Japanese' (Nihongo Kyooiku) and 'The role of the overt expression of first and second person subject in Japanese' (Journal of Pragmatics).

日本語がいっぱい

Elementary Japanese Textbook Nihongo ga IPPAI

発行　2010年1月20日　初版1刷
　　　2018年4月10日　　2刷

定価　3000円+税



絵　Cui Yue Ya

発行者　松本功

装丁　上田真未

印刷製本所　株式会社 ディグ

発行所　株式会社 ひつじ書房

〒112-0011 東京都文京区千石2-1-2 大和ビル2F

Tel.03-5319-4916 Fax.03-5319-4917

郵便振替 00120-8-142852

toiawase@hituzi.co.jp　http://www.hituzi.co.jp/

ISBN978-4-89476-449-1　C1081

# 模範解答
# Standard answers

# 日本語が
# いっぱい

Lee, Duckyoung
Ogi, Naomi
Toma, Masa
Yonezawa, Yoko

ひつじ書房

# Standard answers

These are standard or typical answers only and there are possibilities for different and better answers. If you have any questions or queries, please consult with your instructor.

## Lesson 1

**Grammar Exercise 1**

(1) Watashi wa Suzuki desu. わたしは　すずきです。 (2) Watashi wa gakusei desu. わたしは　がくせいです。 (3) Watashi wa Nihonjin desu. わたしは　にほんじんです。 (4) Yamada san wa sensei desu. やまださんは　せんせいです。

**Grammar Exercise 2**

(1) Kimura san wa sensei desu. きむらさんは　せんせいです。 (2) Honda san wa kaishain desu. ほんださんは　かいしゃいんです。 (3) Yamada san wa isha desu. やまださんは　いしゃです。 (4) Smisu san wa Igirisujin desu. スミスさんは　イギリスじんです。 (5) Shin san wa kankokujin desu. しんさんは　かんこくじんです。

**Grammar Exercise 3**

(1) Kimu san wa sensei desu ka? キムさんは　せんせいですか。 (2) Watashi wa gakusei dewa arimasen. わたしは　がくせいでは　ありません。 (3) Suzuki san wa ginkooin desu ka? すずきさんは　ぎんこういんですか。 (4) Suzuki san wa ginkooin dewa arimasen. すずきさんは　ぎんこういんでは　ありません。 (5) Sukotto san wa Amerikajin dewa arimasen. スコットさんは　アメリカじんでは　ありません。

**Grammar Exercise 4**

(1) Hai. Ono san wa sensei desu. はい。おのさんは　せんせいです。
Iie. Ono san wa sensei dewa arimasen. いいえ。おのさんは　せんせいでは　ありません。

(2) Hai. Kim san wa Kankokujin desu. はい。キムさんは　かんこくじんです。
Iie. Kim san wa Kankokujin dewa arimasen. いいえ。キムさんは　かんこくじんでは　ありません。

(3) Hai. Suzuki san wa daigakusei desu. はい。すずきさんは　だいがくせいです。
Iie. Suzuki san wa daigakusei dewa arimasen. いいえ。すずきさんは　だいがくせいでは　ありません。

(4) Hai, Murakami san wa kaishain desu. はい。むらかみさんは　かいしゃいんです。
Iie, Murakami san wa kaishain dewa ariasen. いいえ。むらかみさんは　かいしゃいんでは　ありません。

(5) Hai, Jon san wa Igirisujin desu. はい、ジョンさんは　イギリスじんです。
Iie, Jon san wa Igirisujin dewa arimasen. いいえ。ジョンさんは　イギリスじんでは　ありません。

**Grammar Exercise 5**

(1) watashi no hon わたしの ほん
(2) watashi no daigaku わたしの だいがく
(3) Tanaka san no kuruma たなかさんの くるま
(4) Mearii no tomodachi メアリーの ともだち
(5) Eigo no sensei えいごの せんせい
(6) Masato no senkoo まさとの せんこう
(7) Nihongo no jisho にほんごの じしょ
(8) watashi no nihongo no sensei no hon わたしの にほんごの せんせいの ほん
(9) Yamada sensei wa watashi no nihongo no sensei desu. やまだせんせいは わたしの にほんごの せんせいです。
(10) Tanaka san wa watashi no tomodachi dewa arimasen たなかさんは わたしの ともだちでは ありません。

**Expression Exercise 1**

Refer to the example.

**Expression Exercise 2**

(1) Konbanwa. こんばんは。 (2) Ittekimasu. / Itterasshai. いってきます。／いっていらっしゃい。 (3) Tadaima. / Okaerinasai. ただいま。／おかえりなさい。 (4) Jaa, mata. じゃあ、また。 (5) Itadakimasu. いただきます。 (6) Oyasuminasai. おやすみ。 (7) Gochisoosama. ごちそうさま。 (8) Sumimasen. すみません。

**Expression Exercise 3**

(1) Watashi wa daigakusei desu. Yamada san mo daigakusei desu.
わたしは　だいがくせいです。やまださんも　だいがくせいです。

(2) Tanaka san wa sensei desu. Kimura san mo sensei desu.
たなかさんは せんせいです。　きむらさんも せんせいです。

(3) Suzuki san wa kaishain desu. Numata san mo kaishain desu.
すずきさんは かいしゃいんです。ぬまたさんも かいしゃいんです。

(4) Sukotto san wa Amerikajin desu. Sumisu san mo Amerikajin desu. Jonson san wa Oosutorariajin desu.
スコットさんは アメリカじんです。スミスさんも アメリカじんです。ジョンソンさんは オーストラリアじんです。

(5) Yamada san wa watashi no tomodachi desu. Honda san mo watashi no tomodachi desu. Nomura san wa watashi no tomodachi dewa arimasen.
やまださんは わたしの ともだちです。 ほんださんも わたしの ともだちです。のむらさんは わたしの ともだちでは ありません。

**Expression Exercise 4**

(1) Sukotto san wa Igirisujin desu. スコットさんは イギリスじんです。
(2) Jon san wa Oosutorariajin desu. ジョンさんは オーストラリアじんです。
(3) Kimu san wa kankokujin desu. キムさんは かんこくじんです。
(4) Foodo san wa amerikajin desu. フォードさんは アメリカじんです。
(5) Rin san wa chuugokujin desu. りんさんは ちゅうごくじんです。

**Pair practice 1**

Refer to the example.

**Pair practice 2**

Refer to the example.

## Lesson 2

**Grammar Exercise 1**

[Speaker A] [Speaker B]

(1) (O) namae wa nan desu ka. (お)なまえは なんですか。→ (Watashino namae wa) Sakamoto desu. さかもとです。
(2) (Go) shusshin wa doko desu ka. (ご)しゅっしんは どこですか。→ Chuugoku desu. ちゅうごくです。
(3) (O) shigoto wa nan desu ka. (お)しごとは なんですか。→ Ginkooin desu. ぎんこういんです。
(4) Senkoo wa nan desu ka. せんこうは なんですか。→ Nihongo desu. にほんごです。
(5) (Go)shumi wa nan desu ka. (ご)しゅみは なんですか。→ Dokusho desu. どくしょです。
(6) (O)sumai wa doko desu ka. (お)すまいは どこですか。→ Sidonii desu. シドニーです。

**Grammar Exercise 2**

(1) Kore wa watashino kuruma desu. これは わたしの くるまです。
(2) Sore wa Suzuki-san no booshi desu. それは すずきさんの ぼうしです。
(3) Are wa Sumisu-san no tokei desu. あれは スミスさんの とけいです。
(4) Kono jisho wa nihongo no jisho desu. このじしょは にほんごの じしょです。
(5) Sono pen wa Nakamura-san no pen desu. そのペンは なかむらさんの ペンです。
(6) Ano ie wa watashi no sensei no ie desu. あのいえは わたしの せんせいの いえです。
(7) Kono kaban wa watashi no kaban dewa arimasen. Ano kaban mo watashi no kaban dewa arimasen.
このかばんは わたしの かばんでは ありません。 あのかばんも わたしの かばんでは ありません。
(8) Ano hito wa Oosutoraria-jin dewa arimasen. Ano hito wa America-jin desu.
あのひとは オーストラリアじんでは ありません。あのひとは アメリカじんです。
(9) A: Are wa shinbun desuka. あれは しんぶんですか。
B: Iie, Are wa shinbun dewa arimasen. Are wa zasshi desu.
いいえ、あれはしんぶんでは ありません。あれはざっしです。
(10) A: Kono kasa wa Yamada san no kasa desuka. このかさは やまださんの かさですか。
B: Hai, soudesu. はい、そうです
(11) A: Sore wa nan desu ka. それは なんですか。
B: Kore wa watashi no nihongo no hon desu. これは わたしのにほんごの ほんです。
(12) A: Are wa nan desu ka. あれは なんですか。
B: Are wa toshokan desu. あれは としょかんです。

**Grammar Exercise 3**

(1) San juu ni さんじゅう に
(2) Roppyaku nana juu ろっぴゃく なな じゅう
(3) Yon hyaku yon juu hachi よんひゃくよんじゅう はち
(4) Kyuu hyaku ichi きゅうひゃく いち
(5) Go sen go hyaku nijyuu yon ごせん ごひゃく にじゅうよん
(6) San zen san byaku san さんぜん さんびゃく さん
(7) Nanaman roku sen hyaku ななまん ろくせん ひゃく
(8) San man ni sen さんまん にせん
(9) Sanjyuu ni man さんじゅうにまん

(10) Juu hachi man san zen じゅうはちまん さんぜん
(11) Kyuuman ni sen hyaku nanajuu Roku きゅうまん にせん ひゃく ななじゅう ろく
(12) Ni juu nana man go sen go hyaku go にじゅうななまん ごせん ごひゃく ご

**Expression Exercise 1**

(1) Goji gofun ごじ ごふん
(2) Shichiji sanjuugofun しちじ さんじゅうごふん
(3) Niji yonjuppun にじ よんじゅっぷん
(4) Juuji sanjuppun じゅうじ さんじゅっぷん
(5) Gozen yoji juppun ごぜん よじ じゅっぷん
(6) Gozen kuji yonjuugofun ごぜん くじ よんじゅうごふん
(7) Gogo hachiji sanjuppun ごご はちじ さんじゅっぷん
(8) Gogo ichiji nijuppun ごご いちじ にじゅっぷん

**Expression Exercise 2**

(1) A: Ima nanji desu ka. いま なんじですか。
B: Juuichiji nijyuugo fun desu じゅういちじ にじゅうごうふんです。
(2) A: Eiga wa nanji desu ka. えいがは なんじですか。
B: Kuji sanjuppun desu. くじさんじゅっぷんです。
(3) A: Paatii wa nanji desuka ぱーてぃーは なんじですか。
B: Gogo shichiji desu. ごご しちじです。
(4) A: Shiken wa nanji desuka しけんは なんじ ですか。
B: Gogo juuji gojuppun desu ごごじゅうじ ごじゅっぷんです。

**Pair practice 1**

Refer to the example.

**Pair practice 2**

Refer to the example.

**Pair practice 3**

Refer to the example.

## Lesson 3

**Grammar Exercise 1**

(1) Watashi no daigaku wa meruborun ni arimasu. わたしのだいがくは メルボルンに あります。
(2) Kokkaigijidoo wa Tookyoo ni arimasu. こっかいぎじどうは とうきょうに あります。
(3) Okada san wa ima Singapooru ni imasu. おかださんは いま シンガポールに います。
(4) Kimura san no okusan wa Amerika ni imasu. きむらさんの おくさんは アメリカに います。
(5) Watashi no kaban wa ofisu ni arimasu. わたしのかばんは オフィスに あります。
(6) Watashi no neko wa Yamada san no ie ni imasu. わたしのねこは やまださんの いえに います。

**Grammar Exercise 2**

(1) Tokei wa sofa (isu) no ue ni arimasu. とけいは ソファ（いす）の うえに あります。
(2) Kasa wa terebi no soba ni arimasu. かさは テレビの そばに あります。
(3) Pen wa teeburu no shita ni arimasu. ペンは テーブルの したに あります。
(4) Booshi wa terebi no ue ni arimasu. ぼうしは テレビの うえに あります。
(5) Ringo wa hako no naka ni arimasu. りんごは はこの なかに あります。
(6) Rajio wa hako no soba ni arimasu. ラジオは はこの そばに あります。

**Grammar Exercise 3**

(1) Watashi no ofisu wa kyooto ni arimasen. わたしの オフィスは きょうとに ありません。
(2) Kokkaigijidoo wa oosaka ni arimasen. こっかいぎじどうは おおさかに ありません。
(3) Ogi san wa ima chuugoku ni imasen. おぎさんは いま ちゅうごくに いません。
(4) Watashi no kaban wa kurumano naka ni arimasen. わたしのかばんは くるまのなかに ありません。
(5) Kimura san wa amerika ni imasen. (Kare) wa Oosutoraria ni imasu.
きむらさんは いま アメリカにいません。（かれ）は オーストラリアに います。

**Grammar Exercise 4**

(1) Q: Pen wa dokoni arimasuka. ペンは どこに ありますか。
A: Teeburu no shita ni arimasu. テーブルの したに あります。
(2) Q: Ringo wa dokoni arimasuka. りんごは どこに ありますか。
A: Terebi no ue ni arimasu. テレビの うえに あります。
(3) Q: Nihongo no jisho wa dokoni arimasuka. にほんごの じしょは どこに ありますか。
A: Watashi no kaban no naka ni arimasu. わたしの かばんの なかに あります。

(4) Q: Saito san wa doko ni imasuka. さいとうさんは　どこに　いますか。
A: Sapporo ni imasu. さっぽろに　います。
(5) Q: Suzuki san wa doko ni imasuka. すずきさんは　どこに　いますか。
A: Kaisha ni imasu. かいしゃに　います。

**Expression Exercise 1**

(1) Watashi no kuruma wa asoko ni arimasu. わたしの　くるまは　あそこに　あります。
(2) Watashi no pen wa soko ni arimasu. わたしの　ペンは　そこに　あります。
(3) Denwa wa asoko ni arimasu. でんわは　あそこに　あります。
(4) Ogi san wa asoko ni imasu. おぎさんは　あそこに　います。
(5) Kimura san no okusan wa koko ni imasu. きむらさんの　おくさんは　ここに　います。
(6) Watashi no hon wa koko ni arimasen. わたしの　ほんは　ここに　ありません。
(7) Yoshida san wa ima koko ni imasen よしださんは　いま　ここに　いません。

**Expression Exercise 2**

(1) Kimura san wa mado no soba ni imasu. きむらさんは　まどのそばに　います。
(2) Inu wa isu no soba ni imasu. いぬは　いすの　そばに　います。
(3) Megane wa teeburu no ue ni arimasu. めがねは　テーブルの　うえに　あります。
(4) Hon wa tsukue no ue ni arimasu. ほんは　つくえの　うえに　あります。
(5) Neko wa terebi no mae ni imasu. ねこは　テレビの　まえに　います。
(6) Koppu wa mado no soba ni arimasu. コップは　まどの　そばに　あります。
(7) Kasa wa teeburu no shita ni arimasu. かさは　テーブルの　したに　あります。

**Expression Exercise 3**

(1) Watashi no kaban wa kuruma no naka ni arimasu. わたしの かばんは くるまのなかに あります。
(2) Nakamurasan no okusan no kuruma wa watashi no kuruma no tonari ni arimasu.
なかむらさんの　おくさんの　くるまは　わたしの　くるまの　となりに　あります。
(3) Daigaku wa kooen no soba ni arimasu. だいがくは　こうえんの　そばにあります。
(4) Honya wa kutsuya no ushiro ni arimasu. ほんやは　くつやの　うしろに　あります。
(5) Basutei wa yuubinkyoku no mae ni arimasu. バスていは　ゆうびんきょくの　まえに　あります。

**Expression Exercise 4**

(1) Watashi wa jitensha ga arimasu. わたしは　じてんしゃが　あります。
(2) Watashi wa kyoodai ga imasu. わたしは　きょうだいが　います。
(3) Tanaka san wa inu ga imasu. たなかさんは　いぬが　います。
(4) Satou san wa oniisan ga imasu. さとうさんは　おにいさんが　います。
(5) Okane ga arimasuka. おかねが　ありますか。
(6) Kondo no shuumatsu konsaato ga arimasu. こんどの　しゅうまつ　コンサートが　あります。
(7) Ashita Nihongo no shiken ga arimasu. あした　にほんごの　しけんが　あります。

**Pair practice 1**

Refer to the example.

**Pair practice 2**

Refer to the example.

**Research**

(1) Biwako wa Shiga ken ni arimasu. びわこは　しがけんに　あります。
(2) Narita kuukouu wa Chiba ken ni arimasu. なりたくうこうは　ちばけんに　あります。
(3) Kusatsu onsen wa Gunma ken ni arimasu. くさつおんせんは　ぐんまけんに　あります。
(4) Genbaku doomu wa Hiroshima ni arimasu. げんばくドームは　ひろしまに　あります。
(5) Matsushima wa Miyagi ken ni arimasu. まつしまは　みやぎけんに　あります。

## Lesson 4

**文法練習1**

(1) りんごを　たべます／りんごを　かいます
(2) アフリカに　いきます
(3) にほんちゃを　のみます
(4) テレビを　みます／テレビを　かいます
(5) ちゅうかりょうりを　たべます
(6) まんがを　よみます

(7) かんこくごを　べんきょうします　　(8) たなかせんせいに　あいます
(9) うちに　かえります　　(10) でんしゃに　のります

## 文法練習２

(1) ほんを　よみますか。　はい、（ほんを）よみます。／いいえ、（ほんを）よみません。
(2) しんぶんを よみますか。　はい、（しんぶんを）よみます。／いいえ、（しんぶんを）よみません。
(3) パーティーに　いきますか。　はい、（パーティーに）いきます。／いいえ、（パーティーに）いきません。
(4) しゅくだいを しますか。　はい、（しゅくだいを）します。／いいえ、（しゅくだいを）しません。
(5) タクシーに　のりますか。　はい、（タクシーに）のります。／いいえ、（タクシーに）のりません。
(6) きっぷを　かいますか。　はい、（きっぷを）かいます。／いいえ、（きっぷを）かいません。
(7) ジュースを のみますか。　はい、（ジュースを）のみます。／いいえ、（ジュースを）のみません。
(8) はがきを　かきますか。　はい、（はがきを）かきます。／いいえ、（はがきを）かきません。

## 文法練習３

(1) A: あした　なにを しますか。　B: にほんごを べんきょうします。
(2) A: きんようび　なにを しますか。　B: えいがを　みます。
(3) A: にちようび　なにを　しますか。　B: ともだちに　あいます。
(4) A: もくようび　なにを しますか。　B: きむらさんの　いえに　いきます。
(5) A: こんばん　なにを　しますか。　B: まんがを　よみます。

## 自然な日本語：練習

(1) そうですね　(2) ええと　(3) そうですね　(4) ええと

## 表現練習１

(1) きむらさんは　たいてい　８じに あさごはんを たべます。　(2) やまださんは　９じ３０ぷん／９じはんに がっこうに　いきます。　(3) おかださんは　４じ３０ぷん／４じはんに　うちに　かえります。　(4) なかむらさんは　１０じ３０ぷん／１０じはんに　ねます。　(5) ジョンさんは　きんようびに　すいえいを　します。　(6) やまださんは　どようびに　かいものを　します。　(7) ほんださんは　にちようびに　テニスを します。　(8) すずきさんは　もくようびに　アルバイトを　します。

## 表現練習２

(1) はなこさんは　なんじに　ひるごはんを たべますか。
→ １２じ３０ぷん／１２じはんに（ひるごはんを）たべます。
(2) はなこさんは　いつ　ざっしを　よみますか。→ かようびに（ざっしを）よみます。
(3) はなこさんは　なんじ(ごろ)に　おちゃを　のみますか。
→ １０じ３０ぷん／１０じはん（ごろ）に（おちゃを）のみます。
(4) はなこさんは　いつ　テニスを　しますか。→ もくようびに（テニスを）します。
(5) はなこさんは　いつ　かいものを　しますか。→ どようびに（かいものを）します。
(6) はなこさんは　なんじ（ごろ）に　ねますか。→ １１じに　ねます。
(7) はなこさんは　いつ　すいえいを　しますか。→ すいようびと　きんようびに（すいえいを）します。
(8) はなこさんは　いつ　アルバイトを　しますか。→ げつようびと　にちようびに　アルバイトを　します。

## 表現練習３

(1) たなかさんは いつも げつようびに しんぶんを かいます。　(2) (わたしは) たまに ３じごろに ケーキを たべます。　(3) かとうさんは ときどき にちようびに ゴルフを します。　(4) (わたしは) たいてい きんようびに にほんごを べんきょうします。　(5) すずきさんは よく おちゃを のみます。　(6) (わたしは) たまに えいがを みます。　(7) やまださんは ときどき にほんの ざっしを よみます。　(8) のむらさんは いつも どようびと にちようびに テニスを します。

## 対話練習１

Refer to the example.

## 対話練習２

Refer to the example.

## 対話練習３

Refer to the example.

## Lesson 5

### 文法練習1

(1) 6じに おきます。 (2) きんようびに プールで およぎます。 (3) デパートで かばんを かいます。 (4) デパートに いきます。 (5) すいようびに にほんに かえります。 (6) 5じに きっさてんで かとうさんに あいます。 (7) どようびに こうえんで サッカーを します。 (8) 4じはんに としょかんで にほんごを べんきょうします。 (9) きむらさんは きんようびに いけぶくろで えいがを みます。

### 文法練習2

(1) きむらさんは 6じに おきます。 (2) よしださんは 10じはんに きっさてんで コーヒーを のみます。 (3) さとうさんは 5じはんに デパートで かいものを します。 (4) はやしさんは げつようびに としょかんで べんきょうします。 (5) すずきさんは こんばん うちで てがみを かきます。 (6) まつださんは まいばん うちで テレビを みます。 (7) たかださんは ごご（よる）8じに きっさてんで ともだちに あいます。（ともだちと コーヒーを のみます。） (8) くどうさんは かようびと もくようびに プールで およぎます。

### 文法練習3

(1) おかださんは あさ（ごぜん）8じに バスで かいしゃに いきます。 (2) たなかさんは きんようびに きむらさんと えいがを みます。 (3) わたしは ともだちと としょかんで にほんごを べんきょうします。 (4) すずきさんは どようびに くるまで シドニーに いきます。 (5) よしださんは にちようびに ひこうきで にほんに いきます。

### 文法練習4

(1) ゆうべ テレビを みましたか。 はい、テレビを みました。／いいえ、テレビを みませんでした。
(2) おととい まちで コーヒーを のみましたか。 はい、コーヒーを のみました。／いいえ、コーヒーを のみませんでした。
(3) ゆうべ にほんごを べんきょうしましたか。 はい、にほんごを べんきょうしました。／いいえ、にほんごを べんきょうしませんでした。
(4) きのう おかださんに あいましたか。 はい、おかださんに あいました。／いいえ、おかださんに あいませんでした。
(5) せんしゅうの どようびに かいものを しましたか。 はい、かいものを しました。／いいえ、かいものを しませんでした。

### 自然な日本語：練習

(1) そうですね。 (2) そうですね。 (3) そうですか。 (4) そうですね。 (5) そうですか。 (6) そうですね。／そうですか。 (7) そうですか。 (8) そうですね。 (9) そうですか。 (10) そうですか。

### 表現練習1

(1) もくようびに いっしょに えいがを みませんか。／～みましょう。／～みましょうか。
(2) いっしょに としょかんで にほんごを べんきょうしませんか。／～べんきょうしましょう。／～べんきょうしましょうか。
(3) きっさてんで いっしょに コーヒーを のみませんか。／～のみましょう。／～のみましょうか。
(4) たいいくかんで いっしょに バドミントンを しませんか。／～しましょう。／～しましょうか。
(5) 3じごろに かとうさんに あいませんか。／～あいましょう。／～あいましょうか。

### 表現練習2

(1) A: いっしょに パーティーに いきませんか。 B: いいですね。いきましょう。
(2) A: いっしょに にほんごを べんきょうしましょうか。 B: いいですね。いっしょに しましょう。
(3) A: いっしょに えいがを みませんか。 B: いいですね。みましょう。
(4) A: いっしょに テニスを しませんか。 B: あ、テニスは ちょっと・・・。さむいです。
(5) A: いっしょに かいものに いきませんか。 B: あ、かいものは ちょっと・・・。おかねが ありません。
(6) A: いっしょに こうえんに いきませんか。 B: いいですね。いきましょう。
(7) A: いっしょに すいえいを しませんか。 B: あ、すいえいは ちょっと・・・。いそがしいです。

**対話練習 1**
Refer to the example.

**対話練習 2**
Refer to the example.

**対話練習 3**
Refer to the example.

**練習しましょう**
Refer to the example.

## Lesson 6

**文法練習 1**

(1) あたらしい ほん　(2) あのほんは あたらしいです。　(3) おおきな たてもの　(4) あのたてものは おおきいです。　(5) ひろい いえ　(6) たなかさんの いえは ひろいです。　(7) ゆうめいな かしゅ　(8) あのかしゅは ゆうめいです。　(9) しんせつな ひと　(10) ならさんは とても しんせつです。

**文法練習 2**

(1) たなかさんの いえは ちいさく ありません。　(2) この じてんしゃは あたらしく ありません。　(3) きょう わたしは げんきでは ありません。　(4) いま としょかんは しずかでは ありません。　(5) この もんだいは むずかしく ありません。　(6) あのひとは しんせつでは ありません。　(7) わたしの いえは だいがくから ちかく ありません。

**文法練習 3**

(1) とうきょうは とても おおきかったです。
(2) わたしの ジャケットは とても たかかったです。
(3) かとうさんの くるまは　はやかったです。
(4) パーティーは とても たのしかったです。
(5) えいがは こわかったです。
(6) すずきさんの いえは おおきかったです。
(7) おかださんは とても しんせつでした。
(8) シドニーは とても にぎやかでした。
(9) きのうの しけんは かんたんでした。
(10) わたしは せんしゅう いそがしかったです。

**文法練習 4**

(1) えいがは おもしろく ありませんでした。
(2) ケーキは おいしく ありませんでした。
(3) わたしは きのう いそがしく ありませんでした。
(4) さとうさんは きのう げんきではありませんでした。
(5) せんせいは しんせつでは ありませんでした。
(6) ビーチは きれいでは ありませんでした。
(7) わたしのだいがくは わたしのいえから あまり とおく ありませんでした。

**自然な日本語：練習**

**練習 1 (Sample)**

(1) そうですか／ええ　ほんとうに　(2) へえ　(3) ええ　ほんとうに／いいですね　(4) よかったですね

**練習 2 (Sample)**

(1) え！すごい！　(2) え！ほんとうですか　(3) そうですか　(4) へえ　(5) うわあ！いいですね

**表現練習 1**

(1) かなしいです。　(2) きもちがいいです。　(3) いたいです。　(4) たのしいです。
(5) げんきです。／つよいです。　(6) たいくつです。　(7) あついです。　(8) さむいです。

**表現練習 2**

(1) わたしは とても いそがしかったです。　(2) にほんは とても とおかったです。
(3) バーベキューは おいしかったです。／たのしかったです。　(4) しけんは とても むずかしかったです。
(5) とうきょうは とても にぎやかでした。　(6) ビーチは とても きれいでした／しずかでした／ひろかったです。
(7) ふくは とても たかかったです。　(8) たなかさんは とても はやかったです。

**表現練習 3**

(1) えいがは（あまり）おもしろく ありませんでした。　(2) けいたいでんわは（あまり）やすく ありませんでした。　(3) りょうりは（あまり）おいしく ありませんでした。　(4) さとうさんは（あまり）しんせつでは ありませんでした。／しんせつじゃ ありませんでした。　(5) おきなわは（あまり）あたたかく ありませんでした。　(6) しけんは（あまり）むずかしくありませんでした。　(7) せんせいは（あまり）きびしく ありませんでした。　(8) そのかしゅは（あまり）じょうずでは ありませんでした。／じょうずじゃ ありませんでした。　(9) たなかさんのくるまは（あまり）はやくありませんでした。　(10) そのいすは（あまり）らくではありませんでした。／らくじゃ ありませんでした。

**対話練習 1**

Refer to the examples.

**対話練習 2**

ささき A: ささきさんの とくちょうは なんですか。
B: ささきさんは はなが おおきいです。

たなか A: たなかさんの とくちょうは なんですか。
B: たなかさんは あしが ながいです／ほそいです。

すずき A: すずきさんの とくちょうは なんですか。
B: すずきさんは せが ひくいです。

やまだ A: やまださんの とくちょうは なんですか。
B: やまださんは みみが おおきいです。

おかだ A: おかださんの とくちょうは なんですか。
B: おかださんは かみが ながいです。

**対話練習 3**

(1) じゅぎょう
A: じゅぎょうは どうでしたか。
B: とても おもしろかったです。
／あまり おもしろくありませんでした。
A: あ、そうですか。

(2) アルバイト
A: アルバイトは どうでしたか。
B: とても いそがしかったです。
／あまり いそがしくありませんでした。
A: あ、そうですか。

(3) しょくじ
A: しょくじは どうでしたか。
B: とても おいしかったです。
／あまり おいしくありませんでした。
A: あ、そうですか。

(4) りょこう
A: りょこうは どうでしたか。
B: とても たのしかったです。
／あまり たのしくありませんでした。
A: あ、そうですか。

(5) テスト
A: テストは どうでしたか。
B: とても むずかしかったです。
／あまり むずかしくありませんでした。
A: あ、そうですか。

(6) コンサート
A: コンサートは どうでしたか。
B: とても たのしかったです。
／あまり たのしくありませんでした。
A: あ、そうですか。

**[Supplementary: At a department store]**

**練習 1**

(1) 家具売り場は　何階ですか。 (2) 時計売り場は　何階ですか。 (3) かばん売り場は　何階ですか。
(4) くつ売り場は　何階ですか。 (5) 階段は　どこですか。 (6) エレベーターは　どこですか。
(7) きっさてんは　どこですか。 (8) エスカレーターは　どこですか。

**練習 2**

(1) くつ売り場は　さんかいに　あります。 (2) 階段は　いっかいの　化粧品売り場の　となりに　あります。
(3) 家具売り場は　よんかいに　あります。 (4) 紳士服売り場は　さんかいに　あります。
(5) きっさてんは　ごかいに　あります。 (6) レストランは　ごかいに　あります。

**練習 3**

Refer to the examples.

**練習 4**

(1) オーストラリアの　セーター　ありますか。 (2) これは　ドイツのですか。 (3) しろいのは　ありますか。
(4) この中国のは　いくらですか。 (5) 安いのは　ありますか。 (6) これは　タイのですか。
(7) 大きいセーター　ありますか。 (8) このぼうしは　にせんごひゃく円です。 (9) 黒いのが　あります。
(10) それは　日本の時計ですか。 (11) 小さいのは　ありますか。 (12) シンガポールのビール　ありますか。
(13) 青いかばん　ありますか。 (14) 韓国のが　あります。

**練習 5**

Refer to the examples.

## Lesson 7

**文法練習 1**

(1) たべない　たべます　(2) いかない　いきます　(3) べんきょうしない　べんきょうします　(4) きかない　ききます　(5) とらない　とります　(6) かわない　かいます　(7) ださない　だします　(8) き

ない　きます　(9) おきない　おきます　(10) こない　きます　(11) よまない　よみます　(12) みない　みます　(13) かえらない　かえります　(14) やすまない　やすみます　(15) でかけない　でかけます　(16) かりない　かります　(17) いない　います　(18) またない　まちます　(19) ねない　ねます　(20) はしらない　はしります

**自然な日本語：練習 1**

(1) わたしは、来年、中国に行きます。そしてわたしは、中国で勉強します。

(2) あなたは、あした出かけますか。

(3) A: きのうのニュース、田中さんは見ましたか。

B: いいえ、わたしは見ませんでした。そのニュースはどんなニュースでしたか。

A: それは、さつじんのニュースでした。さつじんは、このあたりでありました。

B: ええ？それはほんとうですか。　それはこわいですね。

**自然な日本語：練習 2**

(1) たなかです。　(2) あついですね。　(3) わぁ、大きい。　(4) 来年、日本に行きます。

(5) 昨日の夜、先生と晩ごはんを食べました。　(6) 今度/次の日曜日、パーティーに来ますか。

(7) 朝、たいていなんじに起きますか。　(8) A: コーヒーを飲みますか。　B: はい、飲みます。

**表現練習 1**

(1) 今日、山田さんととしょかんで会うつもりです。　(2) 金曜日の夜、えいがをみるつもりです。

(3) 来年、くるまでシドニーに行くつもりです。　(4) 明日、大学に行かないつもりです。

(5) 今晩、岡田さんと会わないつもりです。

**表現練習 2**

(1) きものが／を着たいです。　(2) タイ料理が／を食べたいです。　(3) J－ポップが／を聞きたいです。

(4) 今晩、山田さんに会いたくありません。　(5) さしみを食べたくありません。

**表現練習 3**

(1) おんがくをききたいです。　(2) すしを食べたいです。　(3) 映画を見たいです。

(4) 日本ではたらきたいです。　(5) 旅行がしたいです。

**表現練習 4**

(1) いちがつ　ついたち　（1月1日）　(2) さんがつ　はつか　（3月20日）

(3) じゅういちがつ　いつか　（11月5日）　(4) くがつ　ここのか　（9月9日）

(5) はちがつ　じゅうよっか　（8月14日）　(6) じゅうにがつ　にじゅうよっか　（12月24日）

(7) せんきゅうひゃくきゅうじゅうご　ねん　じゅうにがつ　さんじゅういちにち　（1995年12月31日）

(8) にせん　ねん　くがつ　ここのか　(2000年9月9日)

**表現練習 5**

(1) 四月二十一日です。　(2) 八月十日です。　(3) 十一月二十日に終わります。

(4) (example) 七月六日です。　(5) (example) 三月八日です。

**表現練習 6**

(1) 来週、ともだちに東京で会います。　(2) 私の犬は去年死にました。

(3) あさっては五月二十日月曜日です。　(4) 去年、日本で日本語をべんきょうしました。

(5) 三年前に田中さんはオーストラリアに来ました。

**対話練習 1**

Refer to the examples.

**対話練習 2**

Refer to the examples.

**対話練習 3**

Refer to the examples.

**調べましょう**

1. Spring 春 March, April, May ／ Summer 夏 June, July, August ／ Autumn 秋 September, October, November ／ Winter 冬 December, January, February

2. 梅雨 'rainy season' between the end of Spring and the beginning of Summer ／ さくら 'cherry blossom' Spring ／ 台風 'typhoon' from Summer to Autumn ／ 雪だるま 'snowman' Winter ／ 花火 'firework' Summer,

Autumn ／ 入学式 'school entrance ceremony' Spring ／ 卒業式 'graduation ceremony' Spring ／ 紅葉 'coloured leaves' Autumn ／ 花見 'flower viewing' Spring ／ 新年 'the New Year' Winter ／ 運動会 'field/sports day' Autumn

## Lesson 8

**文法練習1**

(1) まちます まって (2) よびます よんで (3) よみます よんで (4) あいます あって (5) あるきます あるいて (6) とります とって (7) おきます おきて (8) ねます ねて (9) しにます しんで (10) ききます きいて (11) いきます いって (12) とびます とんで (13) いそぎます いそいで (14) はなします はなして (15) べんきょうします べんきょうして (16) きます きて

**文法練習2**

(1) わたしは たいてい 7時半に あさごはんを 食べて 8時半に 大学に／へ 行きます。
(2) わたしは たいてい 10時半に シャワーを あびて 11時に ねます。
(3) わたしは きのう アルバイトを して 4時半に 家に 帰りました。
(4) わたしは まいばん 本を 読んで おふろに はいります。
(5) わたしは 先週の日曜日に 車で まちに／へ 行って 買い物を しました。

**自然な日本語：練習1**

(1) わたしは ちょっと 映画が みたいです。 (2) わたしは ちょっと コーヒーが 飲みたいです。
(3) 日本語は ちょっと むずかしいです。 (4) この 車は ちょっと 高いです。
(5) わたしは 今晩 ちょっと 日本語を 勉強します。

**自然な日本語：練習2**

(1) サッカーは ちょっと・・・ (2) 土曜日は ちょっと・・・ (3) あしたは／パーティーは ちょっと・・・
(4) 来週の月曜日は／映画は ちょっと・・・ (5) リングは ちょっと・・・ (6) あしたは ちょっと・・・

**表現練習1**

(1) 6時に おきてください。 (2) この本を 読んでください。 (3) 窓を 開けてください。 (4) てがみを 書いてください。 (5) 立ってください。 (6) 待ってください。 (7) 急いでください。 (8) ゆっくり 話してください。

**表現練習2**

(1) ペンを 貸してください。 (2) 救急車を 呼んでください。 (3) ケーキを 食べてください。 (4) 窓を開けてください。 (5) 待ってください。

**表現練習3**

(1) A: 公園で バーベキューを しても いいですか。
B: はい、しても いいです。

(2) A: コンサートホールで 携帯電話を 使っても いいですか。
B: いいえ、使っては いけません。

(3) A: このへやに 入っても いいですか。
B: いいえ、入っては いけません

(4) A: ここで 写真を とっても いいですか。
B: はい、とっても いいですよ。

(5) A: 高校生が お酒を 飲んでも いいですか。
B: いいえ、飲んでは いけません。

**表現練習4**

(1) 郵便局に切手を買いに行きます。 (2) 今度の休みに スーザンは 両親に会いに シドニーに 行きます。 (3) きっさてんに 田中さんと コーヒーを飲みに 行きます。 (4) 先週 岡田さんは 町に 映画を見に 行きました。 (5) 来年 木村さんは オーストラリアに 英語を 勉強しに 来ます。 (6) 佐々木さんは ここに 日本語を教えに 来ます。 (7) 先週の週末 友達と 服を買いに シドニーに 行きませんでした。 (8) 先週の土曜日 山田さんは わたしの家に 晩ご飯を食べに 来ませんでした。 (9) 万里の長城を見に 中国に 行きたいです。 (10) 時計と CDプレーヤーを買いに 香港に行きたいです。

## 表現練習５

Sample Answers

(1) 日本語を勉強し／日本人の友達に会い etc. (2) 買い物をし etc. (3) 買い物をし／映画を見／コーヒーを飲み etc. (4) 英語を勉強し／コアラを見 (コアラ 'koala') (5) ご飯をたべ／寝／遊び etc. (6) ピラミッドを見

## 対話練習１

(1) A: たばこを吸ってもいいですか。
B: ええ、吸ってもいいですよ。
or あ、たばこをはちょっと・・・。
A: ありがとうございます。
or そうですか。わかりました。

(2) A: パーティーをしてもいいですか。
B: ええ、してもいいですよ。
or あ、パーティーはちょっと・・・。
A: ありがとうございます。
or そうですか。わかりました。

(3) A: りょうりをしてもいいですか。
B: ええ、してもいいですよ。
or あ、りょうりはちょっと・・・。
A: ありがとうございます。
or そうですか。わかりました。

(4) A: シャワーをあびてもいいですが
B: ええ、あびてもいいですよ。
or あ、シャワーはちょっと・・・。
A: ありがとうございます。
or そうですか。わかりました。

(5) A: コンピューターを使ってもいいですか。
B: ええ、使ってもいいですよ。
or あ、コンピューターはちょっと・・・。
A: ありがとうございます。or そうですか。わかりました。

## 対話練習２

Sample Answers

(1) A: 何時にファックスを送りましょうか
B: 午後2時に送ってください。
A: わかりました。

(2) A: 何時にタクシーを呼びましょうか。
B: 午前9時に呼んでください。
A: わかりました。

(3) A: いつ香港に行きましょうか。
B: 来週の月曜日に行ってください。
A: わかりました。

(4) A: 何時に会議を始めましょうか
B: 午後4時に始めてください。
A: わかりました。

(5) A: 何時に野田さんとお昼ごはんを食べましょうか。
B: １２時半ごろ食べてください。
A: わかりました。

(6) A: いつ木村さんに会ましょうか。
B: あした会ってください。
A: わかりました。

(7) A: 何時に田中さんに電話をかけましょうか。
B: 午前１０時半にかけてください。
A: わかりました。

(8) A: 何時にパーティーを始めましょうか。
B: 午後6時に始めてください。
A: わかりました。

## 対話練習３

Refer to the example.

## 練習しましょう

Sample Answers

(1) 東京で歌舞伎がみたいです。
(2) 大阪で大阪城に行きたいです。
(3) 京都で舞妓さんに会いたいです。
(4) 広島で原爆ドームに行きたいです。

# Lesson 9

## 文法練習１

(1) やすくて (2) にぎやかで (3) おおきくて (4) しずかで (5) ふるくて (6) きれいで
(7) つまらなくて (8) しんせつで (9) むずかしくて (10) りっぱで (11) あつくて (12) じみで
(13) よくて (14) にほんじんで (15) あおくて (16) せんせいで

**文法練習2**

(1) わたしの 車 は、小さくて 古いです。 (2) 東 京 は、大きくて にぎやかです。 (3) あのレストランは、おいしくて 高くないです。 (4) 山本さんの家は、とても広くて きれいです。 (5) わたしのねこは、小さくて かわいいです。 (6) 佐藤さんは、きれいで やさしいです。 (7) 鈴木さんは、 頭 がよくて かっこいいです。／ハンサムです。 (8) ジェームスはイギリス人で、ジェーンはアメリカ人で、ルーシーはオーストラリア人です。 (9) 今日 わたしは 病気で、学校に行きません。 (10) そのワインは、高くて 買いませんでした。

**文法練習3**

(1) わたしは ペンと 本を買いました。 (2) わたしは ハンバーガーと ミートパイを 食べました。 (3) わたしは きょねん 京都と 奈良に 行きました。 (4) これは図書館で あれは 寮 です。 (5) きのう、友達に会って、いっしょに コーヒーを飲みました。 (6) (その)公園は きれいで しずかです。 (7) わたしの 車 は 小さくて、古いです。 (8) よし子さんは かわいくて しんせつです。 (9) きのう 6時に 家に 帰りました。そして シャワーを浴びて 晩ご飯を食べました。 (10) きのう シドニーに 行きました。そこで 野村さんと 岡田さんに 会いました。

**文法練習4**

(1) わたし はあした 田中さんと 木村さんと 山田さんに会います。(2) わたしは きのう 日本語と 経済学を 勉 強しました。(3) わたしは テレビやDVD(ディービーディー)プレーヤーや携帯電話を買いました。(4) 岡田さんは サッカーや ホッケーや 水泳をします。 (5) 野村さんか わたしが 来 週 日本に 行きます。 (6) わたしは 大阪か 京都に／へ 行きます。

**自然な日本語：練 習 1**

(1) すみません。 注 文／お勘 定 お願いします。 (2) すみません！／ありがとう（ございます）。 (3) あ、すみません。なにか おとしましたよ。（なにか 'something'） (4) あっ、すみません！ (5) あ、すみません。

**表現練習1**

(1) のんで／のんだり　(2) みて／みたり　(3) あって／あったり　(4) まって／まったり
(5) とって／とったり　(6) おきて／おきたり　(7) はなして／はなしたり　(8) きいて／きいたり
(9) いって／いったり　(10) べんきょうして／べんきょうしたり

**表現練習2**

(1) 今 週 末は／今 週 の 週 末は、ドライブをしたり、レストランに行ったりします。(2) きょねん、日本で 友達に会ったり、買い物をしたり しました。 (3) 明日、部屋をそうじしたり、洗濯したりします。 (4) 今夜／今日の夜、家族に電話したり、友達にイーメールを書いたりします。 (5) 週 末 は たいてい ビーチに行ったり、映画を見たり、まちでコーヒーを飲んだりします。

**表現練習3**

(1) やすそうです。 (2) にぎやかそうです。 (3) あまそうです。 (4) しずかそうです。 (5) にがそうです。 (6) きれいそうです。 (7) まずそうです。 (8) しんせつそうです。 (9) あたたかそうです。 (10) りっぱそうです。 (11) さむそうです。 (12) ひまそうです。 (13) よさそうです。 (14) 上手そうです。

**表現練習4**

(1) このコートは、あたたかそうですね。 (2) そとは、さむそうですね。 (3) この時計は、高そうですね。
(4) このケーキは、あまそうですね。 (5) この映画は、おもしろそうですね。 (6) この 車 は、速そうですね。
(7) この映画は、こわそうですね。 (8) このいすは／ソファーは、らくそうですね。

**対話練習1**

〜さんの へやは どうですか。→ ふるくて くらいです。／ひろくて あかるいです。／せまいけど、きれいです。 ect.
〜さんの 大学は どうですか。→ あたらしくて おおきいです。／ふるくて きたないです。／ちいさいけど、学生がおおいです。etc.
〜さんの 車 は どうですか。→ あたらしくて はでです。／小さいけど、はやいです／大きくて おそいです。etc.
〜さんの けいたい電話は どうですか。→じみで おもいです。／あたらしくて きれいです。／ちいさいけど、おもいです。etc.
〜さんの 高校は どうでしたか。→ あたらしくて ひろかったです。／ふるくて くらかったです。／おおきいけど、しずかでした。etc.

## 対話練習２

Refer to the example.

## 調べましょう

(1) b　(2) e　(3) a　(4) f　(5) c　(6) d

# Lesson 10

## 文法練習１

(1) もちます　もった　(2) さけびます　さけんだ　(3) よみます　よんだ　(4) あいます　あった　(5) みがきます　みがいた　(6) かります　かりた　(7) かえします　かえした　(8) かえります　かえった　(9) あけます　あけた　(10) のります　のった　(11) べんきょうします　べんきょうした　(12) きます　きた

## 文法練習２

(1) この本は とても おもしろい。 (2) 私 の 車 は 古い。 (3) テストは 難 しかった。 (4) きのうは とても 忙 しかった。 (5) ここは いつも 静かだ。 (6) 私 は すしが 好きだ。 (7) さとしは とても まじめだ。 (8) あの人は 私 の 妹 だよ。 (9) 田中さんは 去年まで 学生だった。 (10) 東 京 は とても にぎやかだった。

## 文法練習３

(1) まりは いつも 朝ご飯を 食べない。 (2) 私 は パーティーに 行かない。 (3) 私 は テレビを 見ない。 (4) そのかばんを 買わなかった。 (5) 田中さんに 会わなかった。 (6) さとしは きょう 学校に 来なかった。 (7) あした テストは ない。 (8) きのう テストは なかった。

## 文法練習４

(1) きょうは 寒くない。 (2) 私 の 車 は 新 しくない。 (3) このいすは 楽じゃない。 (4) さしみは 好きじゃない。 (5) 私 の部屋は 大きくない。 (6) しげるは 学生では なかったよ。 (7) なおこは あまり まじめじゃなかった。 (8) この映画は あまり おもしろくなかったね。

## 自然な日本語：練 習 １

(1) まさとくんは エレナと 町で コーヒーを飲んでいますよ。 (2) シドニーで 新 しいかばんを 買いましたよ。
(3) 私 は 9時から 10時半まで クラスがあります。 (4) あした 鈴木先生に 電話を して ください。
(5) まさと君は 日本に 行かないと 思う。

## 自然な日本語：練 習 ２

(1) 私 学校 行きません。 (2) 私 もう 岡田さんに 会いません。 (3) 私 この映画 見ません。
(4) 田中さん 来ました。 (5) 私 魚 とても好きです。 (6) 私 昨日 田中さんに 手紙 書きました。
(7) この映画 とても おもしろかったですね。 (8) みかさん 昨日 学校に来ませんでした。

## 表現練習１

(1) すしを 食べたことが あります。 (2) 日本の時代劇を 見た ことがあります。 (3) お酒を 飲んだ ことが あります。 (4) 日本の 小 説 を 読んだ ことが あります。 (5) サーフィンを した ことが あります。

## 表現練習２

(1) この 車 が 一番 大きいです。 (2) 飛行機が 一番 大きい／はやいです。 (3) オーストラリアが 一番 大きいです。(4) この時計が この店で 一番 たかいです。 (5) まゆみさんが クラスで 一番 小さいです。

## 表現練習３

(1) 田中さんは 新 しい 車 を 買うと 思います。 (2) 田中さんは 昨日 シドニーに 行かなかったと 思います。
(3) 木村さんは 去年 学生だったと 思います。 (4) この 車 は そんなに 高くない と思います。 (5) テストは 簡単だったと 思います。 (6) 田中さんは このクラスで 一番 背が高いと 思います。

## 対話練習１

(1) A: 日本のまんがを 読んだことが ありますか。　(2) A: 日本語で Eメールを 書いたことがありますか。

B: はい、あります。or いいえ、ありません。
A: そうですか。どうでしたか。or そうですか。
B: おもしろかったです。／おもしろくありませんでした。

(3) A: ＢＢＱをしたことがありますか。
B: はい、あります。or いいえ、ありません。
A: そうですか。どこでしましたか。or そうですか。
B: 湖の近くの公園でしました。

(5) A: サーフィンをしたことがありますか。
B: はい、あります。or いいえ、ありません。
A: どうでしたか。or そうですか。
B: ちょっとこわかったけど、おもしろかったです。

B: はい、あります。or いいえ、ありません。
A: そうですか。どうでしたか。or そうですか。
B: かんたんでした。／難しかったです。

(4) A: カラオケをしたことがありますか。
B: はい、あります。or いいえ、ありません。
A: どうでしたか。or そうですか。
B: とても楽しかったです。

(6) A: ディズニーランドに行ったことがありますか。
B: はい、あります。or いいえ、ありません。
A: どうでしたか。or そうですか。
B: ひとがたくさんいて、とてもにぎやかでした。

対話練習２

Refer to the example

調べましょう

日本: 面積、337,853km$^2$／人口、約1億2650万人(126,500,000)／国花、桜と菊 (cherry blossom and chrysanthemum : Although Japan does not have an official national flower, these two flowers unofficially are recognized as such)／首都、東京／一番大きい都市、東京都市圏(Tokyo metropolitan area)／一番高い山、富士山／一番長い川、信濃川／公式言語、日本語／その他の言語、アイヌ語、琉球語、など

## Lesson 11

文法練習１

(1) 明日、札幌は雪が降るでしょう/雪でしょう。気温は1度ぐらいで、寒いでしょう。
(2) 明日、大阪は雨が降るでしょう/雨でしょう。気温は14度ぐらいで、涼しいでしょう。
(3) 明日、福岡は雨が降るでしょう/雨でしょう。気温は18度ぐらいで、暖かいでしょう。
(4) 明日、広島はくもるでしょう/くもりでしょう。気温は15度ぐらいで、(少し)涼しいでしょう。
(5) 明日、青森は晴れるでしょう/晴れでしょう。気温は7度ぐらいで、(少し)寒いでしょう。

文法練習２

(1) お疲れさま。仕事、疲れたでしょう。(2) (大丈夫ですか)。重いでしょう。(3) (外は) 寒かったでしょう。(4) (お帰りなさい。)暑かったでしょう。(5) どうでしたか。(あのレストランの料理)、おいしかったでしょう。(6) (昨日の夜)怖かったでしょう。(7) 初めての運転、おもしろかったでしょう／緊張したでしょう。(8) エッセイ、大変だったでしょう／眠いでしょう。

文法練習３

(1) 今日は日曜日だから、学校に行きません。(2) 車がないから／車を持っていないから、バスでシドニーに行きます。(3) 高かったから、そのカバンを買いませんでした。(4) 天気がいいから、公園に行きましょう。(5) 日本のアニメが好きだから、ぜんぶ見ました。

文法練習４

(1) 今食べます。おなかがすいていますから。(2) 今晩、うちで勉強します。もうすぐテストがありますから。(3) 海/海岸に行きます。今、休みですから。(4) 寝ます。疲れていますから。

自然な日本語：練習１

(1) すみません。明日はちょっと･･･ (2) すみません。日曜日はちょっと･･･ (3) お茶、もし良かったら･･･／お茶を入れたんですけど･･･ (4) (あの、/すみません) (うちに) 帰りたいんですけど･･･ (5) (あの、) これ、つまらないものですが･･･

自然な日本語：練習２

(1) わあ/まあ、きれい！ありがとう。(2) あら、山田さん、こんにちは。(3) わあ／まあ、大きい(りんご)！おいしそう！ (4) わあっ、びっくりした！ (5) わあ/まあ、(このお酒) おいしい！

### 表現練習１

(1) 話しています　(2) 買っています　(3) 待っています　(4) 泳いでいます
(5) 遊んでいます　(6) 走っています　(7) 書いています　(8) 聞いています
(9) 食べています　(10) 見ています　(11) 勉強しています　(12) 歩いています

### 表現練習２

(1) 私は今 家でばんごはんを食べています。
(2) 田中さんは今図書館で勉強しています。
(3) 山田さんは友達を待っています。
(4) 先生は漢字を書いています。
(5) 弟は公園で遊んでいます。
(6) 岡田さんは今コーヒーを飲んでいません。
(7) 加藤さんは手紙を書いていました。
(8) 野村さんは昨日の夜１０時に家でテレビを見ていました。

### 表現練習３

(1) ジョンが試験に受かったかどうか、知っていますか。
(2) これが私の本かどうか、わかりません。
(3) 図書館が遠いかどうか、わかりません。
(4) 来週クラス／授業があるかどうか、知っていますか。
(5) 田中さんがもうお昼ごはんを食べたかどうか、知っていますか。
(6) 席があるかどうか、調べます。
(7) この答えが正しいかどうか、わかりません。

### 表現練習４

(1) 母は、公務員です。
(2) 奥さんは、今どこ／どちらですか。
(3) お子さんは、どこの／どちらの学校に行っていますか。
(4) 祖母は、テレビを見ています。
(5) お兄さんのご趣味は何ですか。
(6) 主人／夫は会社員です。
(7) 祖父は、今ロンドンにいます。
(8) 妹さんは、何歳／おいくつですか。

### 対話練習１

Refer to the example.

### 対話練習２

You: 〜さんは　今　何をしていますか。

Y.P.: 家で　サンドイッチを　食べています。／へやで　おんがくを　聞いています。／家で寝ています。／まちの　プールで　泳いでいます・水泳をしています。／まちで　買い物を　しています。／まちで　アルバイトを　しています。／家で　お茶を　飲んでいます。／まちで　岡田さんを　待っています。／大学のテニスコートで　テニスをしています。

### 対話練習３

All conversations start with 'A: いま どこに いますか。'

(1)
B: カナダに います。
A: 何をしていますか。
B: スキーを　しています。
A: わあ、かっこいいですね。

(2)
B: パリに います。
A: 何をしていますか。
B: 赤ワインを飲んで、ケーキを食べています。
A: わあ、いいですね。フランスのワインは、おいしいでしょう。

(3)
B: オーストラリアに います。
A: 何をしていますか。
B: エアーズロックやカンガルーを、見ています。
A: わあ、すごいですね。写真をとって、見せてくださいね。

(4)
B: 東京に います。
A: 何をしていますか。
B: 家族に　手紙を書いています。
A: そうですか。〜さんは、やさしいですね。

(5)
B: ハワイに います。
A: 何をしていますか。
B: サーフィンを　しています。
A: わあ、すごいですね。私はサーフィンを、したことがありません。

(6)
B: エジプトに います。
B: ピラミッドを、見ています。
A: わあ、本当ですか。大きいでしょう。

(7)
B: サモアに います。
A: 何をしていますか。
B: ダンスをしています。
A: わあ、すてきですね。

(8)
B: 香港に います。
A: 何をしていますか。
B: 買い物を　しています。
A: わあ、いいですね。私も香港に行きたいです。

**調べましょう**

Entrance 玄関; Garden 庭; Living room 居間; Closet 押入れ; Alcove 床の間; Bathroom 風呂場; Mat in living room 畳 ; Corridor 廊下 ; Stairs 階段; Japanese style room 日本間・和室; Drawing room 応接間・客間; Kitchen 台 所; Toilet お手洗い・トイレ; Heated table 火燵

## Lesson 12

**文法練習１**

(1) 本田さんは風邪を引いたと聞きました。 (2) 木村さんのあかちゃんは、かわいいと思います。 (3) 田中さんが好きだと、ラブレターに書きました。 (4) 吉田さんはとても親切だと聞きました。 (5) 松田さんは、東京は寒いと言いました。 (6) 新しい家は買わないと木村さんに伝えてください。 (7) 会議は２時だと田中さんに伝えてください。

**文法練習２**

(1) 鈴木さんは 今 熱があるそうです。（熱がある= have a fever） (2) 佐藤さんは親切だそうです。 (3) 野田さんは、昨日テニスをしたそうです。 (4) よしこさんは高校生だそうです。 (5) しげるさんは 今朝６時半に起きたそうです。

**文法練習３**

(1) 岡田さんは、このケーキはおいしいと言いました。 (2) 私は、先週結婚したと はがきに書きました。 (3) 今日の朝、町で事故があったそうです。 (4) 木村さんは有名な作曲家だそうです。 (5) この映画はおもしろくないと山田さんに伝えてください。 (6) 私はここで待っているとみんなに言ってください。 (7) 私は、あしたは雨だろうと聞きました。

**自然な日本語：練習１**

(1) → 魚ですか。魚はちょっと・・・。／→ 魚ですか。ええ、大好きです。

(2) → １２時半ですか。その時間はちょっと・・・。／→ 昼ごはんですか。いいですね。

(3) → あのカフェですか。よさそうですね。／→ コーヒーですか。いいですね。行きましょう。

(4) → 写真ですか。いいですよ。

(5) → トイレですか。トイレは５階にありますよ。

(6) → 日本語のテストですか。来週の木曜日ですよ。

(7) → パリですか。いいですね。／→ ワインですか。フランスのワインはおいしいでしょう。

(8) → 来週ですか。それは急ですね。 （急 = sudden）／→ アフリカですか。遠いですね。

**表現練習１**

(1) ここに、お名前をお書きください。 (2) 少々お待ちください。(少々 a bit) (3) 日本語でお話ください。 (4) これはフランスのワインです。お試しください。 (5) このりんごをお召し上がりください。 (6) 午後７時ごろ、おいでください。 (7) こちらをご覧ください。

**表現練習２**

Refer to the examples.

**表現練習３**

(1) 田中さんは、そう言いました。 (2) この車をどう思いますか。 (3) 私もそう思います。 (4) これは、どういう／どんな映画ですか。 (5) こういう／こんな映画は好きじゃありません。 (6) こういう／こんな食べ物は初めてです。

**対話練習１**

(1) A: 田中さん、機嫌が悪いですね。
B: ええ、車がこわれたそうです。
A: あ、そうですか。それは大変でしたね。

(2) A: 田中さん、疲れていますね。
B: ええ、１０時間もアルバイトしたそうですよ。
A: わあ、それは大変でしたね。

(3) A: 田中さん、笑っていますね。
B: ええ、テストで１００点とったそうです。
A: わあ、すごいですね。

(4) A: 田中さん、昨日、クラスに来ませんでしたね。
B: ええ、病気だったそうです。
A: そうですか。大丈夫でしょうか。

(5) A: 田中さん、ゆうべ、パーティーに来ませんでしたね。
B: ええ、忙しかったそうです。
A: あ、そうですか。残念でしたね。

**対話練習２**

Refer to the example.

**対話練習３**

All conversation starts with 'You：もしもし、[your name]と申しますが、直美さん、いらっしゃいますか。'

(1) Y.P.： はい、私ですが・・・。
You： ああ、直美さん、こんばんは。
Y.P.： こんばんは。
You： 明日のことなんですが、大学の図書館で、待っていますね。
Y.P.： 大学の図書館ですね。わかりました。どうもありがとう。
You： じゃ、明日。おやすみなさい。
Y.P.： おやすみなさい。

(2) Y.P.： 直美ですか。直美は、いま、出かけています。１０時までアルバイトなんです。
You： そうですか。
Y.P.： 何か伝えましょうか。
You： あ、はい。明日のことなんですが、１０時に本田さんが学校に来るとお伝えください。
Y.P.： １０時ですね。わかりました。そう伝えます。
You： よろしくお願いします。では、失礼します。
Y.P.： 失礼します。

(3) Y.P.： 姉ですか。ええと、姉は、いま、部屋で勉強しています。ちょっと待ってください。呼んできます。
You： あ、すみません。
Y.P.： はい、電話、変わりました。直美です。
You： あ、直美さん、こんにちは。
Y.P.： こんにちは。
You： あの〜、山田さんのことなんですが、昨日、山田さんに会いませんでした。
Y.P.： あ、そうだったんですか。はい、わかりました。 (closing is the same as (1))

(4) Y.P.： 直美ですか。直美は、買い物に行って、まだ帰ってきていないんですよ。
You： そうですか。
Y.P.： 何か伝えましょうか。
You： あ、はい。明日のことなんですが、映画は４時からだとお伝えください。
Y.P.： 映画は４時からですね。わかりました。そう伝えます。 (closing is the same as (2))

(5) Y.P.： 直美ですか。直美は、いま、出かけています。今どこにいるか、ちょっとわかりません。
You： そうですか。
Y.P.： 何か伝えましょうか。
You： あ、はい来週のことなんですが、来週、テストはないとお伝えください。
Y.P.： 来週、テストはないんですね。わかりました。そう伝えます。 (closing is the same as (2))

**調べましょう**

(a) 公衆電話 (b) 携帯電話 (c) 電話番号 (d) 電話帳 (e) 留守番電話 (f) 伝言 (g) 電話をかける／する
(h) 電話をもらう (i) 木村さんに電話をかける／する (j) 話中 (k) 長距離電話 (l) 国際電話

**練習（れんしゅう）しましょう**

(a) ゼロさんの　ななよんろくさんの　ろくさんきゅうはち

(b) ゼロろくの　ろくいちにごの　さんにゼロご

(c) ゼロにごの　さんにさんよん　いちななにご

(d) ゼロさんゼロよん　ごろくよんろく　よんゼロななきゅう

(e) はちいちの　さんの　ろくさんろくはちの　さんいちさんに

(f) ろくいちの　にの　さんにろくごの　なななゼロご

(g) 電話番号（でんわばんごう）は何番（なんばん）ですか。電話番号（でんわばんごう）をおしえてください。

(h) 私（わたし）の電話番号（でんわばんごう）は、ゼロよんゼロいち　ごよんごさん　ゼロゼロろくです。

(i) 消防署（しょうぼうしょ）の電話番号（でんわばんごう）を知（し）っていますか。

(j) 消防署（しょうぼうしょ）の電話番号（でんわばんごう）は　いちいちきゅうです。

(k) 田中（たなか）さんの　電話番号（でんわばんごう）は、ゼロにの　きゅうごよんななの　いちにさんよんです。

## Lesson 13

**文法練習（ぶんぽうれんしゅう）1**

(1) 何（なに）を (2) 誰（だれ）が (3) 何時（なんじ）に (4) どこで (5) どう (6) どこ (7) なぜ/どうして (8) 何（なに）を

**文法練習（ぶんぽうれんしゅう）2**

(1) Q: こんばん、何（なに）をしますか。
A: 家（いえ）でテレビを見（み）ます。

(2) Q: 今日（きょう）は、何時（なんじ）に朝（あさ）ご飯（はん）を食（た）べましたか。
A: ７時（じ）に食（た）べました。

(3) Q: だれが、この本（ほん）を書（か）きましたか。
A: 私（わたし）の先生（せんせい）が書（か）きました。

(4) Q: これはだれの車（くるま）ですか。
A: 父（ちち）の車（くるま）です。

(5) Q: 試験（しけん）はいつですか。
A: 来週（らいしゅう）の水曜日（すいようび）です。

(6) Q: 映画（えいが）はどうでしたか。
A: とてもおもしろかったです。

(7) Q: この車（くるま）は、いくらでしたか。
A: １２０万円（まんえん）でした。

(8) Q: どうして新（あたら）しい車（くるま）を買（か）いましたか。
A: 宝（たから）くじに当（あ）たりましたから！
(宝（たから）くじに当（あ）たる 'win lottery')

(9) Q: いつ木村（きむら）さんに会（あ）いましたか。
A: 月曜日（げつようび）に会（あ）いました。

(10) Q: 山田（やまだ）さんは、時計（とけい）をいくつ持（も）っていますか。
A: 二（ふた）つ持（も）っています。

**文法練習（ぶんぽうれんしゅう）3**

(1) → はい、見（み）ませんでした。
→ いいえ、見（み）ました。

(2) → はい、来（き）ませんでした。
→ いいえ、来（き）ました。

(3) → はい、降（ふ）りませんでした。
→ いいえ、降（ふ）りました。

(4) → はい、電話（でんわ）しませんでした。
→ いいえ、電話（でんわ）しました。

(5) → はい、会（あ）いませんでした。
→ いいえ、会（あ）いました。

(6) → はい、おもしろくありませんでした。
→ いいえ、おもしろかったです。

(7) → はい、学生（がくせい）ではありませんでした。
→ いいえ、学生（がくせい）でした。

(8) → はい、食（た）べません。
→ いいえ、食（た）べます。

**文法練習（ぶんぽうれんしゅう）4**

(1) 今晩（こんばん）、木村（きむら）さんもいっしょに食事（しょくじ）をするんですか。

(2) この映画（えいが）はもう３回（かい）見（み）たんです。

(3) きのう、頭（あたま）が痛（いた）くて学校（がっこう）に来（こ）なかったんです。

(4) ここで、この車（くるま）が一番速（いちばんはや）いんです。

(5) この町（まち）は、ほんとうに賑（にぎ）やかなんですね。

(6) 田中（たなか）さんは、とても親切（しんせつ）だったんです。

(7) これは私（わたし）のテレビなんです。

(8) あの人（ひと）は去年（きょねん）、私（わたし）の先生（せんせい）だったんです。

**自然（しぜん）な日本語（にほんご）：練習（れんしゅう）1**

(1) 去年（きょねん）、木村（きむら）さんは日本（にほん）にいましたけど、弟（おとうと）さんはいませんでした。 (2) 昨日（きのう）、初（はじ）めて野村（のむら）さんに会（あ）いましたけど、とても親切（しんせつ）でした。 (3) 先週（せんしゅう）、新（あたら）しい自転車（じてんしゃ）を買（か）いましたけど、日本製（にほんせい）でした。

(4) この映画（えいが）を見（み）たいんですけど・・・。 (5) ゆみさん、とてもかわいいですけど・・・。

## 表現練習 1

(1) ・戸田さんは木村さんに、本をあげました。
・木村さんは戸田さんに、本をもらいました。

(2) ・しげるさんは 私 に、ぼうしをくれました。
・ 私 はしげるさんに、ぼうしをもらいました。

(3) ・ 私 はまゆみさんに、ケーキをあげました。
・まゆみ cannot be the subject.

(4) ・坂田さんは和田さんに、りんごをもらいました。
・和田さんは坂田さんに、りんごをあげました。

(5) ・戸田さんは高田さんに、花をもらいました。
・高田さんは戸田さんに、花をあげました。

## 表現練習 2

(1) ここで写真を撮らないでください。 (2) この公園で、野球をしないでください。 (3) 運転中、電話をしないでください。 (4) ここに 車 を停めないでください。 (5) 絵をさわらないでください。

## 表現練習 3

(1) そんなこと、言わないでください。 (2) 遠慮しないでください。 (3) 泣かないでください。 (4) 行かないでください。 (5) 教科書を忘れないでください。 (6) 図書館で、大声で話さないでください。 (7) 冗談を言わないでください。

## 表現練習 4

(1) これも田中さんの 車 だし、あれも田中さんのです。 (2) 今日はコーヒーも飲んだし、ハンバーガーも食べました。 (3) 東 京 にも行ったし、京都にも行きました。でも、札幌には行きませんでした。 (4) 今日は日曜日だし、ゆっくり休んでください。 (5) 山本さんはハンサムだし、お金もあるし、本当にうらやましいです。 (6) おなかもすいたし、晩ご飯を食べましょう。 (7) 宿 題も終わったし、テレビを見ましょう。

## 表現練習 5

(1) 就 職 、おめでとう！ (2) お大事に。 (3) あけましておめでとうございます。 (4) このたびは、ご 愁 傷 さまでした。／お悔やみ申し上げます。 (5) 結婚、おめでとう！

## 対話練習 1

Refer to the example.

## 対話練習 2

All conversations start with ‘どうしたんですか’. There is more than one possibility for the comment.

＜出来事＞
・猫が死んだんです。
・あした面接があるんです。／あしたお見合いがあるんです。
・ふられたんです。／試験の点数がわるいんです。
・あした 大事な試験があるんです。
・コンピューターが壊れたんです。

＜コメント＞
→ 泣かないでください。
→ 緊張しないでください。
→ 落ち込まないでください。
→ 遅くまで 勉 強 しないでください。
→ 心配しないでください。

## 練 習しましょう

Refer to the example.

# Lesson 14

## 文法練習 1

(1) 私 があした会う (2) 木村さんに会った (3) この本を書いた (4) 大学から遠い (5) 髪が長い (6) 日本料理が好きな (7) 日本でとても有名な (8) 医者の (9) 去 年 私 の日本語の先生だった

## 文法練習 2

(1) 戸田さんは、 私 がシドニーで会った人です。 (2) これは 私 がよく行くきっさてんです。 (3) ギターをひいている人は、 私 の友達です。 (4) これは 私 が去年住んでいだ家です。 (5) これは鈴木さんが書いた手紙です。

**文法練習３**

私は　きのう　(i) 去年　札幌から来た　田中さんと　(ii) 上野の 私 の家で　(iii) 私 が京都で買ったお茶を飲みました。

**自然な日本語：練 習 1**

(1) ね・ね　(2) ね　(3) よ　(4) よ　(5) よ／ね　(6) よ　(7) ね・よ　(8) ね・ね　(9) よ (10) ね

**表 現 練 習 1**

(1) テレビでも見たら (どう)？　(2) 音楽でも聴いたらどうですか。　(3) 料理でもしたら (どう)？
(4) 部屋のそうじでもしたら？　(5) 旅行にでも行ったらどうですか。

**表 現 練 習 2**

(1) 書いてくれませんか。　(2) 行ってくれない？　(3) 書いていただけませんか。　(4) 読んでくれない？

**表 現 練 習 3**

(1) A: ごめん。この日本語の手紙、ちょっと読んでくれない？
B: あ、いいよ。　or ごめん。 私 も分からない。

(2) A: いっしょに図書館に行ってくれない？
B: あ、いいよ。
or ごめん、今ちょっと急いでいるから…。

(3) A: ごめん。ちょっとゆっくり話してくれない？
B: うん、わかった。

(4) A: ごめん。ちょっとペン貸してくれない？
B: いいよ、はい。 or ごめん、私 も持ってない。

(5) A: ごめん。ちょっと塩とってくれない？
B: はい、どうぞ。

(6) A: ごめん。ちょっと窓あけてくれない？
B: あ、いいよ。

(7) A: ごめん。ちょっとヒーターつけてくれない？
B: あ、いいよ。

**表 現 練 習 4**

(1) ペンが３本あります。　(2) じしょが５冊あります。　(3) シーディーが２３枚あります。
(4) ぼうしが４つあります。　(5) ねこが３匹と犬が６匹います。

**表 現 練 習 5**

(1) 今朝、りんご３つを食べました。　(2) 昨日、５人の友達に会いました。　(3) 今日、コーヒーを２杯飲みました。(4) 田中さんは昨日、映画を２本見ました。　(5) 私 は猫７匹をかっています（もっています）。

**対話練習１**

～さんがよく行くショッピングセンターは、どこですか。／～さんがいつも見るテレビ番組は、何ですか。／～さんがよくするスポーツは、何ですか。／～さんがよく作る食べ物は、何ですか。／～さんが、いつも友達と行くきっさてんは、どこですか。／～さんがよく聞く音楽は、何ですか。

**対話練習２**

A: おいしい日本料理が食べたいです。
B: 駅前の日本料理屋に行ってみたら、どうですか。

A: 宿 題 が 難 しいです。
B: 先生に質問したら、どうですか。

A: 暑いです。
B: 窓を開けたら、どうですか。

A: 日本人の彼氏／彼女がほしいです。
B: 日本に行ったら、どうですか。

A: コアラが見たいです。
B: オーストラリアに行ったら、どうですか。

A: 日本語を 勉 強 したいです。
B: 日本語のクラスをとったら、どうですか。

**対話練習３**

A: 日本語の辞書が何冊ありますか。
B: ２冊あります。／１冊もありません。

A: 兄 弟 は何人いますか。
B: ３人います。／１人もいません。

A: 日本の歌のＣＤが、何枚ありますか。
B: ５０枚あります。／１枚もありません。

A: 犬を何匹、飼っていますか。
B: ２匹飼っています。／１匹も飼っていません。

A: コンピューターが何台ありますか。
B: ３台あります。／１台もありません。

A: 今月、映画を何本見ましたか。
B: ６本見ました。／１本も見ていません。

**調べましょう**

Bakery パン屋 ／ Bank 銀行 ／ Book shop 本屋 ／ Butcher 肉屋 ／ Cake shop ケーキ屋 ／ Convenience store コンビニエンスストア ／ Coffee shop きっさてん ／ Deli 弁当屋 ／ Electric shop 電気屋 ／ Family restaurant ファミリーレストラン ／ Fish shop 魚屋 ／ Florist 花屋 ／ Hospital 病院 ／ Pharmacy 薬屋・薬局 ／ Post office 郵便局 ／ Police box 交番 ／ Shoe shop くつ屋 ／ Stationary shop 文房具屋 ／ Supermarket スーパー ／ Sushi shop すし屋 ／ Toy shop おもちゃ屋 ／ Vegetable shop 八百屋

**練習しましょう**

Hospital 病院：まっすぐ行って、１つ目の信号を左に曲がってください。そうすると、右に病院があります。／ Cake ケーキ屋： まっすぐ行って、１つ目の信号を右に曲がってください。そうすると、左にケーキ屋があります。薬局のとなりです。 ／ Sushi すし屋：まっすぐ行って、１つ目の信号を右に曲がってください。次の信号をまっすぐ行ってください。そうすると、左にすし屋があります。 ／ Soba そば屋：(see the expressions for Sushi shop and add) すし屋は、そば屋のとなりです。 ／ Convenience store コンビニエンスストア： まっすぐ行って、２つ目の信号を右に曲がってください。そうすると、左にコンビニエンスストアがあります。 ／ Florist 花屋：まっすぐ行って、２つ目の信号を右に曲がってください。そうすると、右に花屋があります。／ Bank 銀行：(see the expressions for Florist and add) 銀行は花屋のとなりです。 ／ Butcher 肉屋：まっすぐ行って、２つ目の信号を右に曲がって、しばらくまっすぐ行ってください。そうすると、右に肉屋があります。 ／ Police 交番： まっすぐ行って、２つ目の信号を左に曲がってください。そうすると、右に交番があります。 ／ Book 本屋：(see the expressions for Police and add) 本屋は、交番のとなりです。 ／ Post office 郵便局：まっすぐ行って、２つ目の信号を右に曲がって、しばらく歩いてください。そうすると、左に郵便局があります。／ Fish 魚屋：まっすぐ行って、３つ目の信号を右に曲がってください。そうすると、右に魚屋があります。 ／ Supermarket スーパー：(see the expressions for Fish shop and add) スーパーは魚屋のとなりです。 ／ Family restaurant ファミリーレストラン： (see the expressions for Fish shop and add) ファミリーレストランは魚屋のとなりのとなりです。

## Lesson 15

**文法練習１**

(1) A: 昨日、その店で何か買いましたか。
B: はい、買いました。
A: 何を買いましたか？
B: ペンとＣＤを買いました。

(2) 休みの間、どこかへ行きましたか。
(3) 今晩、何か作りたいです。
(4) 私の本はこの部屋のどこかにあります。
(5) その話をだれかにしましたか？
(6) いつか田中さんに会いたいです。

**文法練習２**

(1) 昨日、その店で、何も買いませんでした。 (2) 休みの間、どこにも行きませんでした。 (3) 今晩、何も作りません。 (4) 私の本は、この部屋のどこにもありません。 (5) どこにも行きたくありません。 (6) それはだれにも話しませんでした。 (7) 昨日、だれにも会いませんでした。

**文法練習３**

(1) A: 何を食べたいですか。
B: 何でもいいです。

(2) A: どこで、食べたいですか。
B: どこでもいいです。

(3) A: いつ、食べたいですか。
B: いつでもいいです。

(4) A: だれと、食べたいですか。
B: だれでもいいです。

(5) 何でも１００円です。

**自然な日本語：練習１**

(1) A: きょう、学校 行く？
B: うん、行くよ。

(2) A: いい天気だね。
B: そうだね。

(3) A: いま 何時？
B: いま？ 3時だよ。

(4) A: ゆうべ、田中さんに会った？
B: 田中さん？うん、会ったよ。

(5) A: 日本、行ったことある？
B: ううん、ない。

(6) A: さしみ、好き？
B: あ、食べるけど、あまり好きじゃない。

(7) A: 映画、どうだった？
B: とてもおもしろかったよ。

(8) A: あの人、誰？
B: たかし君のお父さんだよ。

(9) A: あの建物、何？
B: あれ？ あれは、図書館だよ。

(10) A: あした、いっしょに勉強しよう。
B: うん、そうしよう。

(11) A: 日本にいる田中さんに、手紙 書こうか。
B: いいね。

**表現練習１**

(1) このシャツは私に大きすぎます。 (2) この宝石は高すぎます。 (3) このケーキはあますぎます。 (4) 食べすぎました。 (5) このテストは、むずかしすぎます。 (6) ゆうべは、飲みすぎました。 (7) このごろ、いそがしすぎます。 (8) この電車は混みすぎです。 (9) 今日は起きるのが、おそすぎました。

**表現練習２**

(1) 食事ですか。じゃあ、ハンバーガーにしましょうか。 (2) 映画ですか。じゃあ、「００７」にしましょうか。
(3) ピクニックですか。じゃあ、湖の近くの公園にしましょうか。
(4) ピクニックですか。じゃあ今週の土曜日にしましょうか。
(5) あしたですか。じゃあ、夜８時にしましょうか。 (6) あしたですか。じゃあ、図書館の前にしましょうか。

**表現練習３**

(1) あしたテストなので、今晩は勉強しなければなりません。(2) 今日は雨が降っているので、車で学校に行かなければなりません。 (3) 来年、旅行したいので、たくさんお金を稼がなければなりません。 (4) お金がないので、アルバイトをしなければなりません。 (5) あした、友達が家に来るので、家をそうじしなければなりません。 (6) あした、朝が早いので、今晩は早く寝なければなりません。 (7) 車が故障したので、学校に歩いていかなければなりません。

**対話練習１**

Refer to the example.

**対話練習２**

さとし： きょうは、どこ行く？
まり： 私は、どこでもいいけど・・・。
さとし： そう。じゃあ、原宿にでも行こうか。
まり： いいね。ここから原宿までどのくらいかかる？
さとし： 電車で１時間半ぐらいかかると思う。
まり： ずいぶん遠いね。
さとし： うん。でも、とても楽しいと思うよ。

[クレープの店で]
さとし： まり、よく食べるね。
まり： とてもおいしい。
さとし： でも、もう５枚目だよ。
まり： まだ大丈夫よ。
さとし： ・・・

[原宿で]
まり： うわー、いろんなお店があるね。
さとし： そうだね。まり、おなか空いた？
まり： うん。少し空いた。
さとし： じゃ、何か食べない？
まり： そうね。
さとし： 何にしようか。
まり： そうね、私は何でもいいけど・・・。
さとし： じゃあ、せっかく原宿にいるから クレープにしない？
まり： あ、いいね。そうしよう。

**調しましょう**

Refer to the example.

## Lesson 16

### 文法練習1

| | | | | |
|---|---|---|---|---|
| 行く | 行ったら | 行くと | 行けば | 行くなら |
| 行かない | 行かなかったら | 行かないと | 行かなければ | 行かないなら |
| 食べる | 食べたら | 食べると | 食べれば | 食べるなら |
| する | したら | すると | すれば | するなら |
| 来る | 来たら | 来ると | 来れば | 来るなら |
| 高い | 高かったら | 高いと | 高ければ | 高いなら |
| 静かな | 静かだったら | 静かだと | 静かであれば | 静かなら |
| 学生だ | 学生だったら | 学生だと | 学生であれば | 学生なら |

### 文法練習2

(1) 着いたら　(2) 足すと　(3) 日本料理なら　(4) 話せば　(5) 終わったら　(6) 終わると　(7) 買うなら

### 自然な日本語：練習

(1) つけてあげました。　(2) 教えてくれました。　(3) なおしてもらいました。　(4) 買ってくれました。
(5) 買ってもらいました。

### 表現練習1

(1) 北海道のほうが東京より広いです。(2) 日本は、7月のほうが12月より暑いです。　(3) 山田さんのほうが、中田さんより背が高いです。(4) 本田さんの車のほうが、田中さんの車より新しいです。(5) てんぷら定食のほうがスパゲッティーより高いです。

### 表現練習2

(1) A: バスケットボールと、野球ボールと、どちらが大きいですか。
　B: バスケットボールのほうが野球ボールより、ずっと大きいです。
(2) A: たかし君のへやと、まなぶ君のへやと、どちらがきれいですか。
　B: たかし君のへやのほうが、まなぶ君のへやより、ずっときれいです。
(3) A: すしとてんぷらと、どちらが高いですか。
　B: てんぷらのほうが高いです。
(4) A: 東京から名古屋までと、東京から大阪までと、どちらが遠いですか。
　B: 東京から大阪までのほうが、遠いです。
(5) A: 山田さんと中田さんと、どちらが背が高いですか。
　B: 山田さんのほうが、背が高いです。

### 表現練習3

(1) 学校に行く前、7時半に朝御飯を食べます。／7時半に朝御飯を食べた後、学校に行きます。(2) 友達に会う前に、買い物をします。／買い物をした後、友達に会います。　(3) 寝る前に、薬を飲みます。／薬を飲んだ後、寝ます。(4) 走る前に、たくさん水を飲みます。／たくさん水を飲んだ後、走ります。(5) 昨日、映画を見に行く前に、宿題をしました。／昨日、宿題をした後、映画を見に行きました。

### 表現練習4

(1) まさとさんは、塾に行って毎日遅くまで勉強したって聞きました。(2) 日本語はあまり難しくないって書きました。　(3) 岡田さんは、この映画はおもしろいって言いました。(4) 野村さんは、昨日東京は雨だったって言いました。(5) 花子さんに、今日私は忙しいって伝えてください。　(6) このコンピューター、安かったって。　(7) 田中さん、来週の月曜日に、インドネシアに行くって。

### 表現練習5

(1) 私は日本料理をよく食べます。すしとか、てんぷらとか。　(2) 私はトトロとかナウシカとか、日本のアニメをよく見ます。(3) 昨日、友達に会いました。田中さんとか、川田さんとか。(4) いろんな国に行きたいです。

中国とかインドとか。(5) 週末は、映画を見るとかケーキを作るとか、いろいろしました。(6) 休みの間、いろいろする予定です。アルバイトするとか旅行するとか。

**対話練習1**

Refer to the example.

(1) ゆうべ晩ご飯の後　(2) ゆうべ寝る前　(3) このクラスに来る前　(4) このクラスが終わった後

**対話練習2**

Refer to the following expressions.

(1) 来る／来ない／来た／来なかった　(2) 洗濯する／洗濯しない／洗濯した／洗濯しなかった　(3) そうじする／そうじしない／そうじした／そうじしなかった　(4) 書く／書かない／書いた／書かなかった　(5) 会う／会わない／会った／会わなかった　(6) 起きる／起きない／起きた／起きなかった　(7) 寝る／寝ない／寝た／寝なかった (8) 食べる／食べない／食べた／食べなかった (9) 見る／見ない／見た／見なかった (10) 行く／行かない／行った／行かなかった　(11) 買う／買わない／買った／買わなかった

**対話練習3**

Refer to the example. For (4) and (5), use 'ドライブを<u>するのと</u>、家でDVDを<u>見るのと</u>' and '買い物を<u>するのと</u>、映画を<u>見るのと</u>' respectively.

**調べましょう**

1. Kindergarten 幼稚園 ／ Primary school 小学校 (1〜6年生) ／ Junior high school 中学校 (1〜3年生) ／ Senior high school 高校 (高等学校) (1〜3年生) ／ University (undergraduate) 大学 (1〜4年生) ／ Postgraduate (M.A.) 大学院修士課程 ／ Postgraduate (PhD) 大学院博士課程

2. Art 美術／ Chemistry 化学／ English 英語／ Ethics 倫理／ Geography 地理／ Home science 家庭科／ Japanese as a national language 国語／ Japanese history 日本史／ Mathematics 数学／ Music 音楽／ Physical education 体育／ Physics 物理／ World history 世界史

## Lesson 17

**文法練習1**

(1) きのう、ひとりで映画を見に行きました。(2) 先週、日本から両親が来ました。(3) いま、町で、友達と買い物をしています。(4) 来年、大学で歴史を勉強します。(5) いま、鈴木さんは、アメリカにいます。(6) 戸田さんは、ここに来ています。 (7) 姉は今、アルバイトに行っています。(8) 山田さんは、お母さんにとてもよく似ています。

**文法練習2**

(1) はい、もう、読みました。/ いいえ、まだ、読んでいません。(2) はい、もう、終わりました。/ いいえ、まだ、終わっていません。 (3) はい、もう、聞きました。/ いいえ、まだ、聞いていません。 (4) はい、もう、電話しました。/ いいえ、まだ、電話していません。 (5) はい、もう、見ました。/ いいえ、まだ、見ていません。 (6) はい、もう、送りました。/ いいえ、まだ、送っていません。 (7) はい、もう、会いました。/ いいえ、まだ、会っていません。 (8) はい、もう、行きました。/ いいえ、まだ、行っていません。

**自然な日本語：練習1**

(1) ねこ → ニャーニャー ／ からす → カーカー ／ うし → モーモー ／ ぶた → ブーブー

(2) のど → からから ／ 雨 → ざあざあ／ 日本語 → ぺらぺら ／ 文句 → ぶつぶつ ／ おなか → ぺこぺこ

**自然な日本語：練習2**

(1) のどがからからです。水をください。 (2) そとは雨が、ざあざあ降っています。(3) おなかがぺこぺこだったので、ひとりで晩ごはんを食べました。 (4) 山田さんはフランス語がぺらぺらです。 (5) とてもおかしかったので、げらげら笑いました。

**表現練習1**

(1) 歯が痛いです。　(2) 熱が(38.5度)あります。　(3) せきが出ます。

(4) 寒気がします。　(5) おなかが痛いです。

**表現練習２**

(1) – (a) 警察署に行ったほうがいいですよ。 (2) – (c) 地図を見たほうがいいですよ。 (3) – (f) 病院に行ったほうがいいですよ。 (4) – (b) 学校で習ったほうがいいですよ。 (5) – (e) 早く寝たほうがいいですよ。 (6) – (h) 今晩、勉強したほうがいいですよ。 (7) – (g) 禁煙したほうがいいですよ。 (8) – (i) 厚着にしたほうがいいですよ。

**表現練習３**

(1) レストランの中で、たばこを吸わないほうがいいですよ。 (2) 鈴木さんは昼寝をしているので、部屋に行かないほうがいいですよ。 (3) この水は古いので、飲まないほうがいいですよ。 (4) 運動しすぎないほうがいいですよ。 (5) 寝すぎないほうがいいですよ。

**表現練習４**

(1) 田中さんは、猫を７匹も飼っています。 (2) あした、テストが５時間もあります。 (3) 田中さんは、背丈が１９０cmもあります。 (4) 野村さんの背丈は、１７５cmはあるでしょう。(5) この車、１５０万円はすると思いますよ。 (6) 昨日のパーティーに、５人しか来ませんでした。 (7) コーヒーをまだ半分しか飲んでいません。 (8) 朝はたいていミルクしか飲みません。何も食べません。

**対話練習１**

A: クラスに遅れています。
B: 走ったほうがいいですよ。

A: 財布をなくしました。
B: 警察に行ったほうがいいですよ。

A: 寒いです。
B: 厚着にしたほうがいいですよ。

A: あした、日本語のオーラルテストがあります。
B: きょう、たくさん練習したほうがいいですよ。

A: 熱があります。
B: 病院に行ったほうがいいですよ。

A: 日本語をりゅうちょうに話したいです。
B: 日本人の友達と、話したほうがいいですよ。

**対話練習２**

A: のどが痛いです。
B: カラオケをしないほうがいいですよ。

A: テレビを見すぎて、目がつかれています。
B: 今日はあまり目を使わないほうがいいですよ。

A: とても疲れています。
B: 仕事をしすぎないほうがいいですよ。

A: 昨日、ワインを飲みすぎました。
B: あまり飲みすぎないほうがいいですよ。

A: 二日酔いです。
B: 今日は出かけないほうがいいですよ。

A: 銀行口座に、ぜんぜんお金がありません。
B: お金を使わないほうがいいですよ。

**対話練習３**

(1) A: あした試験だけど、もう勉強した？
B: 勉強？うん、もうしたよ。
or 勉強？ううん、まだしていない。

(2) A: この映画、おもしろそうだけど、もう見た？
B: この映画？うん、もう見たよ。
or この映画？ううん、まだみていない。

(3) A: 今日、母の日だけど、プレゼント、もう買った？
B: プレゼント？うん、もう買ったよ。
or プレゼント？ううん、まだ買っていない。

(4) A: 運転免許をとるのは難しいって聞いたけど、もうとった？
B: 運転免許？うん、もうとったよ。
or ううん、まだとっていない。

(5) A: 来週、出発だけど、もう切符、予約した？
B: 切符？うん、もう予約したよ。
or 切符？ううん、まだ予約していない。

(6) A: 今日、お父さんの誕生日だけど、京都のお父さんに、もう電話した？
B: 電話？うん、もうしたよ。
or 電話？ううん、まだしていない。

(7) A: もうすぐ晩ごはんだけど、もう作った？
B: 晩ごはん？うん、もう作ったよ。
or 晩ごはん？ううん、まだ作っていない。

(8) A: 今日の新聞、もう読んだ？
B: 新聞？うん、読んだよ。
or 新聞？ううん、まだ読んでいない。

**調べましょう**

(1) hair 髪の毛／ eyes 目／nose 鼻／ ears 耳／ mouth 口／ head 頭 ／ eyelash まつ毛 ／ cheek 頬／ teeth 歯／ face 顔／ eyelid まぶた／ chin あご／ forehead おでこ ／ eyebrow 眉毛／ tongue 舌／ neck 首

(2)　arms 腕／hand 手／elbow 肘／stomach おなか／bottom お尻／knee 膝／feet 足／shoulder 肩／thighs 太もも／ankle 足首／chest 胸／fingers 指／heel かかと／toe つま先

### 練習しましょう

**鼻・目・鼻・目・耳・口・手・足**

## Lesson 18

### 文法練習 1

(1) このごろ、だいぶ寒くなってきましたね。(2) 来週、日本から山田さんが訪ねてきます。(3) 昨日、町に、中村さんと行ってきました。(4) 猫は、三浦さんに、連いていきました。(5) 鈴木さんの車が、遠ざかっていきました。

### 文法練習 2

(1) 高田さんは、ご飯をぜんぶたべてしまいました。(2) 今日は誰にも会いたくないと思っていたら、道で知っている人に会ってしまいました。(3) 疲れていたので、いつの間にか寝てしまいました。(4) 前田さんが明日パーティーに来るかどうか、電話して聞いてみます。(5) となりの家がうるさいので、窓をあけて見てみました。(6) おいしいかどうか、味見をしてみてください。(7) 今晩は、好きな映画を見たいので、早く宿題を済ませておきます。(8) 暑いから、窓を開けておきましょう。(9) 野村さんに電話しましたが、いなかったので、留守番電話にメッセージを残しておきました。(10) パーティーの食べ物は、すでに用意してありますよ。

### 文法練習 3

(1) 読める　読めます　読めない　(2) 言える　言えます　言えない　(3) 信じられる　信じられます　信じられない　(4) 泳げる　泳げます　泳げない　(5) 寝られる　寝られます　寝られない　(6) 勉強できる　勉強できます　勉強できない　(7) 来られる　来られます　来られない

### 文法練習 4

(1) 日本語の本が読めますか。はい、読めます。／いいえ、読めません。(2) 自転車に乗れますか。はい、乗れます。／いいえ、乗れません。(3) 日本語で手紙が書けません。(4) 田中さんはいそがしいので、私は田中さんに会えません。(5) その車は高かったので、買えませんでした。(6) 木村さんはゴルフはできますが、テニスはできません。(7) なおこさんは、フランス語は話せますが、英語は話せません。

### 文法練習 5

(1) インドネシア語ができますか。はい、できます。／いいえ、できません。(2) 野球ができますか。はい、できます。／いいえ、できません。(3) 木村さんは、泳ぐことができません。(4) あなたはこの部屋に入ることができません。(5) 田中さんは、ホッケーはできますが、テニスはできません。(6) 私は英語を話すことはできますが、スペイン語を話すことはできません。

### 自然な日本語：練習 1

(1) 田中さんと同じクラスで勉強できる etc. (2) 山田さんがうそをつく etc. (うそをつく＝lie) (3) ヨーロッパへ旅行に行く etc. (4) 日曜日に仕事する etc. (5) そんなことを言う etc. (6) 南の島にハネムーンだ etc. (7) 川田さんが、仕事をやめる etc. (8) あんな人の言うことを聞く etc.

### 表現練習 1

(1) まだ少し寒いです。etc. (2) まだ眠いです。etc. (3) ぜんぜん勉強していません。etc. (4) どうして人気があるんでしょうか。etc. (5) 昨日は、熱があった etc. (6) 今日はクリスマスな etc. (7) 雨がざあざあ降っていた etc.

### 表現練習 2

(1) 田中さんは忙しくても、毎日仕事の後で、水泳に行きます。(2) 明日雨が降っても、つりに行きます。(3) いくらたくさん食べても、野村さんは太りません。(4) いくら寒くても、鈴木さんは靴下をはきません。(5) それは簡単です。小学生でも知っています。

### 表現練習３

(1) 暑くなりました。 (2) 暇でしたが、忙しくなりました。 (3) ４月になりました。 (4) 寒くなりました。 (5) 一生懸命勉強して、医者になりました。 (6) 部屋がきれいになりました。 (7) ご飯を食べて、おなかがいっぱいになりました。 (8) 夜になりました。 (9) 将来は日本語の先生になりたいです。

### 表現練習４

(1) 日本語の授業、なかなかおもしろいですよ。／そろそろ授業が始まる時間ですね。 (2) あのレストラン、なかなかおいしいですよ。／そろそろレストランが閉まる時間ですね。 (3) 鈴木さん、なかなか来ませんね。／そろそろ鈴木さんが来る時間ですね。 (4) ジョンさんは、日本語がなかなか上手ですよ。 (5) もう遅いし、そろそろ帰りましょうか。 (6) 妹は、ピアノをなかなか上手に弾きます。 (7) 疲れたから、そろそろ寝ます。 (8) 昨日のテストは、なかなか難しかったですよ。／そろそろテストの時期ですね。 (9) みちこさんは、歌がなかなか上手です。 (10) 母は、携帯電話の使い方がなかなか覚えられません。／そろそろ新しい携帯電話を買ったほうがいいですね。

### 対話練習１

Refer to the example and the following translation of the given prompts.

Languages: Chinese 中国語／English 英語／French フランス語／ Indonesian インドネシア語／Korean 韓国語／Spanish スペイン語／Thai タイ語／Vietnamese ベトナム語

Sports: baseball 野球／cricket クリケット／hockey ホッケー／karate 空手／rugby ラグビー／soccer サッカー／swimming 水泳／ tennis テニス

Things: driving a car 車が運転できる／eating nattou 納豆が食べられる／playing the piano ピアノが弾ける／playing the guitar ギターが弾ける／singing songs 歌が歌える／riding bicycle 自転車に乗れる／writing email in Japanese 日本語でイーメールが書ける／dancing ダンスができる

### 対話練習２

Refer to the example.

### 対話練習３

Refer to the example.

### やってみましょう

・歌舞伎 (iii) 男性 (iv) 女形 ・能 (ii) 面 (iii) 侍/庶民 ・文楽 (i) 人形 (ii) 三味線

・落語 (i) １人で (ii) 高座 (iii) 扇子、手ぬぐい ・漫才 (i) 関西 (ii) ２人

## Lesson 19

### 文法練習１

(1) もうすぐ、雨がふりそうですね。It looks like it will rain soon. (2) 日本は、きのう雨が降ったそうですね。I heard that it rained in Japan yesterday. (3) このかばんは高いから、買わないかもしれません。This bag is expensive, so I may not buy it. (4) 最近、雨が全然降っていないそうです。I heard that it hasn't rain at all recently. (5) 私は忙しいから、今夜パーティーに行けないかもしれません。I am busy, so I may not be able to go to the party tonight. (6) あしたの天気は雪だそうです。I heard that tomorrow's weather is snow. (7) あしたの天気は雪らしいです。Apparently, tomorrow's weather is snow. (8) 鈴木さんはもう朝ごはんを食べたらしい。Apparently, Mr Suzuki has already had breakfast. (9) これは加藤さんの車かもしれないよ。This may be Mr Kato's car. (10) どこにも行かないで、家で休んだほうが楽かもしれない。It may be easier to have a rest at home without going out anywhere.

### 文法練習２

(1) 鈴木さんはまじめな学生のようですね。Mr Suzuki seems a serious student. (2) 映画は８時に始まるようだ。It seems that the movie will start at 8 O'clock. (3) 今度のテストは難しいみたいだ。It seems that the next text is difficult. (4) 田中さんは忙しくて会議に行けないみたい(だ)。It seems that Mr Tanaka is busy and cannot got to the meeting.

(5) 鈴木さんは、お金持ちみたいだよ。Mr Suzuki seems a rich man. (6) 田中さんは日本人だから、この漢字が読めるはずです。Mr Tanaka is Japanese, so he is supposed to be able to read this kanji. (7) 今日は休みだから、木村さんは家にいるはずです。As today is an off day, Mr Kimura is supposed to be at home.

**文法練習3**

(1) この船は、木村さんによって作られました。(2) この歌は、日本人によく知られている。(3) このカメラは、たくさんの人に使われています。(4) 遅くおきたので、お父さんに叱られました。(5) みんなに馬鹿にされました。(6) そんなことを言ったら、人に笑われますよ。(7) 田中先生に、「静かにしなさい」と言われました。(8) となりの人に、一晩中うるさくされました。

**自然な日本語：練習1**

(1) (私は) 昼ごはんを食べました、田中さんと。(2) (私)、見たよ、あの映画。(3) 大学生じゃありません、木村さんは。(4) 見てください、この写真を。(5) 田中さんの？このかばん。(6) 山田さんに会いましたか、先週末に。(7) 何した？ゆうべ。(8) 本当に好きです、日本語が。(9) 行ったことある？日本。(10) 難しいね、漢字は。

**表現練習1**

(1) 読もう (2) 歩こう (3) 起きよう (4) 買おう (5) 帰ろう (6) 開けよう (7) 勉強しよう

**表現練習2**

(1) あとでいっしょにお茶を飲もう。(2) 明日、いっしょにテニスをしよう。(3) 今夜、いっしょに水泳をしよう。(4) 授業の後で、いっしょに図書館に行こう。(5) 明日、いっしょに学校に行こう。(6) 金曜日に、いっしょに買い物をしよう。(7) 日曜日に、いっしょにバーベキューをしよう。(8) 授業の後で、いっしょにサッカーをしよう。

**表現練習3**

(1) 木村さんは、家で今、コーヒーを飲もうとしています。(2) 図書館で山田さんに会おうと思っています。(3) 田中さんは、ちょうど電話しようとしていました。(4) 弟は、寒いときでも、靴下をはこうとしません。(5) ちょうど出かけようと思っていたんです。(6) その時計はとても高かったので、誰も買おうとしませんでした。(7) 兄はとても疲れていて、動こうとしません。

**表現練習4**

(1) 野村さんはサンドイッチを食べながら、テレビを見ています。(2) 山田さんは、音楽を聞きながら、本を読んでいます。(3) 黒田さんは、ギターをひきながら、歌を歌っています。(4) 田中さんは、バイトをしながら、学校に通っています。(5) 本田さんは、アイスクリームを食べながら、道を歩いています。

**表現練習5**

(1) 今、京都駅に着いたばかりです。(2) 木村さんは、手紙を書き始めたばかりです。(3) 日本語を勉強し始めたばかりですから、まだあまり話せません。(4) 弟は遊んでばかりいて、全然勉強しません。(5) 肉ばかり食べないで、野菜も食べたほうがいいですよ。(6) さっきアルバイトから帰ったばかりで、とても疲れています。(7) 会議は今、始まったばかりです。毎日会議ばかりで、もういやになりました。

**対話練習1**

Refer to the examples. Use the following volitional forms: 映画を見よう／晩ご飯を食べよう／海に行こう／ドライブをしよう・ドライブに行こう

**対話練習2**

(1)
A: 音楽を聞きながら、よく勉強しますか。
B: はい、よくしますよ。(or いいえ、あまりしません。)

(2)
A: 晩ご飯を食べながら、テレビを見ますか。
B: はい、よく見ます。(or いいえ、あまり見ません。)

(3)
A: 道を歩きながら、よくものを食べますか。
B: はい、よく食べます。
(or いいえ、あまり食べません。)

(4)
A: 悲しい映画を見ながら、よく泣きますか。
B: はい、よく泣きます。(or いいえ、あまり泣きません。)

(5)

A: コーヒーやお茶を飲みながら、よくチョコレートを食べますか。

B: はい、よく食べます。
(or いいえ、あまり食べません。)

(6)

A: 寝ながら、よくいびきをかきますか。

B: はい、よくかきます。(or いいえ、あまりかきません。)

**対話練習3**

Refer to the example.

**練習しましょう**

Refer to the example.

## Lesson 20

**文法練習1**

(1) 社長がお話しになりました。 (2) その寿司は、課長の奥さんがお作りになりました。 (3) 鈴木先生はたいてい6時にお宅にお帰りになります。(宅 'home') (4) 山田先生は手紙をお書きになりませんでした。(5) 先生もこのペンをお使いになったよ。 (6) 社長は車にお乗りにならなかった。

**文法練習2**

(1) 社長も会議にいらっしゃいました。(2) 課長がそうおっしゃいました。(3) 鈴木先生は週末に、たいていなにをなさいますか。 (4) この映画、もうご覧になりましたか。 (5) 山田先生は、朝ご飯を召し上がりません。(6) 山田先生は、今、どこにいらっしゃいますか。 (7) 山田先生は部屋で手紙を書かれています。

**文法練習3**

(1) そのかばん、私がお持ちします。 (2) この英語のチェック、お願いします。 (3) ちょっと先生に申し上げたいことがあるのですが・・・。 (4) それは、私がいたします。 (5) じゃ、お返事、お待ちしています。

**文法練習4**

(1) レストランは7階にございます。 (2) 質問はございませんか。 (3) 木村社長はあの方でございます。 (4) きのうのパーティー、人がたくさん来ましたね。 (5) 山田先生は部屋で手紙を書いていらっしゃるよ。(6) 8時にテレビをご覧になってください。 (7) これは、先生がお書きになった本ですか。

**自然な日本語：練習**

(1) 田中さんに、お会いできて、よかったですね。／田中さんに会えて、よかったね。(2) では、あした午後4時頃、お電話いたします。／じゃあ、あした午前4時頃、電話するね。(3) ここで、お待ちしております。／ここで、待ってるよ。 (4) 魚料理は、お好きですか。／魚料理、好き？ (5) 申し訳ありません。こちらでは、おタバコはちょっと・・・。／ここで、タバコ吸わないで。

**表現練習1**

(1) 今夜、花子さんとお茶を飲むことにしました。 (2) 週末にゆかさんと映画に行くことにしました。(3) 休みの間、中国に行くことになりました。 (4) 来年から、日本語を教えることになりました。(5) 毎日学校の後で、水泳に行くことにしました。 (6) 来年、日本語を勉強するために、日本へ行くことになりました。 (7) 週末に、富士山へ行くことにしました。 (8) お酒をやめることにしました。 (9) 明日、買い物に行くことになりました。 (10) 新幹線で、京都に行くことになりました。

**表現練習2**

(1) 佐藤先生に、私のエッセイを読んでいただきたいです。(2) 父に車を買ってもらいたいです。 (3) ジェニーさんに英語を教えてもらいたいです。 (4) 宿題を手伝ってほしいです。 (5) 加藤さんに、私が作ったすしを食べてもらいたいです。 (6) A: この本、図書館に返してほしいんだけど、いい？ B: うん、いいよ。 (7) A: この書類、チェックしてほしいんだけど、いい？ B: ごめん、今ちょっと忙しくて・・・。

**表現練習３**

(1) 靴をはいたまま、家に入ってしまいました。(2) たけしは、出かけたまま帰ってきていません。(3) 窓を開けたまま出かけてしまいました。 (4) 電気をつけたまま寝ました。 (5) メガネをかけたまま寝ています。

**表現練習４**

(1) とても疲れていたので、シャワーを浴びないで寝てしまいました。(2) 田中さんは、私に何も言わないで家に帰りました。(3) 本を見ないで、私の質問に答えてください。(4) 重要な試験があるので、寝ないで１０時間、勉強しました。 (5) 昨日、野球の試合を見に行きました。でも、チケットが売り切れていたので、試合を見ないで家に帰らなければなりませんでした。

**対話練習１**

Refer to the example.

**対話練習２**

A: 〜さん、ちょっと鉛筆かしてほしいんだけど。
B: 鉛筆？うん、いいよ。何本？
A: ２本なんだけど。
B: ２本ね。いいよ。はい、どうぞ。
A: ありがとう。

A: 〜さん、ちょっと日本語の作文をチェックしてもらいたいんだけど、いい？
B: 作文？うん、いいよ。いつまでにしてほしいの？
A: 来週の水曜日に提出したいんだけど・・・。
B: 来週の水曜日ね。オーケー。じゃあ、その前に、返すよ。
A: ほんと？ありがとう。助かる。

A: 〜さん、明日の朝、起こしてほしいんだけど。
B: 明日の朝？いいよ。何時に起こしてほしいの？
A: ６時なんだけど。
B: ６時？いいよ。ぼくは毎日６時に起きるから。
A: ありがとう。助かる。

A: 〜さん、買い物に一緒に来てもらいたいんだけど。
B: 買い物？うん、いいよ。いつ？
A: 今週の土曜日なんだけど。
B: 土曜日。オーケー。大丈夫だよ。
A: あ、ほんと。ありがとう。

A: 〜さん、ちょっと買い物に行ってきてほしいんだけど。
B: 買い物？いいよ。何を買ってきてほしいの？
A: パーティーのための、飲み物なんだけど・・・。
B: 飲み物ね。オーケー。何本ぐらい？
A: そうね。１５本ぐらい。
B: １５本ね。わかった。
A: ありがとう。助かる。

**対話練習３**

Refer to the example.

**調べましょう**

花火 fireworks, 夏 ／ 月 moon, 秋 ／ 桜 cherry blossoms, 春 ／ 書初 new year's writing, 冬 ／ 秋刀魚 mackerel pike, 秋 ／ 初雪 the first snow of the year, 冬 ／ 蛍 firefly, 夏 ／ 枯れる wither, 冬 ／ 鈴虫 a bell ring insect, 秋 ／ かき氷 shaved ice, 夏 ／ 五月晴 early summer fine weather, 夏

[終わり]